I0820228

Praise for

VIOLENT SAVIORS

"Easterly writes about freedom, something that economists too often forget in their pursuit of growth and living standards. That life is about more than money and that there can be no price on the loss of freedom is a lesson that has taken the world three hundred years to learn. Adam Smith got it right, unlike most of the economists who followed him. Easterly's deep scholarship brings the story to life, celebrating the few who saw clearly, some familiar, many not. An innovative and exhilarating read."

—Angus Deaton, winner of the Nobel Prize in Economics

"Easterly has done it again, sharply revising what we thought we knew, but didn't. He shows us the startling unity among tyrannies we imagined were distinct. A triumph of liberal thought."

—Deirdre McCloskey, Cato Institute

"*Violent Saviors* is Bill Easterly's masterpiece. It brilliantly weaves together the self-serving and arrogant histories of the conquests, enslavements, and destructive 'assistance' the West has imposed on the Rest, showing the common patronizing thread that connects them, and traces all these hideous histories to the philosophies that justified them, which Easterly masterfully dissects. But amidst the horrors and ugliness, there is hope: Some thinkers and actors, from Adam Smith to Easterly himself, insistently teach us to respect individual dignity and promote freedom as the cornerstone of all human flourishing. And Easterly reminds us that the long arc of history is on their side."

—Charles Calomiris, Columbia Business School

"It is a central tenet of economics that markets produce more efficient outcomes than planning because markets aggregate information from innumerable voluntary exchanges, while planning is based on decision-making by a small group of experts who cannot help but bring along their normative values. This powerful idea has a drawback, however; it leaves little role for experts, and experts have strong incentives to embrace big roles for experts. The tension between voluntary consent and expert judgment has produced not only levels of prosperity that were unimaginable at the founding of the discipline of economics 250 years ago but also human tragedies at vast scale. If you want to understand how this tension developed, and why it gave rise to both prosperity and tragedy, you must read *Violent Saviors*."

—Stephen Haber, Stanford University

VIOLENT SAVIORS

VIOLENT SAVIORS

THE WEST'S CONQUEST OF THE REST

WILLIAM EASTERLY

BASIC BOOKS
New York

Basic Books
Hachette Book Group
1290 Avenue of the Americas, New York, NY 10104
www.basicbooks.com

Printed in the United States of America

First Edition: November 2025

Published by Basic Books, an imprint of Hachette Book Group, Inc. The Basic Books name and logo is a registered trademark of the Hachette Book Group.

The Hachette Speakers Bureau provides a wide range of authors for speaking events. To find out more, go to www.hachettespeakersbureau.com or email HachetteSpeakers@hbgusa.com.

Basic books may be purchased in bulk for business, educational, or promotional use. For more information, please contact your local bookseller or the Hachette Book Group Special Markets Department at special.markets@hbgusa.com.

The publisher is not responsible for websites (or their content) that are not owned by the publisher.

Print book interior design by Bart Dawson.

Library of Congress Cataloging-in-Publication Data has been applied for.

ISBNs: 9781541675759 (hardcover), 9781541675742 (ebook)

LSC-C

Printing 1, 2025

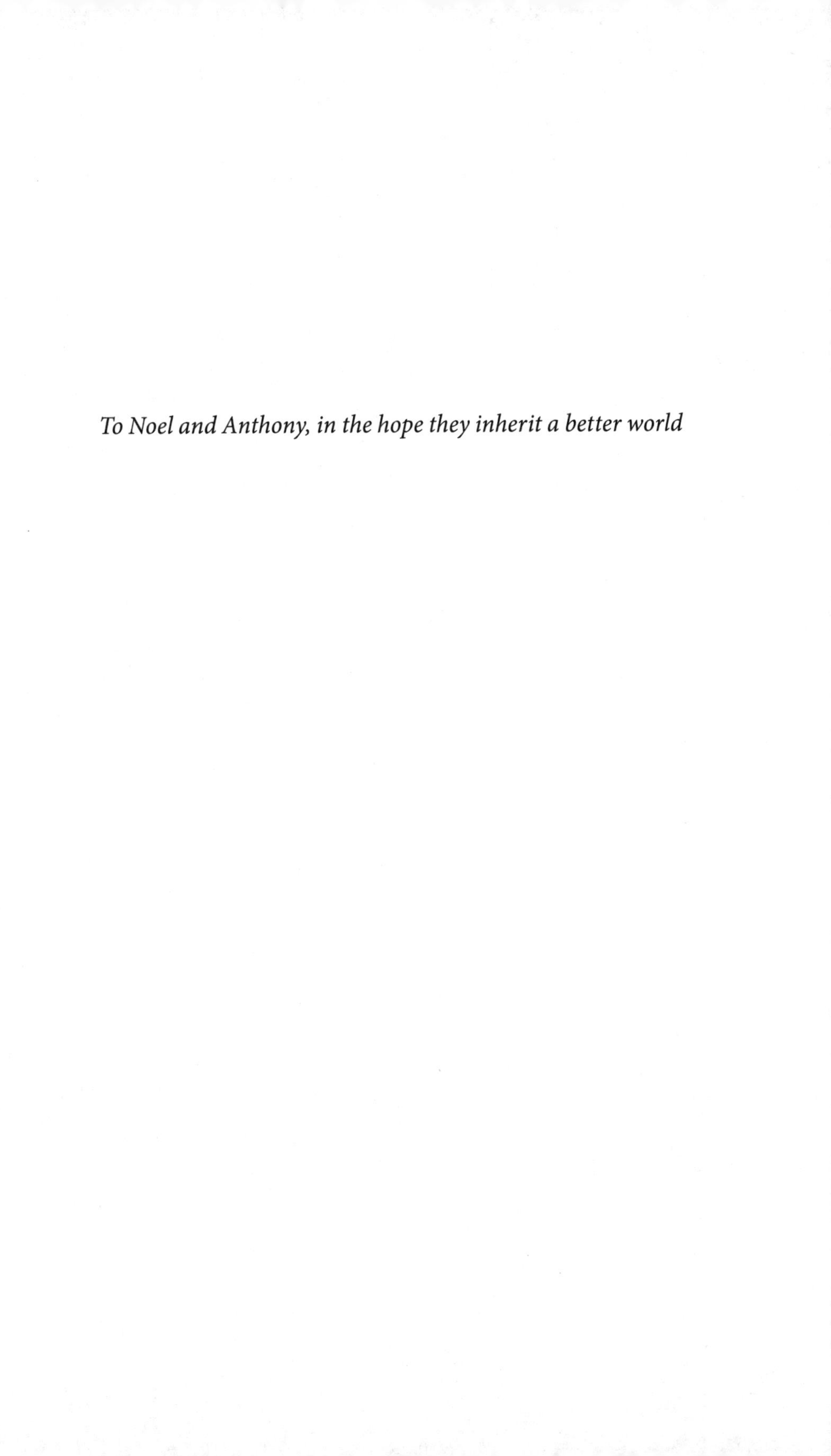

To Noel and Anthony, in the hope they inherit a better world

Contents

VIOLENT SAVIORS

Preface

> We know what is good for you better than you know yourself and we are going to make you do it.
>
> —LIBERAL ECONOMIST WILLIAM GRAHAM SUMNER, 1899, IN A SPEECH PROTESTING AMERICAN COLONIZATION OF THE PHILIPPINES

In 1972, Ugandan President Idi Amin expelled Ugandans of Asian origin from Uganda. Many became refugees in camps in Britain.

A twenty-six-year-old Ugandan refugee named Mahmood Mamdani described his experiences in one of the camps in London in a book published in 1973. The camp directors announced one day with thirteen hours' notice that they were moving fifty refugees to another camp sixty miles from London. Some of those to be moved already had jobs in London. Mamdani and fellow refugees refused to move. They said in a petition to the camp authorities, "We protest at being treated as objects or, at best, as cattle."

Managers of refugee camps don't often have to contend with refugees who demand a voice in what happens to them. The Uganda Resettlement Board in Britain was unlucky in that one of the refugees—Mamdani—was a Harvard graduate student who had already been involved in the civil rights campaigns in America. He would go on to become a famous professor of government at Columbia and at Makerere University in Uganda. Mamdani was successful in getting press coverage of the refugee revolt.

There ensued a battle of wills between the board and the refugees. Mamdani realized that what angered the Uganda Resettlement Board was refugees wanting to run their own lives. As he said in his book the following year, "The crux of the matter was that we had refused to act as refugees, as helpless, well-behaved children, totally devoid of initiative, indiscriminately grateful for anything that may come their way."

Mamdani acknowledged that material aid to the refugees had been generous, even including a Christmas turkey. But it was not enough to compensate them for not having a say in their own fate: "Circumstances deprived us of our possessions, but not yet of our self-respect. For that last possession, our humanity, we were willing to fight."

In the end, the Resettlement Board moved some but left the most diehard protesters alone.[1]

To use the ponderous jargon of modern academics and economic development workers, Mamdani was expressing a demand for agency. *Agency* here roughly means the right to consent to your own progress, to simply have a voice in what affects you. It is the widespread desire of adults to not be treated as children. (Actually, my anecdotal experience as a father and grandfather makes me think that not even children like to be treated as children.)

Agency is often seen as a rather arcane concern for people experiencing extreme deprivation. Aid agencies make some effort to recognize agency by deploying even more ponderous jargon like *empowerment*, *community-driven development*, *participatory development*, *partnerships for development*, *country-led development*, and *consultations with stakeholders and civil society*. It is hard to see how the intended beneficiaries of aid really get a voice from all this. Most development debaters turn with relief away from such buzzwords to seek lower poverty rates or a higher number of Christmas turkeys.

But is material poverty relief a reliable indicator that people will be better off, if they have no agency to say so? Should poverty rates and GDP be the only measure of progress? Maybe GDP increases that happened through forced labor, forced resettlement, and violent land seizures in aid projects, as well as by supporting autocrats, jailing political protesters, shooting demonstrators, and intervening with the Western military, were not exactly equivalent to GDP increases that happen more consensually.

It is disturbing that modern development lacks a vision to decide whether violent development is a good or bad thing. It occurred to me that help might be available from four centuries of commentators on the development violence known as colonialism.

I have also been much influenced by colleagues from developing countries who related their experience with some development people telling them what was good for their countries without giving them a voice. As my Ghanaian colleague Yaw Nyarko shared in a comment on a preliminary draft of this book, he has often heard Western development people say, "Well, we should do those [development actions] to those Africans, and those Africans need this." But Nyarko notes, "There are no Africans in the room. We haven't asked those people." In fact, Nyarko says, "We didn't ask to be saved." Throughout my career, I have heard similar comments from many of my colleagues, underscoring how condescension was as bad to them as material poverty.[2] But these colleagues and I myself certainly do not reject development efforts altogether. The question is how to discriminate between good and bad development. I could look for possible answers in the long history of liberalism, the ideology defined by a love for the freedom to choose and an aversion to coercion and paternalism.

I was aware that liberal economists played a key role in this debate, as they offered consensual exchanges in the marketplace as one of the main ways that people realize agency in a mutually beneficial way. They saw that moral bans on coercion were necessary for trade to play this beneficial role.

I had not fully anticipated how central the demand for agency would be to the story from the beginning. For centuries liberal thinkers across the globe grappled with the demand for agency during the long history of colonialism, including American Indian removal, slavery, and the conquest of Asia and Africa. Liberals seldom used the modern word *agency*, but they used more evocative words such as *consent*, *liberty*, *democracy*, *self-determination*, *voice*, *individual freedom*, the *consent of the governed*, *equal rights*, and the *right to choose*. The liberals linked the demand for agency to other nonmaterial demands, like the demand for dignity and respect. Since *agency* is a modern word, I will usually use the word *consent* instead of *agency* throughout this history.

The value placed on material progress has always been and will always be widely shared, including by this author. The point is not to reject material values altogether. The point is that for four hundred years there has been something else besides a demand for material income—the demand for agency and dignity—and those voices also deserve to be heard. Throughout history, conquerors claimed to increase the material progress of colonial subjects while taking away their agency. But these claims have often been met by skepticism by liberals, not to mention by the colonial subjects themselves. Their simple point was that development without consent is not necessarily progress.

If there seems to be a selection bias in this history toward violence in development, it is because this is a history of violence in development. So this history is not representative of aid and development efforts in general. In this history, the liberals used the most extreme violations of consent as counterexamples to the assertion that material betterment was sufficient to show progress. But the liberal critique of violent development efforts does not aim to tarnish all development efforts. It seeks to eliminate the worst forms of violence, to make it more possible for development to be benevolent. The progress against coercion was as important as the progress against poverty to improved human well-being. Development could then wind up at today's less extreme, even if still problematic, denial of agency.

Who was in the West and the Rest would be flexibly defined by self-labeled members of the former. It usually means Western Europe and its settler offshoots in Canada, the US, Australia, and New Zealand. Sometimes it means only upper-class white males even within Western nations. The Rest is everybody else.

The indignant response to conquest in the name of progress by some people in the Rest and liberals in the West shows that agency, far from being a meaningless buzzword, has been at the heart of the development debate for four centuries. Mamdani's revolt in the refugee camp had a lot to do with this history. As he said at the time, "The victors always seem to forget that the vanquished have a longer historical memory."[3]

1

Our Conquest of Them for Their Own Good

A Native American man in what later became Massachusetts appealed to philanthropists in England in 1629: "Come over and help us."

The Massachusetts Bay Colony featured this man on their seal after King Charles I granted them a charter to New England in 1629. The five-word appeal for help issues from his mouth. He is mostly naked and carrying a bow and arrow, fitting the image that the English had of American Indians. The native man points the arrow downward, signaling that the Indians peacefully welcomed the helpful settlers from the Massachusetts Bay Colony.

Nobody knows the Indigenous man's name or tribal affiliation or anything else about him, perhaps because he was entirely fictional.

The seal accurately reflects the ideas of John Winthrop, the first governor of the Massachusetts Bay Colony that began large-scale settlement in New England. In the winter of 1628–1629, Winthrop had sought to reassure would-be settlers about the noble mission of the colony. Before leaving England for New England, Winthrop set out to answer possible objections to the colony—of which a big one was that "we have no warrant to enter upon that land, which hath been so long possessed by others."[1]

But Winthrop argued that the conquerors did have a right to the land because of their ability to improve it. Surely, God had not intended "a whole Continent as fruitful and convenient for the use of man to lie waste without any improvement." Instead, God had given man an improvement mission in the book of Genesis, namely to "increase and multiply, and replenish the earth and subdue it." The natives in New England had failed to fulfill God's mission. "This savage people" did not develop the land or themselves: "They enclose no land, neither have they any settled habitation, nor any tame cattle to improve the land by."

Winthrop expounded an idea of enormous importance for illiberal thought in the next four centuries. He argued it was lawful for the people who would improve the land, the English, to take the territory from those who had failed to improve it, the Indians, for the sake of global improvement. This book will call this idea the Development Right of Conquest. It confers the right to conquer lands on those who bring material progress to these lands.

But what about development for the Indians? Winthrop in 1629 reassured his audience that the English seizure of Indian land was actually beneficial for the Indians, because the English would teach them the arts of improvement. Although settlement would only leave the Indians part of their former lands, he said, they would "learn from us to improve a part to more use than before they could do the whole." Such a knowledge transfer "will yield them more benefit than all that land which we have from them." God wanted the English to offer religious as well as secular salvation to the Indians, because "the Gospel should be preached to all nations." The Development Right of Conquest would often apply to people as well as land. The developers had the right to subjugate people as long as they benefited those people.[2]

But what did those to be saved think about this? Winthrop thought his offer of development was appealing enough that "we shall come in with the good leave of the natives."[3]

However, Winthrop thought it was possible that the natives might not appreciate the Gospel: "We know not whether those

Barbarians will receive it at first or no." Just in case the natives did not agree to their own salvation, Winthrop planned to have an army. The colony's soldiers would have enough guns and fortifications so that five hundred settlers could defeat three thousand Indians, Winthrop promised.[4]

A fateful us and them had entered the lexicon of progress. The idea of "us" conquering "them" for their own good—the imaginative and fateful mixture of coercion, paternalism, and superiority—was destined for a momentous career for the next four centuries. The West's conquest of the Rest in the name of progress would spawn many competing notions of what progress really is.

The most drastic form of the Development Right of Conquest was the one that applied to the land rather than to people. Suppose the Indigenous people were unable or unwilling to develop, or maybe Western conquerors simply did not care about them. Then the conquerors could console themselves that they were still furthering global progress by making the conquered lands more productive. They could at least save the land if they could not save the people. They could then justify the replacement of the unprogressive people by progressive people in the name of progress.

In Winthrop there is an early sighting of the Western policy of population removal, which would fatefully develop over the next four centuries. What is today called ethnic cleansing went on to figure importantly in debates about progress—specifically on what to do with Indians and Black people inside Western societies.

Winthrop was willing to consider such population removal. In 1634, members of the Pequot tribe killed an English trader after he had taken two Pequots captive to be his guides. This eventually led to war between the English and the Pequots. The English had been asking the Pequots to accept white settlers along the Mystic River in Connecticut and the Pequots had said, *No thanks*. The Pequots apparently did not have as much demand for white saviors as they were supposed to. Whether the land wanted to be saved, it didn't say.

The thirty thousand Pequots were a constraint to English expansion as one of the most powerful tribes in the area. However, a smallpox epidemic had already made them more vulnerable to conquest. Although the introduction of Europeans' diseases to the Indians was not intentional or understood by John Winthrop, he saw the epidemic as a good thing: "God hath consumed the natives with a miraculous plague, whereby the greater part of the country is left voide of inhabitants."[5]

The English enlisted the Narragansett and Mohegan Indians, enemies of the Pequots, to their side. The crucial battle that decided the war took place on May 26, 1637, at a Pequot fortified village named Mistick near the Mystic River. The English set fire to the fort. They and their Indian allies shot those fleeing the fire. Of the four hundred Pequots in the village, only five survived. John Winthrop noted that 150 of the slain were elderly men or women and children. Winthrop also notes that the English divided up Pequot women and children who survived the war among the Narragansetts, the Mohegans, other Indian allies, and English settlers. He also wrote that when Pequot captives escaped and then were recaptured, the English branded them on the shoulder. Winthrop himself took the wife of a Pequot chief named Mononotto as a servant. She had requested only of the whites that they not "abuse her body" or take away her children. Winthrop reassured a correspondent that "I have taken charge of her," presumably nonabusively.[6]

Winthrop reports that he also sent fifteen Pequot boys and two women into slavery in the Caribbean. He later noted that Massachusetts received in exchange for the Pequot slaves some cotton, tobacco, salt, and Black slaves.[7]

The 1638 Treaty of Hartford that ended the war represented only the winners. The English, the Mohegan leader Uncas, and the Narragansett leader Miantonomo all agreed that any remaining Pequot holdouts should either be captured and sent to the English, beheaded on the spot, or divided between Mohegans and Narragansetts. The two tribal leaders and the English then agreed that the Pequots divided up between the two tribes "shall no more be called Pequots but Narragansetts and Mohegans."[8]

In terms of material progress, Winthrop's faith in the English improvement mission went on to be spectacularly confirmed. From around the time that Winthrop wrote to the present, the per capita income of what is now the United States increased more than sixty-fold. For nearly four centuries, Americans' income doubled about every sixty years (Figure 1).[9]

Over a century later, Adam Smith in *The Wealth of Nations* agreed with Winthrop's confidence that conquest of the Americas had led and would lead to material progress. Smith describes how "the colony of a civilized nation which takes possession either of a waste country, or of one so thinly inhabited that the natives easily give place to the new settlers, advances more rapidly to wealth and greatness than any other human society."[10]

A defender of Winthrop today might point also to material progress among Native Americans. Figure 1 also shows a bar representing Native American median household income today. Native Americans today are 29 percent poorer than the US national median. There is no data on what Indian incomes were like in Winthrop's day, but some heroic guesses about seventeenth-century incomes found that most nations' and regions' average incomes were about the same as for the Europeans that would make up the future United States. Rough estimates also suggest Western Europeans had many technologies that Native Americans did not, which would also suggest that Native American per capita income was at a lower level than that of Western Europeans. So a working assumption could be that Indian incomes were at least no higher than the US average in the seventeenth century. If this is true, then Native American incomes are at least forty-four times higher today than in 1650.[11]

A small remnant of the Pequot tribe called the Mashantucket (Western) Pequot Tribal Nation has survived to the present day. Today's Pequots have prospered as owners of the Foxwoods Resort Casino in Connecticut. The Mashantucket Pequot Reservation today has a population of 117 individuals with a median household income of $158,750. This income is 2.44 times the same number for the US population.[12]

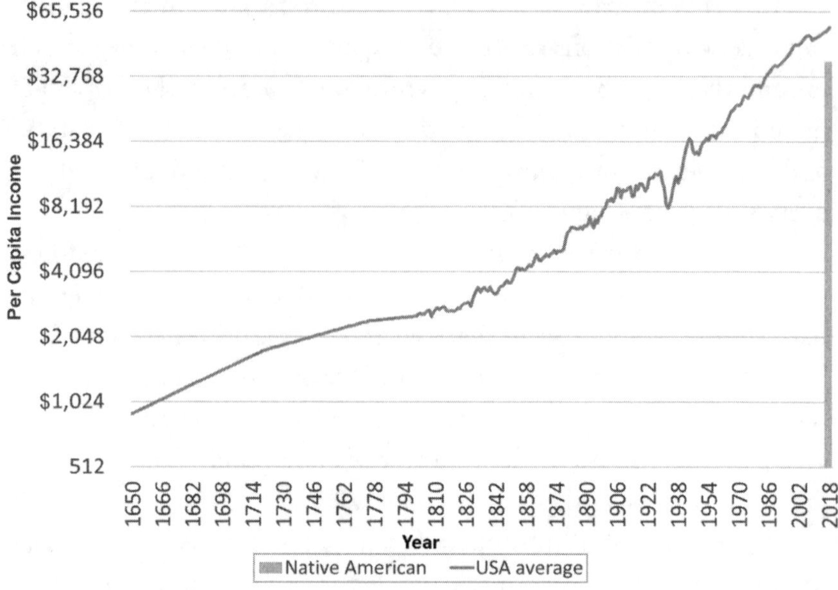

Figure 1. US and Native American income in US dollars, 2011, using a logarithmic scale where every unit increase represents a doubling of income. Source: US per capita income, MPD 2020; Native American median household income as a ratio to US median household income, US Census Bureau, American Community Survey, 2020.

But maybe the Development Right of Conquest was not justified by the later material progress. Maybe economists should not tell the conquered to just be quiet and enjoy the GDP. The most important European skeptic of benevolent conquest was the same one who had noticed the material success of the American settlers, Adam Smith. He noted in *The Wealth of Nations* in 1776 that Columbus and the Spanish had also claimed they were benefiting the natives. The conquerors had the "pious purpose of converting them to Christianity." But the Spanish imposed the alleged benefits of Christianity by taking "possession of the countries of which the inhabitants were plainly incapable of defending themselves." So Spanish settlers with no constraints on their violence had simply pursued their own self-interest by "plundering of the defenseless natives." Smith then generalized the critique to include other European conquests in the Americas since the Spanish. "The savage injustice of the Europeans" in conquest and settlement had been "ruinous and destructive to several of those unfortunate countries."[13]

The disjuncture between Smith's statements of American wealth and greatness and his critique of American savage injustice is the problem this book seeks to address.

In the middle of his critique of conquest, Smith offered the alternative that changed history and that could have changed history a lot more—commerce. Both sides could have realized great mutual gains from exchange: "The commodities of Europe were almost all new to America, and many of those of America were new to Europe." There could have been "a new set of exchanges" Smith lamented, "which should naturally have proved as advantageous to the new, as it certainly did to the old continent." Smith compared two motivations for Europeans seeking contacts with the rest of the world. One was a "project of commerce"; the other was "a project of conquest." Smith insisted commerce would have been better than conquest. But this didn't happen, because Europeans chose conquest.[14]

Winthrop had raised the idea of exchanging civilization for land with the Indians. But Winthrop's idea of exchange was not voluntary. For Smith, in contrast, the very definition of exchange involves consent. If both sides do not consent to the exchange, it is not really an exchange. To violate "the right to free commerce" is to violate Smith's most cherished value—the right to choose.

Trade allows everyone to make their own choices, not have others choose for them. Each side to an exchange decides on their own wants, Smith says, and then both sides benefit: "Whoever offers to another a bargain of any kind, proposes to do this. Give me that which I want, and you shall have this which you want, is the meaning of every such offer." Implicit in your right to choose is also whether you want to trade with me at all, if you do not consider my offer much of a bargain.[15]

Smith described what he saw as the "obvious and simple system of natural liberty." If any one sentence launched the ideology known as liberalism, it was this one: "Every man, as long as he does not violate the laws of justice, is left perfectly free to pursue his own interest his own way."[16]

He had already denounced paternalism seventeen years earlier in *The Theory of Moral Sentiments*: "Every man is, no doubt, by nature, first and principally recommended to his own care; and as he is fitter to take care of himself than of any other person, it is fit and right that it should be so." There is some ambiguity here, as there would often be in liberalism, between whether he is fitter to take care of himself and whether it is right that he take care of himself. The anti-liberals would dispute the former, but liberals would often insist on the moral rightness of self-determination anyway. This was partly because well-being was purely subjective for each individual; no outside caregiver could judge it: "Every man feels his own pleasures and his own pains more sensibly than those of other people." To use the modern language, Smith is getting close to a demand for agency and calling for respect of that demand.[17]

Smith did not argue for a zero amount of coercion. In his system of natural liberty, Smith acknowledged three legitimate purposes for state coercion: defense against foreign invasion, protecting "every member of the society from the injustice or oppression of every other member of it," and providing public works and institutions. Coercion would be necessary to raise taxes for these purposes, and coercion would be needed to fight foreign invasion and domestic oppression. Here was also an implicit critique of the Development Right of Conquest. Smith envisioned a world where every society had a collective right to fight back against foreign conquest, with no exceptions for conquest for the sake of progress.[18]

Smith did not have in mind only European nations when he discussed national self-defense. Smith made clear that he thought it unjust that non-European nations were conquered. During his critique of the West's conquest of the Americas, he said that Western military superiority enabled them "to commit with impunity every sort of injustice in those remote countries."

Then he made a remarkable prophecy of how the conquered nations would someday be able to assert their right to self-defense:

> Hereafter, perhaps, the natives of those countries may grow stronger, or those of Europe may grow weaker; and the inhabitants of all the different quarters of the world may arrive at that equality of courage and force which, by inspiring mutual fear, can alone overawe the injustice of independent nations into some sort of respect for the rights of one another.

Trade would spread knowledge and technological improvement, making self-defense possible for non-European nations. "Mutual communication of knowledge, and of all sorts of improvements" would happen through "an extensive commerce from all countries to all countries."[19]

Two opposing ideas were emerging in the seventeenth and eighteenth centuries. Winthrop's Development Right of Conquest for the next two centuries justified Western conquest of Native Americans, enslavement of Africans, and colonization of everyone else. This disputes the modern view that the idea of development emerged only after the end of colonialism and in opposition to it. The real, much longer history of development challenges this view. The most influential Western thinkers of the past centuries saw colonialism as a means to development, not its opposite. Progress justified force.

In contrast, there is the seed of anti-colonialism in Smith, with his explicit mention of "independent nations" and the national "rights of one another," and his opposition to "force." The vision is that commerce would replace conquest. Smith had begun to formulate a right to consent to your own progress. For Smith, the main mechanism for consent was a market economy.

The dueling visions were of illiberalism versus liberalism, conquest versus commerce, coercion versus consent, paternalism versus self-determination, and ethnic superiority versus equality. These visions continue to contend today, albeit in less extreme forms. The debate was not always quite as simple as good versus evil. Illiberal thinkers' idea of objective progress would help make economics more of a science by making possible tests of measurable predictions. And Smith and his heirs still celebrated material progress and scientifically searched for ways to achieve it.[20]

And liberals were usually better at attacking their opponents' solutions than offering their own. Liberal thinkers would struggle to articulate what individual and collective mechanisms were desirable for consent besides market exchange. Liberals were much clearer on the negative of what was coercion than on the positive of what was consent. Yet the liberals' negative and sometimes hesitant vision turned out to be constructive anyway.

The central point of this book is that these three ideas of consent, self-determination, and equality made possible positive-sum gains from commerce between groups and individuals. The opposing ideas of coercion, paternalism, and racism yielded a negative-sum world of conquest. Smith and his heirs showed how progress did not have to be at the expense of somebody else. They argued material progress alone was not enough. They argued it was necessary for material improvement to have some moral boundaries in order to make possible the positive-sum gains of commerce.

Conquerors liked ideas about benevolent conquest, and those ideas in turn made conquest more likely. The liberals would not find it easy to overcome these incentives. Moreover, liberals had trouble resisting a paternalistic role for themselves in helping the oppressed. Yet against extremely long odds, the right to consent achieved major victories over the Development Right of Conquest. Liberals helped end slavery, extermination of Indigenous peoples, and colonialism.

The big picture is shown in Figure 2. Some forms of violence got worse before they got better, but eventually commerce replaced conquest and consent replaced coercion.[21]

Both the milder and harsher variants of the Development Right of Conquest were part of the momentous debate. The milder version is what Winthrop first embraced: conquering the Indians for their own good, seeing it as possible to civilize them. But then Winthrop

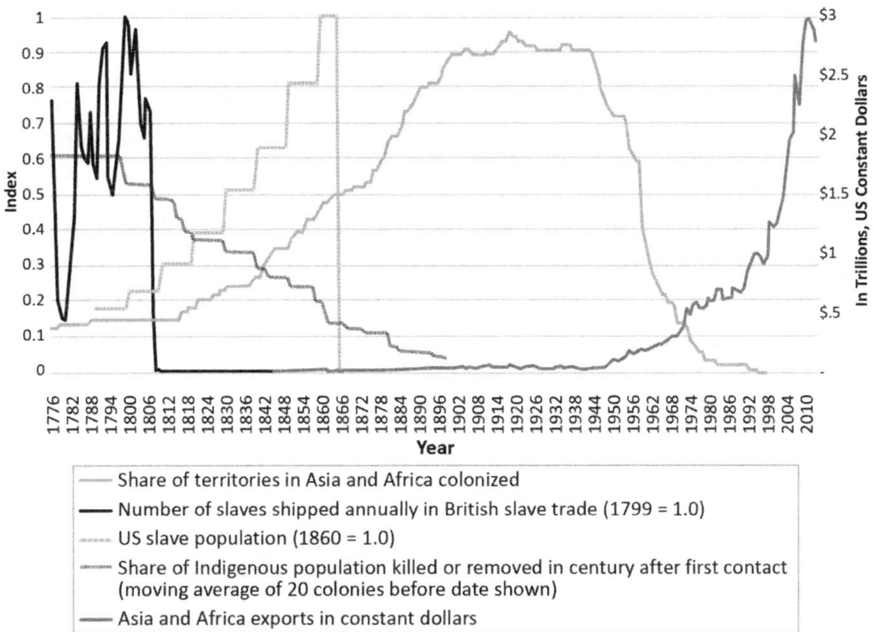

Figure 2. From coercion to consent.

invokes a harsher variant in which improving the Indians is no longer the goal, but just improving the land and removing the Indians out of the way. Winthrop did not explain how his embrace of slavery related to progress, but another future variant of the Development Right of Conquest would be enslaving some Africans to work for the slaves' own higher consumption. But these slaves would never graduate, remaining permanently subordinate. And if even that didn't work, Black people were to be removed somewhere else.

In the rest of the book, the history of the Development Right of Conquest will be traced in four parts. In Part I, the dueling visions of progress in the Enlightenment see some well-intentioned philosophers (represented by Condorcet) justify conquest and removal for progress. Liberals see the Development Right of Conquest as morally objectionable. Smith and Immanuel Kant see true progress as requiring that individuals define their own progress.

In Part II, from 1776 to 1865, there are three broad types of Western illiberal policies: (1) colonial conquest, (2) population removal, and (3) forced labor. The liberals set out their moral critique of these policies (often not very consistently) and their hope to reverse them.

During this time, the West's conquest of the peoples in the Rest is on the rise. Such conquest is justified by the hope of eventually civilizing the locals (the beginnings of British empire in West Africa, Napoleon's attempted conquest of Russia, and the attempt to civilize Indians). Population removal seeks only to develop the land and gives up on civilizing the "savages" (American Indian removal and attempted colonization of American Black people back to Africa). The third type of conquest, forced labor, does not try to civilize Black people; development for them entails only some rise in their material consumption and permanent subordination (the slave trade and slavery).

However, such egregious justifications of violence generate resistance from both its victims and moral reformers. Commerce is an appealing alternative for the economists Adam Smith, Benjamin Constant, Harriet Martineau, and John Stuart Mill. Members of oppressed groups like ex-slave Quobna Ottobah Cugoano, Cherokee preacher David Brown, female reformer Lydia Maria Child, and ex-slaves Frederick Douglass and Harriet Jacobs resist conquest, population removal, and forced labor. There are uneven but eloquent assertions of agency, dignity, and the right to consent for victimized peoples. The United States commits to a liberal foreign policy of nonintervention in the affairs of other nations, albeit only in Europe. Removal and colonization of American Black people is defeated. After the initial wave of population removal in the US, Canada, Australia, and New Zealand, there are no further large-scale European settlements in the Rest that have majority replacement of local people with Europeans (although the defeat of both colonization of Black people and Old World Indigenous removal probably also reflected feasibility rather than just liberal ideals). Liberals lose on Indian removal and nonsettler types of colonial conquests, signifying their overall failure to defeat the Development Right of Conquest. Yet, there are more moral successes for liberals in this period than there will be for a long time afterward. This period ends with the enormous triumph of the right to consent in the abolition of slavery.

In Part III, covering 1865 to 1945, all three types of illiberal policies spread, economists mostly abandon liberal morality, and there are more feeble liberal responses, with virtually no victories. The crucial background is the apogee of colonialism. Commerce expands but without moral constraints on plunder. The US forsakes its ideal of nonintervention. Colonial nonsettler conquests include US conquest of the Philippines, the Partition of Africa, and colonial mandates after World War I. Instances of population removal include conquest of the American West in the late 1800s, eugenics practiced against "white trash" and Eastern European immigrants in the US and UK, and Hitler's genocidal violence against Jews and Eastern Europeans. Forced labor comes back in Leopold's Congo and some other colonies, never to be defeated while colonialism lasts.

Economists far outside the mainstream like William Graham Sumner, E. D. Morel, Paul Reinsch, and Ludwig von Mises barely keep the ideal of consensual trade alive. A diverse band of resisters including Zitkala-Ša, Sixto López, Rabindranath Tagore, W. E. B. Du Bois, and William Monroe Trotter are marginalized, or obscured, or ignored, or all three. Freedom steadily regresses, culminating in the shocking nadir of liberty: the outbreak of World War II. Liberalism has to fight for its very survival.

In Part IV, from 1945 to the present, there are major victories, albeit partial, for liberal ideals. The worst forms of the three policies end. Colonialism ends, and the surge in commerce partially restores agency of the intended beneficiaries. Economists Milton Friedman, P. T. Bauer, and Amartya Sen revive the ideal of individual freedom as an end in itself.

Yet the legacy of the past is still here. While obviously not equating modern development efforts with slavery, genocide, and colonialism, the question remains of what violations of consent today in the name of progress should be out of bounds.

Liberal values are the hero. The hero's quest for freedom in development emerges in the eighteenth century. Yet there are major setbacks for the hero in the late nineteenth century and first half of the twentieth century, seemingly indicating the failure of the quest. But then in the latter part of the twentieth century, the quest is finally (partly) successful. The hero remains scarred by the traumas of the journey but still inspires continued heroism for the future.

PART I

TWO KINDS OF PROGRESS

These vast lands are inhabited partly by numerous peoples who only await assistance from us to become civilized . . . .

—Marquis de Condorcet, 1793

2

The Expert and the Economist

In 1793, the French economist the Marquis de Condorcet gave the best exposition yet of one of the best and worst ideas in intellectual history: the idea of the West developing the Rest.

Condorcet's vision contrasted with that of Adam Smith. Although far less known than Smith, Condorcet represented ideas that were often more successful than Smith's, and that remain dominant today. Condorcet and Smith had much in common. They both agreed that progress did not justify conquest in the past. Condorcet was sometimes more progressive than Smith on equal rights. But Condorcet had faith in enlightened experts to guide progress in the future, which Smith did not share. And Smith offered an ideal of individual consent through commerce that Condorcet did not share.

The dispute was anything but theoretical. In the late eighteenth century, European settlers were subjugating Indigenous peoples in North America. The British East India Company was consolidating its rule in India. Condorcet and Smith debated how their principles applied to this expansion of the West's conquest of the Rest.

The debate suffered from some confusion between morality and science, what today would be called normative and positive economics. Condorcet and like-minded experts then and later predicted that conquest would facilitate material progress but implied that is also what should happen. Smith and his later followers also spent much time examining what would increase the material wealth of nations but set out liberal rules to determine what was just or unjust progress.

There was still much to clear up and left for the future. Did the right to consent refer to groups or to individuals? Were collective rights and individual rights going to conflict? Movements for collective self-determination could (and often did) violate the rights to individual self-determination. How to establish the conditions for consent?

The illiberal side gets some credit for advancing development economics as a science, with an inspiring vision of progress against material poverty. All of today's economists (including this author) are heirs to this vision. While it might be possible to pursue both consent and material progress, the vision failed when it justified violence in the name of progress.

It is understandable that those who wanted lands in the Rest liked the idea of development through conquest. Yet Condorcet was not a cynical justifier of conquest out of his own self-interest. Condorcet is interesting precisely because he was so altruistic and well intentioned. It is even better for the promoters of conquest to have altruists on their side.

In his 1793 essay "The Sketch of Human Progress," Condorcet first offered an inspiring vision of a fight against the misery of the world's least fortunate people. Condorcet said there were many "nations of the earth" in which "development has been arrested." Fortunately, Condorcet said, there was a "science for predicting the progress of the human race, for directing and hastening it," based upon "the history of the progress already achieved." Condorcet uses interchangeably the words *development*, *progress*, and *civilization*.[1]

If some developers hastened progress, then "the vast gulf that separates" civilized nations from uncivilized nations would gradually disappear. Such progress would mean that each generation and each person would increasingly "be better able to satisfy his needs." The "average length of human life will be increased." Anticipating modern development reports, Condorcet imagined "a progress that can be represented with some accuracy in figures or on a graph." To Condorcet, material progress could be objectively measured and promoted. It was a benevolent and inspiring vision of economic development. Condorcet's classic essay offers an early example of economists' fight against global poverty that inspires so many (including this author) today.[2]

But it was the West who had to develop the Rest. The people in the Rest could not develop themselves. According to Condorcet, they were still "vegetating in the infant condition of early times." They represented "the infancy of the human race." The infancy metaphor was very common among Western thinkers looking at other peoples, and it was destined to last. The picture was of children in need of the wise guidance of a father in order to grow up into full development. They had failed to develop on their own and were still stuck in "their condition of apathy," in their "indolence of body and mind," and in their "superstition."[3]

Our own development success made us fit to be the developers of the Rest, Condorcet said. For us, "the wonders of the arts, the discoveries in the sciences and the efforts of reason" had put us at an "immense distance" from "these men close to nature."[4]

(Note that when I say "we" and "they" here, I am quoting or paraphrasing Condorcet. It is Condorcet speaking and not me. The same will be true for all other uses of the word "we" in this book; it is always someone whom I am quoting or paraphrasing who is speaking and not me.)

Condorcet was a member of the Physiocrats, the French economists that share credit with Adam Smith for founding the whole field of economics. He also found time during his career to be a mathematician, government official, and revolutionary leader. Condorcet was the last of the great French Enlightenment thinkers known as the *philosophes*.

The Marquis de Condorcet, Jean-Antoine-Nicolas Caritat, was born on September 17, 1743, two decades after Smith's birth. He inherited the not-very-exalted noble title from his father, a cavalry captain who died when he was five weeks old. His talent for mathematics led to his discovery by one of the leading *philosophes*, Jean le Rond d'Alembert.

Some remarkable women helped launch Condorcet's career. A few aristocratic hostesses sponsored the salons of Paris where the French Enlightenment took shape. Julie de Lespinasse, who was d'Alembert's girlfriend, first invited Condorcet to her salon in Paris in 1769. She mothered the shy, awkward, frail, friendless, poorly spoken, and uncouth twenty-year-old recently arrived from the provinces. Her advice was practical: Don't chew your fingernails, and don't show up at the salon with chalk on your ears. The salon of Julie de Lespinasse noted Condorcet's unusual combination of shyness and passion, of calm analysis and rash tantrums, nicknaming him "the enraged sheep."[5]

Condorcet had a gift for attracting women to help him. Another new friend, Amélie Suard, advised him on his tempestuous love life. He would need a lot of advice. First was his love affair with Madame Suard herself. He lived with her and her husband for seven years in what a biographer calls a "chaste ménage à trois." Second, he fell in love with Madame de Meulan, the wife of a tax collector in Paris. Then suddenly Condorcet at the age of thirty-nine eloped with the eighteen-year-old niece of Amélie Suard herself. Madame Suard rescued her niece and hushed up the scandal.[6]

Finally, at the age of forty-three, in December 1786, Condorcet married the twenty-year-old Sophie de Grouchy. Grouchy was a formidable intellect in her own right. She was an early example of a long tradition in which women restricted to traditional roles still managed to find some voice through their husbands. She and Condorcet set up their own salon, to which they attracted such prestigious intellects as Thomas Jefferson. After Condorcet founded a school to promote Enlightenment ideas called the Lycée, Grouchy became known as the Venus of the Lyceum—perhaps reflecting male tendencies to concentrate a little too much on Sophie's physical beauty.[7]

Condorcet was a remarkable forerunner in the cause of women's rights. The debate on rights for women would sometimes (although never quite enough) intersect with rights for the Rest throughout this book.

Two scholars note that Condorcet's radical views on women's rights came after marrying Sophie. Before the "Sketch," Condorcet had already written in 1790 a remarkable piece in which he saw equal rights for women as necessarily following from universal rights—including equal rights for different races—invoking the classic reciprocity argument: "Anyone who votes against the rights of another, whatever his religion, colour or sex, automatically forfeits his own."[8]

Condorcet's astonishing advocacy of women's equality was far in advance of most other Enlightenment thinkers, including Smith. But Condorcet would be hampered by his general problems defining what rights actually were. It doesn't help for women to have equal rights to men if men don't have rights to begin with.

Condorcet and Grouchy had many links to Adam Smith. Condorcet had attracted interest from another formidable salon hostess, the Duchess d'Enville. She was an eager consumer of the latest advances in social and natural sciences and became an adviser of leading Physiocrats from behind the scenes. Her son, Duke de La Rochefoucauld, was the same age as Condorcet. The duke would himself become a Physiocrat and became friends with Condorcet. None of them foresaw how these friendships would end in acrimony, betrayal, and murder almost three decades later.[9]

Condorcet's connection with the Duchess d'Enville was important, because earlier she had been a key sponsor of Adam Smith's introduction to the salons of Paris in 1766. Smith had met her and her son in Geneva on Smith's one and only trip to the European continent; they would remain friends and correspondents. Smith's temporary residence in Paris in the Faubourg Saint-Germain neighborhood was near the town house of the duchess and her son. Thanks to the duchess, the forty-three-year-old Smith was visiting the Lespinasse salon that Condorcet would later attend. Smith somehow managed to participate despite his inability to make his French intelligible to actual Frenchmen. His French was so awful that the

Duchess d'Enville started learning English to be able to converse with Smith.[10]

There would be lifelong connections between Condorcet and Smith. Smith would later own a copy of Condorcet's *Life of Turgot*, in which in turn Condorcet saluted *The Wealth of Nations* as "a work, unfortunately for the happiness of mankind, hitherto too little known in Europe." Condorcet's 1793 "Sketch," written after Smith's death in 1790, would celebrate the new science of political economy, advanced by "Smith and more particularly the French economists."[11]

As for Sophie de Grouchy, she drafted a commentary on Smith's *Theory of Moral Sentiments* in 1791. After Condorcet's death, she would publish this commentary together with her own translation of Smith's book in 1798.[12]

The first striking thing to notice about Condorcet and Smith is how similar they were. Both condemned past European conquests in the Rest, criticized colonial monopolies, and advocated free trade.

At first, Condorcet seemed well on his way to being an icon for equal rights of the West and the Rest. In the historical section of the "Sketch," Condorcet condemned the Spanish and Portuguese conquerors of the New World in words similar to those of Smith. In these conquests, the "unfortunate creatures who lived in these new lands were treated as though they were not human beings." The conquistadors were "greedy and barbarous men." Condorcet prescribed a reversal of such oppression in the Americas to achieve true progress in the future. He called for Europe to end "her oppressive and avaricious system of monopoly." She should call "upon all people to share her independence, freedom and enlightenment." As these passages show, it is not quite so simple as bad guy Condorcet versus good guy Smith.[13]

After establishing his impressive credentials on universal rights, however, Condorcet made the crucial swerve that would make him the vanguard of illiberalism rather than liberalism for the West's debate on the Rest. In the forward-looking part of the "Sketch," in the space of three remarkable pages, Condorcet set out an anti-liberal approach to the progress of the Rest that would have many echoes over the next two centuries. There would be a drastic change from what had already happened and the progress Condorcet envisioned in the future.

In the first pages of the "Sketch," Condorcet made clear that the purpose of the historical analysis of progress was to prescribe actions that bring progress. The analysis "will instruct us about the means we should employ" for future progress. The "should" words here transported Condorcet to prescription rather than description.[14]

The crucial shift occurred when he considered a range of peoples in the Americas, Asia, and Africa, differentiated by their potential for progress. While Europeans had oppressed those peoples in the past, now, after the advent of enlightenment, he saw the Europeans as the bearers of progress and freedom for Asians and Africans. Condorcet had a "we" (Europeans) and a "them" (Asians and Africans). We would become the agents of progress for them: "We shall become for them useful instruments or generous liberators." The good news for them was that we brought liberation. The bad news for them was that we got to define what liberation was.

The words "for them" were so important. The choices were going to be made for them rather than by them. Condorcet assigned the leading actor role in development to Westerners. The "for them" philosophy would have enormous consequences for the future of progress.

Condorcet had a lot of trust in European benevolence. The key break with the sorry history of colonialism was that the formerly oppressive European settlers had now become enlightened. The European settlers were no longer seeking "to amass treasure by brigandry and deceit." We European settlers were now the agents of progress. We offered the Asians and Africans "the truths that will promote their happiness," and we would be "teaching them about their interests and their rights."[15]

Us teaching them their rights is perhaps the most important phrase in Condorcet's whole future vision of the progress of the Rest. He had suggested that enlightened men define rights already in an article on despotism he wrote in 1789: "The best way to procure a complete declaration of rights would be to encourage enlightened men to each draw up, separately, a model for one." The committee of enlightened men would then reconcile differences among themselves. This article on the word *despotism* was rather condescendingly subtitled: "For the Benefit of Those Who Pronounce This Word Without Understanding It." Maybe the victims of despotism understand it pretty well. But Condorcet overexplains despotism and rights. The Europeans would convey to the non-Europeans the correct definition of their rights, which did not include the right not to have someone else define your rights.[16]

Some Indigenous peoples would not survive this definition of rights. European settlers' efforts in the New World to civilize the locals might succeed. Or the efforts might fail, in which case the Europeans would have caused the extinction of Indigenous peoples: "Will not the European population in these colonies, spreading rapidly over that enormous land, either civilise or bring about the disappearance, even without conquest, of the savage nations who still inhabit vast tracts of its land?"[17]

Condorcet tended to get incoherent whenever his notion of progress became contradictory. Either the European settlers in the Americas would succeed in civilizing the natives or they wouldn't. In the latter case, Condorcet embraced the Development Right of Conquest applied to the land rather than to the people. For European settlers to develop the land, the uncivilizable people had to disappear. But Condorcet claimed the disappearance would somehow happen "without conquest." Perhaps he meant assimilation of the conquered by the conquerors, but the assimilation was still not optional.

While Indians in America were already disappearing, Condorcet more shockingly considered the disappearance of groups in Africa and Asia that had not yet happened. Condorcet defined four different groups inhabiting the "vast lands" of Asia and Africa, sorted by their potential for progress. The first group consisted of "numerous peoples who only await assistance from us to become civilised." The second group was "nations oppressed by sacred despots or dull-witted conquerors." Condorcet did not include Europeans among the dull-witted conquerors from whom the locals wanted liberation. The Europeans would conquer the locals to free them from conquest by somebody else.

The first two groups allegedly wanted European settlers to come to civilize them and to liberate them from any local despots, which would make the rapid progress of these groups possible. At this point, the Europeans' development mission applied to the conquered people rather than the lands. The settlers were going to assist the locals rather than replace them.

Things looked very different for the next two groups. The third group consisted of "tribes living in a condition of almost total savagery." This group was more backward. The fourth group was made up of "conquering hordes who know no other law but force, no other profession but piracy." This group was apparently too lawless to appreciate or receive the blessings of civilization. The forecast for groups three and four in Africa and Asia was ominous: "The progress of these two last classes of people will be slower and stormier; and perhaps it will even be that, reduced in number as they are driven back by civilized nations, they will finally disappear imperceptibly before them or merge into them."[18]

Was Condorcet advocating extermination of some Indigenous peoples? Condorcet embodied the confusion between descriptive and prescriptive economics that would haunt the development debate for the next two centuries. Today, for example, some might predict that greater assimilation of Native Americans would increase GDP but never address whether that prediction makes such assimilation desirable.

Was Condorcet predicting what would happen, or was he recommending what should happen? On one hand he was describing progress that had already happened and using this record to predict future progress. He wants "a science for predicting the progress of the human race."[19]

On the other hand, on the same page where he began his analysis of non-Europeans, he described his idea of progress as "the means to individual welfare." A few pages after these passages, he celebrated "the real advantages that should result from this progress," which would lead to "the absolute perfection of the human race," which would lead to the "happiness of human beings." Words like "individual welfare," "perfection," and "happiness" are normative. He said Europeans brought "sweet blessings of civilization" to the rest of the world.[20]

Omitting further reference to the sad outlook for natives in America and groups three and four in Africa and Asia, Condorcet returned to the cheerful prospect for development of those in the Rest who were willing to be led by us European *philosophes*. There was again a "we" and a "they": "The progress of these peoples is likely to be more rapid and certain than our own," because they are so lucky to "receive from us" all "those simple truths and infallible methods" for progress. Now "all that they need to do is to follow the expositions and proofs that appear in our speeches and writings."[21]

Condorcet's summary picture of the progress of the Rest was full of contradictions. He saw the great powers as establishing "equality between societies" and offering "respect for the independence of weak states," yet he was describing European conquest and settlement of native lands in America, Africa, and Asia and the disappearing of some native groups.[22]

To justify these contradictions, Condorcet could have noted that there might be conflicting goals, of the West fostering material progress in the Rest versus respecting the rights of their people. Condorcet did not go in this direction. A few pages later in the "Sketch," Condorcet insisted that all goals were consistent with each other. Progress featured "the reconciliation, the identification of the interests of each with the interests of all." His vision had no conflicting interests of different peoples: There was only "the human race" who would be "emancipated from its shackles," overcoming the "enemies of its progress," and "advancing with a firm and sure step along the path of truth, virtue and happiness!"[23]

Everything went together: "Nature has linked together in an unbreakable chain truth, happiness and virtue." A century and a half later, the great liberal Isaiah Berlin would cite the "unbreakable chain" quote of Condorcet as one of the roots of the totalitarian ideologies of the twentieth century. Condorcet saw only one truth, one goal, one interest. Berlin lamented how unintentional this was, because Condorcet was "one of the best men who ever lived."[24]

Condorcet's resolution of the contradictions was given by his nearly limitless faith in enlightened men to figure it all out. In an article in 1786, Condorcet had explained: "Let men be enlightened, and soon you will see the good emerge effortlessly from the common will." In a 1790 article, he had similarly celebrated "enlightened men of all countries" who made up "only a single body, ruled by the same principles, and heading toward a single goal." These men were everywhere the "peaceful apostles" of "reason and freedom." They were "superior to the inhabitant of the forests of Ohio." Such apostles of reason were also superior to "ordinary people" not much advanced beyond the Indigenous people in Ohio. These commoners "have often simply substituted degrading vices for the brutality of the savage."[25]

We European experts could not just do nothing. We had to make progress happen. Condorcet wanted us to be guided by "maxims that favour action and energy." We had "to learn how to recognise and so to destroy, by force of reason," any "tyranny and superstition." For Condorcet, the experts were to be in charge of defining and achieving rights and boosting material incomes, without questioning their right to be in charge.[26]

Smith had a different view on the role of experts. As we saw in the previous chapter, Adam Smith had already offered a different vision of the West and the Rest before Condorcet wrote his "Sketch." Smith's critique of the West's conquest of the Rest was central to his thought. It came in the middle of his crucial rejection of mercantilism in Book Four of *The Wealth of Nations*, which was among his biggest contributions to economic thinking at the time. What later became known as mercantilism was the view that a nation's wealth consisted of its reserves of gold and silver, which it should increase by promoting exports and restricting imports. A trade surplus of exports over imports would result in an inflow of more gold and silver.[27]

The policy experts of Smith's time treated reserves of precious metals as an objective measure of progress. Although Condorcet was not a mercantilist, he shared their notion of some tangible index of progress that the experts could seek to increase. In contrast, Smith did not offer any single measure of progress to replace mercantilism.

Smith said the mercantilists' measure of progress was nonsense. He ridicules those who thought that "to heap up gold and silver in any country is supposed to be the readiest way to enrich it." They thought that "to multiply those metals is the great object of national industry and commerce." From this stupid point of view, "it necessarily became the great object of political economy to diminish as much as possible the importation of foreign goods." For Smith, "the mercantile system" sought to maximize domestic production, as if it were "the ultimate end and object of all industry and commerce."

Mercantilist views are still around today, as if the object of policy should be to make everything at home. Smith's original insight is as compelling as ever. If achieving trade surpluses is the goal, there is an unresolvable conflict between nations. If one nation is running a surplus, one or more other nations must be running a trade deficit. Mercantilism sees trade as a zero-sum game. Policymakers compete with each other to make their nation the one with the trade surplus by restricting imports. The competition will kill off international trade and both sides will be worse off.[28]

Smith defined progress by what people wanted rather than by what the mercantilist experts said they should want. Trade "carries out that surplus part of the produce of their land and labour for which there is no demand among them, and brings back in return for it something else for which there is a demand." The crucial word here is "demand."[29]

Smith now suddenly brought up the conquest of America as an example of his key anti-mercantilist point: "It is not by the importation of gold and silver that the discovery of America has enriched Europe." The enrichment was the opportunity to realize new gains from trade, which should have benefited both sides. The two sides had different goods to offer and different wants for those goods, the ideal conditions for beneficial trade. Like mercantilism, conquest took what could have been a positive-sum game and made it into a zero-sum game.

Beginning with the Spanish, the mania for precious metals motivated conquest instead of commerce, as they seized "possession of the countries of which the inhabitants were plainly incapable of defending themselves." They got gold through "the plundering of the defenceless natives," until the natives were "stript of all that they had." According to the mercantilist definition of success, brutal conquest was indeed successful.[30]

Smith took particular relish in denouncing the Spanish, a safe attack to make in eighteenth-century Britain. But later in the chapter, Smith extended the critique to all European conquerors in both Asia and the Americas. He saw that "the discovery of America, and that of a passage to the East Indies by the Cape of Good Hope, are the two greatest and most important events recorded in the history of mankind." The possibility of trade would seem to make these events beneficial to both sides: "By uniting in some measure the most distant parts of the world, by enabling them to relieve one another's wants, to increase one another's enjoyments, and to encourage one another's industry, their general tendency would seem to be beneficial." But the Europeans' conquest ruined the benefits for the non-European side: "To the natives, however, both of the East and West Indies, all the commercial benefits which can have resulted from those events have been sunk and lost . . . ."[31]

Smith was hardly an anti-colonial saint. Like virtually every European writer in the eighteenth century, Smith referred to the American natives (although not to the Aztecs or Incans) as "savages." Moreover, Smith spent a lot of time in *The Wealth of Nations* describing the development successes of the European settler colonies compared to the "savages" as a descriptive fact, and relatively little time on moral condemnation. Perhaps because of this, Smith's normative critique of conquest was overlooked by many readers then (and now).

Despite Smith's fierce critique of the Spanish conquest of the Americas, he described even this conquest as progress by objective measures like population: "The progress even of the Spanish colonies, however, in population and improvement, has certainly been very rapid and very great." If the Spanish had not come, it would have been impossible for these lands to "have been so much improved or so well cultivated as at present." On one hand, he noted "the cruel destruction of the natives." On the other hand, he pointed out that the lands of the Incas and Aztec were "more populous now than they ever were before" and this population now had better development potential because "the Spanish creoles are in many respects superior to the ancient Indians." Smith singled out the future United States as an even greater success: "But there are no colonies of which the progress has been more rapid than that of the English in North America. Plenty of good land, and liberty to manage their own affairs their own way, seem to be the two great causes of the prosperity of all new colonies." He omitted noticing that the plenitude of land came from somebody else, and that this somebody else did not have liberty.[32]

Smith repeatedly used the words *progress*, *improvement*, and *prosperity* in ways similar to modern uses of the phrase *economic development*. Like Condorcet, Smith was often not that clear whether this was what should have happened as opposed to what did happen. And Smith's main contribution was correctly seen as making the case for liberty because it facilitated material progress.

But the crucial distinction between Condorcet and Smith is that Condorcet saw European settlers as agents of progress for non-Europeans, while Smith saw the settlers as benefiting only themselves. Smith never claimed that European settlement was good for the natives, either in the present or the future. Smith was deeply skeptical about those who claimed to be acting in the interests of others.

The other critical difference between Condorcet and Smith is on individual freedom. Throughout *The Wealth of Nations*, Smith insisted on individual freedom of choice in all market transactions as an end in itself. In his critique of British policy toward the European settlers in North America, Smith saw free trade as a moral good. The British banned the settlers from constructing steel furnaces or other manufactures, forcing them to buy manufactured goods from British merchants. Smith was appalled at this violation of the settlers' freedom even though the policy's empirical effect on their prosperity was small: It was "a manifest violation of the most sacred rights of mankind."[33]

Variations on the noun "choice" or verb "choose" occur forty-eight times in *The Wealth of Nations*, usually referring to individual choice. Smith mentions "consent" twenty-four times.[34]

Interestingly for the subsequent history of philanthropy, Smith thought even the recipients of charity should be free to choose. He noted that charitable foundations offering college scholarships decided which college the recipients should go to. He thought the students should choose and that this would force the colleges to provide something worth choosing.[35]

In contrast to Condorcet, Smith doubted the *philosophes* knew what was best for everyone else. Whoever thought they knew what was best for others was just suffering from "innumerable delusions." "No human wisdom or knowledge could ever be sufficient" for "superintending the industry of private people."[36]

Smith's moral critique of the experts puts the two most famous passages of *The Wealth of Nations* in a different-from-usual light. Both are about self-interest:

> It is not from the benevolence of the butcher, the brewer, or the baker that we expect our dinner, but from their regard to their own interest. We address ourselves, not to their humanity, but to their self-love, and never talk to them of our own necessities, but of their advantages.[37]

The butcher offers himself as a selfish trader. He is not a savior. We are OK with that. In Smith's most famous quote, the trader

> intends only his own gain; and he is in this, as in many other cases, led by an invisible hand to promote an end which was no part of his intention. Nor is it always the worse for the society that it was no part of it. By pursuing his own interest, he frequently promotes that of the society more effectually than when he really intends to promote it.[38]

In contrast, Smith doubted the claims of some merchants to be selfless: "I have never known much good done by those who affected to trade for the public good." Smith's great paradox was that the selfish do more good than the saviors do. Many readers of Smith ever since have expressed disbelief that others' self-interest could be so benevolent for us. In fact, reviewing Smith's views outside of these famous quotes, he was actually saying to these readers: You are right.[39]

Smith insisted the evaluation of progress needed normative guidelines, a theory of justice. He had already set forth his theory of justice in 1759 in *The Theory of Moral Sentiments.* He periodically revised his first classic until his death in 1790. In the space of two pages in *The Theory of Moral Sentiments*, Smith sought to outline moral principles that would guide the future course of economics. That he did not succeed is one of the tragedies of intellectual history.

He asked us to imagine an "impartial spectator," who is neutral between us and the other party we are dealing with. A transaction is just if this impartial spectator would approve. Our transaction with another person might use force "to take from him what is of real use to him merely because it may be of equal or of more use to us," but this would fail the test: "No impartial spectator can go along with" such robbery.

The impartial spectator allows us to see things from the other side. What is important is not how "we may naturally appear to ourselves." What matters is how "we naturally appear to others." The spectator directs us to dealings in which our "self-love" is constrained to be "something which other men can go along with." The impartial spectator is a test of reciprocity—would you be okay with him doing to you what you are doing to him? If yes, then it is just. If no, then it is unjust. This reciprocity principle was destined for a long career in liberal thought.[40]

Trade by mutual agreement passes the reciprocity test—we respect the other's right to agree to the trade just as they respected our right to agree. The invisible hand requires mutual assent for our selfishness to be beneficial.

Similarly, the positive role that profit incentives play in economic prosperity holds only if they are constrained by freedom. Yes, profits are "useful and proper for rousing the industry and attention of mankind." Yes, "success in every sort of business" is "the reward most proper for encouraging industry, prudence, and circumspection." But profit incentives for robbery also exist, and these are not "proper." Our stealing the lands of others could have a balance sheet identical to an enterprise based on voluntary exchange. The impartial observer cannot tell the difference between proper and improper profit by some objective indicator like our rate of profit. The observer needs to know whether we are using force. For Smith, profits were proper only if they come from voluntary market transactions for land, labor, capital, or goods.[41]

Smith was *not* claiming that justice is in our own individual self-interest. Justice is not self-enforcing. I may well be worse off by not stealing: "It could not surely be better for you, that I should possess what is my own, than that you should possess it." Sometimes crime does pay. So justice can only be a purely moral principle: We ought "to abstain from whatever belongs to" someone else.[42]

Smith made clear that he was applying the analysis of injustice to our interactions with faraway parts of the earth, not just within our own societies. In a famous passage, he imagined how a Briton would feel if "the great empire of China, with all its myriads of inhabitants, was suddenly swallowed up by an earthquake." Sadly, "provided he never saw them, he will snore with the most profound security over the ruin of a hundred millions of his brethren." He would care a lot more about any "paltry misfortune of his own."

This is usually where the quote stops, but what Smith said next is the most important part. Would it really be okay for the Briton to act on his indifference to others? Should he prevent a tiny loss for himself by ruining a hundred million Chinese? According to Smith, only a villain full of the "greatest depravity and corruption" could say yes. No matter how little the Briton cared about the distant others, justice required that he not gain at the expense of those others.[43]

In a passage seventeen years later in *The Wealth of Nations*, Smith used the earthquake metaphor again on another set of British villains who sacrificed others for their own gains—the East India Company officials and traders colonizing India. Every company official wanted to loot India and then get out of India. The day after leaving India with his loot, the official would not care if India "was swallowed up by an earthquake." Again, Smith applied principles of justice to Europeans' interactions with the rest of the world and not just with each other.[44]

One quake-like disaster in India occurred shortly before Smith wrote these words. In 1770, a horrific drought and famine struck the Indian region of Bengal. Rice production fell by 70 percent. Peasants ate leaves and grass. They sold their children to pay the astronomical prices for rice. In the middle of this, the East India Company maintained its heavy taxes. Company soldiers set up scaffolds in the countryside to hang anyone who resisted the revenue assessments, which for some peasants the company raised by 10 percent. As a company official said, the revenues were "violently kept up to their former standards." In the midst of one of the worst famines in Bengal history, East India Company revenue did not decline. Its share price even went up. The famine killed about one-fifth of the population.[45]

Smith indeed thought the Company's heavy taxation of starving peasants had turned "that dearth into a famine." The East India Company left Bengal only with "want, famine, and mortality." The Company had "exactly the same tendency" as other colonial governments to be "so perfectly destructive a system."[46]

The famine was not the only disaster the colonial rule caused in India. The British from the beginning had destroyed opportunities for mutual gains from trade. In 1755, "the spirit of war and conquest seems to have taken possession of" East India Company officials in

India, Smith said, and it seemed "never since to have left them." By this time they had "acquired the revenues of a rich and extensive territory," which included Madras, Pondicherry, and Calcutta (the capital of Bengal). By 1773, the company had "extended either their dominion or their depredations over a vast accession of some of the richest and most fertile countries in India," with the result that "all was wasted and destroyed."[47]

The East India Company now commanded "obedience only by the military force with which they are accompanied." Once again for Smith, the crucial issue was force versus choice. Indians had not agreed to what the company called trade.

The trade the company offered Indians at the point of a gun aimed to sell British goods at the highest possible price an armed monopoly could impose, Smith noted. Then the armed monopoly would buy Indian goods at the cheapest possible price. The East India Company's "military and despotical" rule excluded any competitors who might offer Indians a better deal. Colonial rulers acted in "the interest of monopoly," which perverted "Justice." Their policy was "to harass and ruin those who interfere with them in any branch of commerce."[48]

Smith was more convincing on what was wrong than on how to fix it. Smith's implied recommendations were so far only negative—don't conquer, don't steal, don't destroy, don't oppress, don't starve, don't kill. And he did not say how to enforce even these negative principles.

A critic of Smith pointed out this lacuna for the case of India. The poet William Julius Mickle in 1779 criticized Smith's idea of replacing the East India Company with "free trade with Asia." What was Smith's plan to protect the traders from robbery and expropriation? Mickle thought that the naive Smith just assumed away the problem: "It is, according to the Doctor, as safe to settle in, and trade with India, as to take a counting-house near London-bridge, or to buy a peck of peas at Covent-Garden." Some liberals in the future would be tempted to embrace colonialism for the sake of enforcing free trade and other individual rights.[49]

Smith did not even have a plan for ending British colonialism. Smith was alert as always to incentives, such as the incentives for Britain to maintain colonialism. "The private interest of the governing part" of the colonizing country wanted colonial opportunities for political patronage and enrichment. The bad incentives existed even though replacing colonial monopolies with free trade with independent nations would be in the economic interest of the majority of Britons, Smith said. But Britons also had a nonmaterial want for national status. The majority still supported empire, because losing an empire would be "mortifying to the pride of every nation."

So Smith saw no hope for replacing colonialism with independence for colonial subjects. Voluntary renunciation of conquests was "a measure as never was, and never will be, adopted by any nation in the world," whatever "the most visionary enthusiasts" might want.[50]

But blaming Smith for not having an expert plan is to misunderstand Smith. Progress did not come from experts. Even the success of free markets at home in Britain was not due to expert advice. As Smith wrote, the system "from which so many advantages are derived, is not originally the effect of any human wisdom." Nobody "foresees and intends that general opulence to which it gives occasion." The trading system just evolved by some combination of historical and geographic accidents.[51]

Smith believed markets functioned with nobody guiding the outcome, hence the "invisible hand." The institutions that supported markets had also emerged without anyone intending the results.

As the political scientist Jennifer Pitts (whose work this chapter partially exposits) pithily summarizes Smith's relentless skepticism about those European experts:

> Smith reminds us, to live under a good system is not necessarily to understand how it evolved, or even exactly how it works: even if Europeans benefited from a fortunate set of circumstances to produce relatively free and effective

> governments, they might not be in a position to export those institutions.[52]

In contrast to Condorcet's celebration of Western agents of progress, Smith saw us experts as rather pathetic. We solution-mongers suffered from "a certain spirit of system" in which we "value the means more than the end," in which we fell in love with our own "view to perfect and improve a certain beautiful and orderly system." Supposedly, we were "eager to promote the happiness of our fellow–creatures." But Smith did not trust us reformers to know what others want, as we lacked "any immediate sense or feeling of what they either suffer or enjoy."[53]

Smith wrote a remarkably fierce passage against the philosophers' claims to be able to engineer what is best for others. He added it to his revision of *The Theory of Moral Sentiments* right before his death in 1790:

> The man of system, on the contrary, is apt to be very wise in his own conceit; and is often so enamored with the supposed beauty of his own ideal plan of government, that he cannot suffer the smallest deviation from any part of it.

The problem yet again is that the man of system does not allow the intended beneficiaries of the system to reject the system. In one of intellectual history's most important passages, Smith identified the reformer's key delusion:

> He seems to imagine that he can arrange the different members of a great society with as much ease as the hand arranges the different pieces upon a chessboard.

But there is a big difference between chess pieces and humans. Chess pieces cannot move themselves. However, human pieces want to make their own moves, different from what the reformer "might chuse to impress upon" them. The man of system does not realize that the chess pieces might want to run their own lives.[54]

The *philosophe*'s central illiberalism was to think he alone was qualified to say what was best for others and should therefore force his solution on them. Smith says that for the guys with the great reform idea "to insist upon establishing, and upon establishing all at once, and in spite of all opposition, everything which that idea may seem to require, must often be the highest degree of arrogance." They "entertain no doubt of the immense superiority of their own judgment."[55]

Condorcet had focused on whether the people in the Rest were fit to develop themselves. Smith questioned how fit *philosophes* in the West were to develop anyone else. The issue was not whether they were fit to be free, but whether we were fit to coerce them.

There is some evidence that Smith may have been reacting here to the French Physiocrats. Although Condorcet had not yet written his "Sketch of Progress," other Physiocrats had prefigured Condorcet's endorsement of salvation by force. Smith in *The Wealth of Nations* had already criticized the Physiocrats for excessive faith in their own solutions. The Physiocrats wanted to force on society a "certain precise regimen," Smith said, "the exact regimen of perfect liberty and perfect justice." Smith rejected something like what today would be called shock therapy. Smith's denunciation of drastic reforms, even when they imposed his own principles, was a crucial difference between him and Condorcet.[56]

Smith had in his library four pamphlets written by Condorcet in the early stages of the French revolution about constitutional reform, as late as September 1789. In one, Condorcet proposed a legislative chamber made up of wise men, which he said in Britain would have included Adam Smith.

As for Condorcet, he failed to get to a conception of individual freedom to choose. In an article on freedom he wrote in 1793 and 1794, he did see freedom as missing when there was coercion: "I am not free as I no longer have the power to determine my course of action."[57]

So far, so good. Yet Condorcet could not quite resist his characteristic instinct to tell individuals which kind of freedom was good for them. He saw freedom as listening to reason, doing what was objectively the useful thing. If the individual was instead ruled by passions then he didn't cut it as a free person: "Freedom ceases when there is just one desire to which the will succumbs automatically."[58]

In his "Sketch of Progress," Condorcet described one area where passion often ruled. He denounced those whose excessive childbearing was "foolishly to encumber the world with useless and wretched beings." Instead of individuals making these bad fertility choices, "their aim should be to promote the general welfare of the human race, or of the society in which they live or of the family to which they belong." It is the philosopher who tells the family how they should behave in their own interest. This opened the door to coercion of individuals for the sake of the general welfare. Advocacy of compulsion in the name of lowering population growth would recur throughout the history of development.[59]

Who makes the rules on whether individuals are really free? Condorcet answered this in his Freedom article. Historically, Condorcet thought, people had not gotten to the right ideal of freedom on their own. They could not be trusted to fight for the right kind of individual rights. They had only "a vague sense of these rights," based only on "customs respected for superstitious reasons." Once again, Condorcet put Enlightenment intellectuals in charge. Once again, their job was defining what "rights" should mean for others. Condorcet congratulated himself and his fellow *philosophes* on "an extensive, and already very precise, understanding of the rights of man."[60]

Smith's critique of intellectual arrogance is compelling in principle. Nevertheless, the passivity implicit in this critique made Smith's idea of humility the hardest sell imaginable to economists. Experts have an incentive to embrace a big role for experts. Smith's ideas have a fatal flaw for intellectuals then and now: They do not give intellectuals anything to do. He seemed to be saying that the intellectuals should just shut the f— up and let people run their own lives.

Condorcet did not shut up. The French Revolution had made clear his attitude toward violence in the name of progress before he wrote the "Sketch." He had become president of the Legislative Assembly in February 1792. He would not be a Jacobin, and he did not advocate the escalating violence, but he accommodated himself to it. From September 2 through September 7, 1792, revolutionary mobs massacred one thousand prisoners whom the Committee of Vigilance had just arrested as suspected royalists. The murdered included forty-three teenage boys and more than forty supposedly royalist prostitutes.[61]

On September 4, 1792, the mobs also lynched La Rochefoucauld, Condorcet's old friend and fellow Physiocrat. The mob paraded his body in front of the coach of his mother the Duchess d'Enville, who had been the favorite society hostess of both Condorcet and Smith.[62]

On these murders of the prisoners and his friend La Rochefoucauld, Condorcet just blathered. "We must draw a curtain over these events whose number and consequences it would be too difficult to appreciate just now." He saw "a naturally good and generous people" as somehow "constrained to devote itself to such vengeance."[63]

The Duchess d'Enville did not appreciate that Condorcet called her son's murderers naturally good and generous. She threw her bust of Condorcet on the manure pile.[64]

In November 1792, Condorcet further justified the use of force in the revolution. There was the "necessity and the obligation" to obey "not one's own reason," but instead "the collective reason of the greatest number." The collective could force submission when it was just imposing reason. Who would define what was reason was already clear: the philosophers.[65]

In a 1793 letter, Condorcet was torn on the violence for progress. He wrote, "The French Revolution was certainly much bloodier than would have been desirable for the happiness and swift emancipation of humankind."[66] Condorcet compared peaceful and violent change in his "Sketch of Progress." Violent revolutions were "swifter and more thorough." They bought "freedom and happiness," paying "the price of transient evils." Peaceful revolution would avoid such evils, "but it might be at the price of long delaying the harvest of the fruits."[67]

In another 1793 piece, "On Revolution," Condorcet further justified violence for progress. He said that "opposition from the defenders of royalty and abuse soon required the adoption of harsh measures necessitated by circumstances." He thought that "the counter-revolutionaries" just appealed to reciprocity to embarrass him. They said if Condorcet had joined the revolution to protect his own rights, he should respect the same rights for his opponents.

Condorcet's rejoinder to the reciprocity argument was one of those tortured passages he came up with whenever he needed to reconcile the irreconcilable. Yes, the new social pact was to be "founded on mutual assurance of those rights." But wait, these rights did not "apply to those individuals wishing to dissolve the pact." Condorcet announced that "our treatment of them is constrained only by limitations to the exercise of our natural right to defend ourselves." What were these limitations? Well there really weren't any. "If a more important right is threatened," Condorcet says, "we need to sacrifice another, less important, right in order to preserve it." Our right to impose the correct answer trumped the individual's rights to choose the answer.[68]

"Let us make revolutionary laws," Condorcet said, in a foreshadowing of Lenin, "but only to advance the moment when we no longer need them." The revolutionaries did not intend "to shed more blood," but only "to bring the revolution to fruition and to speed up its conclusion."[69]

But the revolutionary violence kept getting more and more extreme. Eventually Condorcet had had enough. In June 1793, he denounced the arrests of moderate legislators and the censorship of the press. On July 8, a member of the National Convention denounced him in turn, and the Convention ordered his arrest. Condorcet went into hiding with a Parisian landlady, Madame Vernet, where he remained until March 1794. It was during this time undercover that he wrote the "Sketch of Progress."[70]

His wife, Sophie, now again played an important role. Condorcet had started to write a tedious defense of his role in the revolution, but Sophie persuaded him that this had little social value. She convinced him to return to a long-standing project on the history of progress, and so he wrote the "Sketch" as a summary for this never-to-be-completed project. She took him books during clandestine visits.[71]

She was also to prove indispensable in editing the "Sketch" (with some added passages on women's rights that she probably inserted) and seeing it published. Although Sophie helped make the "Sketch" the success that it would be, later intellectual historians failed to note her role. Not for the last time, a female participant in the debate on progress did not get enough—or really any—credit.[72]

In March 1794, meanwhile, another announcement threatened anybody hiding Condorcet with the guillotine. To protect his landlady, Madame Vernet, Condorcet fled into the countryside. His former friend Amelie Suard and her husband refused him refuge when he arrived at their home south of Paris on March 27. They may have feared for their own safety, or they may have hated Condorcet for his failure to condemn the murder of La Rochefoucauld. Or maybe they just wanted to avoid Condorcet running off with another one of their nieces.[73]

Condorcet's bumbling disguise as a worker on his own estate did not fool the locals, who had the suspicious character arrested. On March 29, 1794, at the age of fifty, he was found dead in his jail cell. Nobody ever established whether it was a suicide or an execution.[74]

Condorcet had left behind a eulogy for himself at the end of the "Sketch." He found it "consoling for the philosopher" that he leaves behind the fruits of "his efforts to assist the progress of reason." Characteristically for Condorcet, he saw the other expert philosophers and himself as having a starring role in progress.[75]

Condorcet was most problematic when he considered the two versions of the Development Right of Conquest: develop the people, or develop the land and acquiesce in the disappearance of the people. The way Condorcet almost accidentally backed into the second would be a bitter legacy of his approach.

Smith had challenged the developers' claims of superiority, their blindness to their own self-interest, and their willingness to use violent means to attain good ends.

Condorcet never became famous, but his ideas would appear in works of those who did. When Karl Marx issued his famous dictum "The philosophers have only interpreted the world. . . . The point is to change it," he was speaking like Condorcet.[76] When Harry S. Truman launched the modern era of development in 1949 by saying "We must embark on a bold new program for making the benefits of our scientific advances and industrial progress available for the improvement and growth of underdeveloped areas," he was unknowingly channeling Condorcet. Virtually all development economists, including this author, are in some way heirs to Condorcet.

Unlike Condorcet, Smith would become famous. But the fight between Smith's defense of consent and Condorcet's neglect of it would last for more than two centuries, with Smith's side usually losing. Smith had created only an ideal that a minority of liberal advocates would keep passing along from one generation to the next.

3

The Demand for Dignity

Even more than Adam Smith, Immanuel Kant gave a hearing to the arguments for the Development Right of Conquest and then forcefully rejected them. He denounced European seizures of Indigenous lands in South Africa, North America, and Australia. He denounced colonial exploitation of India and the Spice Islands, and the enslavement of Africans. Like Smith, he identified commerce as the moral alternative to conquest. But where Kant stands out is his formulation of a universal right to dignity.

An idea that I had not anticipated when I began this project is the importance of a demand for dignity. I started to notice how some modern discussions of development identified a need for dignity. But what does dignity mean, and what determines it? What did liberals have to say about dignity? At that point, I discovered Kant's writings on dignity.[1]

Kant was the first major thinker in the West to see the violation of consent as a violation of dignity. For Kant, to see some human beings as a means to progress for somebody else is to not respect them as human beings choosing their own objectives. In the liberal tradition so forcefully advanced by Kant, the quest for respect would be as important as the quest to escape poverty. When the Universal Declaration of Human Rights in 1948 declared that "all human beings are born free and equal in dignity and rights," it articulated ideals already present in Kant's writings more than a century and a half earlier.[2]

What is dignity? It is a word usually defined only in terms of other words that also need definition, such as "respect" or "honor." As so often with liberal ideals, dignity is perhaps easiest to define in terms of its opposites: contempt, humiliation, degradation, disrespect, dishonor, insult, condescension, patronization. All these words have a visceral charge that would be clear to many peoples and cultures.

Smith, in *The Theory of Moral Sentiments* in 1759, had already identified an individual's demand for dignity that was separate from his or her demand for material consumption. He saw it in opposition to oppression. Smith thought an oppressed individual had a passionate resentment for "the whole baseness of the injustice which has been done to him." Acting on such a passion would "defend us against injuries, to assert our rank and dignity in the world." We have a separate passion "to provide for the support and necessities of the body." The demand for dignity and the demand for material consumption were two different dimensions of our well-being. Elsewhere in the same work, he evocatively describes how "what chiefly enrages us against the man who injures or insults us, is the little account which he seems to make of us."[3]

But Smith stopped well short of the modern idea of equal dignity for everyone and did not spell out freedom as determinant of dignity. This would be up to Kant. Kant was born less than a year after Smith, in 1724, in Königsberg on the Baltic Sea. Königsberg was then part of Prussia; today, it is part of Russia and known as Kaliningrad.[4]

Like Smith, Kant was a critic of empire. In a work published in 1797, Kant asks whether colonial development of the lands of American Indians, "Hottentots" (as the Khoikhoi were then called by the Dutch) in South Africa, and Aboriginal people of Australia justified conquest of those lands. Kant noted the Europeans either took the land by force or by fraudulent purchases. Kant considered the rationale in words very close to those of John Winthrop, only substituting "nature" for "God." Kant spelled out others' argument that we should be allowed to conquer since nature "abhors a vacuum." Therefore, nature allegedly demanded our settlement on lands that "would have otherwise remained uninhabited by civilized people." The argument was that it was to "the world's advantage" that "these crude peoples will become civilized" thanks to our conquest.

Or maybe not. Although Kant noted sardonically that "sufficient specious reasons to justify the use of force are available," he thought it was pretty "easy to see through this veil of injustice." He noted that these bad arguments were like others that "sanction any means to good ends." He mocked the "supposedly good intentions," which cannot really "wash away the stain of injustice in the means used for them." The unavoidable conclusion was that "such a way of acquiring land is therefore to be repudiated."[5]

Kant in his writings counterbalanced what it means to be human against violations of dignity:

> As a person (homo noumenon) he is not to be valued merely as a means to the ends of others or even to his own ends, but as an end in itself, that is, he possesses a dignity (an absolute inner worth) by which he exacts respect for himself from all other rational beings in the world.[6]

Kant's usually tortured syntax was not going to give him much of a future in the refrigerator magnet industry. But the reader can still tease out the crucial points. Humans have an inherent dignity that they demand be respected by others. They want never to be used as a means to somebody else's end; they want always to be an end in themselves. They want never to be sacrificed for the sake of an abstract goal like progress or civilization or development. Development was made for man and not man for development.

So Kant formulated a revolutionary new principle based on human dignity: "So act that you use humanity" to be "always at the same time as an end, never merely as a means."[7]

You are always to treat everyone else as humans, whose well-being is an end in itself. You are never to dehumanize them by seeing them only as a means to some goal of your own, even if it is called progress or development.

Mutual respect for dignity was one application of Kant's famous "categorical imperative," that you should "act only according to that maxim through which you can at the same time will that it become a universal law." This famous imperative is related to Smith's impartial spectator in formulating the principle of reciprocity. Follow the maxims that you would want to be applied to you. You want your dignity respected, so you should respect everyone else's.[8]

Kant is not sufficiently recognized as an economic thinker. Kant partly had in mind economic exchanges when he asserted the mutual right to dignity and the categorical imperative. His example of economic exchange was a loan—you give me money today in exchange for me giving you money as repayment tomorrow. But what if I get a loan from you when I plan to cheat you out of repayment? This treats you the lender as a means to my enrichment. Mutual respect of dignity is necessary for economic exchanges. The categorical imperative is violated by the cheating borrower. If everyone behaved like him, Kant said, then there would be no market for loans.[9]

Another economics example that Kant gave of violating others' dignity was disrespecting their property rights. He included "attacks on the freedom and property of others." Kant saw that when I violate others' economic rights, I am violating the principle of respecting individuals as ends in themselves instead of just as a means to my own goals.[10]

Dignity is a nonnegotiable goal. Seeing material consumption and dignity just as competing ends that can be traded off against each other does not get it right either: "What is elevated above any price, and hence allows of no equivalent, has a dignity." Kant condemned the many attempts to offer material progress as compensation to others for their loss of dignity. The very act of you offering to buy me out disrespects my dignity. My dignity is not for sale.[11]

Kant even included my political right to participate in making the rules as part of my dignity. I should get "respect" for my "autonomy" in helping with "legislating" the rules. I want the political right to consent to the laws applying to me, so I should respect the same rights for you.[12]

Crucially for the future of Western philanthropy, Kant identified the paternalism of rich benefactors as a violation of dignity. The philanthropists preferred to give to the poor rather than recognize the rights of the poor: "They do not want to subject themselves to the rights of people, but to view them simply as objects of their magnanimity." I have a right to my own property; it is not something I beg you to give me: "What properly belongs to me must not be accorded me as something I beg for."[13]

Kant was not only a pioneer on the concept of dignity. Kant should be seen as one of the founders of liberalism because of his absolute commitment to individual freedom for everyone. The universally right law is that which "enables the freedom of each individual's will to coexist with the freedom of everyone else."[14]

Kant in the end was close to articulating the modern idea of self-determination as freedom: Freedom is "independence from being constrained by another's choice." It is the individual "being his own master."

Kant also offered a remarkable commitment to "innate equality" of the "original right" of all humans to "innate freedom." He rejected the group hierarchy behind the Development Right of Conquest. Kant's linking of the words "dignity," "respect," "autonomy," "independence," "equality," and "freedom" was momentous for the debate on progress, even if it was still a little too vague to be a reference to the full set of political and economic freedoms that lay far in the future.[15]

Despite Kant's clarity on principles, he did not see easy solutions on political institutions that would deliver equal dignity: "This is therefore the most difficult of all tasks, and a perfect solution is impossible." In a phrase that the twentieth-century liberal Isaiah Berlin loved to quote, Kant said that "nothing straight can be constructed from such warped wood as that which man is made of."

Again the liberals were a lot better on what was wrong than on how to fix it.[16]

Kant's idea of equality was about equal dignity and rights and not about equal outcomes. Indeed, he had doubted the development potential of Black people early in his career. In 1764, he quoted David Hume on some rather dubious empirical work on Black people and white people, saying that there was not a single example of a Black person who had "accomplished something great in art or science or shown any other praiseworthy quality." Whites, in contrast, "earn respect in the world" by their accomplishments. He thought the two races had unequal "capacities of mind."[17]

Kant also doubted the capacity of women. A woman "does not possess certain lofty insights," Kant wrote, "she is beautiful and engaging, and that is enough."[18]

Kant did not repeat these views two decades later in his career as he was writing about equal dignity, but nor did he renounce them. Yet importantly for the huge debate on whether non-whites and non-males were fit to be free, he did not take away the right to self-determination even from groups he expected to have inferior outcomes.[19]

Even though Kant did not know how to achieve equal dignity, and even though he doubted the ability of women and Black people to participate in progress, he still could renounce gratuitous and unjust violence. In a 1795 work on his hopes for "perpetual peace," Kant condemned the "behavior of civilized, especially commercial, states in our part of the world" for

> the injustice they show in visiting foreign lands and peoples (which with them is tantamount to conquering them) goes to horrifying lengths. When America, the negro countries, the Spice Islands, the Cape, and so forth were discovered, they were, to them, countries belonging to no one, since they counted the inhabitants as nothing.

Like Smith, Kant denounced the European colonizers of India:

> In the East Indies (Hindustan), they brought in foreign soldiers under the pretext of merely proposing to set up trading posts, but with them oppression of the inhabitants, incitement of the various Indian states to widespread wars, famine, rebellions, treachery, and the whole litany of troubles that oppress the human race.

Kant also denounced "the cruelest and most calculated slavery" in the sugar-producing colonies in the Caribbean. Counting individuals as nothing was precisely what violated Kant's dignity principle.[20]

Like Smith, Kant saw global commerce as the peaceful alternative to colonial violence. Each nation could offer "to engage in commerce with any other," as its traders traveled the world. The Europeans should have limited themselves to just "seek commerce with the old inhabitants. In this way distant parts of the world can enter peaceably into relations with one another." Like Smith, Kant foresaw a world in which commerce would replace conquest, where mutual recognition of dignity would replace a zero-sum world of disrespect and contempt for others. It would take a couple more centuries to move in that direction.[21]

PART II

LIBERALS DOUBT EMPIRE, 1776–1865

It has been recorded as a principle in our legislation, that commerce itself shall have its moral boundaries.

—Abolitionist Thomas Clarkson in 1808, celebrating the British abolition of the slave trade

4

Smith and Allies Challenge the Slave Trade

The Age of Enlightenment was also the Age of Slavery. Slavery was the biggest violation of Adam Smith's free market principles in British policy during his lifetime. Defenders of slavery creatively argued that enslaved Africans were materially better off than those back in Africa that had escaped this blessing. Surprisingly, Smith agreed with this claim. But he explained why he thought this was not enough to justify slavery. For liberals, slavery was the most extreme demonstration of how material improvement was not necessarily development. Smith was the first in an age of economists addressing moral questions. He responded to slavery's violence in the name of progress; his successors would campaign for abolition in the British Empire and in the United States. Smith's alternative to slavery was a market for free labor that led to positive-sum gains for both workers and employers. The role of slavery in free market ideas, and the role of free market ideas in the campaign against slavery, have not been sufficiently appreciated.

The number of Africans that British slave traders carried across the Atlantic surged in the eighteenth century. Britain became the single-largest slave trading nation over this period, in most decades accounting for more than 40 percent of the traffic.

Eighty-eight percent of British slaves went to the Caribbean. The brutal conditions in the sugarcane plantations caused such high slave mortality that slaveholders needed continual flows of replacements. The single largest destination for British slave exports was Jamaica, accounting for 38 percent of total British slave exports during the history of the slave trade.[1]

The lack of consent of the slaves to slavery and the brutal coercion by slave owners were not abstract concepts. On April 7, 1760, a massive slave revolt broke out in Jamaica. Over the course of the revolt, the slave rebels killed sixty whites. The British suppression of the revolt killed over five hundred Black men and women. The British did not manage to end the insurrection until October 1761.[2]

A slave named Tacky led the initial phase of the rebellion, so it is known as Tacky's Revolt. The etymology of his name suggests he had belonged to a royal lineage in a kingdom in what is now Ghana. Tacky died in battle early on, but the revolt did not depend on only one leader.[3]

The British forces tried to suppress the decentralized rebellion with severe punishments. One local white noted how they executed prisoners—"what they bring in alive we burn and some we hang in Gibbets." The British wanted to "leave a Terrour on the Minds of all the other Negros for the future." The British burned the rebel Quaco at the stake, like many others. They hanged some other rebels, Scipio, Harry, and Cuffee, then had their heads cut off and fixed on poles. The British Army pushed Black men, women, and children off cliffs. One observer noted, "We had Two that were hung up in Chains alive & Starv'd to Death. They hung a great while [and] one of them kept his Speech and Senses 9 days & a few Hours."[4]

Not long after Tacky's Revolt, on Wednesday, February 16, 1763, thirty-nine-year-old Professor Adam Smith at the University of Glasgow, Scotland, rose to address his students at 7:30 in the morning. He was very aware of the violence inherent in slavery. Possibly alluding to Tacky's Revolt, he explained to his students that slaves were "put to death in prodigious numbers on the least appearance of insurrection." The slaves were hung up with "an iron collar such as they use for the dogs, in which they will hang 6 or 7 days till they die of hunger."[5]

In the previous day's lecture, on Tuesday, February 15, 1763, Smith noted, "The authority of the masters over the slaves" is "unbounded." In the West Indies, he noted, "it was a customary thing for the master to give the slaves a whipping" in the morning. The European citizens were the masters, and they knew their profits increased the greater was their "power over their slaves."

Smith noted how slavery violated the reciprocity required for justice. Although white citizens in the British Caribbean made laws protecting their own rights, he noted sadly, they never made laws to protect the rights of slaves. On the contrary, they favored laws to strengthen even further "the authority of the masters and reduce the slaves to a more absolute subjection."[6]

The site of Smith's university, Glasgow, itself participated in the slave system. Smith had arrived a quarter century earlier as a fourteen-year-old student in Glasgow. The city at that time was a major entrepôt for slave-grown tobacco and sugar from the Americas. Glasgow shipped tobacco and sugar to other British ports and to France, Germany, and Russia in exchange for goods for export to the Americas.[7]

Adam Smith would never become well known for his moral critique of slavery. This was partly his own fault, as his strongest denunciations of slavery were in his nonpublic lectures in Glasgow. The quotes of lectures here are from two manuscripts of student notes on Smith's lectures discovered much later—one in 1895 and the other in 1958. Indications are that the first set of notes could have circulated for sale at the time, and his students could have told others about his ideas, but otherwise there was no way for Smith's views to have influenced public debate. In any case, the notes help us understand Smith's thinking that underlay some of his sparser public writings on slavery.[8]

In *The Wealth of Nations*, Smith noted that the labor of the slave "can be squeezed out of him by violence only" by the slave owner, "and not by any interest of his own" that he would choose for himself.

The West Indian slave owners actually enjoyed the violence, Smith believed, out of a "love to domineer."[9]

He had denounced violence in *The Theory of Moral Sentiments* in 1759. When violence prevails over justice, "what indignation does it not excite in the breast of every human spectator?" Smith imagined the impartial spectator having "compassion for the sufferings of the innocent," but "furious resentment against the success of the oppressor."[10]

The word "violence" was one of Smith's favorite terms of abuse. It appears forty-eight times in *The Theory of Moral Sentiments* in 1759, and forty-two times in *The Wealth of Nations* in 1776.

The renunciation of violence was the key to beneficial economic transactions. Smith condemned contracts based on violence in a lecture to his students on January 21, 1763. "A man who by forcible confinement or other violence" forces others to make a contract with him violates the others' "liberty." Smith said such contracts were not really contracts. "Now all such contracts or obligations which are forced from one by duresse," which are "extorted by fear," are null and void. A contract needs to be voluntary in order to be valid.

In the next sentence, Smith gave a shocking illustration of an involuntary contract: rape. Rape—both literal and metaphorical—would appear many times in liberal arguments. Smith suggested only the death penalty for the rapist could give justice to the victim for "the injury done her." Again, consent was the critical test. One could distinguish rape from love only by knowing whether there was compulsion or consent.[11]

Smith expounded further on the theme of men coercing women. In earlier times in Western Europe, Smith noted in a lecture on February 8, 1763, there had also been coercion in marriages. In those times, the wife was "greatly under the subjection of the husband." The laws were "made by men" and therefore were "very severe on the women, who can have no remedy for this oppression."[12]

In that same lecture, Smith drew a parallel between the men's oppression of their wives and oppression of their slaves. In ancient

Rome, the man of the house had the power to punish his slaves, which included even the power to kill them. And he "had the same power over his wife." Smith stressed again the parallel between wives and slaves: "The father possessed a power over his whole family, wife, children, and slaves, which was not much less than supreme." But eventually in Europe, "the husband and the wife came to be much more equal in their power," and then they both entered the marriage voluntarily. Marriage was now formed thankfully "merely by the consent of the parties." The wives no longer faced the death penalty for disobeying their husbands.[13]

Smith did not acknowledge how much women still lacked equal rights in Western Europe. Liberal thinkers in this book did not usually cover themselves with glory fighting for women's rights. But at least Smith's discussion of women's right to consent in marriage shows how much he viewed consent as universally desirable. For Smith, the desirability of free choice was not limited to market transactions.

On February 15, 1763, Smith discussed sexual relations within slavery. He described marriages of slaves as involuntary. The slave owner forced sex on the female slaves to breed more slaves. If the female slave was not producing enough slave children with her present mate, Smith said, the master would force her to give up that mate and take another. (Smith did not mention explicitly that the master sometimes chose himself to be the imposed mate. He only referred darkly to "prostitution" on the slave plantations.) The master violated the slaves' right to choose marriage, to choose sex, to choose whether to have children.[14]

Smith's critique of coercion intersected with his advocacy of free markets. Slavery was the absence of a free market for labor. It violated the slave's right to choose to work when he wanted, to keep the proceeds of selling his own labor services, and to choose the buyer of his labor.

For "slaves under the absolute and arbitrary power of their master," Smith said, there were no such rights to free commerce. The slave had no recourse if the master forced on him "the most severe and insupportable work," including "the most severe and grievous tasks imaginable," an accurate description of the work on sugar plantations.

Slavery was theft: "The fruit of all his labors, which were exacted in the most rigorous manner, went to his master." The master fed the slave "nothing more than was barely necessary for his maintenance, as a horse or other work animal." The slave "could enter into no contract without either the express or the tacit consent of his master."[15]

In *The Wealth of Nations*, Smith discussed the freedom of British workers to choose their own contracts. "Every man's interest would prompt him to seek" what he thought was "the advantageous" employment. Workers would choose "to shun" what they thought was "the disadvantageous employment," which to British workers included working on sugar plantations.[16]

Smith could not emphasize the ideals of free labor enough. The free worker owned himself; this was "the most sacred and inviolable" property right of all. To restrict him from supplying his labor wherever and whenever he wanted was a "violation of this most sacred property." Liberty should exist for both workers and employers to enter into contracts with each other based on the free choice of each side. Any restriction was "a manifest encroachment upon the just liberty" of both workers and employers.[17]

Many later readers would see these quotes as being about excessive government regulation, which indeed they were. Readers today see these quotes only as part of the debate between Smith and those to his left on the political spectrum. In Smith's lifetime, however, they also were part of the debate between Smith and those to his right who defended slavery.

The slave owners claimed in response to Smith that they had raised the material well-being of slaves. However, Smith's critique of slavery was about its moral violation of liberty for slaves, not about its material consequences for the slaves. In *The Theory of Moral Sentiments*, he referred to slavery in ancient Greece as "the vilest of all states." It was vile to sell slaves, "man, woman, and child, like so many herds of cattle, to the highest bidder in the market."[18]

Slaves responded to the disrespect of their rights by disrespecting the enslavers, as he said in *The Theory of Moral Sentiments* in 1759. "Nations of heroes" in Africa found themselves subjected to European slave traders. The slavers' "brutality, and baseness," said Smith, justly earned them "the contempt of the vanquished."[19]

Celebrating the just contempt of heroic slaves for their owners was radical. In 1764, this passage provoked a Virginia slave owner to respond to Smith. Arthur Lee was a member of the prominent Lee family that later produced Robert E. Lee. Lee said in defense of West Indian and North American slave owners: How could Mr. Smith "reflect on the inhabitants, in such opprobrious terms?" Was it necessary, Lee said plaintively, "that the Americans should be debased into monsters?"

Lee's argument was that slavery improved the material well-being of the slaves. He compared their consumption to that of peasants in Scotland and Ireland. By comparison, "the habitations of the negroes are palaces, and their living luxurious," Lee claimed. Therefore "the condition of those slaves is far happier than that of the Scotch or Irish vulgar." Lee wanted the evaluation of slavery to depend only on the material condition of the slaves.[20]

The argument that slavery was materially good for the slaves sounds so preposterous to modern ears that it is worth documenting how widespread it was. The argument was not new when Lee made it in 1764. In 1746, an official of the slave-trading Royal African Company named Malachy Postlethwayt had argued the slaves' "condition is much bettered than what it was in their own country." He cited the planters' incentives to safeguard the slaves' "healths and lives" to preserve the planters' own labor supply to grow sugar. Postlethwayt noted the slaves' condition was no worse than that of coal miners in European countries.[21]

Jamaican planter Edward Long later made a similar claim in his *History of Jamaica*, published in 1774: The planters had the incentive to treat slaves humanely. Since the slaves were such valuable property, therefore "too much care cannot be taken of them."

Long imagined that the slaves saw their owner as "their common friend and father." Regrettably, some slaves needed help to overcome "a savage, intractable humour." The slave owner then applied a little "coercion of punishment" for their own good.

Long appealed to facts on the ground in Jamaica to argue that slaves enjoyed better material well-being than English workers. The "House Negroes" got more meat and drink than the poor workers in England did, for "half the work." Even the slaves in the fields got "frequent intervals of recreation."

Long also claimed the Jamaican African slaves were better off than Africans still in Africa. His evidence for this was that he had "once interrogated a Negroe" about whether he wanted to go back to Africa. The sample of one said no, that in Jamaica "he had food and clothing as much as he wanted," and "a good house." Back in Africa, he said, he "would be destitute and helpless."[22]

These claims sound ludicrous today. Most people would see the slavers as too biased to trust their evidence for material betterment caused by slavery. Nevertheless, the slavery proponents here set up a clever trap. Most of their opponents took the bait and just fiercely disagreed that the slaves' material consumption was higher than that of free workers. However, this put the opponents right where the slavery advocates wanted them, debating just the empirical facts, such as slave diets. If the opponents objected to slave owners' claims of high slave consumption as biased, the slave owners could respond that a moral agenda also biased abolitionists' claims of low slave consumption.

Maybe somewhere and sometimes slave consumption was higher than that of some miserable free workers, or maybe sometimes higher than it had somewhere been in Africa. Modern economic historians have given a view of slave consumption as sometimes above consumption of free workers.[23]

Maybe some reforms that offered nutritional supplements to the slaves could make this true if it was not already. Indeed, Long argued for reforms in Jamaica to improve the material condition of the slaves. Therefore, if material consumption was a measure of progress, and anything that achieved progress was good, then slavers thought they could justify slavery.

Smith responded in *The Wealth of Nations* to the general claim that slaves were materially better off than the British peasants. He actually thought the claim was correct. For slaves in the West Indies and the American South, Smith said, we must not think their consumption of food or other essentials was worse than the lower class in England. It was in "the interest of their master that they should be fed well," just like he had an incentive to feed his cattle.[24]

If Smith conceded slaves could be materially better off than free workers, did that mean slavery was OK? Smith's answer in this passage of *The Wealth of Nations* was that the slaves "as they are in a state of slavery, are, no doubt, in a worse condition than the poorest people either in Scotland or Ireland."[25]

The benevolent-slavery thinkers defined *condition* to mean only material consumption. But Smith defined *condition* to include freedom. Smith denied that material betterment for slaves—even if it happened—was actually betterment.

Other opponents of slavery also emphasized the lack of consent of slaves to slavery. A key breakthrough used the consent versus compulsion itself to decide whether slaves were better off. A bishop named William Warburton in 1766 asked the slave owners: If you offer so much benevolence to the slaves, why do you have to force them to take it?

Warburton's ideal of freedom to choose allowed him to see slavery from the viewpoint of the slaves. Slave owners had torn slaves from their "native country by fraud and violence" yet claimed they "thereby became the happier." However, slaves had not chosen this happy outcome, as Warburton mocked the slavers: "Did your slaves ever complain to you of their unhappiness amidst their native woods and deserts?" Once enslaved in America, "did they ever cease complaining of their condition under you, their lordly masters?"

Warburton asked the supposed saviors of Africans, "Who are you who pretend to judge of another man's happiness?" His conclusion for the slave owners was to "let your slaves judge for themselves what it is which makes their own happiness." The liberal emphasis on individuals' right to choose for themselves covered Black as well as white people. It was a far more effective critique of slavery than arguing about slaves' material consumption.[26]

In Britain, twelve men launched an effort to abolish the slave trade on May 22, 1787. One would become a leading British campaigner against the slave trade, Thomas Clarkson. He quoted Warburton's crucial argument in 1786, in a book entitled *An Essay on the Slavery and Commerce of the Human Species, Particularly the African*. Clarkson then offered an even better rejoinder based on the reciprocity principle. If slave owners thought slavery was so great, why would not "any one of them make himself a slave?"[27] The choices of slave owners themselves were also evidence against benevolent slavery.

The Whig leader Charles James Fox later noted during parliamentary debate that whites kept claiming "that the Africans were less happy at home" than in the slave Caribbean. However, "what right had we to be judges of their condition?" Had anybody asked them? "They would tell us a very different tale, if they were asked."[28]

But abolitionists like Clarkson and Fox did not actually ask slaves to tell their very different tale. Clarkson's speaking tour against the slave trade did not feature ex-slaves.[29]

An image designed by the potter and abolitionist Josiah Wedgwood reflects how many abolitionists saw the slaves. It shows a slave in chains kneeling and asking, "Am I not a man and a brother"? The hypothetical slave asking to be saved by the abolitionists sounds like the hypothetical Massachusetts Indian that asked to be saved by John Winthrop's settlers. Abolitionists battling against the slave owners' paternalism had their own form of paternalism. It would take a long time (possibly forever) for white critics of paternalism to overcome their own paternalism by letting the patronized speak for themselves.[30]

Yet some former slaves did want to give their own testimony on the slave trade. And the success of their books in the London market suggested the general intellectual public was more interested than the abolitionists in hearing ex-slaves speak. The most successful ex-slave narrative was published in 1789 by Olaudah Equiano, also known by his slave name of Gustavus Vassa. He titled it *The Interesting Narrative of the Life of Olaudah Equiano, or Gustavus Vassa, the African. Written by Himself.* It turned out to be a best seller that made Equiano rich. A US edition was printed, and it appeared in German, Dutch, and Russian. Eight more editions appeared in Equiano's lifetime. Equiano's five-year-long book tour through Britain and Ireland boosted sales of his book and gave him his own direct access to white audiences.[31]

To be fair to Thomas Clarkson, he did at least write a letter of introduction for Equiano to visit Cambridge University on his book tour, describing him as a "very honest, ingenious, and industrious African." Clarkson asked his Cambridge contact to help promote Equiano's book sales.[32] Clarkson was listed as one of the subscribers to Equiano's book, committed to purchasing two copies.[33] On the minus side of the ledger, Clarkson's two-volume 1808 history of the abolitionist movement did not mention Equiano.[34]

Equiano in his book focused on the atrocities of the slave trade, not on those of slavery itself. In this he was typical of the late eighteenth-century British abolitionist movement, where the "abolition" sought was of the slave trade and not of slavery itself.[35] Abolition of slavery was apparently too radical for even the most committed abolitionists.

However, another ex-slave named Quobna Ottobah Cugoano in 1787 had published a more radical book in London, titled *Thoughts and Sentiments on the Evil and Wicked Traffic of the Slavery and Commerce of the Human Species.* The phrase "the Slavery and Commerce of the Human Species" is a quote from Clarkson's book title. He quoted a number of passages from Clarkson. The admiration did not become reciprocal—unlike Equiano, Cugoano did not succeed in getting Clarkson to publicly recommend him. Clarkson was not listed as one of the subscribers to Cugoano's revised and shortened version in 1791. Cugoano's book was printed by the same printer used by the Society for Effecting the Abolition of the Slave Trade, but apparently without any support from the society.[36]

Cugoano had been born in 1757 in a Fante village in the chiefdom of Agimaque and Assinee, near the coast of what is now Ghana. African slave raiders kidnapped him from his village at the age of thirteen and sold him to European slave traders in 1770. It was a rare first-person narrative of slavery to reach English readers:[37]

> I was early snatched away from my native country, with about eighteen or twenty more boys and girls, as we were playing in a field. We lived but a few days journey from the coast where we were kidnapped, and as we were decoyed and drove along, we were soon conducted to a factory.[38]

The European traders at the factory (slave-trading station) put him on a slave ship to the Caribbean. Cugoano said it was agonizing that as he sailed there was no way to get word back to his family what had happened.

Cugoano's slave ship landed in Grenada, where a certain Alexander Campbell purchased him. In 1772, Campbell took Cugoano to England, where he managed to escape. He found employment as a servant to prominent painters Richard and Maria Cosway. Richard Cosway produced a 1784 engraving of Cugoano waiting on him and Maria.[39]

Cugoano wrote in his book in 1787 that even "if the argument was even true" that slaves were materially better off than in Africa, it still "could afford no just and warrantable matter for any society of men to hold slaves." Cugoano thought it was just wrong to even argue about Africans' material consumption before and after enslavement like that of a "cow or a horse."[40]

Cugoano agreed that he himself had gotten some benefits in England from "learning and principles unknown to the people of my native country."[41] He acknowledged that England had some superior technologies to offer him. He still had not chosen to be a slave to get those benefits.[42]

Cugoano shared Smith's critique of conquest versus commerce. If the exchange between Britain and Africa had been consensual, if Africa were "not annually ravished and laid waste," Cugoano said, there could have been a "profitable trade carried on with the Africans."

Therefore, now the British should just "abolish the slavery and oppression of the Africans," Cugoano insisted. Let Great Britain offer their "arts and sciences" to any willing takcrs on the coast of Guinea. The Africans would voluntarily use such knowledge "to improve their lands, and make use of that industry as the nature of their country might require." Then Africans could choose whether to trade the fruits of their improvement with Britons.[43]

Cugoano invoked the principle of the Golden Rule, which was similar to Smith's and Kant's ideals of reciprocity as part of justice. "And as ye would that men should do to you, do ye also to them likewise." The British would not like it if "African pirates" had "made excursions on the coast of Great-Britain" to "carry off their sons and their daughters, wives and friends, to a perpetual and barbarous slavery." The British "have no better right to steal, kidnap, buy, and carry away and sell the Africans, than the Africans would have to carry away any of the Europeans in the same barbarous and unlawful manner." There was also no slaveholder who "would like to have himself enslaved, and to be treated as a dog, and sold like a beast." Again, the liberal skeptic asked, if slavery is so great, why don't you want it for yourself?[44]

Cugoano had a lot less success than Equiano with his book, perhaps because white readers saw it as too extreme. There were three issues in 1787, a French translation, and a revised edition in 1791. But the book got no reviews in the London press. After 1791, there is no further historical record of Cugoano.[45]

Unlike Cugoano, the white campaigners against the slave trade had access to influential people. The moral principles noted by both the white liberals and Cugoano soon entered parliamentary debates on slavery. The most famous abolitionist was William Wilberforce, who on May 12, 1789, introduced in Parliament a motion to end the slave trade. It failed to pass.[46]

On April 18, 1791, Wilberforce again motioned for abolition of the slave trade. Wilberforce yet again used the choices of slaves as evidence against claims that Black people were happier as slaves. If a slave had saved enough money, Wilberforce said sarcastically, "did he not always purchase his release from this situation of superior happiness?"[47]

Other voices in the parliamentary debate echoed the liberal skepticism based on choices of white and Black people. A certain James Martin asked: If we do not want slavery for ourselves, "how could we consistently entail an eternal slavery upon others?"[48]

The liberals still faced long odds against the slaveholding interests. Abolition again failed in 1791. It kept failing for the next fifteen years. The war with France distracted Parliament. As the British establishment opposed the radicalism of the French Revolution, other radical ideas like abolition lost support.

However, as would happen again in the history of liberalism, the lunatic fringe in one period saw their ideas become mainstream in the next period. On March 25, 1807, at twelve noon, Wilberforce's bill at last became law, abolishing the British slave trade. It was the first major victory for the liberals.[49]

Thomas Clarkson described the key insight and the key accomplishment of the abolitionists of the slave trade: "We have lived . . . to see the day, when it has been recorded as a principle in our legislation, that commerce itself shall have its moral boundaries."[50]

Sadly, successors to Smith mismanaged his legacy on the moral boundaries to commerce. The political environment after Smith's death helped obscure his moral vision of economics. In Scotland on August 30, 1793, a lawyer named Thomas Muir was put on trial for (among other things) complaining in a Smithian way about high taxes. The court found him guilty of sedition and sentenced him to fourteen years' transportation to the new penal colony of Australia.[51]

The same Scottish courts in early 1794 accused Smith's own student Dugald Stewart of seditious writings. The Terror of the French Revolution motivated the Scottish authorities to repress radical sentiments at home.[52]

Smith had died on July 17, 1790, at the age of sixty-seven. In a move that has broken the hearts of Smith fans since, Smith destroyed more than eighteen volumes of his unpublished manuscripts before his death. Apparently, the volumes included the development of his Glasgow lectures on government into a book, which Smith had been promising to complete for more than thirty years. As late as 1785, Smith had written about the book to his friend La Rochefoucauld (the same one that a mob later lynched in the French Revolution, which Condorcet failed to condemn). Smith told La Rochefoucauld that he had already had his notes "put into tolerable good order." Smith was suffering from some major writer's block. As noted above, these lectures included some of his most radical critiques of slavery.[53]

Had Smith feared that political radicals would misuse Smith's own radical critiques? Dugald Stewart thought so. But Stewart's own frightening experience with sedition accusations may have biased his supposition about Smith.

Around the same time as the Scottish sedition trials began in 1793, Stewart read his memoir "Account of the Life and Writings of Adam Smith" to the Royal Society of Edinburgh. Stewart felt a need to defend his late teacher against sedition. He denied emphatically that Smith had any intention "to unhinge established institutions, or to inflame the passions of the multitude." He said Smith did not deserve his reputation for "extreme" judgments.

Stewart said Smith just meant to give technical policy advice on freedom as good for "national wealth." He had not intended to advocate "political freedom," which was not the business of economists. As the great intellectual historian Emma Rothschild wrote: "Stewart's description of the instrumental value of freedom corresponds to very little which Smith himself wrote."[54]

Stewart was excessively eager in a time of revolutionary crisis to downplay the moral radicalism of Smith. In this, sadly for the future of economics, and sadly for the future of slavery and colonial oppression, Stewart was all too successful.

Later generations would see the founder of economics as having founded only a positive science, without normative judgments. Supporters or opponents of Smith would debate mainly or only his empirical predictions about free markets being good for well-being, as defined by some supposedly objective measure of wealth or income. They would lose Smith's great emphasis on freedom as an end in itself.

Nevertheless, some of Smith's economist heirs kept hope alive. Smith's student Dugald Stewart had a Scottish student named James Mill. Mill in turn had a son and student, John Stuart Mill, who became the greatest liberal economist of the nineteenth century. Smith's intellectual great-grandson John Stuart Mill would later renew the fight against slavery.[55]

Before that point, liberals would have to confront new claims of benevolent conquests for progress. One of these new conquests had been blundered into by the abolitionists themselves.

5

The West Invents the Rest

On May 10, 1787, the first British mission for the economic development of Africa reached Frenchman's Bay in Sierra Leone. Twenty-five years later, on September 16, 1812, Napoleon's invasion of Russia reached Moscow. In what strange world could these two events be connected?

A new Condorcet type of development expert thought they knew the answer. Economists, philanthropists, and abolitionists had come up with a plan for Africans, both those in England and those still in Africa. The plan for Black people in England flirted at first with the same kind of removal that was happening with Indians in America. This same class of experts, including one French economist in particular who had had a plan for Africa, also saw Eastern Europe and Russia as a less civilized area in need of their advice. They would see connections between many uncivilized peoples in need of plans for progress, carelessly stumbling into greatly expanded conquests of the less developed by the more developed. West Africa would be left with the beginnings of the British Empire there. Russia would be left with a never-ending resentment of Western condescension, as one of its greatest novelists would later express.

The West's great lumping of diverse regions and peoples into the Rest had begun. The new international class of economists defined the Rest as the less developed areas (making up most of the globe) where the West should make progress happen, including by conquest.

Development differences between regions were not imaginary. Table 1 shows a calculation of technology levels of the continents in 1500. The technologies include firearms, oceangoing ships, the wheel, horse-powered vehicles, the magnetic compass, printing, and the presence of iron and steel. The index measures percent of advanced technologies used in each region.[1]

Region	Technology Index, 1500
Western Europe	0.91
Eastern Europe	0.81
Africa	0.32
Asia	0.70
Oceania	0.12
Americas	0.14

Table 1. Averages for technology levels in 1500. Source: Comin, Easterly, and Gong.

There is indeed a large technology gap between Western Europe and Africa, Oceania, and the pre-Columbian Americas. The technological lag of Asia behind Western Europe is less marked, while the gap between Western and Eastern Europe is small.

Table 2 shows a rough calculation of per capita income levels three centuries later originally done by the economic historian Angus Maddison. Unlike the previous table, income per capita now reflects the effects of European settlement in what Maddison called "Western Offshoots" (Australia, Canada, New Zealand, and the United States) and in Latin America. In Western Europe, the industrial revolution has begun. The gap between Western and Eastern Europe is now large. Lumping together Eastern Europe and sub-Saharan Africa on the basis of per capita income alone in the early nineteenth century (probably not too different from the late eighteenth century) is not completely crazy. There is a more pronounced gap between Western Offshoots and Western Europe, on one hand, and everyone else on the other hand. Hence the division between the West and the Rest. It was not too different from the modern breakdown between developed and developing countries.[2]

Region	Income in 1820
Western Offshoots (Australia, Canada, New Zealand, United States)	$2,513
Western Europe	$2,307
Asia (East)	$1,089
Middle East	$974
Latin America	$953
Asia (South and Southeast)	$929
Eastern Europe	$818
Sub-Saharan Africa	$800

Table 2. Per capita income in the early 1800s. Source: Maddison.

Among the new experts was a French economist named Pierre Samuel du Pont de Nemours, who intended to be a connector between plans for progress in such disparate regions as West Africa and Eastern Europe. In 1771, Du Pont had proposed a scheme in West Africa in which the cheap "cultivation of sugar established among the Negroes in their own country" would drive slave-grown Caribbean sugar out of business. Du Pont expected his scheme would prove Africans were fit to be free because "we would have made them industrious cultivators." We could be benevolent civilizers instead of "senseless and cruel oppressors." Du Pont had contributed to the great lumping by treating African slaves and Africans in Africa as one homogeneous mass who needed to prove they were fit to be free.[3]

To get things rolling, Du Pont said, we should "create a few peaceful settlements on the coast of Africa." Du Pont mixed idealism with condescension. We will "say to the negroes; friends, you see that cane, cut it, pass it between the two rolls that we offer you, make the juice boil in the boiler like this." Du Pont offers that "we shall pay you well for the syrup that results" from his rather obvious instructions.[4]

Somehow French Enlightenment thinkers could not resist the Africa sugar plan. Condorcet, in the middle of his celebration of European colonization for progress in 1793, envisioned how "the sugar industry, establishing itself throughout the immense continent of Africa, will destroy the shameful exploitation which has corrupted and depopulated that continent for the last two centuries." Setting up a profitable sugar industry without slavery would convince the slave owners and traders that abolition was in their own interest. "Will not France hasten to imitate such undertakings dictated by philanthropy and the true self-interest of Europe alike?"[5]

Back in 1788, Condorcet had written bylaws for a "Society of the Friends of Negroes," of which he was elected chairman the following year. They contained the usual Condorcet paradox of remarkably advanced views on justice for all mixed with his fatal affection for experts to define what justice was. The experts would solve slavery by task force. The expert committee would "assemble all the facts and vouch for their authenticity, collect all the proposals for changing the present system, examine them, subject them to calculation, look for any information they may be lacking and obtain it, pose questions, find the answers and compare them, and finally form a considered plan of action, implement it and maybe even conduct some experiments."[6]

Only Condorcet's task force could offer "plans which are sufficiently detailed and based on facts and calculations." The committee would also enlighten slave owners "about their interests." The committee would consult the slave owners so the plan could benefit "from their enlightenment and their experience." Through these consultations, "the Society will attempt to discover, balance and accommodate the interests of all concerned." Characteristically, Condorcet thought of Europeans—even slave owners—as the agents of progress on slavery.[7]

This was the mindset that led to the Sierra Leone project. Du Pont shared Condorcet's view of thinkers in the West as God's gift to the Rest. And Du Pont was himself a member of the Physiocrats' group of economists in France that had produced Condorcet, who was four years younger than Du Pont. Like other development consultants then or now, Du Pont thought expertise in one part of the developing world qualified him to offer advice to others. Du Pont was one evocative example of the West lumping diverse regions and peoples into the Rest.

Du Pont had written a treatise in 1769 on French colonial policy in India. The French government thought Du Pont was also qualified enough to be offered the job of colonial administrator of Mauritius in 1774. Much later in his career, in 1817, he would comment on development plans for the Cherokees in the US.[8]

Du Pont would also offer advice in 1774 to Eastern Europe, when the Physiocrats sent him to Poland on what sounds a lot like a development mission. The New York University historian Larry Wolff, in a classic 1994 book (on which the Du Pont and Eastern Europe part of this chapter is based), described this event as part of the invention of Eastern Europe.

Du Pont's main assignment in Poland was to advise a commission reforming Polish education. As Du Pont was about to depart Paris in the spring of 1774, he gave a farewell speech to a dinner of his fellow Physiocrats in Paris. He showed his characteristic condescension. Poland wants "to be guided by your counsels," Du Pont told his fellow Physiocrats. Poland "has caused me to envision the honor of creating a nation by public instruction."

The farewell dinner in Paris gave more warning signs of Du Pont's savior complex. "My friends, my dear friends, shed some tears at my departure," Du Pont said at the dinner. Somebody might have to carry back from Poland "my worn out body, as it will be after twelve years of the career that opens itself before me." It would be a battle, said Du Pont, to confront such savagery:

> I go to Poland to swim in the void . . . struggling in space with efforts as prodigious as they are useless. I go into a land of intrigues, jealousies, cabals, despots, slaves, proud ones, inconstant ones, weak ones, and madmen.

Upon arrival in Warsaw, Du Pont started work immediately on reforming education in Poland. He dismissed the Poles' own plan for parish schools. He proposed instead founding an academy to teach the works of the Physiocrats. A Polish observer noted that "no professor here has undertaken to conform to this plan" that emerged from "the enflamed head of Du Pont."

Du Pont blamed the Poles for failing to appreciate how great his ideas were. "The people of Poland are still serf and savage," he noted regretfully, and "what difficulties to take them out of" that condition! Du Pont said his main contribution was that "I have made on this point some memorandums." Du Pont was already starting the tradition of writing development reports that nobody reads.

Getting nowhere, Du Pont was relieved to get an offer back in Paris later in 1774 for a post in the French government. He departed Warsaw after a stay of three months, not quite the twelve years' battle to the death for Polish progress that he had promised.[9]

The Physiocrats had already sent one of their number to Russia prior to Du Pont's mission to Poland. The economist Pierre-Paul Lemercier de La Rivière had arrived in Saint Petersburg in 1767. He had just published a book on economics, and he also brought recent experience from another part of the less developed world as the administrator of the slave colony of Martinique. The Physiocrats sent him to advise Catherine the Great "with some assistants we have given him, to plant there economic legislation." Lemercier himself had in mind something like what two centuries later in Russia would be called shock therapy: "Everything remains to be done in that land; or to say it better still, everything remains to be undone and redone."

Catherine did not appreciate Lemercier's approach to economic advice. As she later wrote to Voltaire, Lemercier supposed "that we walked on four paws, and who very politely gave himself the trouble of coming from Martinique to stand us up on our hind feet." Twenty years after Lemercier's visit, Catherine was still complaining about him to the French ambassador Louis-Philippe de Ségur in 1787: "[He] got it into his head that I had called him to help me govern the empire, to draw us out of the darkness of barbarism by the expansiveness of his lights."[10]

Ségur himself had exclaimed on his way to Saint Petersburg: "When one enters Poland, one believes one has left Europe entirely." Noting the "dirty villages" and "cottages little different from savage huts," he felt he had "been moved back ten centuries." When Ségur got to Russia, he described it as a half-civilized place, a mixture of "the age of barbarism and that of civilization, the tenth and the eighteenth centuries, the manners of Asia and those of Europe, coarse Scythians and polished Europeans, a brilliant, proud nobility, and a people plunged in servitude." The "Scythians" Ségur saw reminded him of "demi-savage figures" he had seen carved on ancient Roman ruins.[11]

Indeed the label "Scythians" was borrowed by Western European thinkers from the ancient Greek historian Herodotus (490/480–425 BCE), who so named the barbarian people north of the Black Sea. Some eighteenth-century thinkers applied the name "Scythians" to all of Eastern Europe, until the label gave way to another more lasting designation also borrowed from ancient history—the Slavs.[12]

The career of an American world traveler named John Ledyard gives further insight into how the Enlightenment era promiscuously lumped together Eastern Europeans with other uncivilized peoples. Ledyard was born in 1751 in Groton, Connecticut, the son of a sea captain who worked in the Caribbean trade.[13]

Ledyard in 1772 began his career at a school in New Hampshire. A Congregationalist minister, Eleazar Wheelock, had started Moor's Charity School a few years earlier to Christianize and civilize America's own less developed people, the Native Americans. Wheelock's first big success was a convert to Christianity from the Mohegan tribe named Samson Occom. The Europeanized Occom then successfully toured England to raise funds for Moor's Charity School.

One who responded to Samson Occom's appeals was an evangelical Christian and one of England's richest men, John Thornton. Thornton's son, Henry, would later help start the philanthropic colony in Sierra Leone. At the beginning, the school gave courses to thirty-five Indian boys and ten girls on farming, Christianity, and Greek and Hebrew. Wheelock expected the students to go back to their communities to propagate true religion, advanced technology, and difficult languages nobody needed. Meanwhile, Occom and Wheelock had fallen out soon after Occom's return from Britain, with Occom complaining that Wheelock had abandoned him to poverty. Wheelock in turn denounced Occom: "I have taken much pains to purge the Indian out of him, but after all a little of it will sometimes appear."

Wheelock's other Indian students proved to be even less enthusiastic about Wheelock purging the Indian out of them. Wheelock shifted the school's objective to training white missionaries to the Indians. He refounded the school in 1769 with a new name taken from one of its patrons, the earl of Dartmouth. It is today Dartmouth College.[14]

The twenty-one-year-old John Ledyard in April 1772 attended the Dartmouth courses on civilizing the natives and then spent time among the Iroquois. He would for the rest of his career compare Russians and other so-called backward peoples to American Indians.[15]

Adding further to his development qualifications, Ledyard joined from 1776 to 1780 the third and final voyage of Captain James Cook. The expedition made stops in southern Africa, Tasmania, New Zealand, Tahiti, Hawaii, southern China, Cochin China (Vietnam), and Alaska. In Alaska he encountered Russian fur traders. Another stop in Kamchatka gave Ledyard further exposure to Russians.[16]

These last encounters made Ledyard want to explore Russia and Siberia. He finally made it to Saint Petersburg in 1787, where he wrote to Thomas Jefferson about how he had encountered "a Scythian at the table that belongs to the royal society of Physicians here." Ledyard told Jefferson, "The moment the savage knew me & my designs he became my friend."[17] Ledyard's new "savage" friend offered to help him with his planned expedition to Siberia.

A little bit like an American teenager today wandering the Third World on a gap year, Ledyard enthusiastically lumped together the peoples he encountered. Encountering "Tartars" on his journey in the city of Kazan on the Volga, Ledyard compared "the thick lip" and "broad flat nose" to Africans. The red-painted nails of the Tartar women reminded him of the Cochin Chinese (Vietnamese) he had seen on the Cook expedition. Further analysis of facial features led Ledyard to compare the Tartars with "the Chinese, the Negroes, and the Jews."[18]

Ledyard also wrote his friend Jefferson "how universally" the Tartars "resemble the aborigines of America." He observed how "the cloak of civilization sits as ill" upon the Russian Tartars as upon "our American tartars." He recalled being part of the Dartmouth "efforts to convert our Tartars to think and act like us," which he noted had had less than glorious success, with the relapse of even the most advanced convert, Samson Occom, into Indian-ness.[19]

Traveling farther into Russia, getting more excited by the mile, Ledyard in his journal remembered he had read how "the Scythians scalped their Enemies." Drawing another connection from his own experience, Ledyard then recalled how when the Hawaiians had killed Captain Cook, "they had cut off all [of his] Hair." Then of course there was scalping by American Indians. The practice of scalping allowed Ledyard to lump together Russian-Scythians, Pacific Islanders, and Native Americans.[20]

Like Ségur, Ledyard also got excited by an analysis of Russia's uncivilized Kalmuck people (which he spelled *Calmuc*), whom he identified as a branch of the Tartars. He became more precise on their racial differences from whites, calculating that "the ears of Calmuc and Mongul Tartars, project uniformly and universally farther from their heads than those of the Europeans." In an early example of empirical work in development, Ledyard drew a sample of three Tartar individuals and found an average ear projection of one and a half inches. Less precisely, Ledyard asserted that the Kalmuck ears "were by no means extraordinary examples—the ears of the Chinese are the same."[21]

As for the Jews Ledyard encountered in the borderlands of Russia and Poland, they also seemed to him "Asiatics." Their villages were miserable, full of poverty and dirt. This was "a proper situation for them"; indeed he thought "they ought to be placed between the borders of every Nation."[22]

As Ledyard got deep into Siberia, the Russian Tsarina Catherine the Great heard about his explorations. In December 1787, she ordered Ledyard arrested and expelled westward from the Russian Empire. The sources do not make clear why. "Regarding Ledyard," Catherine said cryptically, "discovery for others is not always discovery for us."[23]

A rather sore loser, Ledyard said as he left the Russian Empire: "I quit it gladly for the Godlike Regions of the West." Ledyard thought he was now qualified, based on "the little Tour I have made," to prove "the inferiority of the Eastern to the Western World." He had not previously comprehended "so vast a difference" between the two. Even Eastern European imports had showed him a difference in taste that "divides both Poland & Russia from the Genius of Europe." Imports from France consisted of "painted Gewgaws" and toys. The French fitted out her caravans to Eastern Europe the same as she did "her ships for the Coast of Africa."[24]

Back in Paris on July 4, 1788, Ledyard wrote a letter to Jefferson. After being "banished by the Empriss of Russia," Ledyard wrote about himself in the third person, "he is now on his way to Africa to see what he can do with that continent." Africa was never to find out what Ledyard could do with it, as he died suddenly in Cairo on January 10, 1789, at the age of thirty-seven.[25]

Meanwhile, back in Paris, Du Pont in 1774 had returned to his own Africa plan. He wrote the French government a memo recommending his experimental colony in West Africa. Nothing happened. Twenty-two years later, Du Pont was still pushing the plan in a proposal to the French revolutionary government. As often happened with Du Pont's memos, his plan went nowhere.[26]

Du Pont had failed to become the influential civilizing expert he hoped to be. While Du Pont had failed to become the Father of Polish Progress, he had more impact on the global economy as a literal father. His son founded what is still today the giant DuPont corporation.

Meanwhile, Du Pont's Africa scheme had gotten new life with a botanist named Henry Smeathman, who had spent four years around the Sierra Leone Peninsula beginning in 1771, studying local flora and fauna. He married the daughter of a chief. After she died, he married another chief's daughter, who also died. His botanical studies led him by 1783 to conclude that the area could produce "an immense quantity" of rice, cotton, tobacco, and sugar for export. Smeathman thought it was "one of the most extraordinary facts in the annals of mankind" that European slave traders for nearly three centuries had failed to notice they could profit more from buying African products from willing sellers than by kidnapping slaves.

His plan would correct that inexplicable oversight, forming a settlement in Sierra Leone where African production would take off with European techniques, education, and government. The plan would therefore "emancipate and civilize every year, some thousands of slaves," which would strike at the root of the European slave trade.

Smeathman was a much more talented aid promoter than Du Pont. It is unclear if Smeathman had heard of Du Pont's plan, or if it was a case of not-so-great minds thinking alike.

Smeathman in 1783 set an example for future aid promoters when he said he would not delay things by "foreseeing and answering any objections" to his scheme. Surely, any such objections would be "of very little moment when opposed to a plan of such magnitude." Humility was not a conspicuous feature of early expert approaches to African progress.

In 1783, Smeathman visited Paris to sell his plan for "civilizing Africa" to Benjamin Franklin, who declined to help sell others on the scheme. But British abolitionists fighting for the end of the slave trade loved the idea of an experiment to prove the superiority of African free labor to African slave labor. Smeathman had luck with one of the leading abolitionists, Granville Sharp.[27]

Sharp now joined the growing band of would-be saviors for Africans. In 1783, Sharp wrote a "Memorandum on a late Proposal for a New Settlement to be made on the Coast of AFRICA" referring to Smeathman's proposal. But he altered the plan with some even better ideas. One of Sharp's alterations was democratic self-government of the settlement. At the same time, "the settlers must not refuse to admit a Governor . . . of the King's appointment." The settlement should also "obtain the consent (and association, if possible) of the native inhabitants."[28]

Sharp's concern for the consent of Africans to be civilized was as salutary as it was rare. However, other promoters of the project did not share Sharp's priority on Africans' agreement to their own progress. Sharp himself did not explain how to reconcile self-government of outside settlers, the King's authority to rule, and the agreement of local Africans.[29]

Sharp further developed his own plan in another tract in 1786, even including a scheme for a paper currency in the settlement. On the paper currency, as apparently with other details, Sharp surprised himself on how easy it was to solve development problems:

> The advantages appear to me so great and extraordinary, that I can hardly give credit, as I proceed, to my own estimate of them, and am inclined to suspect that I am, in some way or other, enormously mistaken; but as I cannot yet find out my error . . .[30]

Sharp's failed attempt to doubt himself would have some bad consequences. But self-confidence is good for aid promotion. Sharp would secure financing, British government backing, and settlers for his experimental colony.

Sharp had to make some strategic alliances, first with Smeathman. Smeathman in May 1786 had already gotten on his side the British Treasury and a London philanthropic group called the Committee for the Relief of the Black Poor. He promised this committee that he would take care of London's Black poor "forever" by resettling them in Sierra Leone.

London's Black poor included those who had gained freedom by fleeing to the British side in the American Revolutionary War and then made their way to London. Many such free Black people in

London were in poverty, and many white Londoners were worried about their potential for crime.

In January 1786, the Committee for the Relief of the Black Poor stated its intent to "effectually relieve them." It mobilized support from Londoners by proposing the emigration of this potential criminal class. In February, the Committee even tried to get support from West Indian slave owners by tying its plan to a possible new law "to prevent any Foreign Blacks being brought to this Country to remain." The planters were enthusiastic about this attempt to shut an escape valve out of slavery.

At this point, the plan came close to embracing the removal of Black people from England back to Africa. The idea of removing uncivilized people from civilized societies had already come up under John Winthrop in 1629, and it would come up again for Black and Indigenous people in America.

Perhaps being allied with slave owners was embarrassing for Granville Sharp and the other abolitionists, and the committee dropped the proposal for banning Black immigration to England. But the committee still advertised a softer objective of getting rid of Black people.[31]

The Treasury agreed to pay Smeathman, whose creditors were chasing him around London, fourteen pounds for every resettled Black poor person. The relief committee endorsed the idea that "no place" was "so fit and proper" for these London Black people as "the Grain Coast of Africa." The committee was sure the Smeathman–Sharp plan would provide "the necessaries of life" for the Black settlers with only "moderate labour," and so their lives would be "rendered very comfortable." The House of Commons on July 6, 1786, approved the plan "for the Relief of a Number of distressed Black Persons, and Persons of Colour, now in this Country, and for sending them to such Place beyond the Seas as shall by His Majesty be thought best adapted for that Purpose."[32]

Everyone seemed enthusiastic about the plan for the free Black people except for the free Black people. There were an estimated fourteen to twenty thousand Black people in Britain. By November 22,

1786, only 259 would-be settlers had come on board the transports scheduled to leave for Sierra Leone. Shortly before sailing on April 9, 1787, the number had increased to 344 Black people. The settlers also included 115 white people, some of whom were specialists in health, agriculture, textiles, and education.[33]

At this point, the ex-slave Quobna Ottobah Cugoano got involved. Cugoano understood that the project was motivated in part by a desire for removal of Black people. The Sierra Leone promoters' embrace of this goal had not endeared would-be settlers to the plan. Cugoano caught on to this agenda right away: Many English whites just wanted the Black people "to be hurried away" by any possible means.[34]

Moreover, Cugoano noticed that Sierra Leone was right in the middle of the slave trade, supported by British forts. There was a British slave fort on Bance Island inside the estuary chosen for the settlement. How could the same British government both promote and fight slavery at the same time and in the same place? "Can it be readily conceived that government would establish a free colony for them nearly on the spot," Cugoano worried, "while it supports its forts and garrisons . . . to carry others into captivity and slavery?" The slavers understandably deterred ex-slaves in Britain from volunteering for Sierra Leone.[35]

As a devout Christian, Cugoano saw some advantages to the Sierra Leone plan because "some encouragement could be given to send able school masters, and intelligent ministers, who would be faithful and able to teach the Christian religion. This would be doing great good to the Africans, and be a kind restitution for the great injuries that they have suffered." But Cugoano did raise the rather neglected question of West Africans' consent to the blessings-of-civilization plan. Cugoano noticed the organizers had not actually consulted any Sierra Leoneans on whether they wanted to be civilized, despite Granville Sharp's mention of local consent. No "treaty of agreement" had "been first made with the inhabitants of Africa." This is not what Cugoano had had in mind for voluntary exchange between Britons and Africans. Cugoano summarized that the plan had not "altogether met with the credulous approbation of the Africans here" in Britain.[36]

Once on board the ships prior to sailing to Sierra Leone, things apparently got worse for the few Black people who had volunteered (although there are some conflicting reports). They complained of insufficient food, beds, and clothing. A letter of January 4, 1787, signed by Black representatives complained that "their poverty is made the pretense for their transportation," and that their treatment by whites on the ships was "little short of the discipline of Guinea-men [slave ships]." Another letter from the Black settlers on March 24 protested that the white organizers were treating Black people like slaves.[37]

All this Black discontent increased Cugoano's worries back in England even more. He now recommended calling it all off. Those free Black people still on board "had better swim to shore, if they can, to preserve their lives and liberties in Britain."[38]

Finally, the ships sailed to arrive in the estuary of the Sierra Leone River on May 10, 1787. The commander of one of the ships managed to sign a treaty with a local named King Tom for purchasing land for the settlement, which Sharp named the Province of Freedom. The British concept of land purchase had no local counterpart, however, and King Tom had dubious authority in that area anyway.[39]

Arrival coincided with the start of the rainy season. Heavy rainstorms washed away the seeds planted by settlers. The storms blew down the tents under which the hapless settlers were trying to shelter. Disease was also at its worst in the rainy season. By mid-September, 122 settlers had died. The provisions brought from England ran out.

A Black settler named Abraham Elliot Griffith quickly wrote back to Sharp. "I am sorry, and very sorry indeed, to inform you, dear Sir, that this country does not agree with us at all," Griffith wrote. "It was really a very great pity ever we came to the country," he lamented.[40]

Validating some of Cugoano's earlier fears, King Tom in early 1788 grabbed two settlers and sold them to a passing French slaver. More re-enslavement was in store. In June 1788, five Black settlers robbed a store of the British slave traders on Bance Island. The traders demanded that the colony hand them over for justice, which the other settlers did. A jury found the five men guilty and sentenced them to "banishment," which turned out to be re-enslavement. The traders carried out the sentence by selling the five Black settlers to another French slave ship bound for the Caribbean. Meanwhile, many of the remaining settlers survived only by working for the one local industry that provided an adequate living—the slave trade.[41]

Finally, at the end of 1789, after chronic conflict between settlers and locals, another local chief named King Jimmy razed the settlement down to the ground. The local British slave traders gave refuge to the eighty-seven surviving settlers.[42]

Sierra Leone's demonstration of the superiority of free labor did not turn out to be as convincing as Granville Sharp had hoped. A Caribbean slave trader, Gilbert Francklyn, noted in 1789 that Sharp's project was supposed to make ex-slaves "perfectly happy." Yet he noted that of the surviving Black poor in the Province of Freedom, "there was scarce one who did not express his wish to quit his new abode, his estate and his liberty." Compared to that disaster, Francklyn thought the Sierra Leone settlers would be willing to return to "pristine slavery, in the sugar colonies." With this kind of outcome, Francklyn thought, maybe slavery was good for Black people after all.[43]

Such were the dangers of a demonstration project to refute slavery. It was perilous to let an empirical debate trump the moral argument for freedom. Whites were not required to achieve great things in someone else's development experiment to prove they should not be slaves.

The abolitionists had sought to prove slaves and ex-slaves were fit to develop themselves. However, the abolitionists were not skeptical enough about their own ability to develop anyone else. After the fiasco of the Province of Freedom, parliamentary opponents of abolishing the slave trade mocked Granville Sharp as "that philanthropic genius."[44]

Granville Sharp's failed project would need British government intervention, which led to the establishment of Crown rule over

Sierra Leone. Sharp had unintentionally accelerated the British colonization of tropical Africa.

Meanwhile, in other areas to be developed, Du Pont's and the Physiocrats' condescending view of Eastern Europe also had fateful consequences. The Physiocrats had not had the power to impose their advice on Poland, and even less on Russia. But in the next generation Napoleon seems to have been inspired by their example. Historian Larry Wolff notes that Napoleon in his invasion of Russia in 1812 used the idea of development as part of the justification for conquest.

We have some record of what he was thinking in the memoir of his aide-de-camp, Philippe-Paul de Ségur, the son of the condescending former French ambassador to Catherine the Great, Louis-Philippe de Ségur. Ségur Jr. recorded Napoleon musing he was the "champion of the civilization" of the advanced part of Europe, confronting the "rude ignorance" of Russia.[45] Another French officer (ironically) cited "the civilisation which we were introducing into Russia."[46] Ségur himself, much like his father, observed the Russians were "still in but the first stage of civilization."[47] He noted the continuity from the effort of the previous century, when "either from philanthropy or vanity, Europe was eager in contributing to civilize" the Russians. Napoleon was the perfect man for "so great an enterprise."[48]

The critical moment of the invasion was when Napoleon arrived in undefended Moscow expecting to receive the surrender of the Russian army. Instead, the Russians were burning down their own city in an attempt to catch the French army in the fire. Ségur recorded Napoleon's reaction as he gazed on Moscow on September 16, 1812: "What a horrible sight! To do it themselves!" Napoleon's conclusion was similar to that of previous amateur anthropologists: "These are indeed Scythians!"[49]

What did Russians think of all this? As usual, the voices of those to be civilized are seldom heard. One spectacular exception came along a little more than half a century later. Leo Tolstoy looked back on this moment in *War and Peace*, showing the deep scar it left behind in his psyche. Tolstoy had served as an officer in the Russian army in 1854 during another Western incursion into Russia in the

Crimean War. Tolstoy was an early example of how some people in the Rest would react to being lumped together into an uncivilized mass in need of civilizing by the West.[50]

Tolstoy's historical fiction was partly based on the memoirs of Ségur. Tolstoy described Napoleon's invasion as similar to that of Alexander the Great marching into "the Scythian state." Tolstoy had Napoleon announce, "I will show them the meaning of true civilization."[51]

In case anyone missed Tolstoy's sarcasm about Napoleon's attempted conquest for civilization, Tolstoy closed *War and Peace* with a nonfictional essay to expound his own views further. He saw Napoleon's notion of "civilization" as a dangerous "abstraction," which allowed a conqueror to think he was on the side of progress. The "people occupying the small northwest corner of a large continent," said Tolstoy bitterly, were the ones who got to define what was progress. As for Western scholars, Tolstoy said, it had been "natural and pleasant for them to think" that their ideas on progress were "the basis for the movement of all mankind." Some Western ideas wound up in favor of "killing a man in recognition of his rights."[52]

The subsequent history of Africans and Eastern Europeans illustrates how perilous it is for the West to see you as backward. The carnage of the slave trade and colonialism in Africa had many decades yet to run. The Slavs formerly known as Scythians would be the targets of early twentieth-century US immigration restrictions. Hitler would later justify his genocidal fury against Poland and Russia with previous Western ideas on the backward Slavs. Russian leaders from Lenin to Putin would have a furious reaction to Western condescension. They used this history to justify their own ferociously anti-liberal ideas at home and to claim leadership of the anti-colonial revolt of the Rest against the West, which would include many Sierra Leoneans rebelling against the colonialism that began in 1787.

Before all that, another determined liberal thinker challenged the idea of conquest for progress.

6

Benjamin Constant Critiques Conquest

Where were the liberals as the West began to apply the Development Right of Conquest to Africa and Russia? Not for the first or last time, Western coercion of the Rest provoked the response of a liberal critic within the West itself. The liberal opposition to empire begun by Smith and Kant continued with a French economist named Benjamin Constant. The liberal opposition to conquest for progress also influenced the foreign policy of the young new government of the United States.

Yet liberal anti-imperialism would be increasingly under threat as the nineteenth century proceeded. One of the British economist heirs to Adam Smith went over to the other side, supporting the Development Right of Conquest. A French liberal heir to Constant came out in favor of French colonialism in Algeria.

In 1813 Constant published a critique that anticipated Tolstoy's on "Enlightened Wars." Writing right after the failure of Napoleon's invasion of Russia, Constant published *The Spirit of Conquest and Usurpation and Their Relation to European Civilization*. The pamphlet was a publishing success. By April 1814, there had already been three editions published in Paris, and an edition had appeared in London.[1]

Born twenty-eight years after Du Pont, Constant was from the post-Enlightenment generation in France that succeeded the Physiocrats. Constant had studied at the University of Edinburgh in 1783, which exposed him to the ideas of Adam Smith and the Scottish Enlightenment.[2]

In *The Spirit of Conquest*, Constant denounced the French Enlightenment notion of wars for progress. They had invented "a pretext for war previously unknown." They claimed to be "freeing peoples from the yoke of their governments." As Tolstoy had said, the result was just a lot of killing. Constant saw Napoleon's justification for conquest as cynical, with his "lying protestations of respect for the rights of men." Constant saw the paternalistic conquest as "the worst of all conquests," because it is so "hypocritical."[3]

In *The Spirit of Conquest*, Constant went to some length to analyze and refute the conquest-for-progress idea. He was one of the first to identify the violation of dignity as a big part of the problem. Every nation had a "sense of its own value and dignity." Even if you, the conqueror, brought improvement to such a nation, the problem was that "you impose your own improvement upon it by force." The loss of national dignity trumped any supposed improvements from conquest. Conquest here saw a demand for dignity that was collective rather than individual.[4]

Constant's full title of *The Spirit of Conquest* emphasized its "Relation to European Civilization." Constant had Napoleon's conquests in Europe in mind. Yet Constant also referred to worldwide colonial conquests "in order to acquire remote countries," in which Europeans "send their armies from one pole to the other." The colonizers also violated the collective rights of the conquered: "It is one thing to defend one's fatherland, another to attack people who themselves have a fatherland to defend."[5]

Despite some inconsistencies, Constant denounced the hierarchal ranking that justified Western coercion of the Rest. In an 1829 essay, Constant asserted equality of groups as a moral principle rather than an empirical claim. Constant actually was not sure whether there were physiological differences between peoples, although he was sure that all peoples were capable of progress. But he saw clearly that the claims of racial differences were often a pretext for oppression.[6]

Constant presented forcefully the central liberal critique of the colonizers, that they could not be trusted with the unchecked power that their supposed superiority purportedly gave them: "It is too easy to leap from the recognized inferiority of one race and the superiority of another, to the servitude of the first." The superiority claims had been "repeated for three hundred years in order to maintain the most illegitimate oppression and the most execrable ferocity."[7]

Constant was an outstanding liberal heir to some other Enlightenment thinkers (including Smith and Kant), who had offered all along a less condescending, less grandiose, and less violent way for the West to think about progress of the Rest. Like Smith, Constant almost got to the idea of a liberal international order based on free trade and mutual respect for sovereignty, even for non-European nations. He was opposed to military intervention in other nations even if it was meant to spread freedom.

But the anti-imperialist liberals were getting increasingly lonely in Western Europe. Jennifer Pitts sees Constant as an exception to "the emergence of support for the violent conquest and despotic rule of non-Europeans in the mid-nineteenth century" by liberal thinkers. As so often in the history of liberalism, it seems miraculous that anticonquest liberal ideas survived at all.[8]

An illustrative pro-imperial case is the Scottish economist James Mill (1773–1836), a contemporary of Constant. Mill was a student of Adam Smith's student Dugald Stewart. Mill is also important because of his effect on his more famous and influential son, John Stuart Mill. Unlike Smith, the elder Mill was an enthusiast for British colonization of India in the name of development: "The English government in India, with all its vices, is a blessing of unspeakable magnitude to the population of Hindustan." The English brought peace, he argued in 1810. In another 1810 article, he declared that "mild and paternal" English rule would attract European settlers. European industry would flourish "under the protecting hand of a

British government on the spot," leading to a "more vast and precious produce." Like Condorcet, and unlike Smith and Constant, Mill believed that whatever led to higher material production was right. In 1819, he actually became an employee of the East India Company, who presumably liked his views.[9]

Mill was one of the first to succumb to what would be a perpetual liberal temptation—to opt for colonialism because it could provide the good government necessary for commerce to flourish in the colonies. Mill could not go along with Smith's preference for leaving people alone. He declared altruistically: "We earnestly hope, for the sake of the natives, that it will not be found necessary to leave them to their own direction."[10]

Mill, like many Western thinkers over the next century, did not perceive a demand for self-determination in the Rest. In testimony to the House of Commons in 1831, Mill said, "I consider that the feeling of degradation, from being governed by foreigners, is a feeling altogether European. I believe it has little or no existence in any part of Asia." It is not very clear on what he based this statement. Responding to an incredulous interrogator, Mill acknowledged he had never been to India and had not read anything written by Indians on the subject of being ruled by foreigners.[11]

In contrast to Mill, Constant's great contribution to liberalism was to identify both the collective quest for national liberty from conquest and the desire for individual liberty. Constant was one of the first thinkers to identify the possible conflicts between collective freedom and individual freedom. In 1819 at the Athénée Royal in Paris, he gave the lecture for which he is best known among specialists: "The Liberty of the Ancients Compared with That of the Moderns."[12]

For Constant, the modern notion of liberty was the way that the English, French, and Americans saw it. This notion of liberty was about individual rights against coercion. It was first defined by negatives: "to be neither arrested, detained, put to death or maltreated in any way by the arbitrary will of one or more individuals." Modern liberty was about individual rights to free speech, choice of occupation, and property rights: "It is the right of everyone to express their opinion, choose a profession and practise it, to dispose of property, and even to abuse it." Importantly for the history of population removal in the West, Constant saw freedom of choice applying to where to live: Modern liberty gave individuals the right "to come and go without permission, and without having to account for their motives or undertakings." Also on the list of rights was individuals' freedom "simply to occupy their days or hours in a way which is most compatible with their inclinations or whims."

The right to one's own whims suggests a radically subjective definition of well-being, which would not show up in mainstream economics until decades later. Nobody else can objectively say what is in my interest. I don't have to account for my motives or undertakings to anybody else. I choose for myself, and that's the end of it. Lastly, Constant saw the modern notion of liberty as including political rights for individuals, through elections or petitions.[13]

In contrast, liberty for the ancients was collective rather than individual. Freedom for them was collective exercise of "complete sovereignty." Citizens collectively deliberated "over war and peace" and "forming alliances with foreign governments." Greek city-states chose war to not "be conquered," to preserve "their independence." Constant said, "This was the constant interest, the almost habitual occupation of the free states of antiquity."[14]

Constant was insightful on the clash between the two kinds of liberty. Individual liberty had to be sacrificed to the war effort. For the ancients, therefore, collective freedom was compatible with "the complete subjection of the individual to the authority of the community." They had so little respect for individual rights that they accepted slavery.[15]

Collective versus individual liberty was also related to conquest versus commerce: "War and commerce are only two different means of achieving the same end, that of getting what one wants." Constant was a true heir to Adam Smith in seeing the "mutual agreement" of commerce as superior to zero-sum conflict. Compared to war, commerce was "a milder and surer means of engaging the interest of others to agree to what suits his own." He thus endorsed the invisible hand in which trade reconciled the interest of the nation's and individual's own interests with that of others.

Constant embraced laissez-faire and condemned government intervention in markets. He celebrated individual self-determination as a happy outcome coming from unfettered commerce: "Commerce supplies their needs, satisfies their desires, without the intervention of the authorities."

Like Smith and Kant, Constant prophesied that "an age must come in which commerce replaces war." Constant saw this prophecy already coming true in his own time: "We have reached this age." Constant turned out to be right that international trade would expand a lot between European nations as well as with the United States. Peaceful interaction through commerce was increasingly an option right up to the eve of World War I. But declaring a permanent replacement of conquest by commerce was a bit premature.[16]

Although Constant forcefully argued for modern individual liberty against having only national freedom, he still saw the latter as a value worth pursuing. His condemnation of conquest had already recognized nations' collective rights not to be invaded. In his 1819 lecture, he looked for a liberal combination of individual and collective rights: "Therefore, Sirs, far from renouncing either of the two sorts of freedom which I have described to you, it is necessary, as I have shown, to learn to combine the two together." Constant had little to say about how to do this combination, which would bedevil liberal thinkers for the next two centuries and still does today. But he is notable among liberals for insisting that both individual and collective freedom from outside control are desirable, that one without the other is not acceptable. Adam Smith had gone in this direction but James Mill certainly had not.[17]

Like many liberals then and later, Constant applied his notions of freedom rather inconsistently to the Rest. As a legislator in the 1820s, Constant condemned the slave trade (in which French merchants were still engaged). But like the Wilberforce generation in Britain, he did not move to the greater cause of ending slavery itself. He called for equal rights for free Black people in the French colony of Martinique but stopped short of considering the rights of the slaves there.[18]

Although Constant had denounced the hypocrisy of conquerors with a civilizing mission (like Napoleon), Constant did see progress as desirable. He agreed that "civilization is in the destiny of the human species"; it was preferable to "savage life." He said, "One cannot and should not stop it."[19]

Even after condemning Western conquests around the world, Constant had an ambiguous view of the French seizure of Algiers in 1830. He denounced the conquest as an "affair of royal vanity." But his patriotism in this case trumped his anti-imperialism: "Let us wish ardently for the military successes of our brave compatriots." Contrary to his previous writings, Constant was open to the notion that the right to sovereignty did not hold for a bad government; he praised "the ruin of a den of pirates." He didn't think the French had to respect "sovereignty in a barbarian." Constant died in December 1830 before France's colonial plans for Algeria had fully developed.[20]

The liberal opposition to colonialism was increasingly fragile. The next great thinker in the French liberal line of succession, Alexis de Tocqueville (1805–1859), supported the colonization of Algeria by French settlers and armies in the 1830s and 1840s. Tocqueville did so mainly because of a desire to promote the international standing of France: He wanted to "raise a great monument to our country's glory on the African coast." Much as he regretted it, he said this required violence against the locals.[21]

Tocqueville's tortured commentary on Algeria still recognized some liberal principles. Most notably, he rejected the conquest for progress narrative. He ridiculed the British for pretending their conquests were good for the conquered: "What I cannot get over is their perpetual attempts to prove that they act in the interest of a principle, or for the good of the natives." He acknowledged that European settlers' claims to be superior beings were "so mortifying to the self-respect of the Indigenous people that more anger resulted from that than from any political oppression." Yet after all that, he still accepted the need for brutal violence for the glory of France. It was not easy for liberals to go against powerful interests in their own countries.[22]

A more faithful heir to liberal anti-imperialism during the Algeria debate was Algerian. Hamdan ben Othman Khodja (ca. 1773–1842) was a local scholar and businessman. He published a book in 1833 with an epigraph from Benjamin Constant. He denounced the double standard in which free nations in Europe advocated self-determination for Poland but not Algeria. "When my eyes return to the country of Algiers," Khodja said, "I see its wretched inhabitants placed under the yoke of despotism, extermination, and all the scourges of war, and all these horrors committed in the name of free France." End the hypocrisy, he demanded, because "Algerians, too, have rights that should permit them to enjoy liberty and all the advantages that European nations enjoy." The most reliable defenders of rights were often going to be those who fought for their own rights.[23]

The French settlement and colonization of Algeria would go ahead. Although Constant's ideas had lost the debate in France on colonialism, there was at least one Western nation at the time that did renounce both conquests for liberation in Europe and colonial conquests in Asia or Africa. The infant United States had tried to follow a neutral foreign policy ever since George Washington called for it in his farewell address in 1796.[24]

Secretary of State John Quincy Adams in 1821 gave one of the most eloquent statements of this policy. Adams's own background set him up well to debate conquest. The son of the second president of the US, John Adams, he had an inside view of many of the big events of the period. He was the US minister to Russia at the time of Napoleon's invasion in 1812 and followed the war from Saint Petersburg. Adams met Benjamin Constant in Paris and London in 1815 and 1816 and was aware of his writings. Adams called Constant "invariably a friend of liberty."[25]

As secretary of state, Adams discussed America's role in the world in a speech celebrating the Fourth of July in 1821. His position on nonconquest was similar to that of Constant. The Declaration of Independence had "demolished at a stroke the lawfulness of all governments founded upon conquest." While Adams expressed sympathy for the cause of freedom, he emphatically rejected any American military intervention to advance the cause:

> Wherever the standard of freedom and independence has been or shall be unfurled, there will her heart, her benedictions and her prayers be. But she goes not abroad in search of monsters to destroy. She is the well-wisher to the freedom and independence of all. She is the champion and vindicator only of her own.[26]

Was this just what a later generation would condemn as isolationist? But Adams was not simply trying to attend to America's self-interest. He thought that American interventions abroad would become tyrannical and therefore harmful to others. Her policy would shift "from liberty to force." He presciently worried that "she might become the dictatress of the world."

Adams insisted that America respected a liberal international order, similar to what Smith, Kant, and Constant had begun to sketch out. America held out to other nations "the hand of honest friendship, of equal freedom, of generous reciprocity." She had always "respected the independence of other nations." She had renounced paternalism as well as coercion, having "abstained from interference in the concerns of others" even on behalf of her most cherished principles.[27]

Like Smith and Constant, Adams saw commerce as the alternative to conquest. In the same address, he said American policy since independence had been to "form connexions of friendship and of commerce with foreign nations."[28]

Adams's ringing denunciations also applied to colonial conquests—sort of. In the Fourth of July address, he equivocated: "Colonial subjection is compatible with the essential purposes of civil government, only when the condition of the subordinate state is from its weakness incompetent to its own protection." The rationale for one power conquering you was to protect you from being conquered by some other power.[29]

In a letter seven months later, Adams went much further opposing colonialism. The letter to Edward Everett (the influential editor of *The North American Review* and a future politician) explained what he had meant to say about colonialism in his Fourth of July address. He anticipated an American debate on "whether we too shall annex to our federative government a great system of colonial establishments." Now his denunciation of colonialism was as forceful as anything Smith, Kant, or Constant had said. He had demonstrated in the address that "colonial establishments cannot fulfil" a "just purpose." He had proven the justice of the contemporaneous struggles of South American colonies for independence from Spain. He had looked forward to "the downfall of the British Empire in India." The address had showed that "great colonial establishments are but mighty engines of wrong," which humanity should abolish just as it should abolish slavery.

It's not easy to find these remarkable anti-colonial demonstrations in the public address, perhaps because they are not there. Nor did Adams make them public at this point. He implored Edward Everett to keep the letter confidential, to show it only to one other trusted confidant. Adams was going to successfully run for president in 1824, and maybe these positions were a little too radical for the electorate. Anti-colonial liberalism in America was at least still alive in secret.[30]

Even in secret, John Quincy Adams had one rather important omission from his condemnation of colonial conquests. He did not apply it to the British/American conquests of Indian nations. He didn't even see this as conquest. In the Fourth of July address, he had a not-completely-accurate account of how the first settlers of Massachusetts had "purchased from the Indian natives the right of settlement upon the soil." In a later passage in the address, the Indians disappear from the picture altogether, as the settlers "civilize the wilderness and fill with human life the solitudes of this immense continent."[31]

Adams thus embodied some of the contradictions of the victory for liberal anti-imperialism in the US. The nation would refrain from conquest outside North America for many more decades, but these liberal restraints did not apply to continental expansion. The contradictions would lead to some tortured debates on Indian policy in America.

7

The Civilizing Plan for the Creek Indians

Success finally is no longer doubtful." So wrote the US government agent Benjamin Hawkins to Thomas Jefferson in 1803 about a government program of economic development he was running among the Creek Indians in what is now Georgia and Alabama.[1]

Hawkins was a former senator from North Carolina and a Princeton graduate. Hawkins had been teaching the Creeks, formerly hunters, how to farm, raise cattle, and produce handicrafts. What became known as his Plan of Civilization had multiple objectives. It would above all improve the well-being of the Creeks. It would achieve peace on the frontier. Because farming took less land than hunting, the plan would free up Creek lands to satisfy the demands of white American settlers. The success or failure of the plan for the Creeks was to determine the fate of many.[2]

The flood of Europeans settling the United States, Australia, Canada, and New Zealand forced Anglo-American thinkers and leaders to confront the dilemma of how to treat native peoples of those lands. The answer was again giving the Indians development aid in exchange for their land, as Winthrop and Condorcet had. It began sounding more and more like some modern rhetoric that is perpetually hopeful that development will solve all problems and reconcile all interests, no matter how much it has previously failed to do so.

The reader may suspect already that the Creek plan was not going to be a great success. This may unfairly imply Indian development efforts always failed. Cherokee development was more successful and will be discussed in the next chapter. But the Creek case illustrates what backup plan experts had in mind if civilizing efforts were unsuccessful. Such a failure could be either because the Indians were unable or unwilling to do what whites defined as development—or because the white developers were a tad incompetent. That the white developers preferred the first to the second explanation is an important part of the story. In the wake of the plan's failure, many white thinkers shifted to the mandate of developing the land rather than the people. Removing the Indians and taking their land would then be justified in the name of progress. What was at the time called "extermination" began to emerge in Anglo-American thought.

Alison Bashford and Joyce Chaplin note that the terrifying word *extermination* had two meanings in the late eighteenth and early nineteenth centuries. One was the way that it is understood today: the elimination of a whole group. The other was removal of the group from the place under discussion to somewhere else.[3]

The development justification for conquering Indians had been restated numerous times since Winthrop. The great English philosopher John Locke in 1689 endorsed the idea of development as a basis for land rights in his *Two Treatises of Government*, which otherwise is a classic statement of liberal ideals, such as the consent of the governed. God had commanded man to "subdue the earth, i.e. improve it." Whoever "in obedience to this command of God, subdued, tilled and sowed any part of it" could claim that part of it as their property. God made this rule to give the land to "the industrious and rational" so that the earth would not remain "uncultivated." Locke applied this principle to "the wild woods and uncultivated waste of America, left to nature, without any improvement, tillage or husbandry," where "the needy and wretched inhabitants" get no more from a thousand acres than the English got from ten acres in

Devonshire. Locke encouraged the English settler to "plant in some in-land, vacant places of America." Like Winthrop, Locke thought the English occupation of the Indians' land was actually good for the Indians. Arguing by analogy with some other vacant places in Spain, Locke suggested the "inhabitants think themselves beholden to him, who, by his industry on neglected, and consequently waste land, has increased the stock of corn, which they wanted."[4]

The right to conquer for development also made it into the extremely influential 1758 book *The Law of Nations*, by Emer de Vattel (1711–1767), which would be gratefully quoted by European settlers in America for many years afterward. The Europeans had found lands "of which the savages stood in no particular need, and of which they made no actual and constant use." The Europeans "were lawfully entitled to take possession of it, and settle it with colonies." Vattel did not argue that this process was actually good for whom he called the savages. In an earlier passage in *The Law of Nations*, he declared that any people who inhabit fertile land, fail to cultivate it, and plunder their neighbors "deserve to be extirpated as savage and pernicious beasts." Vattel applied these principles to declare lawful the conquest of North America.[5]

Critics of the development right to Indians' land emerged early on. In 1726, Jonathan Swift was already mocking the idea in *Gulliver's Travels.* Upon Gulliver's arrival in the land of the gentle Houyhnhnms, he "took out some Toys, which Travellers usually carry for Presents to the Savage Indians of America." In Swift's satire, Gulliver explains to his Houyhnhnm host the civilizing rationale for conquest. "Where the People are poor and ignorant," the conquerors "may lawfully put half of them to Death, and make Slaves of the rest, in order to civilize and reduce them from their barbarous Way of Living." Swift was not slow to ridicule the notion that some people had to partially disappear for their own good.[6]

The settlers in America had not asked Indians what they thought of this civilizing solution. Native American voices only occasionally appear in the records. In 1777, some Cherokee chiefs made a treaty under duress giving up five million acres of their land. Even after the treaty, settlers continued to encroach on the Cherokees' remaining lands. One of these chiefs, Onitositah (also known as Old Tassel or Corn Tassel), protested against the endless invasions of Cherokee lands rationalized by a supposed civilizing effort. He addressed the whites: "Much has been advanced on the want of what you term civilization among the Indians." You whites wanted us Indians "to adopt your laws, your religion, your manners and your customs," presumably including respect for others' property rights. However, we Indians "should be better pleased with beholding the good effect of these doctrines in your own practices than with hearing you talk about them." A year after this speech, a white settler murdered Onitositah.[7]

The leaders of the new nation were aware of the criticisms of their treatment of the Indians. Enlightenment critiques of conquest may have partially gotten through. Secretary of War Henry Knox suggested to George Washington in 1789 that the nation maintain the "respect which every nation sacredly owes to its own reputation" by adopting a program for "the civilization of the Indians." Instead "of exterminating a part of the human race," we could offer "our Knowledge of cultivation, and the arts, to the Aboriginals of the Country." Development was the answer to the question the Indians were not asking.[8]

Washington adopted Knox's suggestions in his 1791 message to Congress. He proposed, "Rational experiments should be made" for the Indians, "for imparting to them the blessings of civilization." Such a program, he agreed with Knox, would be "honorable to the national character."[9]

The Washington administration had already broached the idea of civilization among the Creek Indians. Washington negotiated the Treaty of New York with the Creeks in 1790 to end incessant conflicts between them and Georgian frontiersmen. The idea of exchanging civilization for land came to the rescue. In return for the Creeks giving up some of their land, the treaty offered aid so "that the Creek nation may be led to a greater degree of civilization." To support a transition from hunting to farming, "the United States will from time to time furnish gratuitously the said nation with useful domestic animals and implements of husbandry." If civilizing did not work, Washington wrote the Marquis de Lafayette after the treaty that any Indian rebels "can be easily chastised or even extirpated if it shall become necessary."[10]

Washington in 1796 gave a fuller explanation to the Indians of his plans for them. In a speech to Cherokee chiefs in Philadelphia, he set out his civilizing policy. He might have taken it as a warning when he noted that "many good men have considered how the condition of the Indian natives of the country might be improved; and many attempts have been made to effect it." And all this had been "nearly fruitless."

But the development idea from the beginning has been remarkably resilient to failure, as each new development thinker is sure they can finally get it right. Like a modern TED Talk, Washington's speech to the chiefs confidently declared, "I also have thought much on this subject," and I have finally found the "one path" to material abundance. "In this path I wish all the Indian nations to walk," Washington said rather forcefully.

Washington detailed his one path for the Indians—keeping sheep, cattle, and hogs, using plows, growing corn, wheat, flax, and cotton, selling crops to whites. The women could learn spinning and weaving. The potential was exciting: "You can vastly increase your crops." Like a classic enthusiast for development aid, Washington promised the chiefs that success was easier than it looked. If they just "make the attempt," they "will find every obstacle easy to be removed." But if the chiefs could not make it work, Washington warned in 1796, the US "may think it vain to make any further attempts to better the condition of any Indian tribe."[11]

Washington announced to the Cherokee chiefs that he was sending Benjamin Hawkins as his principal agent to the Southern tribes. "His whole time will be employed in contriving how to do you good," Washington assured the chiefs, "and you will therefore act wisely to follow his advice."[12]

Hawkins would supervise other agents among the Cherokees. The forty-two-year-old Hawkins moved to Creek country in 1796 to himself take charge of the Plan of Civilization there.[13]

Hawkins was fully devoted to the civilization effort. He had previously served as a commissioner to negotiate treaties with the Southern tribes. In 1786, Hawkins had written his friend Thomas Jefferson on how "there is nothing I have more at heart than the preservation of them."[14]

In 1800, Hawkins filed a report with the War Department on the aid program after its first four years. As he summarized the report in a letter to Thomas Jefferson in early 1800, the spinning and weaving by the Creeks had clothed three hundred women and children. The livestock program had achieved the raising of one thousand beef cattle and three hundred hogs for the market. In a subsequent letter to Jefferson in 1800, Hawkins promised further details that would show him that "the plan has unquestionably succeeded."[15]

On March 1, 1801, as Jefferson was about to be inaugurated president, Hawkins sent him the promised update. He reported that he had established two nurseries of peach trees. Hawkins calculated he had distributed five thousand peach trees from the nurseries since his arrival among the Creeks five years earlier. The Creeks began to accept the peach trees, Hawkins said.[16]

The War Department had sent Hawkins seventy plows, of which he got the Creeks to use fifty. Hawkins had introduced production of oil from hickory nuts and acorns in 1797. As he wrote in 1801, one trader was on his way to New Orleans to sell 240 gallons of the Creeks' hickory oil.

Hawkins paid special attention to programs for women. He had delivered in 1801 eighty spinning wheels to the Creek women. Eight looms were in operation, Hawkins said in his report, although white women operated four of them. He noted three Indian women had clothed themselves already with the outputs of the spinning wheels and looms.

Hawkins noted that there were two blacksmiths in Creek country, although they also supplied white customers. He reminded the readers that the Treaty of Colerain in 1796, which Hawkins had negotiated, had promised the Creeks blacksmiths in return for them giving up some of their land.[17]

Jefferson gave a report on the overall Indian civilization effort to Congress at the end of 1801, attaching Hawkins's report. "The continued efforts to introduce among them the implements and the practice of husbandry and of the household arts have not been without success," Jefferson told Congress. The Indians were realizing the superiority of farming to hunting. "Already we are able to announce," Jefferson enthused, that "instead of that constant diminution of numbers produced by their wars and their wants, some of them begin to experience an increase of population." Jefferson had blamed the Indians' population decrease on their backward ways rather than the depredations of white settlers, so the answer was the civilization plan.[18]

In 1803, Jefferson wrote Hawkins that he was under pressure from the Georgians to deliver yet more Creek land for white settlers. He also noted the Georgians were suspicious that Hawkins was too favorable to the Creeks. Jefferson implored Hawkins to increase his efforts. He had to get the Creeks to give up more land in return for civilizing aid. Hawkins had to persuade the Creeks that this exchange "will be for the good of both" sides.[19]

In desperation, Hawkins wrote back to Jefferson in 1803 that "success finally is no longer doubtful," as quoted at the beginning of this chapter. Hawkins' evidence for this success was rather underwhelming—after seven years in the field, his recommendations on livestock, agriculture, and household manufactures "begin to be the general theme of conversation" among the Creeks. He hoped that the Creeks "will become honest and peaceable neighbors," and therefore "they can and will spare their superfluous land." He hoped that one more land cession by the Creeks to Georgians would buy ten or twenty more years of peace "to perfect our plan of civilization." Hawkins defensively referred Jefferson back to his earlier report that "will shew you the course I have pursued and am pursuing to attain" the goal of Indian civilization.[20]

This was not exactly a rigorous evaluation of the civilizing effort among the Creeks. In one of history's first aid debates, the Frenchman Louis LeClerc de Milford emerged as a critic of Hawkins. Milford had lived in Creek country from the 1770s through 1790s. As he pointed out in a book he published in France in 1802, even some of Hawkins's modest claims of progress were about things that the Creeks were already doing on their own. Despite the frequent emphasis of American leaders on Indians as hunters, many Indian tribes, including the Creeks, had been practicing agriculture for centuries.[21]

Milford had observed during his time among the Creeks before the plan that they already owned a lot of livestock. As for the famous five thousand peach trees that Hawkins bragged about in his 1801 report, Milford commented sardonically: "The author has no doubt forgotten, or never known, that the Creeks have such an enormous quantity of peach trees that one encounters them at every turn." Milford's caustic evaluation of the Hawkins report was that "nothing, or practically nothing, in this article is true." As is often the fate of aid critics, Milford was ignored.[22]

Instead of evaluating what the plan had already achieved, Hawkins made claims about what was happening in the present or would happen in the future. Perhaps the modest achievements so far ("three Indian women had clothed themselves") should be seen as the start of something bigger.

Hawkins was fond of gerunds like "going" or "becoming." As Hawkins told Jefferson in 1800, "The benevolent plan of the government, is going successfully into operation, among the Creeks." Jefferson followed suit in his 1801 message to Congress: The Indians "are becoming more and more sensible of the superiority" of farming over hunting.[23]

Laura Freschi and I in the modern aid debate noted in 2010 how aid defenders sometimes offer a "gerund defense." Whatever your doubts about how much progress has already happened, the defense suggests, please let me assure you that progress is happening now. You cannot test this in the present; you will only be able to look back on some future date for whether progress had really been happening—at which point I can reassure you with a new gerund that progress is now happening. A gerund remains prominent today in naming the very object of development efforts—the developing countries.[24]

Thomas Jefferson repeated the gerund defense four years later in his 1805 message to Congress: "Our Indian neighbors are advancing." Once again, Jefferson reiterated, the Indians "are becoming sensible" of how farming is better than hunting. (And he noted to Congress, as a more tangible accomplishment, that the Creeks did give up the piece of land he had demanded of Hawkins in 1803.[25])

Jefferson's successor, James Madison, would continue the gerund defense four years later in his 1809 State of the Union address. "The just and benevolent system continued toward" the Indians, Madison said, "is more and more advancing habits favorable to their civilization and happiness."[26]

The defenses by Jefferson and Madison of their Indian plans seemed to work on some observers. The peripatetic development promoter Pierre Samuel du Pont de Nemours in 1817 would note how "the excellent Jefferson and his worthy successor Mr. Madison" had had plans to give "the Cherokees greater ease and make them happier." He shifted into the future tense on whether these plans work: "There will be more Cherokees, and above all happy Cherokees."[27]

Another variation on gerunds was Hawkins's assertion in the 1800 letter to Jefferson that the Creeks "begin to be attentive to the raising of stock." This is doubly hard to verify—that something is beginning in the present tense, and that what is beginning is an unmeasurable outcome—the attentiveness of the Creeks. Hawkins was quoting himself accurately—he had used the phrase that the Creeks "begin to be attentive to" some part of the civilization plan five times in his 1800 report on the plan to the War Department.[28]

Perhaps this was because Hawkins could only report more gerunds than results. His intensive town-by-town, household-by-household visits led him only to individual, underwhelming reports like that on his 1799 visit to the town of Hill-au-bee, where he talked to four "half breeds" and to Au-wil-au-gee, the wife of

O-pi-o-che-tus-tun-nug-gee: "These Indians promised the agent, in 1799, to begin and fence their fields." To sum up rather unfairly the claims of the beleaguered Mr. Hawkins, his defense was that the Creeks were beginning to think about following his advice to begin doing what they were already doing.[29]

The Creeks' problem was not a shortage of white advice; it was a shortage of white respect for their land rights. Whites kept taking more and more of their lands. Hawkins under government pressure would force the Creeks to make four major land transfers to whites during his time with them (1796, 1802, 1805, and 1814). None of these land cessions stopped the further encroachment of settlers on the remaining Creek lands.[30]

Nobody was demanding that white Americans give up their own ways as a condition of keeping their land. The Cherokee chief Old Tassel had appealed to reciprocity back in 1777: "You say: Why do not the Indians till the ground and live as we do? May we not, with equal propriety, ask, Why the white people do not hunt and live as we do?"[31]

Hawkins promised the Creeks they could keep their lands if they adopted his plan. However, he did not keep the promise even when he claimed the plan was succeeding. It was not surprising, therefore, that Creek resistance to Hawkins emerged.

The opposition was in the background all along. In Hawkins's 1800 report on the Plan of Civilization, he expressed exasperation about how the opposition to the plan prevailed "more or less in every town in the nation." He complained, "The plainest proposition for ameliorating their condition is immediately opposed."[32]

Hawkins attributed Creek resistance to his plans to an irrational attachment to the old ways. In 1797, he tried to explain to Secretary of War James McHenry how the Creeks had a surprising lack of appreciation for "the pains taken to better their condition." (The pains included his delivery to them of two reams of paper, twine for ten fishing nets and two seines, and some garden seeds—in return for their land cession in 1796.) Resistance to such efforts could be due only to "their obstinate perseverance in their old habits." The

Creek men had been "bred in habits proudly indolent and insolent." The Creeks had to "be humbled to the level of rational life."

Hawkins could get some chiefs on his side by enriching them with gifts. He reported to the secretary of war in 1797 that he had taken the government money for the Creek civilization plan and divided it among those friendly town chiefs "who faithfully exerted themselves for the honour and interest of their country." The civilization plan could conceivably have had some attractive things to offer some Creeks. Of course, the friendly chiefs also knew military resistance would lead to even faster loss of their lands, while cooperation could give at least temporary relief.[33]

Other chiefs made a different choice. Hawkins noted in his 1800 report the opposition of the chief of the Creek town of Tallassee, Hoboithle Micco (also known to Americans as Tame King). Tame King had an inexplicable "spirit of contradiction." Hoboithle Micco and a band of warriors in September 1799 chased off a team of white surveyors attempting to mark the boundary between US territory and Spanish Florida.[34]

Hawkins responded furiously. He got Creek warriors on his side to bind and whip Hoboithle Micco and three of his followers. The warriors described their punishment of one of Tame King's followers: "We beat him with sticks until he was on the ground as a dead man, we cut off one of his ears with a part of his cheek and put a sharp stick up his fundament."[35]

Hawkins in his 1800 report bragged about this "exemplary punishment." Hawkins then persuaded his Creek allies to form a national government to make decisions for all Creeks. The Creeks had previously been a heterogeneous collection of towns, each one of which had its independent chief. Their tribal meetings were a consensual forum for discussion, not to enforce conformity between different towns. No town chief had claimed any power to enforce his will on other towns of Creeks. Only a consultative confederacy existed. Now a US-backed Creek national government would enforce the Plan of Civilization on all Creeks. Not for the last time, an aid donor found a native autocrat to be convenient.[36]

Hoboithle Micco continued his defiance. In 1803, he said he still had no desire for a "blacksmith in the nation or weavers to bring them into slavery, no plough or any plantation tools." Jefferson, getting his reports from Hawkins, in 1805 attributed the resistance to the "bigotry" of "anti-philosophers," who incomprehensibly favored their own ways "over the duty" of following rational improvement schemes. Jefferson just could not understand why the Indians were not impressed with his experts.[37]

A further threat to civilizing plans happened north of the Ohio River in 1807. Two brothers with a mother reported to be Creek, the "Shawnee Prophet" Tenskwatawa, and the warrior Tecumseh, were preaching pan-Indian resistance against whites. This worried President Jefferson, and he asked his secretary of war to contact wavering tribes "to recall to their minds" the "paternal policy" he had pursued and that he "still meant to be pursued." Jefferson said plaintively "that we never wished to do them an injury, but on the contrary to give them all the assistance in our power towards improving their condition."[38]

Jefferson warned rebels who were against the civilization plan: "If ever we are constrained to lift the hatchet against any tribe, we will never lay it down till that tribe is exterminated, or driven beyond the Missisipi [*sic*]." Jefferson threatened again that "we shall destroy all of them."[39]

The new president in 1809, James Madison, inherited the tense situation. Hoboithle Micco hoped to influence Madison to hold back white settlers. In a letter to Madison on September 29, 1809, Tame King said the Creeks were getting ever more impoverished. They could not even clothe themselves; they "must and do go naked." The problem was that "the Muscogee [Creek] land is become very small," Hoboithle Micco wrote to Madison. Yet still the settlers encroached onto their lands further by driving in their livestock, building houses, cutting red cedars, even hunting. He asked Madison to "give orders to your officers to prevent this in future."[40]

Madison replied on November 6, 1809, that there were some bad men on both sides. He said Hawkins would prevent encroachments "in future as much as he can." After this tepid promise, President Madison told Hoboithle Micco that the real answer to Creek poverty was more of the same old Plan of Civilization:

> Fence in your Lands, plow as much land as you can, raise corn & Hogs & Cattle. Learn your young Women to card & spin, & let those who are older learn to weave. You will then have food and cloathing and live comfortably.

Even after thirteen years of less-than-glorious success for the Plan of Civilization, Madison informed Tame King he was sure "that his red Children can live well if they will follow his advice." Madison promised the Creek chief once again, "Colo. Hawkins will give you Cards and Spinning-wheels and Looms to weave in."[41]

Hoboithle Micco was not too convinced. In 1811, Tecumseh visited the people his mother reportedly came from—the Creeks—attempting unsuccessfully to persuade them to join his pan-Indian revolt. However, he sowed further divisions between pro- and anti-plan Creeks.[42]

Finally, in 1813, the long-brewing Creek rebellion broke out. It was both a civil war among the Creeks and a war against the whites. Hoboithle Micco became one of the leaders of the rebellion. He now looked on the Creek procivilization leaders "as people of the United States." The rebels, known as the Red Sticks, targeted the most visible emblems of the Plan of Civilization. They destroyed corn, hogs, and cattle and tossed plows and looms into the river.[43]

But the rebel cause was hopeless. In a battle on November 29, 1813, white Georgian soldiers and pro-plan Creeks killed Hoboithle Micco (whom the Georgians called the "greatest conjuror of all the fanatics"). They also razed to the ground Tame King's town of Tallassee.[44]

Andrew Jackson had overall command of the US forces to suppress the rebellion. Jackson finally defeated the Red Sticks at the Battle of Horseshoe Bend on March 27, 1814. In August 1814, Jackson forced the Creeks to sign a treaty that surrendered two-thirds of their remaining lands. Jackson did not allow Hawkins to participate in the treaty negotiations. Hawkins was shocked at the collapse of his life's work. He wrote to a friend, "I often regale myself with tears." Hawkins died a broken man in 1816.[45]

Jefferson told a friend in December 1813 he felt betrayed by the Indians whom "we had been taking so much pains to save and to civilize." He said, "Their unexpected desertion and ferocious barbarities justified extermination." He was saddened particularly that some Creeks, "for whom we had done more than for any other tribe," had joined the pan-Indian revolt. The Creeks now had to submit to "removing to such new settlements beyond the Mississippi as we shall assign them."[46]

As Jefferson foresaw, the solution to the Indian problem now shifted to removal. After the 1813–1814 war, the failure of civilizing plans among the Creeks became the reason for removing the Creeks. The head of the Indian office in the War Department, Thomas L. McKenney, visited the Creeks in 1827. Despite years of civilizing effort, he said, the Creeks were now "habitually drunk." Their "total abandonment to vice demands that the government save them from destruction by removal to the west."[47]

Observers that were more perceptive noted how little incentive the Creeks had to invest in their farms when they expected to lose their lands soon. This was a critical flaw in the Plan of Civilization from the start.[48]

The Indian removal effort now reached its climactic phase in the South. But where were the liberals?

8

The Liberal Fight Against Indian Removal

In 1830, the US Congress debated an Indian Removal Act that would decide the fate of the Southern Indians. The climactic debate finally brought out some who gave the liberal case against removal, including a leader of missionary efforts, a pioneering female reformer, and a young Cherokee preacher. The shift of the debate to the Cherokees was important because Cherokee development was generally considered a success. Would the success of plan A, developing the people, really stop the advent of plan B, to get rid of the people and just develop the land?

Meanwhile, British colonial policy still had to decide whether the same process of European settlement and Indigenous removal would happen in Asia and Africa. The debate would be influenced by the feasibility of European settlement in tropical zones with dense populations. But possibly liberal ideas condemning extermination also influenced the policy choice. There could have been an amoral rationale for replacing Indigenous people with productive European food producers to avoid a Malthusian population crisis worldwide. But one Malthusian who saw this rationale as immoral was Thomas Malthus himself. Liberal objections to removal would thus fail in the US but perhaps by accident succeed in Asia and Africa.

The US debate had sharpened when some of the removal proponents openly shifted to the Development Right of Conquest for the land rather than the people, giving up on the civilizing effort. Democratic politician Lewis Cass, who would become secretary of war under Andrew Jackson in 1831, published an article in January 1830 promoting removal. The failure of civilizing plans revealed that Indians were incapable of development, because of "the institutions, character, and condition of the Indians themselves." On the Indians' rights to the land, they had only those rights "which do not interfere with the obvious designs of Providence." What Providence wanted, Cass said, was that "the earth should be reclaimed from a state of nature and cultivated." The Creator wanted "improvement," as Cass repeated the usual arguments ad nauseum that those who failed to improve their lands lost rights to those lands.[1]

The most prominent opponent of Indian removal was Jeremiah Evarts (1781–1831), the corresponding secretary of the American Board of Commissioners for Foreign Missions (ABCFM). The board was an organization in New England that supported missionaries to the Indians. Although not himself a clergyman or missionary, Evarts was a Yale graduate and longtime advocate and leader of the civilizing and Christianizing efforts among Southern Indians. At first, Evarts did not want to come out against removal, suggesting the missionaries stick to political neutrality.[2]

Even after the election of pro-removal Andrew Jackson as president in the fall of 1828, at least one board member at Evarts's employer, the ABCFM, advocated backing Jackson so as to get government funding for civilizing programs. It was a familiar conflict for aid organizations, between getting government support and denouncing unjust policies by that government.[3]

For Evarts's part, however, Jackson's election in 1828 had finally led him to open opposition to government policy. In the summer of 1829, he began writing and publishing a series of essays opposing removal that would be widely circulated and make him the national leader of the antiremoval cause. He noted the Georgians justified removal by an appeal to Vattel's principle that civilized cultivators could use the land better than a "vagrant, hunting and savage people."[4]

However, Evarts's counterattack against the Georgians' right of taking land from the uncivilizable did not at first deny this right. Unlike Benjamin Hawkins, Evarts was involved in a much more successful civilizing program, that among the Cherokees. Evarts could argue that Indians were civilizable after all. Evarts imagined that "the Cherokees might justly reply" to the Georgians that they were farmers, that they had cattle, houses, mills, looms, furniture, and roads. They could deny they were the "sort of people, as the writers on the laws of nations had in their minds, when they talked of vagrants, hunters, and savages." Evart did not dispute that vagrants should be displaced; he just denied that Cherokees were vagrants.[5]

Evarts's membership in the With-Friends-Like-These club was further demonstrated by his embrace of paternalism (already signaled by presuming to speak for the Cherokees). He saw the federal government as protector of the Cherokees but denied that protectors necessarily oppressed their wards. By way of analogy, he asked whether paternalistic husbands ever abused their wives. Just because the husband had the power, did he ever abuse his wife or seize her inheritance?[6]

Evarts thought the answer was no, but at least one of his female contemporaries thought the answer might be yes. A remarkable but largely unknown reformer named Lydia Maria Child drew connections between her revolt against condescension toward women and her support for Indians' rights. During her long career, she was an early example of one oppressed group supporting rights for another oppressed group.

Child had rediscovered the dignity problem of paternalistic aid and applied it to the Indians. Such condescension was an insult to the Indians, she noted later in her career: "Contempt, whether expressed or implied, alienates all men; but it operates with peculiar force upon Indians, because they have by nature great pride of independence."[7]

Child may have been sensitive to the dignity dimension because of her own history as a woman patronized by men. Lydia Maria

Child was born Lydia Francis in Medford, Massachusetts, on February 11, 1802, just as Hawkins and Jefferson were corresponding about civilizing the Creeks. Both she and her older brother, Convers, showed an enthusiasm for books. But while her father sent Convers to Harvard, he interrupted Lydia's education to pack her off to her older sister's in Maine to help with the housework. In Maine, she encountered the surviving remnants of the once-numerous Abenaki Indians.[8]

In 1829, Child published an amazingly radical view of Indians versus settlers that signaled Child's enrollment in the campaign against Indian removal. The title was *The First Settlers of New-England: Or, Conquest of the Pequods, Narragansets, and Pokanokets, as Related by a Mother to Her Children*. The author of this critique of European "usurpers," from their very beginnings in Massachusetts, identified herself only as "a lady of Massachusetts." There were no reviews of the book, not even in the leading Cherokee newspaper. Child herself apparently made no effort to promote the book, perhaps realizing how hopeless it was to gain an audience for so sweeping a denunciation of European settler ideology. As with other examples of unheard voices, Child's critique in *The First Settlers* might have become influential, if only someone had bothered to listen to some of the victims of coercion and paternalism.[9]

Child began her account with the destruction of the Pequods under John Winthrop. Lest anyone miss the connection of Massachusetts history to the Indian removal debate happening at the time of publication of *The First Settlers*, Child made it clear in a preface. The removal advocates wanted to force the Cherokees to "retire to the western wilds, where they must erelong miserably perish, to gratify the insatiable cupidity of the Georgians." Child insists her critique is highly applicable to the rights of all the Indians in the South, including the Creeks.[10]

In *The First Settlers*, Child was contemptuous of the Winthrop-era belief that God had sanctioned the destruction of the Pequods for the sake of progress. Unlike Evarts, Child denounced the Development Right of Conquest, the claim that "we have a right to take the land of the natives" just "because they do not improve it in the manner we think best." This idea was simply "unjust and unsound." Child invoked the classic reciprocity test: Should the whites who do not occupy and develop their land be forced to surrender it to someone else who could develop it? Of course not; whites would never tolerate such expropriations. Like Smith and Kant, Child also linked the Of Course Not to economics: Such violations of property rights would "subvert all our institutions and incitements to industry or distinction."[11]

The surprising thing about *The First Settlers* is how much space it devotes to women's rights among whites. Child later described her own motivation to support women's rights during her long career: "I was indignant for womankind made chattels personal from the beginning of time, perpetually insulted by literature, law, and custom." And similarly, she rejected white Christian paternalism toward "heathens," referring specifically to the Indians. The Christian nations' "philanthropic labors" among such heathens, she later said, "are nearly deprived of efficacy by an assumption of superiority, a pride of condescension."[12]

Giving a clue as to where she got her sensitivity to Indian dignity, Child gave a visceral example of "humiliating" laws for women. If a woman sought to leave her unfaithful husband, she would lose her children to the custody of him and his paramour. The courts did not want to award more than a "pittance" for alimony so as "to discourage every attempt made by women to emancipate themselves from their thralldom." Even if women remained till death do us part, the husband could still leave her only a pathetic inheritance when he finally died—even if she brought her own property into the marriage. Her loss of economic and social standing in that case would also be "mortifying." The lack of economic and parental rights humiliated women. Just as Child invited readers to empathize with how Cherokees felt about losing their land, she invited them to also empathize about how women felt losing their own money and children.[13]

However liberal Child was, she was still not herself completely free of paternalism. Like Evarts, she was enthusiastic about the civilizing agenda for the Indians. Although she rejected basing Indians' land rights on their capacity for civilization, she still felt the need to deny that Indians were "incapable of becoming a civilized people." As evidence for this, she cited a report of progress among the Cherokees that detailed adoption of Christianity, schools, printing presses, roads, and flourishing agriculture. They also had the classic marker of development in Georgia: "peach orchards."[14]

Unusually, however, Child did show some interest in letting some Indians speak for themselves. For the report on Cherokee development, she actually quoted a young Cherokee named David Brown. He was a beneficiary and proponent of the programs to Christianize and civilize the Indians. Brown was in a role familiar today in development efforts: the local working for a foreign NGO whom nobody listens to.[15]

Brown was born about 1806, or perhaps a little earlier. In 1819, he attended the Brainerd school sponsored by missionaries, and in 1820 he converted to Christianity. Jeremiah Evarts was a regular visitor to the school. David aspired to be a preacher. The missionaries, having identified David as promising, sent him in the summer of 1820 to the Foreign Mission School in Cornwall, Connecticut. David studied there for two years and then spent another year at Andover Theological Seminary in Massachusetts. By the summer and fall of 1823, the well-trained young campaigner was giving talks on the state of the Indians in towns throughout Massachusetts.[16]

As secretary of the American Board of Commissioners for Foreign Missions, Jeremiah Evarts encountered Brown at these talks. A big moment came on December 11, 1823, when Evarts and Brown traveled together to Worcester, Massachusetts. Evarts spoke for fifteen minutes; then Brown spoke for much longer. The collection plates after the talk overflowed with donations for the Indian missions. Evarts and fellow missionary officials realized that featuring an Indian voice was great for mobilizing financial and political support. "David would make the best agent we could have," they decided, and dispatched Brown and Evarts on a joint speaking tour of the eastern United States.[17]

Brown would repeat the talk he had given in Worcester in tour stops in New York; Philadelphia; Baltimore; Washington, DC; Richmond; and many other cities. Thanks to newspaper reports and the providential saving of a full copy of the speech, Brown's words were preserved. It was a rare survival of an Indian voice. On one hand, Brown was a fan of the Christianizing and civilizing mission among the Southern Indians. He offered the audience "my warmest gratitude to the benevolent of New England, for their exertions to send the blessings of civilization and the Gospel to my nation." He told the benevolent whites, "Your missionaries are much beloved by my countrymen." He also conveyed that "much gratitude is due to the government of the United States for its generosity, especially of late, toward the Indians." The Cherokees had appropriated such private and public funds for fifteen schools that enrolled hundreds of children.[18]

Brown announced his support for "every effort to have the Indian civilized, and above all evangelized." Brown portrayed the white missionaries as having the starring role in this effort. "These almoners of benevolence," he said, "have already gone to carry the glad tidings of Salvation to the children of the forest." Brown, like Evarts, offered a rejoinder to the Development Right of Conquest just by emphasizing how much the Indians were already developed.[19]

Brown also wrote in 1825 a paean to progress among the Cherokees. His report was widely circulated, and it was this that Lydia Maria Child quoted four years later. There is a noticeable shift away from the emphasis on white saviors in his 1823 speech to a portrayal of development led by Cherokees in his 1825 report.

Brown portrayed commerce as an alternative to conquest. On the local rivers leading out of Cherokee territory, Brown noted, "Cherokee commerce floats." It was "the natives" who had succeeded at trading with neighboring states and exporting cotton down the Tennessee River to the Mississippi down to New Orleans. In case you missed the point on who should get the credit for trade, Brown told the reader, "Nearly all the merchants in the nation are native Cherokees."

Brown now shifted from the third person to a proud first-person plural. He celebrated good economic management: "We are out of debt, and our public revenue is in a flourishing condition." He noted the republican principles of "our system of government." Brown's celebration of the spirit of independence among the Cherokees also saw them as in charge of their own development.[20]

Most importantly of all, David Brown saw material development among the Cherokees as a success. In a result that seemed to keep John Winthrop's promise from two centuries earlier, Brown noted how knowledge of agriculture had spread among the Cherokees. They were "producing Indian corn, cotton, tobacco, wheat, oats, indigo, sweet and Irish potatoes," and they had apple and peach orchards. Not only agriculture but also "industry and commercial enterprise are extending themselves in every part."[21]

Despite his enthusiasm for the civilizing effort, however, Brown was a fierce critic of Europeans' seizures of Indian lands. In his speech in Massachusetts in 1823, Brown declared the Indians had been "driven from their lawful possessions" by the white "usurpers of their dominions." His own father had taught him about these "wrongs and losses sustained by" the Indians. His mother had celebrated the Indian warriors who had died "defending the rights of our country." Although Brown also condemned "the cruelty and depredations" of some Indian warriors who had murdered "many innocent and Christian people," he said a greater "indignation rises within me, at the impious and savage procedure of Europeans." The European savages had more recently shown their true face in the "destruction of the Creeks" under Andrew Jackson. Brown also referred to the Indian removal that had already happened as of 1823, mentioning Southern Indians already driven west of the Mississippi "who are now far removed from the land of their fathers, some of whom with sorrow and deep regret have turned their faces toward the setting of the sun."

Whatever the progress of the civilizing effort among the Indians, Brown saw the violation of Indian rights as not being betterment at all. As Brown told his white audience: "As things have been in America for three hundred years, better would it have been had the natives never seen even the shadow of a white man."[22]

As pressure on the Cherokees to leave for the West increased, Brown began to openly condemn removal. Unlike Evarts, Brown rejected the idea of the Development Right of Conquest in all its varieties.

His crucial moment came in a letter he published in a missionary magazine in 1825. Brown forcefully articulated the core liberal principle of reciprocity: "How would the Georgians receive a proposition from the Cherokees to exchange the land they now hold, (which originally belonged to the Cherokees) for a tract of country near the Rocky Mountains?" Just as the Georgians would reject this proposition, so did the Cherokees. The Cherokees "love their birth right possessions" just like everyone else, Brown insisted. The Cherokees wanted agency just as the Georgians did. Putting it all together, Brown wanted Cherokees and whites to have mutual recognition of land rights, and to interact peaceably through trade.[23]

Brown had his own blind spots on consent versus coercion. He admitted that some Cherokees owned slaves, but he claimed that they were "generally well treated, and they much prefer living in the nation, to a residence in the United States." Despite his opposition to removal for Indians, he advocated removal of freed Black people back to Africa: "The Cherokees will, at no distant day, cooperate with the humane efforts of those who are liberating and sending this proscribed race to the land of their fathers."[24]

Brown's contribution to the Indian-removal debate was tragically to be very brief. He referred already to his own health problems in the 1825 report on progress. Brown battled tuberculosis until his death on September 15, 1829.[25]

Meanwhile, Evarts in late 1829 and early 1830 mobilized Northern supporters to flood Congress with antiremoval petitions, but it was in vain. On May 28, 1830, President Jackson signed the decisive Indian Removal Act after it passed Congress. Evarts was worn out and ill after the intense antiremoval campaign, and he died on May 10, 1831. The antiremoval movement fell apart after his death.

These events led to the US government's eventual forced march of the Cherokees and other Southern tribes westward in the winter of 1838–1839, the famous "Trail of Tears."[26]

In the last year before his death, Evarts seemed liberated to become more radical, now that he had already lost. In an article he published in October 1830, Evarts finally denounced the Development Right of Conquest. He confronted the supposed development mandate directly: "We shall be asked, whether this continent should be left in a state of perpetual wildness, covered with interminable forests, and unsubdued by the labor of man?" Now he insisted, at least hypothetically, that if a group "should pertinaciously refuse to sell their lands, or to admit strangers," then he thought "that no code of political morality" should force them to do so, any more than Europeans should be forced to give up their own lands.[27]

Evarts invoked the reciprocity argument that Brown had used five years earlier. Property rights among whites did not depend on whether they followed someone else's civilizing advice. White people are not required to be farmers instead of hunters in order to "have a title to their own country," Evarts said. It would not be okay for immigrants from France, Germany, and Ireland to take land from white frontiersmen, just because the immigrants were more civilized than the frontiersmen. It would not be okay for the immigrants to set up their own governments. Evarts insisted the rules for whites and Indians should be the same: "The plainest rules of morality forbid us to appropriate to ourselves the property of others without their consent."[28]

Evarts finally renounced the Vattel rule that cultivators should have the right to conquer hunters: "Nations are not to be asked, whether they gain their subsistence by hunting, pasturage, fishing or agriculture, before it can be determined, whether they have a title to their own country or not."[29]

Evarts noted the supposed philanthropic motivations for Indian removal: "Those who urge the removal of the Indians say, that such a measure would be greatly for their advantage." So if removal beyond the Mississippi was so good for them, why hadn't they chosen to move voluntarily? Evarts had finally become a good liberal skeptic. But he had done so too late to stop the Indian Removal Act. The liberal defeat on removal was total.[30]

Still to be decided was whether the same process of European settlement and removal of non-European peoples would happen in large parts of Asia and Africa. One of the most famous of the classical economists, Thomas Malthus, would consider the economic and moral case for such an outcome.

Malthus gave a powerful rationale for disappearing the native people. In 1803, he published a second edition of his famous *An Essay on the Principle of Population*. He acknowledged in this edition that the settler colonies offered a partial solution to his alarm about English population growth outstripping the food supply because of a fixed supply of land. Some of the excess population of England could move to areas of low population density and bring these new lands into food production.

But for Malthus, finding this technical solution to overpopulation was not enough to justify expansions of English settlements in the colonies. The debate had to consider the morality of such expansion because it harmed somebody else:

> There are many parts of the globe, indeed, hitherto uncultivated, and almost unoccupied; but the right of exterminating, or driving into a corner where they must starve, even the inhabitants of these thinly peopled regions, will be questioned in a moral view.[31]

Malthus made clear that he had the United States in mind. A couple of pages before this passage he described "the northern states of America" as places where, because of abundant land for subsistence, nobody bothered with restraining population growth. The result was explosive population growth in which the population doubled every twenty-five years. The consequence of this rapid population growth was not famine, as in the usual Malthusian story. The unacceptable consequences were those for the native population. Right after the above passage, Malthus noted that "if America continue increasing," then "the Indians will be driven further and further back into the country, till the whole race is ultimately exterminated."[32]

For Malthus, the colonial solution to excess population growth in Europe was no solution at all. His preferred and morally acceptable solution was to persuade everyone to limit reproduction through late marriage and abstinence within marriage.[33]

Malthus's message, "Don't take land and don't have sex," was probably unlikely to appeal to the white males who made up the electorate in the United States. They preferred ongoing land seizures justified by the land-developing mandate.

Malthus returned to the issue of European settlement and native extermination in a short book he published in 1830. On his usual fear about global population outrunning the food supply, he noted again the possible answer that "many parts of the earth are as yet very thinly peopled, and, under proper management, would allow of a much more rapid increase of food."

Moreover, he doubted that development of non-Europeans was a feasible answer to expand food production. He could not imagine the improvement of their "knowledge, in government, in industry, in arts, and in morals." Such improvement would not happen anytime soon, if ever.[34]

Should European settlers displace the inhabitants in large parts of Asia and Africa, so as to maximize global food production? European colonizers still had to decide. Malthus could have offered his analysis of land scarcity causing famine as a justification for such displacement. But for Malthus, the moral argument was what decided the question. Unlike Condorcet, Malthus made clear his moral objections to such large-scale extermination in the name of progress: "To exterminate the inhabitants of the greatest part of Asia and Africa, is a thought that could not be admitted for a moment."[35]

It is not clear that moral objections decided the outcome in Africa and Asia. Statistical analysis shows that European settlement was most likely on a large scale where (1) the precolonial Indigenous population density was low, (2) Indigenous people were highly susceptible to European diseases, and (3) the climate was temperate, so settlers could apply European farming techniques. All three factors had been favorable for European settlement in North America, Australia, and New Zealand. All three factors were unfavorable in the tropical lands of Asia and Africa. This might be enough to explain why there were no colonial territories in Asia and Africa in which European settlers engaged in removal of the native inhabitants on a large enough scale to become a majority. Colonies in which first contact with Europeans occurred in the nineteenth century (mainly in Asia and Africa) had much lower shares of Indigenous people killed or removed compared to previous centuries (Figure 2).[36]

Algeria was an important case of European settlement, already mentioned in a previous chapter. European settlers made up 7 percent of the population by 1860.[37] The great French liberal commentator on Algeria, Alexis de Tocqueville, said in 1846: "It is not only cruel, but absurd and impracticable, to try to force back or exterminate the natives."[38] Even a liberal gave more emphasis to practicality than morality for why extermination should not happen. Tocqueville expressed stronger liberal sentiments on another occasion in 1847 when he warned that if the settlers treated the Algerians too badly, there would eventually be a remorseless war for survival between the two peoples (a prediction that would come true in the Algerian war for independence in the twentieth century). "May God save us, gentlemen, from such a destiny!" Tocqueville declared. Recalling the unhappy history in this chapter, Tocqueville had a request for his French readers: "Let us not, in the middle of the nineteenth century, begin the history of the conquest of America over again."[39]

By 1861, the permanent undersecretary at the Colonial and India Offices (and Oxford professor of political economy), Herman Merivale, noted that in the Old World, in "the populous and semi-civilized regions, the European appears as a conqueror and a master, rarely in our times as a colonist."[40] (*Colonist* in this context means *settler.*) Condorcet's vision of groups disappearing in Asia and Africa in the name of progress was not going to happen. At least the strong form of the Development Right of Conquest—developing just the land and not the peoples—had not spread. It was a lot easier to be against Indigenous removal in lands Europeans did not want to settle anyway. It was a weak win for liberalism.

Such moral scruples were a bit less prominent in lands that Europeans desired and where large-scale population replacement was feasible. The failure of liberalism in Indian removal policy in North America was stark and never reversed. Tocqueville in 1835's *Democracy in America* had been clearer on the betrayal of liberal values in America than he was in Algeria:

> If they remain savages, they will be driven out as others advance. If they wish to become civilized, contact with more civilized people subjects them to oppression and misery. If they continue to wander from wilderness to wilderness, they will perish. If they try to settle in one place, they will also perish.[41]

Tocqueville offered a sardonic epitaph for the benevolent rhetoric in the Indian civilization plan: "To destroy human beings with greater respect for the laws of humanity would be impossible."[42]

After Indian removal, the US had another removal debate on Black people in America. Would the development of both white and Black people increase by sending the latter back to Africa?

9

What Shall We Do for Black Progress?

In the mid-nineteenth century, there were two major ideas about American Black people that needed to be defeated to give them freedom. White thinkers debated these ideas to address Black progress out of poverty. They are this history's most extreme example of offering material progress while denying the right to consent to your own progress. Violating Black consent did not lead to a very sensible notion of Black progress.

The first idea was that slavery itself was already the best thing that could be done for Black people. The second idea was that Black progress required Black people to leave the United States for a land of their own somewhere else.

The first position would continue the debate on benevolent slavery that had involved Adam Smith. The debate would involve slave owners, classical economists, thinkers, crusaders, former slaves, and politicians who debated the morality and economics of free labor as the crucial showdown over American slavery approached. White women would play a role in the debate, and there was also a rare voice given to a Black woman.

The more novel second idea, called colonization, was more prominent at first after American independence. As hard as it is to imagine today, some white American thinkers advocated partial or total removal of Black people, just as some had advocated it for Indians. It was another instance of the idea of population removal justified by the Development Right of Conquest.

Thomas Jefferson led the way on the second position. In his 1785 *Notes on the State of Virginia*, Jefferson expressed support for freeing the slaves. However, he thought he then had to answer the question: "What further is to be done with them?"[1]

His answer was that American Black people "should be colonized" to some place. Jefferson would figure out which place later. The project would furnish resettled Black people with arms, equipment for handicrafts, food, and domestic animals. Americans would supply military protection at first, anticipating that the natives of the other place might not be so keen on the idea. Jefferson planned to discontinue the economic and military aid to the Black settlers once "they shall have acquired strength." Americans would then finally recognize Black people in this other place as "a free and independent people."

Jefferson's emancipation-plus-colonization plan in 1785 had freed Black females depart when they were eighteen and males at twenty-one, leaving behind any of their young children. Jefferson continued to promote this kind of scheme for the rest of his life. The plan would not be voluntary. In 1811, he wrote, "It may perhaps be doubted whether many of these people would voluntarily consent to such an exchange of situation," but this did not "discourage the experiment."[2]

By 1824, the elderly Jefferson admitted to a correspondent that "the separation of infants from their mothers too would produce some scruples of humanity." But too many scruples would lose sight of how colonization resolved the Negro problem. It would be "straining at a gnat, and swallowing a camel." The only consent that Jefferson worried about was that of slaveholders. Jefferson reassured them that the emancipation of their slaves would be "voluntary."[3]

Africa was a natural place to put the colony. The Black colonists could also then civilize Africa. As the statesman and slave owner

Henry Clay from Kentucky later enthused: "They will carry back to their native soil the rich fruits of religion, civilization, law and liberty." Colonization of Black people in Africa would bring "a signal blessing to that most unfortunate portion of the globe."[4]

The imaginative antebellum thinkers offered the perfect illiberal trifecta: population removal, benevolent slavery, and colonial rule. Although there would be a lot of controversy about the consent of Black people to be colonized, nobody seemed to care about the consent of Africans to be civilized.

The colonizers could claim a little support from Black people themselves. Some free Black people disgusted with white peoples' oppression also proposed a Black homeland in Africa. A free Black merchant and sea captain named Paul Cuffe had explored the prospects for Black emigration to West Africa in 1811. Cuffe traveled to Sierra Leone in 1816 with forty free Black people from the North, although nothing further came of it. Other Black Americans had explored back-to-Africa schemes since the late eighteenth century.

The events that led to Liberia's founding began in 1816. Perhaps fittingly, one of the founders of colonization was drunk when he got the idea. The Virginia legislator Charles Fenton Mercer had learned of Jefferson's colonization scheme during an inebriated conversation with other legislators. He resolved to put it into practice.[5]

Mercer pursued the vision along with other justly forgotten visionaries. They did have a gift for involving much more famous men. Their roster of supporters included or would later include seven US presidents (Thomas Jefferson, James Madison, James Monroe, John Quincy Adams, Andrew Jackson, James Buchanan, and Abraham Lincoln), as well as Henry Clay, Daniel Webster, national anthem author Francis Scott Key, and Supreme Court Chief Justice John Marshall. The founding meeting of what became the American Colonization Society (ACS) took place on December 21, 1816.[6]

The ACS founders equivocated on whether their target was Black people who were already free or slaves to be freed as part of the scheme—and how voluntary it would be for either group. The constitution of the ACS said it was "to promote and execute a plan for colonizing (with their consent) the Free People of Color residing in our Country."[7]

Colonizers also deferred to the consent of slaveholders. Colonization in the South could proceed only as fast as slaveholders freed slaves. Slaveholders did not want any pressure. Putting "Free People of Color" in the ACS mandate avoided too much focus on slavery in the South. In practice, the ACS would resettle both slaves freed by Southern slaveholders and people already free in both North and South.

The ACS got down to action quickly. It dispatched to Africa two white men, the missionary Reverend Samuel Mills and Burlington College math Professor Ebenezer Burgess (who organizers noted also spoke Spanish). In 1818, they cruised the coast just south of the perpetually failing British colony of Sierra Leone, from whose travails they did not learn any lessons. The Spanish-speaking math Professor Burgess gave an enthusiastic report of West Africa's suitability for settlement by American Black people. It was a land overflowing with gold and ivory, he said, offering fertile soil for rice and sugar cane. Reverend Mills was more silent on such prospects, possibly because he died of fever on the voyage.[8]

Whatever the economic prospects for West Africa, the ACS came along at a crucial moment in the debate on slavery. In February 1819, Missouri applied for admission to the Union. Turning it into a slave state would break the tie between the number of slave states and free states. Northerners feared slave-power domination if the South had more votes in the House and Senate. One of the founders of the ACS, Speaker of the House Henry Clay of Kentucky, negotiated a compromise. The admission of free Maine would balance the admission of slave Missouri. In the Louisiana Purchase, the compromise allowed slavery below the latitude of the southern border of Missouri, but banned it forever north of that line. President James Monroe signed the Missouri Compromise on March 6, 1820.[9]

With the Union roiled by slavery, Clay and Monroe hoped colonization could attract support in both North and South. The ACS offered the one thing Northern and Southern whites could agree on: getting rid of Black people. Charles Fenton Mercer advanced his formerly drunken vision of colonization with a bill passed in March 1819 during the Missouri crisis. The bill authorized Monroe to transport Black people from America to West Africa.[10]

An ACS expedition left New York on January 31, 1820, on the ship *Elizabeth*, carrying eighty-six free Black settlers for West Africa. They landed in the area explored by Mills and Burgess. Within six months, forty-nine of the colonists had died from fever. The white ACS Board persisted: "To these dispensations of the Almighty we bow in submission and at the same time resolve to go in the path of duty." They showed not very impressive courage about the sacrifices of other people.[11]

President Monroe ordered a new expedition that left on January 21, 1821, with thirty-three would-be settlers. With support from an American naval officer, the expedition purchased land at gunpoint from local chiefs around Cape Mesurado south of Sierra Leone. The settlers just barely managed to defeat counterattacks from natives not so welcoming to their would-be civilizers.

The ACS kept sending more ships carrying small groups of free Black settlers. Finally, in February 1824, the ACS had a tiny colony worth naming. They renamed the area around Cape Mesurado *Liberia*, after the Latin word *liber* (free). The chief settlement got the name *Monrovia* in honor of the most powerful ACS patron, President James Monroe.[12]

Liberian agriculture did not quite live up to the enthusiastic report of Professor Burgess. Land along the coast featured mangrove swamps; land in the interior had thick forests and undergrowth. The cheap hoes supplied by ACS to new arrivals were of little use to settlers. The ACS rarely provided draft animals, and the animals even more rarely survived. Skills the Black settlers had learned on American farms did not match the new climate and pests.

The ACS gave each new emigrant as much as ten acres of land. It took the land back if the emigrants failed to improve it to ACS standards, which was often. The vision of Liberians growing sugarcane, tobacco, and cotton to compete with slave-grown crops in the Americas failed to materialize.[13]

The mortality on the early voyages would continue to be the biggest problem. From March 1820 to September 1843, there were 4,472 emigrants to Liberia. Of these, 2,198 had died by 1843. Five hundred twenty of the emigrants had left Liberia by that time. Only 1,754 of the emigrants from 1820 to 1843 survived to the end of the period and stayed in Liberia. One modern scholar estimated that Liberia over this period had one of the highest peacetime mortality rates ever recorded from reliable numbers.[14]

The ACS promised its supporters that a solution to the high mortality in Liberia was just around the corner. In 1834, the ACS claimed that this mortality, which was "the great problem which American philanthropy has been working out for twelve years," was finally "solved." The announcement was premature, by a couple of centuries.[15]

At least the ACS kept reliable numbers, which it reported back home. In 1844, the ACS records on the fate of emigrants were read into the Congressional Record. The numbers to confirm that Liberia was a death trap were available to anyone who wanted to check.

Neither Black people nor slaveholders were as enthusiastic about Liberia as they were supposed to be. The 4,472 Black Americans going to Liberia from 1820 to 1843 was a small number relative to the Black population of 2.9 million in 1838. About half of the settlers were slaves whose owners had freed them on condition of going to Liberia, but it was a tiny number relative to the total slave population. Meanwhile, the flow of free Black people to Liberia amounted to only one hundred a year.[16]

Most Black American leaders had turned against emigration to Africa after the all-white ACS took over the idea. In 1817, a leader of the free Black community in Philadelphia named James Forten wrote to Paul Cuffe. Of Black Philadelphians, Forten reported to Cuffe, "not one was willing to go to Africa." Forten chaired an 1817 meeting of Philadelphia Black people, which issued a declaration renouncing colonization. "If the plan of colonizing is intended for our benefit," the declaration said to colonizers, then you might want to know "that it is not asked for by us." The ACS "proffers to those who do not ask for them what it calls benefits, but which they consider injuries."[17]

Twenty years later in Philadelphia, James Forten's daughter, Sarah, was still reporting how little enthusiasm Black Americans had for colonization. In a letter to the white abolitionist Angelina Grimké in 1837, Sarah Forten explained how "colonization is, as you well know, the offspring of Prejudice." Forten told Grimké that she had "never yet met one man or woman of Color who thought better of it than I do." Colonization just told Black people "this is not your Country," Forten said.[18]

Another meeting of free Black people in Richmond in 1817 introduced a rare note of concern about colonization's effects on Africans in Africa. Black American colonists "would be apt to turn the ignorance of the natives to their own advantage, and do them more harm than good." And what would the natives think when they learned that the civilized white Americans had deported the Black Americans that were supposed to be civilization's emissaries? "Tell it not to barbarians, lest they refuse to be civilized."[19]

The anti-interventionist John Quincy Adams also disliked the idea of an American colony because it would be . . . an American colony. In 1819, he worried that the Colonization Society "would smuggle in upon us a system of establishing Colonies beyond [the] sea." As in his later letter in 1822, he did not go public with his opposition to colonialism. He reported his objections only to himself, in his private diary.[20]

One of Adam Smith's classical-economist heirs now entered the debate. Harriet Martineau (1802–1876) gave a favorable reaction at first to colonization. One of history's first female economists, Martineau in Britain in 1832 had written *Illustrations of Political Economy*. She displayed a gift for illustrating economics principles with fictional stories. One of her tales in 1832 contrasted slavery with freedom from the slaves' point of view. Her fictional slave narrator just aspired to "live in the same way that the whites live," to "trade as we like, and be rich, and even be governors."[21]

To Martineau, colonization was a way for American Black people to start from scratch under free institutions. Liberia offered American ex-slaves "a better place" with American institutions. She saw it as offering both collective and individual agency to Black people. In Liberia, Martineau explained, American Black people "will make their own laws," and "guard their own rights." According to the precepts of classical economics, such ideal laws would make it possible for American ex-slaves to "labor, and prosper and be happy. They will become farmers, planters, merchants, or tradespeople." Progress will ensue. Liberals would often be tempted by some deus ex machina for instant liberty and free markets.[22]

But Martineau by 1838 had turned against colonization. On another trip to the South, she said she had learned of most slaves' "horror of going to Liberia," which "appears to me decisive as to the unnaturalness of the scheme." Like a good classical economist, Martineau judged schemes for progress by the choices of the intended beneficiaries.[23]

For their part, many free Black people noted the parallel between Black removal and Indian removal. A meeting in New York in 1831 noted that whites had also promised that Indians' removal would be with Indians' consent. With that promise not kept, this assembly of Black New York asked, "Can they blame us if we attach the same credit to the declaration that they mean to colonize us only with our consent?"[24]

In December 1844, the annexation of Texas set off a new crisis over slavery. Northerners objected to Texas as a slave state. They feared the annexation of the formerly Mexican territory would provoke war with Mexico. Such a war would likely lead to the US conquering yet more territory that could become yet more slave states. The war with Mexico did indeed break out in May 1846 and did lead to the US annexation of Mexican territory from New Mexico to California.[25]

Many Southern leaders feared the reverse outcome—that a slew of free states would emerge out of the Louisiana and Mexican territories. Panicked by the growing abolitionist movement in the North,

Southerners worried about how the dominant free states would impose abolition on them. To counter the abolitionist narrative of slave owners as selfish oppressors, the South needed its own positive ideology about slavery. Most Southern leaders now rejected colonization, because it highlighted the possibility of emancipation. At this point, many Southerners fell back on the first position in the debate on Black progress—slavery itself was the best option for Black people.

The South Carolina slaveholder James Henry Hammond (1807–1864) became one of the loudest advocates of benevolent slavery, resuscitating the British proslavery arguments that Adam Smith had confronted in the late eighteenth century. Hammond was governor of South Carolina from 1842 to 1844 and a senator from 1857 to 1860.

On January 28, 1845, Hammond addressed a letter to the British abolitionist Thomas Clarkson. The one-time protagonist in the campaign to abolish the slave trade in Britain in 1807 was still fighting slavery. Now the aged Clarkson had taken the abolition debate into the next generation and across the Atlantic in 1844 with a letter appealing to American Northerners to recognize the evils of slavery.[26]

Hammond responded furiously to Clarkson, updating previous claims from Clarkson's generation about the benevolence of slavery. Slavers who shipped Africans to be slaves in the South enabled them to move "from barbarism to civilization," Hammond insisted.

Moreover, Southern slaves consumed more than free British laborers, claimed Hammond. The latter were in "frightful destitution." Quoting official British sources, Hammond noted some British workers lived in horrific conditions, in cellars, in tents, or in the open air; some lived as many as ten to a cottage in dire hunger. In contrast, Hammond claimed, "never did a slave starve in America." Slave owners had strong incentives to take care of their slaves. The half-hearted British relief system had weak incentives to take care of British paupers. The British poor did not get "the slightest comfort" from their freedom. The British had no solution to end white poverty in Britain, Hammond gleefully taunted Clarkson, while the slave owners had one to prevent Black poverty in America.

As further evidence, Hammond cited the British Caribbean colonies after the abolition of slavery there in 1833. The economy of the West Indies had collapsed after abolition, and the ex-slaves had miserable incomes, he said. He would never have been so inhumane to his own slaves.[27]

Hammond had self-interest at stake, but some non-slaveholders also argued for the idea of benevolent slavery. Across the Atlantic, the British historian and literary celebrity Thomas Carlyle also looked back to the emancipation of slaves in the British Empire in a series of articles between 1843 and 1850. It distressed him that West Indian Black people after emancipation "refuse to work" on the sugar plantations as before. The sugar economy had declined, and the ex-slaves had fallen into "the abysses of open Beggary." As always, the evidence for benevolent slavery for Black people was their material poverty without slavery. Now he addressed them on their attempt to be free: "You, for your part, have tried it, and failed."[28]

Like Jefferson earlier, the key question for Carlyle to ask the slaves after emancipation was "What to do with you?" Emancipation was fatefully not a good idea unless the emancipators also had a good plan for the ex-slaves.[29]

Carlyle imagined the slaves answering him: "If thou art in very deed my Wiser, may a beneficent instinct lead and impel thee to 'conquer' me, to command me!" Carlyle was clear about the link between paternalism and compulsion: "If thou do know better than I what is good and right," then thou should "force me to do it."[30]

I may even have to kill you in order to save you, Carlyle said. If you resist, "I will flog you; if still in vain, I will at last shoot you,—and make God's Earth . . . free of you." Carlyle's apocalyptic answer to the poverty of ex-slaves in the Caribbean was to either kill them or return them to slavery.[31]

Now a second heir to Adam Smith entered the slavery debate on the same side as Harriet Martineau. The great classical economist John Stuart Mill answered Carlyle in 1850. Mill throughout his long career was one of history's greatest liberal proponents (although sadly not always a consistent one) of "the rights of others," to use his words.

Mill denounced Carlyle's theory of innate differences between white and Black people. Mill was one of the foremost critics of the nineteenth-century rise of scientific racism. He referred to all such theories of non-white racial inferiority as "vulgar." It was so unscientific to just attribute "the diversities of conduct and character to inherent natural differences."

The reasoning was vulgar because it was circular reasoning. The slaves were poor because they were allegedly inferior. Carlyle said he knew they were inferior because they were poor.

Mill instead said that poor incentives for the slaves explained their reluctance to work hard and to invest in the future: "What race would not be indolent and insouciant when things are so arranged, that they derive no advantage from forethought or exertion?" Mill rejected Carlyle's justification of slavery as fit for slaves permanently unfit to choose for themselves.[32]

Some thought the debate between innate inferiority and incentives was an empirical debate about the cause of Black poverty. However, Mill insisted also on the slaves' demand for agency: Nobody should take away someone else's agency based on the supposed material benefits of doing so. Mill actually used the word *agency* elsewhere in his political writings. In 1861, he discussed how much rulers varied in "free agency of their subjects, or the supersession of it by managing their business for them."[33]

Like Smith, Mill compared slave owners coercing Black people with husbands coercing wives. For both Black people and women, Mill celebrated "freedom of individual choice," against the "general presumption, that certain persons are not fit" to choose for themselves. He scorned the self-interest of slave owners and husbands who claimed a right based on their alleged superiority to dominate their slaves and wives.[34]

Mill's wife, Harriet Taylor Mill, influenced these passages. She had written an earlier and briefer article with much the same arguments. She had also compared slavery and oppression of women. She ridiculed those who claimed that women were fine with their husbands' right to coerce them. The men did not appear to consult any actual wives on the matter. Therefore, Mrs. Mill asked, how did they "know that women do not desire equality and freedom?"[35]

Mill gave credit to his wife for much of his writings. What I owe to her, Mill said, is "almost infinite." Most of his readers then and now did not believe him on Harriet Taylor's contribution to his work and gave Mrs. Mill little recognition, continuing the phenomenon of wives of economists (like Condorcet's wife, Sophie de Grouchy) getting a little bit of a voice but getting too little credit for it. It would happen again.[36]

Mill's critique of benevolent slavery was both a demand for agency and a moral critique. Like Smith, Mill believed economists could not talk about whether economic outcomes were desirable without a theory of justice. Material improvement was not enough to judge an outcome as satisfactory; the outcome also had to be just. His definition of justice was "the recognition and observance of the rights of other people."[37]

Another theme of Smith and Kant that Mill picked up was the demand for dignity, which he linked to the demand for agency. Mill thought *dignity* was the best word to describe "the love of liberty and personal independence." This "sense of dignity" was something that "all human beings possess in one form or other." There was some variation across individuals, only imperfectly correlated with education or income. Dignity was essential to happiness. No material reward associated with the elimination of dignity was adequate compensation for such a loss. "It is better to be a human being dissatisfied than a pig satisfied," Mill asserted. Elsewhere, Mill described economics as "absurd" if it assumed that individuals were motivated only by material incentives.[38]

For Mill, dignity was connected to the individual's right to be free from coercion by society or government. He proclaimed that "there is a circle around every individual being, which no government, be it that of one, of a few, or of the many, ought to be permitted to overstep." The people who believed in this space for individuals included anyone "who professes the smallest regard to human freedom or dignity."[39]

These passages on dignity versus coercion did not refer to slavery, but they help us understand why Mill in 1850 was not going to argue with Carlyle about whether the slaves were materially better off than British workers or Caribbean ex-slaves. Mill said, "It is not the facts of the question, so much as the moralities of it, that I care to dispute with your contributor." All that mattered was that slaves had not chosen slavery.

Carlyle understood well this opposition to slavery from classical economists, especially the opposition of Mill. He mocked Mill's "Voluntary Principle." He thought it ridiculous that British Empire officials should leave the fate of West Indian plantations to ex-slaves and sugar consumers making their own decisions on "supply and demand."[40]

Could economists really believe only in just "letting men alone"? Carlyle wondered whether Mill thought "all the Horses also are to be emancipated, and brought to the supply-and-demand principle?"[41]

Carlyle's comparison of ex-slaves to horses shows how much what Mill called his "vulgar" belief in the innate inferiority of the ex-slaves motivated his views on coercion. Deploying another livestock metaphor later in an 1859 letter to his brother, Carlyle rejected Mill's view that it was "a sin to control, or coerce into better methods, human swine in any way."[42]

Carlyle applied the Development Right of Conquest to both the land and the slaves. Before colonization, the Caribbean islands had been nothing but "mere jungle, savagery, poison reptiles and swamp malaria." Our Maker had decided to give "proprietorship" to whoever could get from the islands the "noble produce they were created fit for yielding." Heaven appointed this most efficient producer as "Vicegerent of the Maker." This vicegerent turned out to be "the white European" who got the lands and forced the slaves to produce sugar. Now the ex-slaves revealed again their innate inferiority as "indolent, two-legged cattle." They refused to work for God's sugar mission and chose to produce pumpkins for their own subsistence. The "Eternal Powers" therefore decided that "no black man, who will not work" had "the smallest right" to any of his own land or his own subsistence crops.

Carlyle knew about the tradition of skeptical liberalism that had produced Mill—he saw him as a "sad product of a skeptical eighteenth century." Carlyle coined the phrase "Dismal Science" for Mill's incomprehensibly passive economics of "letting men alone."[43]

Carlyle was clear on his crucial difference with Mill, that Mill's Dismal Science declared that "negro and white" were "on a footing of perfect equality, and subject to no law but that of supply and demand." Carlyle thought this to be "clearly no solution" for Caribbean prosperity.[44]

Carlyle's low view of classical economists also applied to Harriet Martineau, with an added dose of condescension. In later reminiscences, Carlyle said that "her talent" suited her to be "a quite shining Matron of some big Female Establishment, mistress of some immense Dress-Shop." But Martineau's talent "was totally inadequate to grapple with deep spiritual and social questions." He dismissed her views on slavery as "N—— fanaticisms."[45]

"Dismal Science" was to be a lasting slur on economics, although later users of the phrase seldom realized that it had originated from a proslavery polemic. Today people usually identify promarket arguments with the right, and criticism of markets with the left. In 1850, it was the promarket left against the anti-market right.[46]

Mill was aware that his debate with Carlyle in 1850 arrived in America during the slavery crisis provoked by the Mexican-American War. To Mill, Carlyle's benevolent-slavery articles in 1849 and 1850 offered crucial support from a disinterested celebrity to slave owners. "I hardly know of an act by which one person could have done so much mischief as this may possibly do," Mill lamented.[47]

The benevolent slavery proponent James Henry Hammond, like Carlyle, had identified a British classical economist as a key opponent, none other than Harriet Martineau. After traveling through the American South, Martineau denounced the claims of not only benevolent colonization but also benevolent slavery.

Martineau described slavery in her 1837 book *Society in America*. Like Adam Smith, Mr. and Mrs. Mill, and Lydia Maria Child, Martineau compared the oppression of women to slavery for Black people. She noted legal restrictions on the rights of women in the United States. They were required in some states to turn over all their property to their husbands. Martineau wondered, "Whence do governments derive the unjust power of thus disposing of property without the consent of the governed?"

She elaborated: "How obedience to the laws can be required of women, when no woman has, either actually or virtually, given any assent to any law"? Those who claimed to be benevolent autocrats as husbands were almost as ridiculous as the self-proclaimed benevolent slave owners were. The unmarried Martineau singled out one such statement by Mill's father, James Mill, who claimed fathers and husbands adequately represented women's interests. "This statement is not worth another word," Martineau scoffed.

Martineau saw slaves as well as women deprived of the consent of the governed: "Their houses and schools are pulled down," and they are "excluded from the most honorable employments." And this was done to them by their fellow citizens who "declare that all men are born free and equal, and that rulers derive their just powers from the consent of the governed."[48]

For Martineau, the worst case of oppression of women and Black people was the combination of white male slave owners oppressing Black female slaves. Unlike Smith, Martineau was explicit about slave owners forcing sex on their female slaves. Her most sensational story was told to her by a Southern lady who owned "a very pretty mulatto girl." The girl attracted unwelcome attention from a young white man who was staying in the Southern lady's house. The girl begged her lady owner for protection from his advances. At first, the lady gave protection to her slave. The young white man returned a few weeks later to reiterate to the Southern lady his desire for the girl.

"I pitied the young man," Martineau quoted the lady saying at this point, "so I sold the girl to him for 1,500 dollars."[49]

Hammond in 1845 was apoplectic about Martineau's pretty mulatto girl story, and he quickly turned misogynous. "Old maids, like Miss Martineau, linger with such an insatiable relish" on such "scandalous stories," Hammond said. "Miss Martineau with peculiar gusto," like other abolitionists, stigmatized "the whole Slave region as a 'Brothel.'" Hammond avowed that Southern social norms would penalize any slave owner for such intercourse, "if carried on habitually." Yet Hammond himself later admitted he had long-lasting sexual relations with two of his own slaves, Sally and Louisa Johnson, who were mother and daughter.[50]

Moreover, Hammond thought male slaves were "comparatively indifferent" about what happened to their own wives or daughters. And why was this any different from Northern white men having white mistresses? Overall, Hammond affirmed his belief that "our slaves are the happiest three millions of human beings on whom the sun shines."[51]

Martineau on her trips through the South had heard a lot about "the fondness of slaves for slavery." She thought there could have been individual cases of contentment. But as a skeptical liberal economist, she asked, If they liked it so much, why did so many other slaves run away? Southerners just attributed running away to "ingratitude" for the allegedly opulent lifestyle that slave owners had made possible for their slaves. Martineau tried to explain to slave owners that the supposedly high material consumption of slaves, even if true, was not enough—"the extremest pampering, for a lifetime, is no equivalent for rights withheld." The slave owners not only violated human rights, Martineau said; they had "an inability even to comprehend them." James Henry Hammond failed to comprehend the difference between white mistresses and slave mistresses. White women usually had the right not to be sold to their own rapist.[52]

Some abolitionists realized that the most effective testimony on female slaves' lack of rights against rape would come from the female slaves. In a remarkable memoir that could help educate white Americans on whether the South was a brothel, ex-slave Harriet Jacobs detailed her own sexual victimization by her owner in Edenton, North Carolina.[53]

The abolitionist who helped Jacobs get published was the same person who had helped publicize the writings of the Cherokee David Brown. Lydia Maria Child had enlisted in the abolition movement in 1833 with a courageous jeremiad against slavery, titled *An Appeal in Favor of That Class of Americans Called Africans*. In it she cited Harriet Martineau for educating her on the economics of slavery. Martineau in turn saluted Child's sacrifice for the cause after society ostracized her and stopped buying her books.[54]

Child in 1833 was a rare white voice to emphasize Black people fighting for their own liberty, saying they "fought like very tigers for freedom!" This history was suppressed by slave owners: "But they have been hung, and burned, and shot—and their tyrants have been their historians!" But someday those in Africa and in the diaspora would give their own perspective: "When the Africans have writers of their own, we shall hear their efforts for liberty called by the true title of heroism in a glorious cause."[55]

So Child was enthusiastic when Harriet Jacobs approached her in the summer of 1860, just months before the election of Abraham Lincoln. Jacobs asked for editorial help, while the publisher insisted on Child writing the preface as a condition for publication. The extent of Child's editing is unclear. It is always complicated when there is a white gatekeeper for a non-white voice. The memoir, *Incidents in the Life of a Slave Girl*, came out in 1861, just in time for the Civil War. Child mailed copies of the book to Union troops throughout the war.[56]

It is best to let Harriet Jacobs tell her story in her own words: "I now entered on my fifteenth year—a sad epoch in the life of a slave girl. My master began to whisper foul words in my ear." He was a medical doctor whom she gave the pseudonym Dr. Flint. Jacobs went on:

> I was compelled to live under the same roof with him—where I saw a man forty years my senior daily violating the most sacred commandments of nature. He told me I was his property; that I must be subject to his will in all things. My soul revolted against the mean tyranny. But where could I turn for protection? . . . There is no shadow of law to protect her from insult, from violence, or even from death; all these are inflicted by fiends who bear the shape of men.[57]

Jacobs said she had a desperate need "to preserve my self-respect." She used words evocative of her lost battle for respect like *compulsion*, *degradation*, and *humiliation*. Jacobs shifted back and forth between the third person and first person as she described her trauma with Dr. Flint:[58]

> Soon she will learn to tremble when she hears her master's footfall. . . . If God has bestowed beauty upon her, it will prove her greatest curse. That which commands admiration in the white woman only hastens the degradation of the female slave. I know that some are too much brutalized by slavery to feel the humiliation of their position; but many slaves feel it most acutely, and shrink from the memory of it. I cannot tell how much I suffered in the presence of these wrongs, nor how I am still pained by the retrospect. My master met me at every turn, reminding me that I belonged to him, and swearing by heaven and earth that he would compel me to submit to him.[59]

Jacobs was astonished by the benevolent slavery argument that ignored such humiliations for the slave. She quoted a speech by Senator Albert Brown of Mississippi, who claimed that slavery was "a great moral, social, and political blessing; a blessing to the master, and a blessing to the slave!" She had not found Dr. Flint to be a blessing.[60]

She had heard the arguments about how badly off the white poor in Europe were in terms of material consumption compared to slaves. On a later trip to England she visited some of "the poorest poor." She realized "that the condition of even the meanest and most ignorant among them was vastly superior to the condition of the most favored slaves in America." The key difference was that "they were protected by law." For those who were poor but free: "The father, when he closed his cottage door, felt safe with his family around him. No master or overseer could come and take from him his wife, or his daughter."[61]

Harriet Jacobs said that for powerless slave girls, "resistance is hopeless." She wanted nevertheless to find some ways to resist Dr. Flint, however imperfectly. Harriet Jacobs decided to enter into a relationship with another white man in the neighborhood to protect her from Dr. Flint. Again her key issue was finding some kind of freedom from coercion: "It seems less degrading to give one's self, than to submit to compulsion. There is something akin to freedom in having a lover who has no control over you, except that which he gains by kindness and attachment." She had two children by her partner, to whom she gave the pseudonym Mr. Sands. He later became a congressman in Washington.[62]

It turned out Mr. Sands was still not enough to escape Dr. Flint's harassment. She went into hiding in her own neighborhood and then finally escaped to the North.

Harriet Jacobs knew that confessing to the liaison with Mr. Sands in her memoir would ruin her reputation among her readers in the North. She appealed for understanding to the female readers: "O, ye happy women, whose purity has been sheltered from childhood, who have been free to choose the objects of your affection, whose homes are protected by law, do not judge the poor desolate slave girl too severely!" The plea for empathy did not work. She never became a major figure in the abolition movement and lived out the rest of her long life in obscurity.[63]

Another runaway slave named Frederick Douglass would be far more successful in explaining Black people's desire for freedom to white audiences. Douglass was born in 1818 to a slave mother and a white father, possibly his first owner, Aaron Anthony.

Douglass testified to his own demand for dignity and respect. In 1834, his owner rented the sixteen-year-old slave to an even more brutal farmer named Edward Covey. Douglass eventually decided to fight back. He got into a fistfight with Covey, which he later celebrated as a moment of awakening of his need for dignity:

> I WAS A MAN NOW. It recalled to life my crushed self-respect and my self-confidence, and inspired me with a renewed determination to be A FREEMAN. A man, without force, is without the essential dignity of humanity.[64]

Douglass brought the same dignity as a free man to conflicts with racists in the North. After the annual meeting of the American Anti-Slavery Society in New York in May 1850, Douglass took a walk along Battery Park in downtown Manhattan with two white abolitionist sisters, Julia and Eliza Griffiths. A mob beat up Douglass to punish him for his crime of associating with white women. Douglass confessed he was guilty of the crime of being "a man, entitled to all rights, privileges and dignity."[65]

Like Martineau and Jacobs, Douglass discussed the sexual violation of slave women. Again, it was dignity that was at stake. Slavery would "leave her unprotected—a degraded victim to the brutal lust of fiendish overseers, who would pollute, blight, and blast her fair soul—rob her of all dignity."[66]

Douglass was yet another liberal thinker who saw the link between rights for Black people and women. He was sensitive to the needs of white women for dignity, which led him to another radical position: endorsing women's movements for the right to vote. As he later explained in his 1881 autobiography, gratitude for women's participation in the abolition movement led him to pay attention to women's rights. The pioneering suffragist Elizabeth Cady Stanton helped educate him on how the denial of the right to vote perpetuated the "degradation of woman."[67]

Douglass was at the Seneca Falls Convention organized by Stanton in 1848 that was a milestone in launching the women's rights movement. As he wrote at the time, the proceedings were almost entirely conducted by women, who exhibited a marked "dignity." He called out abolitionists for their inconsistency offering rights to Black people but not to women. The case for women's right to vote emerged for Douglass from the principle that "government only is just which governs by the free consent of the governed."[68]

He spelled out further the crucial links between women's consent and dignity twenty-two years later: "Woman is not a consenting party to this Government. She has never been consulted." This made our government "a Government of force." He deplored how "we legislate for woman, and protect her, precisely as we legislate for and protect animals, asking the consent of neither."

He suggested a parallel between the claims of benevolent slavery and benevolent male guidance of women: Women were also subject to "masters" who could "be kind and tender hearted," just as slave masters could possibly be. But "this in nowise mitigates the harshness of the principle."

Finally, he stated the momentous link between consent and dignity: "To deprive her of this right" to consent by voting "is to deprive her of a part of her natural dignity." He also put it in terms of the synonym of *dignity, respect*: "To deny woman her vote is to abridge her natural and social power, and to deprive her of a certain measure of respect."[69]

Of course, Douglass himself had more experience of the allegedly benevolent slavery. Douglass in 1855 recalled a childhood memory of his first owner, Anthony, whipping Douglass's fifteen-year-old aunt, Esther, because she had refused Anthony's advances. He noted how cruel were the wives of slave owners to their husbands' slave offspring. Husbands often sold such children to escape the wives' wrath. So much for the benevolent slavery hypothesis, Douglass said; a man who sold his own offspring "may not be safely relied on for magnanimity." Douglass gibed about a later owner, "Master Thomas was one of the many pious slaveholders who hold slaves for the very charitable purpose of taking care of them." In a speech the same year, Douglass explained to his white audience that "care for the slave as property is no compensation for denial of his personality." Even if you "surround the slave with luxuries," that would only "enhance his torment, and deepen his anguish."[70]

Frederick Douglass next entered the other debate over benevolent colonization, in addition to benevolent slavery. He targeted the longtime colonization promoter Henry Clay, the Kentucky senator. Douglass failed to understand how Clay could reconcile what Clay called Black people's "free and unconstrained volition" with Clay's intent to "gladly send us where he would never see us more." Douglass satirically appreciated that "it would be for our good," that Clay "would make this sacrifice" of sending away his Black fellow residents of Kentucky.

If colonization was really for Black people's own good, and was to be of their own volition, why did they even need Clay telling them to do it? "When we wish to go to Liberia, or elsewhere, we can go without his telling us that he wishes [us] to go." How would Clay feel if a group of Black people wished him off his farm, to go to Liberia, of his own volition? Wouldn't Clay take it as an unforgivable insult? Well, Douglass declared, "our right to stay here is as good of that of Mr. Clay, or of any man-stealer in the land."[71]

For Douglass, the colonization plans sounded nonvoluntary. He was horrified to read in one of Clay's plans (like Jefferson's) that parents with children, some with children ages one to four, "shall be torn away from their children and hurried off to Liberia or somewhere else." The children were to be kept at work for another twenty-eight years, then they in turn would be torn away from their own children and "hurried off to Liberia."[72]

Then Douglass drew the parallel with population removal applied to Indians. Instead of a supposedly voluntary option, Douglass thought Clay's plans for Black people sounded more like "the plundering of the Indians of their territory." Douglass summarized that colonization "next to slavery is the deadliest foe of the colored man."[73]

Now a new and formidable white voice entered the colonization debate. The colonization promoter Henry Clay died on June 29, 1852.

A few days later in a eulogy for Clay, one of his disciples vowed to carry on the colonization cause. Abraham Lincoln in this eulogy approved of Clay's pitch for the movement from twenty-five years earlier as good for civilizing both African Americans and Africans in Africa.[74]

Lincoln in 1852 thought prospects for the success of the plan had only gotten stronger in the decades since the ACS founding. It would allow present and future generations to "succeed in freeing our land from the dangerous presence of slavery," while "restoring a captive people to their long-lost father-land." Lincoln thought colonization was the only way to give Black people equal rights. As he later explained his support for colonization to a group of Black leaders in 1862, the problem was that "even when you cease to be slaves, you are yet far removed from being placed on an equality with the white race."[75]

As the North's conflict with the South escalated over slavery in the Western territories, Lincoln faced further pressure to articulate his views on colonization. In a speech in 1854 on territorial slavery, Lincoln acknowledged that Liberia had not turned out well. Despite his enthusiasm for colonization, he was still debating it inside himself. "If all earthly power were given me," Lincoln imagined, "I should not know what to do" with slavery. Lincoln said his "first impulse would be to free all the slaves, and send them to Liberia,—to their own native land." But Lincoln seemed to be aware of the frightful mortality in Liberia: "If they were all landed there in a day, they would all perish in the next ten days." So "what then?"[76]

Lincoln the politician wanted to end slavery eventually but desperately needed to offer the voters a plan for the ex-slaves. Many white voters in the North feared an influx of freed slaves from the South. Colonization seemed the magic answer. Lincoln's answer to a failed colonization project in one place was to heroically imagine the same approach could still work somewhere else. Although colonization faced huge implementation challenges, Lincoln insisted in 1857, "We shall find a way to do it, however great the task may be."[77]

Meanwhile the debate on option number one for Black people—benevolent slavery—got even more furious. In 1857, the US Supreme

Court under Chief Justice Roger B. Taney endorsed benevolent slavery. The *Dred Scott* decision by Taney announced that Black people were "altogether unfit" for freedom, and so "the negro might justly and lawfully be reduced to slavery for his benefit." It followed that Black people "had no rights which the white man was bound to respect."[78]

Lincoln could have become a footnote to history as an obscure colonization promoter. However, the benevolent-slavery proponents allowed Lincoln to put forward his strongest suit, his moral commitment to freedom.

In 1858, invoking reciprocity like the liberal economists, Lincoln asked the benevolent slave owners if they would want such benevolence themselves. Probably not, he said:

> As a good thing, slavery is strikingly peculiar, in this, that it is the only good thing which no man ever seeks the good of, for himself. Nonsense! Wolves devouring lambs, not because it is good for their own greedy maws, but because it is good for the lambs!!![79]

What about the slave owners' claim to having superior civilization to pass on to their slaves? Even if this were true, Lincoln said, it did not justify slavery. In 1858, Lincoln invoked the classical skeptics' idea of reciprocity to show whites where such civilizing arguments would lead. The argument for civilizing slavery proved more than its advocates wanted it to:

> It proves that among the white races of the world any one might properly be enslaved by any other which had made greater advances in civilization. And, if this rule applies to nations there is no reason why it should not apply to individuals; and it might easily be proved that the wisest man in the world could rightfully reduce all other men and women to bondage.[80]

The debate on benevolent slavery continued after the Civil War broke out in April 1861. Across the Atlantic, the British debated whether to recognize the Confederacy. The Confederacy had sent emissaries to Britain in the summer of 1861 to plead for recognition, hoping that British textile manufacturers would be desperate to keep access to Southern cotton.[81]

John Stuart Mill now sought to influence that decision by again ridiculing claims for benevolent slavery. In February 1862, Mill wrote how the Confederates were "loudly vaunting" slavery as a "civilizing" institution. Slave owners like Hammond and British apologists like Carlyle, Mill said, thought slavery "the fit condition not only for negroes but for the laboring classes of all countries." He mocked Confederate rhetoric that slavery was a "sacred deposit providentially entrusted to the keeping of the Southern Americans, for preservation and extension."[82]

Although it was a narrow escape, Mill's critique would win this round of the battle. No doubt influenced by Union victories as well as by Mill's eloquence, the British government by 1863 had decided not to recognize the Confederacy.[83]

Thanks to Lincoln, however, colonization also continued to be part of the slavery debate during the Civil War. Lincoln still thought he needed a plan for freed slaves as part of his opposition to slavery. Colonization could induce the slave states still in the Union to gradually abolish slavery, Lincoln hoped, while getting rid of freed Black people whom white people were not ready to accept, even in the free states.

Lincoln was so eager to advance colonization that he met with a promoter of one possible site on April 10, 1861, just two days before the battle over Fort Sumter began the Civil War. Having given up on Liberia, colonization enthusiasts were now suggesting Central America. Lincoln was eager to talk to Ambrose W. Thompson, who told Lincoln that he owned several hundred thousand acres in a place called Chiriquí on the Pacific coast of the Isthmus of Panama. Panama was then part of Colombia. Thompson told Lincoln that Chiriquí had both abundant coal deposits and a great harbor, making it ideal for a prosperous colony of American Black people. Lincoln authorized negotiations for "coal and privileges" with Thompson.[84]

The first victory for emancipation with colonization was in the District of Columbia, which was under federal jurisdiction. The emancipation plan, which Congress passed on April 11, 1862, included a provision for colonization of the freed slaves. The ACS was still trying to induce freedmen to go to Liberia. The freedmen did not show much enthusiasm for such a move. "The number known to entertain that desire was one," the ACS reported.[85]

Lincoln still hoped that Central or South America would be more appealing to freed Black people than Liberia had been. In July 1862, he tried again to convince representatives of slave states still in the Union to embrace gradual abolition of slavery, combined with colonization. As Lincoln informed the deeply uninterested border-state men, "Room in South America for colonization, can be obtained cheaply, and in abundance." When "the freed people" heard about this great plan, they "will not be so reluctant to go."[86]

Lincoln referred to the Chiriquí scheme. By August 1862, Senator Samuel Pomeroy of Kansas had offered Lincoln a plan to organize one hundred Black families to go to Chiriquí. A few free Black people were willing to go, including even two sons of colonization critic Frederick Douglass.[87]

That same month, Lincoln advocated the plan in person to a delegation of Black ministers. A Black colony in Chiriquí on the Isthmus of Panama would prosper from its location on the main transit route from the Atlantic to the Pacific. Lincoln enthused: "On both sides there are harbors among the finest in the world. Again, there is evidence of very rich coal mines." It would be "extremely selfish" for free Black people to resist emigration to this paradise, he told the ministers. If only free Black people could begin a Black exodus out of the United States, it would make emancipation possible for their enslaved fellow Black people.

Lincoln admitted to the Black ministers in August 1862 that "the political affairs in Central America are not in quite as satisfactory condition as I wish." Indeed, contacts with Central American governments had found they had no interest in giving up part of their land and sovereignty to Black Americans. But Lincoln promised the Black ministers that he would try again. The Black ministers politely said they would think about it.[88]

Lincoln announced his momentous decision to emancipate slaves in the Confederacy on September 22, 1862. On January 1, 1863, slaves in the rebel states "shall be then, thenceforward, and forever free." He included in the preliminary September proclamation some less inspirational language still promoting his plan for colonization of freed Black people. Just eleven days earlier, the Lincoln administration had signed a contract with Ambrose W. Thompson to buy land for settlement in Chiriquí and to invest in its coal mines.[89]

However, doubters in Congress and the Cabinet now pointed out to Lincoln a few problems with the Chiriquí scheme. Thompson, as it turned out, was offering lands that he did not own. Colombia was having its own civil war. A Smithsonian Institution scientist tested samples from the allegedly rich coal mines of Chiriquí and found them of zero value.

The collapse of the Chiriquí scheme was swift. On September 24, 1862, two days after pushing colonization in the preliminary Emancipation Proclamation, Lincoln suspended the Pomeroy expedition. It was just a week before the hundred free Black families were supposed to depart for Chiriquí. By October 1862, all the backers of Chiriquí had disavowed the plan.[90]

Lincoln refused to give up on colonization. He set an impressive standard for future aid promoters with his ability to promise future success despite present-day failure. On December 1, 1862, just a month before the Emancipation Proclamation was to take effect, Lincoln brought up colonization again in his annual message to Congress. He admitted that "several of the Spanish-American republics have protested against the sending of such colonies to their respective territories." Moreover, he noted that free Black people were not "so willing as I think their interest demands."

For a less fervent believer, these facts might have suggested colonization failure was again likely. But Lincoln went for the classic gerund defense of an unsatisfactory outcome: Black opinion of colonization was "improving."

Lincoln concluded his 1862 annual message with one of his most inspirational passages: "In giving freedom to the slave, we assure freedom to the free—honorable alike in what we give, and what we preserve." The frequent quotations of this beautiful passage (including in Aaron Copland's "Lincoln Portrait," as read by Henry Fonda) rarely mention its context. When Lincoln advocated "freedom" here, he was actually referring to colonization. In the annual message, he had announced his plan for gradual emancipation in the border states with colonization.[91]

Lincoln by then had already moved on to a new site for colonization after Chiriquí. The Charleston businessman Bernard Kock now proposed for colonization an island off the coast of Haiti called Île à Vache (Cow Island). The Haitian government had given Kock exclusive rights to harvest mahogany and other hardwoods on the island, which was seven miles wide and thirteen miles long. Kock wrote a letter to the Lincoln administration in the fall of 1862 offering his "beautiful, healthy, and fertile island" for colonization. There was nobody to get in the way because no Haitians wanted to live on Cow Island. (Liberal skeptics would have asked, Why not?)

Kock would offer employment to the colonists. He would provide houses, schools, churches, and medical care. Kock wrote that he already had purchased sawmills, as well as cotton gins for the planned cotton crop. Farm equipment was already on order. Kock's plan had each male settler getting title to eight acres of land after ten years.

Meanwhile, at Fort Monroe, Virginia, in late 1862, six thousand miserable people had escaped slavery only to see the Union Army put them to work on fortifications. A Quaker report dramatized the poverty of these former slaves—living twelve people to a room, lacking adequate clothing and fuel for heating in the cold winter. Here was the kind of destitution that colonization was supposed to cure.

On December 31, 1862, the day before the Emancipation Proclamation took effect, Lincoln reached agreement with Kock to take five thousand Black Americans from Fort Monroe to Cow Island. After more back-and-forth, 453 of the ex-slaves from Fort Monroe finally shipped to Île à Vache, arriving on June 1, 1863. An early report had them prospering under the "able, wise, and humane direction" of Mr. Kock. The report was not quite accurate.[92]

As a later observer reported, the new settlers on Cow Island were starving on sparse rations of salt pork and corn. No houses existed. Settlers huddled under brush or lay directly on the ground, clothed in rags, plagued by insects and torrential rains. Forty had died. Kock had taken all the settlers' money when they came on board the ship and later stopped paying them the promised wages. Kock soon had to flee from the angry colonists. On learning of the debacle, Lincoln dispatched a ship to bring the survivors home in February 1864.

Lincoln was finally ready to give up. Congress repealed previous colonization clauses in July 1864. So the white dream of Black progress through colonization, which had entranced seven US presidents over eight decades, finally came to an ignominious end on Cow Island. In the end, despite all his hopeful rhetoric on colonization, Lincoln had not been willing to force Black people to leave the US. The resistance of the Black community meant that colonization would have entailed massive violence. In the end, Lincoln's belief in liberty won out over his colonization fantasies. Although his colonization support had threatened the cause of equal rights for Black people, in the end he did far more for the cause of liberty with his denunciation of benevolent slavery. Lincoln in the end did contribute to a new birth of freedom.[93]

10

The Victory of the Man Without a Plan

What was the alternative plan for Black development if both benevolent slavery and colonization were finally defeated? A third way rejected the entire notion of white plans for Black progress.

Liberal thinkers now reached the climactic battle over slavery, this history's most extreme justification of coercion in the name of progress. One liberal thinker's response was to develop further a demand for Black agency that would not only help defeat both slavery and removal of Black people but would give Black people a path of dignity after the end of slavery. Frederick Douglass was that thinker. Douglass has not been sufficiently recognized as a liberal, nor for the critical role of his no-plan argument.

Douglass saw Black people demanding the rights they deserved instead of waiting for white saviors. White preoccupation with plans for Black people after the end of slavery would actually delay the end of slavery. In contrast, Douglass preferred rights without plans to plans without rights. This was what actually worked to defeat slavery. It was liberalism's greatest accomplishment so far.

Douglass also saw how the white preoccupation with relief of Black poverty unintentionally facilitated the retrogression on equal rights that happened after the end of Reconstruction. His vision of

Black self-determination prefigured the rise of the civil rights movement and the fall of colonialism in Africa that would happen a century later.

Douglass first articulated his planless vision at a crucial moment for the debate on slavery. In January 1862, he wrote an article acknowledging white philanthropists' "sincere solicitude for the welfare of the slaves themselves." The philanthropists asked, "What will you do with them?" Douglass shockingly answered: "Do nothing with them." Consistent with Douglass's critique of benevolent slavery and colonization, he pointed out to his well-meaning audience of whites that "your doing with them is their greatest misfortune." You whites should just not "trouble yourselves with any questions as to what shall be done with" the slave. Just "let him alone."[1]

On February 12, 1862, Douglass articulated again the scandalous "do nothing" ideas in a speech to the Emancipation League in Boston. The demand for a solution for freed Black people was itself an obstacle to emancipation. Douglass pointed out that opponents of emancipation loved to ask, "What shall be done with the four million slaves if emancipated?" Such opponents would wait to emancipate until a complete answer was forthcoming, which would be never.

Douglass offered principles instead of plans. Proponents of slavery in the British Empire earlier in the century had sought to derail the abolitionist William Wilberforce by demanding his "plan of Emancipation." Douglass appreciably noted that Wilberforce had simply responded: "Quit stealing."

Douglass respected white philanthropists who wanted answers to Black misery. In a classic appeal to reciprocity, however, he wondered what they would say if roles were reversed. What if Black people required white people to have a plan to end white poverty—or else be slaves? He imagined whites would say "mind your own business." He equally told them, "Leave us to mind ours." Just "let us alone. Do nothing with us." Douglass told his audience in Boston, "We ask nothing at the hands of the American people but simple justice."[2]

Douglass had given more insight into his "do nothing" thinking in that earlier 1862 article. Given Douglass's history with white action consisting of benevolent slavery and colonization, he was not a fan of "do something" thinking. As he noted, "something" usually denied equal rights for Black people:

> When you, our white fellow-countrymen, have attempted to do anything for us, it has generally been to deprive us of some right, power or privilege which you yourself would die before you would submit to have taken from you.[3]

Douglass's idea of rights denied to Black people included the right to agency. He wanted the right to participate in a free labor market, the "right to work." Free labor allowed free choice and self-determination. "We only ask to be allowed to do with ourselves" what we want, Douglass demanded. Douglass continued to draw links between different victims of Western superiority—equal rights should be respected for all men, including "Jews, Gentiles, Barbarian, Sythian."

He saw markets offered a crucial alternative to paternalism. A free labor market, Douglass said, would "let us stand upon our own legs, work with our own hands, and eat bread in the sweat of our own brows."[4] Douglass told white philanthropists that market participation by the former slaves was "the best way to help them," which "is just to let them help themselves."[5]

Likewise in his Boston speech to white philanthropists, Douglass argued that consensual contracts between employers and Black people should replace the coercion of slavery. The answer was to "pay them honest wages for honest work; dispense with the biting lash, and pay the ready cash." The incentive to avoid the lash had been to "benumb and degrade the soul." For the ex-slaves now to respond voluntarily to market incentives was to give them an infinitely more dignified motive "of hope, of self-respect, of honor, and of personal responsibility."[6]

Douglass also advocated political rights, the right to vote for the Black man, an amazingly radical notion in January 1862. Whites should "let him alone if he has a ballot in his hand," where he could "vote for the man whom he thinks will most justly and wisely administer the government which has the power of life and death over him." Douglass demanded equal rights for Black people to consent to what would happen to them: "His right of choice as much deserves respect and protection as your own."[7]

Political rights also included Black people's right to voluntarily emigrate, or not, and to determine their own colonization schemes, if any: "But why not let them go off by themselves? That is a matter we would leave exclusively to themselves."[8]

In another speech in May 1863 in New York City, Douglass reflected on how his no-plan argument had earned him only mockery. He was charged with offering only "abstract ideas" like "one great law of liberty, equality, and fraternity for all Americans without respect to color." Douglass was unrepentant: "I admit the charge."

How well had things turned out for the mockers' practical plans for the slaves? By now, anyone who was not a slave owner recognized the idea of benevolent slavery as nonsense. Both slave owners and ex-slaves had rejected colonization plans. These plans had failed to prevent the Civil War and had led only to repeated colonization fiascoes. Give me principles instead of plans anytime, said Douglass. "Behold, how all to the mocker has gone."[9]

Douglass's "let us alone" philosophy became relevant in a different way after the Civil War. He was a pioneer for the cause of agency and dignity for the recipients of antipoverty relief. Douglass struggled to reconcile charity and dignity, as would many future aid thinkers.

Douglass updated his concerns about white benevolence for the Reconstruction era in an angry Independence Day speech he gave on July 5, 1875, in Washington, DC. He worried about signs of North-South reconciliation that would abandon any Reconstruction principles of "liberty and equality" for Black people. Many Northern whites had gotten enthusiastic about material aid to the ex-slaves in the South. For Douglass, these altruists could not be trusted to defend Black rights and they may have made things worse.

Speaking of African Americans nationwide, Douglass claimed, "We have been injured more than benefited by the efforts of so-called benevolent societies." Douglass hated what today would be called "poverty porn":[10]

> In order to obtain revenue to carry on what they call their work (including, of course, the salaries which they piously vote themselves by the thousand) they draw the most distressing pictures of the black man's character and condition. They keep the public mind constantly upon the poor, wretched negro, and thus damn the whole race to a large measure of contempts with a small degree of pity which is akin to contempt.[11]

Perhaps Douglass was enraged by the insult to his lifelong demand for agency and dignity for Black people. What was most important for Black people was "to be respected." He insisted, "The colored race is capable of living more than a life of absolute dependence, and can think and speak for itself." He stormed on about poverty porn: "The prostrate form, the uncovered head, the cringing attitude, the bated breath, the suppliant, outstretched hand of beggary does not become an American freeman." Douglass made clear his opposition: "We will not consent to be any longer represented in that position."[12]

It was not that easy to navigate the relationship with well-intentioned white abolitionists and philanthropists. Douglass had a conflicted relationship with portrayals of Black dependency and white benevolence. The next year he gave a speech celebrating the dedication of a grateful monument to Lincoln from the Black community. The Freedmen's Monument in Memory of Abraham Lincoln emerged from tortured interactions between white and Black abolitionists and ex-slaves on how to portray Emancipation. It portrayed a slave kneeling to Lincoln in thanks. Douglass in his speech in 1876 gave both praise and criticism of Lincoln (including a note on the president's support for colonization when he "strangely told us that we were to leave the land in which we were born"). But Douglass did not criticize the imagery of the statue.[13]

Then five days later (in a letter to a newspaper only rediscovered recently), he had second thoughts:[14]

> The negro here, though rising, is still on his knees and nude. What I want to see before I die is a monument representing the negro, not couchant on his knees like a four-footed animal, but erect on his feet like a man.[15]

Douglass in his 1875 speech mostly aimed his critique at post-war aid to freed slaves. Despite the pretensions of white philanthropists to be God's gift to Black people, Douglass portrayed them as "broken-down preachers without pulpits, lawyers without clients, professors without chairs, editors without journals." It infuriated Douglass that any random white people, even professional failures, were supposed to be more effective than Black people in helping Black people.[16]

Douglass issued a dramatic Declaration of Independence from white philanthropy, echoing the language of the original. Blacks were ready to "assume among their fellow men the independent and equal position to which the laws of nature and of nature's God entitle them." Whenever any philanthropic organization did not have "the consent of those in whose interest they have been professedly created," it was the right of Black people "to alter or abolish it."[17]

Instead of having white philanthropists in charge of efforts for Black well-being, Douglass called for Black leaders to emerge and take over. Black leaders should just demand equal political and economic rights for Black people: "The burden of our demand upon the American people shall simply be justice and fair play."[18]

But it was not quite so simple as to aid or not to aid. Douglass was sometimes more open to the idea of aid for Black people. Douglass discussed "material aid" for freed slaves in Mississippi in 1886, and this time he said, "There is no degradation, no loss of self-respect, in asking this aid, considering the circumstances of these people." Douglass struggled with balancing respect and material relief just like so many others then and since. Tellingly, however, he saw the aid as compensation rather than charity: "The white people of this nation owe them this help and a great deal more." Douglass seemed to be searching for a way to have aid with respect, rather than just to reject aid in general.[19]

As shocking as his "do nothing with us" argument was, events vindicated Douglass. Practical plans like benevolent slavery and colonization had confirmed only the bad incentives for and the incompetence of whites in developing Black people. Principles without plans actually did lead to positive change. In 1865, the Thirteenth Amendment permanently abolished slavery in the United States. In 1870, the Fifteenth Amendment gave Black people the right to vote. Douglass's vision of rights without plans did defeat plans without rights.

With his distrust of white charity after the Civil War, Douglass also presciently anticipated how the United States would backslide from Reconstruction to Jim Crow over the rest of the nineteenth century. The loss of freedom as a moral guideline for economic thinkers would herald a decline of liberty for peoples in the Rest worldwide.

PART III

THE REGRESS OF LIBERTY, 1865–1945

There are classes in every modern community composed of those who are virtually children, and who require paternal and fostering care, the aim of which should be the highest development of which they are capable.

—Richard T. Ely, cofounder of the American Economic Association, 1898

11

How Economists Forgot Consent

In the spring of 1874, the English economist Alfred Marshall (1842–1924) had a problem. People thought that economists were mainly in the business of passing moral judgments on what should and should not happen in the economy and society. But Marshall wanted economics to be a science, and science is not about moral judgments. He insisted that moral judgment is not what economists should do, saying it is "necessary to keep entirely distinct two questions." The first asks "what consequences will follow" from economic policies. The second "must be decided by our moral judgments, viz., whether an action which produces these consequences is right."

He noted sensibly that economists were well equipped to decide the first but not the second. The economist can give his opinion on the second, "but his special science can give him no commission to do so." American economists forming themselves into the American Economic Association around the same time would similarly reject morals in favor of science.[1]

It was a momentous turning point for economics. Putting economics on a better footing as a science was desirable. But it was costly to lose the emphasis on consent of the classical generation. Respecting agency was a moral commitment. If the economists did not want to make moral judgments, who should make them? Implicitly they would accept the political and moral judgments of their own societies. The first generation of professional economists had not-so-great timing on this. American and Western European policymakers were discovering an ever longer list of people who needed compulsion for the sake of progress: American Black people, Native Americans, Africans, Filipinos, lower-class whites, Jews, Catholics, Hungarians, Chinese, Appalachians, Russians, white trash, Congolese, Cubans, women, Polish, East Indians, West Indians, Slavs, Puerto Ricans, Southern American whites, the Irish, and the feeble-minded. The widespread rejection of liberal constraints on coercion had not-completely-attractive consequences.

The new wave of professional economists in the US and UK embraced or failed to condemn illiberal policies in the three major policy areas for the West developing the Rest:

1. **Colonial Conquest.** US conquest of the Philippines, the Partition of Africa, and colonial mandates after World War I.
2. **Population Replacement.** Conquest of the American West in the late 1800s and eugenics practiced against "white trash" and Eastern European immigrants in the US and UK.
3. **Forced Labor.** Forced labor in Leopold's Congo and in European colonies after World War I.

A few heirs to the liberalism of classical economists remained, but they were not always terribly consistent about liberal ideals. The liberals were marginalized and easily defeated and today they are mostly forgotten. An heir to the classical economists named William Graham Sumner resisted the new imperialism. The crusader E. D. Morel and liberal social scientist Paul Reinsch denounced abuses in the Congo and protested Western hypocrisy after World War I.

The decline of freedom did generate more voices of resistance from the victims. An American Indian woman named Zitkala-Ša, the Filipino leader Emilio Aguinaldo and the thinker Sixto López, the Bengali poet Rabindranath Tagore, and the American social scientist W. E. B. Du Bois all criticized the new White Man's Burden. They got even less of a hearing than classical liberal economists.

It gets worse. As the definition of who was in the Rest kept expanding, the definition of who was in the West kept shrinking. The definition of the West now contained hardly anyone besides upper-class Anglo-Saxon Protestant males. Seldom had so few gotten the right to coerce so many.

The division between the West and the Rest cut through the societies of the West themselves. The policy goal was often not the progress of these groups themselves, but the need to protect the progress of the West against their bad behavior.

A leading American economist named John Commons would call for banning the immigration of "lunatics, idiots, paupers, and Chinese." Commons and other members of the first postclassical generation of economists seem almost like cartoon villains today, but in their time hardly any economists opposed them.[2]

Participants in economic debates who invoked morality just messed things up, Alfred Marshall argued in 1874. The morally minded commentators were often "men who have not the patience, the training, the intelligence, and the knowledge required" for scientific analysis. The moralizers will conceal this "deficiency," by issuing "a vague declamation" that is "a substitute for an elaborately reasoned investigation of the causes which operate in the case under discussion, and of the consequences which follow from them." The moralists will only unnecessarily introduce "the heat of excited feeling" by forgetting the "rigidly scientific character of political economy," thus undermining "scientific calmness and thoroughness." This was much like the modern aversion in economics to ideological arguments, a lot of which is understandable and constructive.[3]

In response to a critic of this first article, Marshall published a second article admitting that most people thought that political economy did teach what "we ought and ought not to do." But "the leading writers" on economics unanimously opposed this role:

"None of the chief authors of the science have defended" moral recommendations by economists. Marshall was defining who were professional economists (the "leading writers" and the "chief authors"). It was the men who brought "scientific calmness" to economics and not the hysterical ones suffering from "the heat of excited feeling."[4]

Marshall was later to play a key role in the founding of the professional association of British economists known today as the Royal Economic Society. On that occasion, in 1890, Marshall set out again his vision of economics as science, which "could be true or false." For him, "the best way to find out what was true was to welcome the criticisms of all people who knew what they were talking about." Marshall was a key figure in what would turn out to be the successful and salutary professionalization of economics.[5]

Crucially, Marshall back in 1874 had said that one thing scientific economists could still comment on was "the belief in the harmfulness of avoidable restraints on liberty of the individual in any form." Marshall thought, "Now the time has come for a discussion of the exceptions to the general rule." Economists then and now recognized that some coercive government actions could be justified to deal with market failures such as monopoly or public goods (as indeed Adam Smith had). But unlike Smith and the classical economists, Marshall insisted the discussion should only be about empirical consequences of restraints on liberty for material outcomes, not about whether liberty was a moral good.[6]

On the other hand, Marshall allowed economists to have a moral preference about the material outcomes like poverty or inequality. To Marshall, they should of course prefer less poverty and more equality and the aim of science should be how to achieve this. Marshall was writing at a time when many contemporaries perceived high inequality in both the UK and the US. Recent estimates confirm a high share of income received by the top 1 percent in the UK and US in the late nineteenth century (and also in the Netherlands and Japan). The picture of high Anglo-American inequality in the late nineteenth century is also confirmed by modern estimates of the Gini coefficient measure of inequality.[7]

Therefore, Marshall had a well-grounded concern about whether the working class shared in economic development, about why poverty coexisted with plenty.

Marshall had thus set out much of what is modern economics—the scientific study of how to relieve poverty. For this, he deserves to be celebrated. But there was something inconsistent about Marshall's definition of economists' role, an inconsistency that still exists today. On one hand, he said economists should not make policy recommendations that require moral judgments. But of course, many economists then and now could not really be so self-denying as to refrain from policy recommendations on how to reduce poverty, nor did many noneconomists want them to so refrain. The tacit assumption remained that whatever did produce higher income and lower material poverty was what should happen, while disavowing the classical economists' moral commitment to consent.

As American economists became more professionalized, they also rejected the moral preference for consent in favor of a preference for equality, as Marshall had. Their path to this point was a little more roundabout than that of the English economists.

On September 9, 1885, a meeting of economists in the Bethesda Parish House in Saratoga Springs, New York, founded the American Economic Association (AEA). The economist who was most instrumental in founding the AEA was Johns Hopkins University Professor Richard T. Ely, after whom the AEA later named the most prestigious lecture series at its annual meetings (until it was renamed in 2020 because of qualms about Ely's views). By 1892, Ely had moved to the University of Wisconsin, where he would lead an influential group of economists.[8]

As with Marshall, Ely's economic analysis and prescriptions would be motivated by very good intentions. He declared that "pauperism is a moral and physical evil, and we ought to do all in our power to remedy it." Poverty "is for the most part a curable disease." He wanted to improve the living standards of the working class. He promoted as solutions to poverty an appealing list of government actions that would be widely endorsed today: "Improved education, . . . better factory legislation, . . . gymnasiums, playgrounds, and parks, increased facilities for making small savings, like postal savings-banks, and more highly developed sanitary legislation and administration."[9]

Ely thus favored "positive aid" from the state. Such aid was "an indispensable condition of human progress." We economists could not simply do nothing and just let markets work with minimal government intervention (laissez-faire). Ely believed that "the doctrine of laissez-faire is unsafe in politics and unsound in morals."[10]

Ely's moral commitment to fighting poverty had motivated him in his campaign to create the AEA. Ely rejected the moral preference for freedom of the classical economists because he wanted a different set of moral guidelines. Unlike Marshall, and unlike most later economists up to the present day, Ely was explicit about the contest of ethics. The contest was between the old ethical commitment to individual freedom and a new ethical commitment to collective efforts for reducing poverty.

Ely in his presentation at Saratoga in 1885 had rejected the classical economists' emphasis on individual consent through voluntary exchange. This commitment to "free contract" had led to the moral belief that the state "ought not to interfere in industrial life." The classical economists thought that "free trade must be received as an ethical dogma, being a practical application of the command, 'Thou shalt not steal.'" Ely was appalled at this moral justification of laissez-faire. In contrast to valuing individual freedom of contract, he preferred the "social ethics" of a more active state fighting poverty.[11]

Ely had no intention of including economists with the old morals in the new AEA. "The fundamental differences between economists are so radical that they cannot all work profitably together," he said. Ely said the old kind of economists "may take their own way, and far be it from us to hinder them, but we must part company."

Part of his motivation for rejecting laissez-faire economists from the AEA was so they wouldn't tarnish popular views of economists: "Intelligent men and women should distinguish between us and certain economists in whom there is little faith." The professional economists would educate these intelligent people on what is "quackery," Ely said, "and it must be our province to expose it and bring it into merited contempt." The AEA economists' works as published in their own journal would help those sufficiently intelligent to reach "an enlightened judgment." Ely wanted to make economics more appealing to the public because "the respect for political economy, as it has been hitherto taught, is very slight." Efforts of economists to be liked (usually unsuccessful) were going to recur up to the present day.[12]

Ely's statements were a little too strong for some of those at the AEA founding meeting. In the end, the meeting adopted a "Statement of Principles" somewhat watered-down and less divisive compared to Ely's original language—but still pretty strong. The key principle was that "we regard the state as an agency whose positive assistance is one of the indispensable conditions of human progress."[13]

Whether all this was scientific was a bit problematic, since the AEA had already taken a position on what the role of the state should be without waiting for the results of any "statistical study." This conflict between advocacy and science eventually got to be embarrassing. In an important turn of phrase, Ely noted how in 1885, "the Statement of Principles seemed like a proclamation of emancipation." It had been greeted with "jubilation." It was an emancipation from the individualist values that implied that "free trade must be received as an ethical dogma." It freed economists to pursue alternative values supporting "social reforms for social uplift." While the classical generation of economists had sought the emancipation of individuals, the postclassical generation sought the emancipation of the economists.[14]

At least Ely was honest. Subsequent generations of economists rarely repeated his candor about the conflict of values. This was partly because the values went underground soon after the AEA founding. The Statement of Principles got quietly dropped in 1892. Ely approvingly quoted one of his correspondents to explain what happened. In 1885 the statement was necessary because "we wanted no doubt as to our unity and who our enemies were." But then, "only a few years later when the victory was won, we no longer wanted a partisan attitude but one of scientific impartiality." Like Marshall, the AEA founders had now successfully defined economics as science, while leaving unstated the moral assumptions behind the policy recommendations of that science.[15]

Now that there was a science, Alfred Marshall considered the causes of what he called "national progress" in his 1890 textbook, *Principles of Economics*. This celebrated textbook went through eight editions by 1920 and was a huge achievement in the history of economic thought. It was the first to suggest the supply and demand graph that is still used in modern Economics 101 textbooks.

Marshall sought to explicate international as well as national inequality. He had an explanation for the "conditions of backward races." Although Marshall admitted that information on "savage tribes" was "scanty and untrustworthy," he was still confident about his explanation of their backwardness. The problem with savages, for Marshall, was they were "never forecasting the distant future, and seldom making provision even for the near future." Their work habits were part of the problem. Although they could have bursts of effort, they were "incapable of keeping themselves long to steady work."

Since innate characteristics of the "savage tribes" were the only determinant of their economic progress, there was zero variation among them. They "show a strange uniformity of general character," Marshall's textbook said, "whatever be their climate and whatever their ancestry." Marshall both repeated the great lumping of Condorcet and Du Pont's generation and anticipated the later lumping together of the Third World.[16]

Marshall explained not only the poverty of non-white races but also the poverty of some whites. The "lower ranks of society" in Britain suffered from the "comparative weakness of their power of distinctly realizing the future," he said. The low saving of the lower classes was not enough to cover the education of their many children.[17]

The different economic outcomes between the upper- and lower-class whites was itself explained by something like an innate racial difference. The ancestors of today's whites included lords and serfs. Marshall thought "the share of servile blood was largest" in the working class. The white poor were not fully white.[18]

Marshall's comparative analysis lumped together the semi-white working class in Britain, the Chinese and other Asians, North American Indians, and the Irish, all of whom "marry recklessly without any thought of the morrow," have too many children, don't save enough, and don't work hard enough. Like children, these disparate groups care more for immediate gratification than for the future. A civilized race, in contrast, will "exert itself for the sake of the future." Hence, the whites became rich and non-whites remained poor. (These last quotes came from a book coauthored by his wife, Mary Paley Marshall, on which more in a moment.)[19]

Marshall was giving up a lot of morality for not much science. Marshall's explanation of poverty is close to being tautological. Anti-advancement preferences explain why some people are not advanced. How does Marshall know that their preferences are anti-advancement? Because they are not advanced.

John Stuart Mill in the previous generation had rejected the tautological innate-differences idea as both bad science and bad morals. Mill had condemned Carlyle for the "vulgar error of imputing every difference which he finds among human beings to an original difference of nature." Mill had rejected Carlyle's justification of slavery as fit for slaves permanently unfit to choose for themselves. The post-classical economists relitigated the Carlyle–Mill debate.[20]

What were the policy implications of the Marshalls' analysis of comparative progress? Since people's preferences for saving, work habits, and family size were innate and unchanging, the main determinant of global progress was the relative population shares of people with good and bad preferences.

The old policies of population removal had become population engineering. If the British working class "multiply more rapidly than those which are morally and physically superior," then the British population quality will deteriorate. The same would happen in America and Australia. The answer would be to restrain population growth of the lower classes.

Marshall also wanted population policies at the global level. The concern for global progress was that rapid non-white population growth threatened to lower the global population share of the superior whites. For example, if the Chinese multiplied faster than whites did, the Marshalls said, then "this spiritless race will overrun portions of the earth that otherwise would have been peopled by English vigor." However, if the population growth of the "spiritless race" could somehow be kept in check, then colonization and overseas settlement would "spread the energy and genius of the English people over the earth."[21]

Sounding like John Winthrop centuries earlier, Marshall in a later work noted that non-whites had been "unable to turn to the best account the advantages of the place in which they live." The English settlers and colonizers in the Rest advanced global economic progress far more than the natives did.[22]

Marshall seemed to be justifying Indigenous removal once again as the earlier generation had. Like them, Marshall's policy objective was more to develop the lands of non-white people rather than to develop the non-white people themselves.

Again, Marshall had some good reasons for rejecting the classical emphasis on freedom. He worried that some in the classical generation had been for "keeping the working classes in their place," using laissez-faire doctrines to undermine desirable factory regulation to improve working conditions. Such simplistic thinkers had been just "parasites" on classical economists. His prime example was Harriet Martineau, whom he blasted:[23]

> Miss Martineau was not an economist in the proper sense of the word: she confessed that she never read more than one chapter of an economic book at a time before writing a story to illustrate economic principles, for fear the pressure on her mind should be too great.[24]

Marshall was twisting the words of Martineau in her autobiography, in which she merely said she focused on one topic at a time.[25]

Marshall's hierarchical view of unequal groups apparently applied to female economists. In some unpublished notes he wrote in May 1894, Marshall noted: "Economics is like a fine chest of tools, which will not turn out anything of value except in skillful hands. This indicates that economics is a subject generally unsuited for advance by women."[26]

If Marshall's views on female economists were a little notable, it is because his wife, Mary Paley Marshall, was a female economist. She was one of the first women to take economics at Cambridge University and later became its first female lecturer on economics. Mary coauthored a textbook with Alfred in 1879, which is quoted above, but that was the last time she got credit for their work together. Subsequently she became an uncredited contributor and commentator to his *Principles* textbook. Later generations of economists (including John Maynard Keynes) were puzzled by Alfred's treatment of Mary. As Austin Robinson (himself the less famous member of an economist couple with Joan Robinson) wondered in 1947, "Why indeed (as Keynes felt bound to ask) did Alfred make a slave of this great woman and not a colleague?"[27]

To be fair, Marshall's views on women were common among men of his generation. Because of his lasting fame, moreover, he has attracted more modern scrutiny than his less prominent opponents. Some observers thought Mary herself chose a subordinate role.

On the other side of the Atlantic, meanwhile, the loss of the right to consent as a constraint on economists was also costly. In books and articles written between 1889 and 1903, Richard T. Ely divided the planet into three groups, not unlike the First World, Second World, and Third World definitions five decades later. There were the civilized, the semicivilized, and the savages. The civilized group had only three members: England, the US, and Germany.[28]

The civilization line went within as well as between societies. Inside the US, Ely saw the "negroes" as "grown up children" and said they "should be treated as such." The solutions for the childlike people—whether they were far off in India or within the US—would come from "the leadership of wise and strong men."[29]

Ely also analyzed the problem of white paupers in America. Like Marshall, Ely was convinced that the white lower class made up its own hereditary group, almost like a separate race. "Sexual licentiousness" characterized "hereditary pauperism," producing too many children who were "physically unable to endure hard work."

Ely did acknowledge some role for nurture as well as nature. He could rescue some poor whites by strong government action, which would force them to work, offer them better education, and induce them to save. The government should recognize the rights of these more hopeful cases only after they had shown some improvement out of pauperism.

Nevertheless, the remaining poor whites were a lost cause due to heredity. The empirical breakthrough that made possible Ely's bold claim was an analysis of degraded paupers in Indianapolis, who were descended from a single ancestor, Ben Ishmael. Mr. Ishmael lived in Kentucky in 1790 when his reproductive crime spree began. Ely noted that his descendants included 121 prostitutes, as well as murderers, thieves, and beggars. Ely's case study of the Tribe of Ishmael was compelling evidence, except for the fact that it was largely fictitious.[30]

This "social refuse" of the "hopelessly lost," Ely said, "must be kept permanently isolated in asylums." He shared the garbage metaphor of "social refuse" with the more common label "white trash," which went back to before the Civil War. Like Mr. Ishmael of Kentucky, white trash proliferated in the South and in the Appalachians. Ely insisted that this must end; the social refuse "should not be allowed to propagate their kind."[31]

Ely's economic analysis then turned a bit misogynist. Currently, there was too much "liberty allowed to vagrant and degraded women," the same ones who produced "a vicious progeny." They should stay in the poorhouse under "the supervision and oversight adequate to their protection." However, the superior whites were the ones who really needed the protection from being seduced by the degraded women, from having the superior race contaminated by inferior whites. He would prohibit the white trash women from marrying. The aim for this group was just to make them slowly disappear. Like Marshall, Ely also embraced population control, effectively updating the old population removal policies of past generations.[32]

Other AEA founders shared Ely's views on the Rest. In 1885, the AEA founders chose as their first president Francis Amasa Walker, the president of the Massachusetts Institute of Technology. Along with other qualifications, Walker brought a lot of experience with less-developed people.

From November 1871 to December 1872, he had been the US commissioner of Indian affairs as conquest of Indian lands in the Western United States was underway. He had no experience with Indian affairs other than visiting a few reservations in the fall of 1871. This was enough to make him an expert on Indian development. In a book he authored in 1874, he noted the long history of failed efforts to civilize Indians. He was aware of some of the previous failed plans for the "advancement in industry and the arts of life" for the Indians. In a rare moment of self-doubt, Walker admitted that this history did "not reflect much credit on the sagacity of the superior race to which have been intrusted the destinies of the red man." However, Walker soon moved on from doubting white saviors. The failure of the civilizing experiments were really the Indians' own fault, reflecting their "sloth" and their lack of "frugality." In this, they were similar to Black people and the poor whites of the South, Walker noted.[33]

US government efforts could make at least some Indians be less slothful and more frugal. The government should confine Indians on reservations under a "rigid reformatory control" which would force them "to learn and practice the arts of industry." The civilizers could not leave it up "to their own choice how miserably they will live." Walker did not want any debate on compulsion: "The right of the government to exact, in this particular, all that the good of the Indian and the good of the general community may require is not to be questioned." Walker insisted that "the most extreme and decided measures" were "necessary to save this race from itself."

As conquest of the West proceeded, Walker had the usual goal of taking over Indian lands for whites. The Indian had no right to stop whites' conquest of land that the Indian "has suffered to remain a wilderness." He should get only some modest compensation for such lands, which would fund the aid-for-civilization program for Indians on the reservations. The aid program was not optional. The only options for Indians were "yield or perish."[34]

Walker differed from Smith and Mill on dignity of people as a goal. Walker explicitly rejected dignity for the Indians as an objective of US policy: "There could be no issue of dignity between a civilized power and a band of irresponsible savages."[35]

Rarely was there a chance for those labeled irresponsible savages to comment on the yield or perish options. Some glimpses emerged later in the century when another policy featured forced removal of Indian children from their parents so that they could be assimilated through education in white-run boarding schools. As an alternative to elimination of non-whites, some of the non-white children could be trained to be white.

An Indian agent at Mescalero, New Mexico, in 1897 reported how desperate Indian parents would drug their children to make them sick or unfit for going to school, hide them out in the bushes, deny having any children, or just defy the order to deliver their children.[36]

An American Indian writer and activist named Zitkala-Ša is a rare voice from those forced to progress by Walker and similar thinkers. She was born as Gertrude Simmons on the Yankton Indian Reservation in 1876 to a white father and Dakota mother. She was herself educated in a white-run boarding school, beginning at the age of eight. In 1897, she became a teacher at the most notorious boarding school for Indians, the Carlisle Indian Industrial School in Pennsylvania, whose slogan was "Kill the Indian and save the man!" She was exactly the kind of assimilated Indian that white developers sought to produce. But Zitkala-Ša became disillusioned and resigned from the school after two years at Carlisle.[37]

Shortly after, she published an article in *The Atlantic* magazine on her experiences. She said her time at the school left her "in no mood to strain [her] eyes in searching for latent good in [her] white co-workers," who included an alcoholic doctor whose Indian patients died from their untreated ailments. She "burned with indignation" as the "missionary creed" of the "large army of white teachers in Indian schools" seemed to involve supporting their own families more than saving Indians. White supporters frequently visited the school to congratulate themselves on how "they were educating the children of the red man!" She was no longer a fan of this "semblance of civilization."[38]

Despite these bitter reflections, Zitkala-Ša still had some ambivalence about the assimilation effort of which she was both beneficiary and victim. As an activist for Indian rights, she needed all the white allies she could get as an assimilated Indian. She was later to change names again to her married name, Gertrude Simmons Bonnin. During World War I, she protested the government closure of the Carlisle School in order to convert it to military use. For Indians, she said, the closure lost them the "educational opportunities only Carlisle can give."[39]

Back to AEA President Walker, he next entered another debate on population engineering: how to respond to the surge of immigrants to the US in the late nineteenth century. In 1896, Walker expressed alarm at the inflow of "vast throngs of ignorant and brutalized peasantry from the countries of eastern and southern Europe." This group, including "millions of Hungarians, Bohemians, Poles, south Italians, and Russian Jews," had "inherited instincts" that made them the "least thrifty" of the Europeans. Why would the US want to admit these "beaten men from beaten races; representing the worst failures in the struggle for existence?"[40]

There was no effort here to civilize the semicivilized Eastern European whites; the goal was just to keep them out to protect the civilization of American whites. The former AEA President Walker had helped launch the immigration restriction movement, which was alarmed by the entry of those called the beaten races and sought to halt such entry. The restrictionists would eventually attain their goal of drastic reductions in immigration from Eastern and Southern

Europe. They got their national (effectively racial) quotas in the Immigration Act of 1924.[41]

Instead of the old advocacy for removing Black people and Indians from the US, immigration controllers would keep the uncivilized people out of the US in the first place. The coercion to keep people out was much less than to expel people already here. Controls on immigration are common in many societies then and now. The most illiberal part of the restriction movement was the invocation of permanent racial characteristics as a basis for restriction. This was deeply insulting to the dignity of the proscribed races, as subsequent events would show.

Walker died in 1897, but another AEA economist, John Commons, took over his cause of immigration restriction. Commons had studied at Johns Hopkins University during Richard T. Ely's time there. After Ely moved to Wisconsin, he got Commons a chair at Wisconsin in 1899. Ely cited Commons's work on immigration as qualification for the chair. Commons later became president of the AEA.[42]

Commons is forgotten today, but in his time his 1907 magnum opus, *Races and Immigrants in America*, was influential. In it, Commons lumped together many different groups into one aggregate of "backward, thriftless, and unintelligent races."[43]

Catholics from Europe were "almost a distinct race," whom Commons compared to Black people. The border of civilization in Europe separated Scandinavia, Britain, Germany, and France from Russia, Austria-Hungary, Italy, and Turkey, partially overlapping with the late eighteenth-century boundary between Western and Eastern Europe. The differences between the "thrifty peasantry" to the north and west and the unthrifty "Latin, Slav, Semitic, and Mongolian races" to the south and east determined the border. Commons had reinvented yet again the West and Rest distinction within Europe.[44]

Commons embraced the theory of innate incapacity for the Rest. For example, the Africans were "indolent," and "improvident," said Commons, with childbearing decisions determined by "strong sexual passion." Their formerly enslaved descendants in America shared these preferences, which Commons thought explained the lack of Black progress over the four decades since emancipation.[45]

He revived the idea of benevolent slavery. Commons thought the antebellum Southern planters had been "friend and protector" to their slaves. Blacks needed compulsion to work: Emancipation had failed to correct the "savagery" of the African diaspora in America.[46]

By way of empirical facts, Commons cited a study of the racial origins of a list of eminent Americans. Out of 14,423 of these eminences, England had produced 10,376. Russia and Poland each accounted for one. None were from Hungary, Africa, or Asia.[47]

Like Ely, Commons also sought to explain poverty among native whites in America. Commons defined the poor-white group geographically, with their region variously identified as the hills, the South, West Virginia, the Appalachians, the frontier, or the Blue Ridge Mountains. This assortment of locations matched the historical use of the "white trash" label (as it still does today). Commons demonstrated excessive childbearing in West Virginia with an extensive sampling of two observations, both mountain couples in the Blue Ridge Mountains. The alarmingly prolific two couples had eighteen and twenty-two children, respectively. Mountaineers were also lazy and spendthrift.[48]

Commons on a few occasions applied his views on innate differences between groups to the sexes. He affirmed that women were not good for factory work because of their "carelessness, ill temper, and unreliability." He wanted to restrain low-quality white women from excessive procreation. The job of higher-quality white women was to raise high-quality white children. Commons approvingly quoted Theodore Roosevelt's critique of "the women," that if they "do not recognize that the greatest thing for any woman is to be a good wife and mother, why that nation has cause to be alarmed about its future."[49]

Commons and Roosevelt expressed some concern that women would not make the right choices on their own. Lawmakers agreed. Forty US states between 1909 and 1919 restricted hours for female workers. Commons later in his career opposed the Equal Rights Amendment because, he said, women's "physiological differences" required laws to protect them. Women were yet another group that needed upper-class white men to protect them.[50]

The postclassical economists' rejection of laissez-faire lines up today with the familiar debate between the left, which wants government intervention and the right, which wants free markets. Yet it lined up historically with a debate less familiar to modern eyes, between the proponents of laissez-faire and advocates of state action on Indian reservations, immigration restrictions, Black segregation, restrictions on women, and eugenics.

What had happened to the liberal opposition to empire? Where were the liberal economists in all this? There were few of them left, and they would be on the fringe for many decades after. Liberals were going to be faced with a great expansion in European empires. The next chapter turns to an example of an American economist in 1898 who opposed American colonization of the Philippines.

12

America in the Philippines and the New Colonial Expansion

On January 16, 1899, the economist William Graham Sumner gave a speech on US colonization of the Philippines. The fifty-eight-year-old Yale professor of political economy came out of early retirement to deliver this speech before the Phi Beta Kappa Society of Yale. On May 1, 1898, during a short war between Spain and the United States, US Admiral George Dewey had defeated a Spanish armada to capture the Philippines. Sumner spoke as the US Senate considered whether to ratify a treaty with Spain that included the US taking possession of the islands. Sumner had joined the American Anti-Imperialist League that advocated rejection of the treaty in the fall of 1898.[1]

The colonization supporters said that they would offer benevolent rule to promote what they called the Filipinos' "national development." To Sumner, it was abhorrent to say, "We know what is good for you better than you know yourself and we are going to make you do it." Now that Americans had ended Spain's oppressive colonial rule in the Philippines, they should just endorse independence. Sumner was an heir to Adam Smith's anti-colonial critique, but such heirs were becoming much rarer and more marginalized.[2]

It was a turning point for America's role in the world, a last chance to pull back from imperialism abroad. America had until then stuck to the liberal nonintervention foreign policy set by George Washington and John Quincy Adams, with admittedly some not-so-tiny exceptions like conquering Indian nations, Liberia, and Mexico. America's new apostasy would be part of a major expansion of colonial empires in the late nineteenth century.

The American Economic Association founders had singled Sumner out as the kind of economist they did not want to be. He was way too much a proponent of laissez-faire both at home and abroad. For his part, he had refused to join the AEA because of its rejection of laissez-faire. In an earlier essay in 1894, Sumner had derided the AEA economists for succumbing to "the greatest folly of which a man can be capable, to sit down with a slate and pencil to plan out a new social world."[3]

Sumner was for nonintervention, for doing nothing, a hard sell at the best of times. But the case for Doing Nothing depends on what Doing Something looks like. Sumner thought that America's newfound colonialism was indeed worse than Doing Nothing.

America's colonization of the Philippines occurred soon after a peak in Western colonial violence. Modern estimates find that the number of new violent conquests peaked in the 1880s, and new violence continued in the 1890s.[4]

In retrospect, the classical economists had left an ambiguous legacy on the morality of colonialism, as we saw with James Mill in the chapter on Benjamin Constant. While Adam Smith had condemned British rule in India, James Mill's son, John Stuart Mill, defended it. In his great classic *On Liberty* in 1859, the younger Mill at first gave one of economists' strongest rebukes to paternalism, which anticipated Sumner's critique. Nobody had the right to coerce an individual for his own good; compulsion was acceptable only to prevent people from harming others. "He cannot rightfully be compelled to do or forbear" actions just because "it will be better for him to do so, because it will make him happier, because, in the opinions of others, to do so would be wise, or even right."[5]

Mill had demonstrated his opposition to paternalism in his arguments against benevolent slavery with Thomas Carlyle. Did he also oppose the paternalism of colonial governments toward their non-white subjects? Right after his soaring defense of individual rights against paternalism in *On Liberty*, Mill made a crucial exception that broke the hearts of some of his later admirers. He denied that the case for liberty applied to "those backward states of society in which the race itself may be considered as in its nonage." Mill argued that "despotism is a legitimate mode of government in dealing with barbarians, provided the end be their improvement, and the means justified by actually effecting that end."[6]

This passage left a lasting stain on liberalism. The Indian essayist Pankaj Mishra in 2020 would cite this passage from Mill to argue that "Liberal ideas in the West" justified colonialism. These ideas "did not seem particularly liberal to the peoples subjugated by British, French and American imperialism in the eighteenth and nineteenth centuries."[7]

How to reconcile this passage with Mill's denunciation of theories of innate racial inferiority? The crucial phrase here is "backward states of society" compared to individuals in "a civilised community." While Mill rejected the idea that some races were innately backward, whole societies could be backward compared to a civilized community. Although not fully spelled out, Mill seems close to the argument still around today that some societies are not ready for political rights. They don't have the unspecified ingredients necessary for a "free and equal discussion." The outcome of political freedom would be bad, because these societies cannot be trusted to implement the institutions that will enable "spontaneous progress." Mill's moral vision on slavery allowed him to reject the slave owners' and Carlyle's claims of material improvement of the slaves as irrelevant. The same vision failed him on colonialism, where improvement justified despotism.

Although this passage does not mention colonization, Mill had made clear elsewhere his favorable reviews of British rule in India.

Like his father, Mill actually worked for the East India Company, and he gave his employer credit for an "amount of good government produced which is truly wonderful considering the circumstances and the materials." Mill enthused that "it has been the destiny of the government of the East India Company to suggest the true theory of the government of a semi-barbarous dependency by a civilized country."[8]

Back at the AEA, many of America's newly professionalized social scientists were with Mill rather than Sumner. The AEA in 1899 appointed a committee to study US policy in the Philippines, as the decision on American colonization was still up for grabs. Led by Cornell Professor Jeremiah Jenks, the committee endorsed autocratic colonial rule in the Philippines: "The desires of the United States Government, expressed by the proper authority, are to be paramount and its decisions final."[9]

Political science associations also gave expressions of support for American imperialism. The annual meeting of the American Academy of Political and Social Science (AAPSS) in 1899 featured a symposium on "The Foreign Policy of the United States: Political and Commercial." Like economists, political scientists were increasingly professionalized as scientists through organizations like the AAPSS, founded in 1889. Yale international law Professor Theodore Woolsey commented in the symposium on US colonialism. The US military should act as "a benevolent despot" to create the environment for development. We should not guarantee political rights for Filipinos. Such rights should "be put out of reach, like edged tools rescued from children's hands," Woolsey said.[10]

Another participant in the AAPSS annual meeting, Alleyne Ireland, published in 1899 a book titled *Tropical Colonization*. In it, Ireland argued that colonizers needed to force Black people in the West Indies and Africa to work. He said that colonizers had no choice but to get Black people out of their "lazy backwardness." Likewise, he opined that Americans in their new colony of the Philippines had to do something to advance the development of Filipinos notorious for their laziness.[11]

Ireland presented another paper on colonialism at the American Political Science Association annual meeting in 1906, "On the Need for a Scientific Study of Colonial Administration." Ireland deplored the "torrent of ignorant and often violently prejudiced writing" produced by those who lacked the scientific credentials that he himself brought to the subject, which included travels to the Caribbean, South America, India, and Ceylon.

Ireland argued that "the subjection of one race under the rule of another" was justifiable because the ruling race would achieve "the right of the world as a whole to enjoy the natural resources of the whole earth." Speaking for The World, Ireland said this global enjoyment could happen only if each territory developed and traded its products internationally.

So, Ireland asked, what if an Indigenous government failed to provide the property rights and contract enforcement necessary for development of its own territory? What if the territory failed to trade internationally? Any government "greatly inferior to the best type" was eligible for takeover. Alleyne Ireland pointed out that "native rule in the tropics" had failed to achieve the "development of the resources of the territory." Therefore, the ruling race must appoint itself to replace native rule. Ireland was most concerned with developing the conquered land rather than the people. However, he claimed that colonizers should also try to achieve "the general betterment" of the subject races.[12]

The case for American rule in the Philippines could also be set to rhyme. Rudyard Kipling published his classic poem "The White Man's Burden" in February 1899 to persuade Americans to embrace their colonial mission in the Philippines. As in modern times, the 1899 development debate included celebrities as well as social scientists.

Instead of the white man doing nothing for the non-white world, he should:

Take up the White Man's burden—
Send forth the best ye breed—
Go bind your sons to exile
To serve your captives' need;
To wait in heavy harness

On fluttered folk and wild—
Your new-caught, sullen peoples,
Half devil and half child.

The West should heroically persevere when the Rest resisted progress:

Take up the White Man's burden—
And reap his old reward:
The blame of those ye better,
The hate of those ye guard—
The cry of hosts ye humour
(Ah, slowly!) toward the light:—
"Why brought ye us from bondage,
Our loved Egyptian night?"

It was light versus darkness. The colonizers brought the West's "light" to replace the Rest's "night."

The white conquerors terrorized the half-devil and half-child people for their own good:

Take up the White Man's Burden—
In patience to abide,
To veil the threat of terror
And check the show of pride;
By open speech and simple,
An hundred times made plain,
To seek another's profit,
And work another's gain.

The Kipling development goals included peace, nutrition, and health:

Take up the White Man's burden—
The savage wars of peace—

Fill full the mouth of Famine
And bid the sickness cease.[13]

Born in Bombay in 1865, Kipling had observed imperial benevolence firsthand in India. Not all the Indian beneficiaries were fans of the empire or of Kipling. A contemporary of Kipling was the Bengali poet Rabindranath Tagore (1861–1941). On December 31, 1900, almost two years after Kipling published "The White Man's Burden," Tagore published in Bengali a poem, "The Sunset of the Century." Where Kipling had seen a picture of nineteenth-century progress, with night giving way to light, Tagore saw the opposite—colonialism was a sunset instead of a sunrise. The red sky to Tagore indicated violence, and the violence did not exactly bring progress: "The sun of the century is setting to-day in clouds of blood— / at the festival of hate to-day, in clashing weapons sounds the maddened, dreadful chant of death." Tagore closed his poem with an apparent reference to Kipling's poem that was not very flattering: "Awakening fear, the poet-mobs howl round, / A chant of quarrelling curs on the burning-ground."[14]

Tagore received the Nobel Prize in Literature in 1913, six years after Kipling got the same award. It was gratifying for him to be recognized. As Tagore had said in a speech in 1908, the British "are behaving as if we do not exist." The British "think and act and rule as if we are huge cyphers." Tagore in 1913 could now celebrate how those giving him the Nobel recognized a two-way flow of good things between East and West, in contrast to Kipling's purported one-way flow from West to East: "The East and the West ever touch each other like twin gems in the circlet of humanity, that they had met long before Kipling was born and will meet long after his name is forgotten."[15]

Tagore would return to the critique of the White Man's Burden during the rest of his long life. In a 1930 speech in New York at which Franklin D. Roosevelt was present, Tagore would at first express thanks for material benefits from the West: "The age belongs to the West and humanity must be grateful to you for your science." But this material progress was not enough to justify the White Man's Burden: "You have exploited those who are helpless and humiliated those who are unfortunate with this gift. A great portion of the world suffers from your civilization." Tagore would experience his own humiliations touring the US because of the insulting behavior of American immigration officials in the wake of the 1924 ban on Asian immigrants. He would cut a 1929 US tour short in protest against such affronts.[16]

Back to the end of the nineteenth century, the US was going to embrace Kipling's view of the White Man's Burden in the Philippines. In June 1898, US President William McKinley sent 12,500 US troops to the Philippines. McKinley's mission for the troops was a little imprecise. They should bring "order and security to the islands while in the possession of the United States." McKinley had still not decided whether to actually rule the islands.[17]

One group that did want political rights for Filipinos was . . . Filipinos. Emilio Aguinaldo had been the leader of a previous Filipino rebellion against the Spanish. In 1898, his rebels helped the Americans defeat the Spanish on land after Dewey's naval victory. Aguinaldo saw the Americans at first as liberators. On June 12, 1898, when he issued a declaration of independence, he gave thanks for "the protection of the Powerful and Humanitarian Nation, the United States of America." In language that echoed the Americans' Declaration of Independence, Aguinaldo asserted Filipinos' "right to be free and independent." As a Filipino thinker named Sixto López later reminded Americans, they were supposed to believe that "all just powers of government are derived from the consent of the governed." How then could they possibly "deny the application of that principle of human right to the Filipinos?"[18]

But McKinley discovered that colonialism played well on the campaign trail for the November 1898 midterm elections. On the eve of the elections, McKinley sent peace commissioners to Paris to negotiate a treaty with the Spanish to end the war. No Filipinos were at the treaty talks. McKinley wrote the commissioners on October 25, 1898, that the US could not simply do nothing about its new conquest—we "cannot let go." Our "duty requires we should take the archipelago." As the devout McKinley later explained to a missionary committee, God told him during his prayers "we could not leave them to themselves," because they "were unfit for self-government." After this divine intervention, McKinley understood that "there was nothing left for us to do but to take them all, and to educate the Filipinos, and uplift and civilize and Christianize them." God himself used the classic "we" and "they" formulation. God also forgot to tell McKinley that devout Filipino Catholics were already Christian.[19]

The US commissioners signed the treaty with Spain ending the war on December 10, 1898. The treaty transferred sovereignty over the Philippines from Spain to the US. In return, the US paid Spain $20 million. A two-thirds majority in the Senate still had to ratify the treaty for it to go into effect.[20]

William Graham Sumner implored the Senate to reject the treaty. Sumner insisted that the US should not take over government of the Philippines. In Sumner's Yale speech in January 1899, he considered whether colonizers offered good government in the tropics. He made clear that independence for Filipinos would not necessarily lead to good government. Bad government was a common feature of self-government around the world.[21]

Nevertheless, Sumner asked, who has the right to decide for others that they are unfit to have political rights? Whites deciding this for non-whites only justified unlimited oppression. "This disposition to decide off-hand that some people are not fit for liberty and self-government" was exactly "what causes tyranny and cruelty." This disposition caused tyranny and cruelty at home toward Black people and Indians, Sumner said.[22]

For Sumner the critical question was not whether non-whites were fit for self-rule, but whether we whites were fit to rule them. By way of illustration, Sumner reminded his audience of a recent lynching of a Black postmaster in South Carolina, on February 22, 1898. A white mob upset at having a Black postmaster, whose name was Frazier B. Baker, set his house on fire. They then murdered Baker and his two-year-old child when they fled the flames. How could we

Americans claim we were bringing good government to Filipinos, when we "Americans cannot assure life, liberty, and the pursuit of happiness to negroes inside of the United States?"[23]

We white thinkers justified our oppression by claiming that "it was all for the best good of the oppressed," Sumner noted. We supposed "we are so much better than others that it is liberty for them to be governed by us." The only protection against such self-interested claims was "the doctrine that all men are equal."[24]

Kipling thought colonial rule brought peace. Sumner asked, Would peace happen when the imperialists really wanted "to take in hand any countries which we do not think capable of self-government?" The peoples we sought to benevolently conquer would arm themselves to resist our benevolence. The White Man's Burden would lead to an endless stream of imperial wars around the world, as indeed it eventually did.[25]

In the century after Benjamin Constant, Sumner was one of the vanishingly few who continued the tradition of liberal economists critiquing conquest in the name of progress. His critique of endless imperial war harked back to John Quincy Adams's defense of the traditional noninterventionist US foreign policy, which McKinley was fatefully reversing.

So Sumner saw only one path out of our self-induced mess of violence and fake altruism in the Philippines: "There is no escape except to give them independence and to let them work out their own salvation or go without it."[26]

Sumner was part of an American Anti-Imperialist League that formed in the fall of 1898 to oppose colonization of the Philippines. The anti-imperialists now sought to persuade senators to reject the treaty with Spain that included US annexation of the Philippines. Sumner and the league narrowly lost that battle on February 6, 1899.[27]

Meanwhile, war broke out on February 4, 1899, between American forces and Aguinaldo and his army. McKinley sought also to win a propaganda war for Filipino and American opinion. To make the case for benevolent American rule against Aguinaldo's fight for self-rule, the President dispatched to the islands an expert commission. The commission included such experts as an ornithologist who had visited the Philippines to study local birds.[28]

The commission decided after arriving in Manila to first issue a proclamation in April 1899 on its plan for the Filipino people. Although the commission promised to consult many Filipinos, the plan had been finished before the consultations began. Civilizing efforts of this era did not conspicuously feature the views of those to be civilized.

While not taking too seriously the views of actual Filipinos like Aguinaldo, the commission would offer paternal guidance to abstract Filipinos. It issued a proclamation on April 4, 1899. Since the commission had just arrived in Manila two days earlier on April 2, 1899, it seems likely the input of locals into the proclamation were limited. The proclamation explained to Filipinos that the US was committed to their "advancement," a concept that the commission also called "national development." Filipinos should see there was "no real conflict between American sovereignty and the rights and liberties of the Philippine people." Americans would be glad to grant such liberties if they were "reconcilable with the maintenance of a wise, just, stable, effective, and economical administration of public affairs," which unfortunately they were not. The US could not grant independence because of their responsibility to both Filipinos and the world.[29]

However, the commissioners promised Filipinos advancement through the construction of roads, railroads, and elementary schools, as well as promotion of domestic and foreign commerce, agriculture, and industry. The development mission justified American rule. The Commission's main report used the words "develop," "developing," or "development" twenty-nine times.

The Commission printed twenty-five thousand copies of their plan for distribution in Manila and the interior, as well as putting up posters. Eventually the commission produced a four-volume report of 1,621 pages.[30] It was Conquest by Development Reports.

Nothing happened at first except reports. The next step for implementing the actions recommended in the commission's report was . . . another commission. McKinley in January 1900 appointed an Ohio judge and future US president named William Howard Taft to head the next commission, which arrived in Manila in June 1900. The ornithologist from the first commission was appointed again to the second.[31]

But some real actions happened this time for the progress of those whom Taft called "our little brown brothers." The Taft Commission again stressed education. It would establish elementary schools, as well as some secondary schools. It also founded schools for nursing and nautical skills, as well as the University of the Philippines in Manila. Taft himself would become the civilian governor of the Philippines.

To help staff the schools, a group of six hundred American teachers arrived in August 1901 on board the ship *Thomas*. One of the Thomasites, as they became known, later wrote to her family. She explained that they were "social assets and emissaries of good will." Results eventually followed, as the literacy rate rose in one generation from 20 to 50 percent.

American doctors, agronomists, engineers, and sanitation specialists soon followed the Thomasites. Manila got a new sewage system and a new hospital. American doctors running sanitation and vaccination campaigns made progress against cholera, malaria, and smallpox. With the advice of the AEA colonial expert Jeremiah Jenks, Taft established a sound currency to replace the chaotic jumble of multiple currencies. Taft also campaigned in the US for Filipino exporters to have access to the American market. He would eventually achieve this objective in 1909 when he himself was president of the US. There then was a surge in Filipino exports.[32]

Like some modern nation-building efforts, the American effort in the Philippines combined military and development interventions. The aim was to show the military invasion as benevolent. But after the war with Filipino independence fighters began, reports of American atrocities emerged.

The anti-imperialists now had a new line of attack: White rule violated non-white human rights. As Kipling's "White Man's Burden" appeared in February 1899, the Americans were engaged in the Battle of Caloocan versus Filipino fighters. Five soldiers from Kansas accused their commander in this battle of ordering the execution of Filipino prisoners of war. Other less conscience-stricken soldiers embraced the violent version of the White Man's Burden. Armed with Krag-Jørgensen rifles, the soldiers sang as they marched:

Underneath the starry flag,
Civilize them with a Krag.[33]

Atrocities on both sides increased after Aguinaldo shifted to guerrilla war at the end of 1899. After seeing or hearing of comrades killed by Filipino insurgents masquerading as civilians, American soldiers embraced a more brutal war. "No more prisoners," a soldier wrote, "we will kill wounded and all of them." Another American soldier wrote of a retaliatory attack in which "we got orders to spare no one." The soldiers obeyed orders: "We went in and killed every native we met, men, women and children." General Arthur MacArthur (father of Douglas) declared martial law in the Philippines in December 1900, announcing that captured guerrillas would not have the rights of prisoners of war. Both the guerrillas and their civilian supporters could face the death penalty. The American forces torched whole villages if they suspected any villager of supporting the guerrillas. One American officer suggested that "the judicious application of the torch is the most humane way of waging such a war."[34]

American soldiers captured Aguinaldo on March 23, 1901, but other insurgent leaders continued the war. The rebels killed forty-eight US soldiers at Balangiga on Samar Island. In retaliation, Brigadier General Jacob Smith ordered Major Littleton Tazewell Waller to turn Samar into "a howling wilderness." Smith instructed Waller, "I want no prisoners. I wish you to kill and burn, the more you kill and the more you burn the better you will please me." Smith spelled it out: "I want all persons killed who are capable of bearing arms." Waller asked Smith what was the minimum age to kill potential arms-bearing males, and Smith replied, "Ten years." In one well-documented incident, Waller in January 1902 executed eleven of the army's Filipino porters whom he suspected of disloyalty.[35]

Meanwhile, Brigadier General J. Franklin Bell sought to destroy the insurgents led by General Miguel Malvar in the province of Batangas on Luzon Island in January 1902. Bell instituted a new policy: concentration camps. He would force civilian Filipinos to move into the camps with their livestock and other possessions. Any male of arms-bearing age outside the "protected zones" would be arrested or "shot if he runs away," Bell announced. Bell sought to deny Malvar's guerrillas their civilian support, a strategy common to later counterinsurgency campaigns elsewhere. More than three hundred thousand people wound up in the camps. About eleven thousand of the camp inhabitants died from malnutrition, cholera, or malaria in the unsanitary sites.[36]

The Anti-Imperialist League had appealed to the voters to reject a second term for McKinley and his imperial mission in the 1900 elections, but they lost that battle. Although the league had lost both the 1899 treaty vote and the 1900 presidential election, they did not give up. Most of all, they continued to publicize the human rights violations by American forces.

The anti-imperialists now could deploy their own literary celebrity to counter Kipling's poetic fantasies of benevolent imperialism. In February 1901, Mark Twain published an essay, "To the Person Sitting in Darkness." He quoted a report from General Arthur MacArthur in November 1900. Twain pointed out how the American side suffered 268 killed and 750 wounded, while the Filipinos suffered 3,227 killed and 694 wounded. The skewed ratio of killed to wounded confirmed the American take-no-prisoners campaign.

Twain lampooned Kipling's metaphor on how the West's "light" would replace the Rest's "night." The Americans indeed brought "Torches of Progress and Enlightenment" to the people that "sit in darkness." However, they used the Torches to burn down villages. Bringing this kind of "light," Twain wondered if we should "go on conferring our Civilization upon the peoples that sit in darkness, or shall we give those poor things a rest?"

Twain ratcheted up his mockery of the "light" metaphor:

> The Blessings of Civilization are all right, and a good commercial property; there could not be a better, in a dim light. In the right kind of a light, and at a proper distance, with the goods a little out of focus, they furnish this desirable exhibit to the Gentlemen who Sit in Darkness: LOVE, LAW AND ORDER, JUSTICE, LIBERTY, GENTLENESS, EQUALITY, CHRISTIANITY, HONORABLE DEALING, PROTECTION TO THE WEAK, MERCY, TEMPERANCE, EDUCATION,—and so on.
>
> There. Is it good? Sir, it is pie. It will bring into camp any idiot that sits in darkness anywhere.

Would white Americans want such light for themselves? Twain invoked the classical reciprocity argument. He imagined Filipinos wondering about the double standard: "Is it, perhaps, possible that there are two kinds of Civilization—one for home consumption and one for the heathen market?"[37]

A dissident social scientist echoed Twain's language about the Blessings of Civilization in a less comedic tone three months later at the Fifth Annual Meeting of the American Academy of Political and Social Science on April 12–13, 1901:

> War, murder, slavery, extermination and debauchery—this has again and again been the result of carrying civilization and the blessed gospel to the isles of the sea and the heathen without the law.[38]

The words were from the Black social scientist W. E. B. Du Bois, who was just beginning his illustrious career. In his 1903 classic *The Souls of Black Folk*, Du Bois was surprisingly open at first to the case for a Development Right of Conquest: "It is possible, and sometimes best, that a partially undeveloped people should be ruled by the best of their stronger and better neighbors for their own good."

But the fatal flaw was that the rulers could not be trusted to put the interests of the ruled above their own self-interest. Putting the weak at the mercy of the strong creates a temptation for tyranny "which human nature seldom has withstood and seldom will withstand."[39]

Du Bois anticipated many debates to come in the new century: "The problem of the twentieth century is the problem of the color-line,—the relation of the darker to the lighter races of men in Asia and Africa, in America and the islands of the sea."[40]

Meanwhile, Bell's concentration camp strategy succeeded at defeating guerilla commander Miguel Malvar in the province of Batangas. On April 16, 1902, Malvar surrendered, ending the last major resistance to American rule. Some 4,234 American soldiers and 20,000 Filipino soldiers died in the war. Filipino civilian deaths were hard to estimate, perhaps around 200,000. On July 4, 1902, President Theodore Roosevelt announced the war was over and turned the Philippines over to American civilian rule.[41]

William Graham Sumner lost the argument for liberal nonintervention abroad. McKinley, Roosevelt, and Taft had decisively embraced an expanded US mission to the world. Their justification for America as savior was to influence the next American president after Taft, Woodrow Wilson.

Another economist in the Anti-Imperialist League foresaw the consequences for the cause of liberalism of the US embrace of colonialism in the Philippines. Like Sumner, University of Chicago Professor J. Laurence Laughlin had declined to join the new American Economics Association and preferred the free market economics of the classical generation. He founded the Chicago Department of Economics and thus was a precursor of the Chicago School that would produce Milton Friedman.[42]

Laughlin was another member of that ever-more-slender band of anti-imperialist liberal economists. In a tract in 1899 he had embraced the "liberty party" that advocated "self-government," and "liberty for all men in all lands" to apply to Filipinos. He hedged a little on having "no more of our presence over there than is necessary to protect the islands from foreign aggression" and "to assure the rights of liberty and property to foreigners." But he forcefully rejected the "royalist party" who would "create a relation of master and subject races," which "is vitally opposed to all the principles of free institutions." This was the "great moral issue" for his generation.

Crucially, Laughlin quoted Lincoln on the dangers of hypocrisy. He said what Lincoln said about slavery could be said about the US conquest of the Philippines: "I hate it because it deprives our republican example of its just influence in the world; enables the enemies of free institutions, with plausibility, to taunt us as hypocrites."[43]

Laughlin was to be all too correct in predicting that the enemies of freedom would exploit the Western hypocrisy on free institutions in the Philippines, not to mention in the West's expanded colonial empires worldwide.

It would get even worse. Not only was colonialism expanding, but also events in the Congo would herald a new formulation of benevolent slavery under colonialism.

13

Leopold's Congo and the Revival of Benevolent Slavery

Economic rights affect human rights. That was the insight of a British human rights campaigner and unofficial liberal economist named E. D. Morel, who campaigned against the Belgian King Leopold's reign of terror in the Congo in the late 1890s and early 1900s. King Leopold's men were forcing the Congolese to bring them ivory and rubber under the threat of whipping, chopping off hands, and killing. Morel argued such violence followed from the failure of the Belgians to recognize property rights and freedom of exchange for the Congolese, with Leopold giving a monopoly of trade to his own agents. It was the worst case of white oppression of Black people since the end of slavery. With forced labor, Leopold perpetrated a more malevolent exploitation of the Congo than the Americans did in the Philippines. The Congo at that point was Leopold's own personal colony and not a colony of the Belgian state.

Forced labor would be a recurrent issue in colonialism after this. Morel's Congo campaign was another major installment in the liberal critique of forced labor that went back to the benevolent-slavery rebuttals of Smith and Mill. The liberals in this round would be less successful than in the previous one. The use of forced labor in colonies would ultimately undermine the appeal of liberalism to people in the Rest, with fateful consequences in the twentieth century. At the time, there was little effort to hear the victims of forced labor, even by reformers. Some Congolese villagers were quoted by missionaries but lacked a forum otherwise to give their viewpoints.

Respecting economic rights and thereby human rights was a necessary condition for markets to be benevolent, Morel argued. Reducing violence required economic reforms. Most observers of the great campaign against Leopold's atrocities in the Congo failed to appreciate the economics of human rights violations.

Perhaps the moral reformers as usual were a little unfair to their opponents, portraying them at their worst. Leopold gave the advocates the invaluable gift of himself as a cartoon villain. Morel exploited this gift in an international campaign against the Congo atrocities.

King Leopold began with strong claims for his benevolence in the Congo. In 1876, the Belgian king called a conference on the exploration of Africa. He inspired conference delegates with his call "to open to civilization the only portion of our globe to which it has not yet penetrated." He used the venerable light-versus-darkness metaphor. He wanted "to pierce the darkness which envelopes entire populations." It was, he said, a crusade "worthy of this century of progress."[1]

To adjudicate the claims for African territory that Leopold disrupted, the colonial powers convened the Berlin Conference of 1884–1885. The Berlin delegates agreed on the goal of "furthering the moral and material well-being of the native populations." They offered this progress to the Africans they were conquering.

All the nations at the conference recognized King Leopold's nascent Congo Free State, including the United States, France, Germany, and Britain. Leopold and other participants in the conference made a commitment to free trade in the Congo Basin.[2]

A few doubters wondered whether colonizers of Africa were progressive. In February 1899, the same month as Kipling published his poem "The White Man's Burden," the author of another literary masterpiece signaled his doubts. Joseph Conrad in *Heart of Darkness* continued the metaphor war of light versus darkness. Kipling and Twain had argued about whether white men really brought the light to replace the night in the Philippines. Now Conrad joined the argument on which side represented darkness in King Leopold's Congo Free State.

Marlow, the narrator in *Heart of Darkness*, gets a job traveling to the heart of Africa with "the Company," modeled on Leopold's monopoly trading companies in the Congo. Marlow's aunt embarrasses him by viewing him as an "emissary of light," an "apostle" to save "those ignorant millions from their horrid ways." When he arrives in the Congo, he hears of Mr. Kurtz, the chief of the Inner Station. The station is far up the Congo River, in the heart of ivory country. Kurtz collects as much ivory as all the other European agents put together.

Few of Conrad's readers realize how much Kurtz starts off as a kind of development economist. Another agent in the Congo tells Marlow that Kurtz is "an emissary of pity, and science, and progress." Indeed, a certain International Society for the Suppression of Savage Customs commissioned Kurtz to write a report on the Congo. When Marlow and Kurtz finally meet, Kurtz shows him the report. In the first paragraph, Kurtz argues that whites, "from the point of development we had arrived at," had a lot to offer the "savages." Kurtz enthuses that "by the simple exercise of our will we can exert a power for good practically unbounded."[3]

Conrad reveals how this unbounded power for good turned out in one of the most notorious scenes in world literature. Marlow first glimpses Kurtz's Inner Station from afar, where he sees some posts around the station topped by ornamental balls. When he gets closer, he sees that the balls are actually human heads impaled on stakes.[4]

Conrad gives us our first hint of Congo economics. Marlow hears from another European about Kurtz's methods for trading for ivory with the natives. Even when Kurtz ran out of trading goods, he still had plenty of ammunition. He and his local henchmen collected ivory at gunpoint, "killing whom he jolly well pleased." Marlow sees that Kurtz had added a handwritten postscript to his progress report for the International Society for the Suppression of Savage Customs: "Exterminate all the brutes!" Attending Kurtz on his deathbed, Marlow hears his last words: "'The horror! The horror!" Kurtz was not the light; he was the darkness.[5]

By the time Conrad published *Heart of Darkness*, reports of Belgian atrocities in the Congo were multiplying. An article in an American magazine, republished in a British periodical, gave a report from 1895 of a Belgian captain named Léon Rom at the Stanley Falls station deep in the Congo interior. Rom had decorated his flowerbeds with the heads of twenty-one Congolese killed by a punitive expedition, which may have inspired the Kurtz character for Conrad. Three other atrocity reports by missionaries from 1895 to 1897 generated fierce debates in the British press, which was already following events in the Congo. In *The Times* alone, there were 257 articles with *Congo* in the headline or byline from 1889 to 1899.[6]

An article in *The Times* on May 14, 1897, gave firsthand account from a Swedish missionary in the Congo, E. V. Sjöblom, of Belgian troops rampaging through the interior. Sjöblom also gave his account to British human rights advocates at a meeting of the Aborigines' Protection Society, on May 12, 1897. The troops, made up of local auxiliaries, killed Congolese villagers and cut off the hands of the dead. The troops spared the lives of some villagers but cut off their hands. The local troops smoked the hands to prove to the Belgians how many they had killed. Severed and smoked hands were going to be the symbol of the horrors in the Congo. A later Belgian critic called the monuments built by King Leopold with his Congo profits "the Arches of the Severed Hands."

What was going on? Sjöblom reported it was all part of the collection of wild rubber for export from the Congo. The Belgians demanded a quota of collected rubber from each village and killed or mutilated villagers that failed to meet their quota. Villagers had to roam far afield to find enough rubber. Some wound up dying of starvation before the Belgians could kill them. Sjöblom noted that the locals responded to the Belgian agents of progress by asking, "Why did the white man ever find his way to my country?"[7]

King Leopold offered in 1896 one of the classic solutions to any aid controversy—a commission. His Natives Protection Commission would investigate any violence against the natives and report such abuses directly to the governor-general for correction. Nothing changed.[8]

King Leopold in a speech published in 1898 further defended his mission against critics. His "firm and parental" rule only forced the insufficiently inclined Congolese to work hard for Congo's own "development of civilization." Previously, the nonhardworking natives produced barely enough for their own subsistence. Prosperity in the Congo, resulting from the imposition of hard work on the locals by the Free State, would serve both "the interests of whites and negroes." Leopold was reviving the theory of benevolent slavery that liberals had seemingly defeated with American emancipation. Leopold said he was bringing "all the blessings of Christian civilization" to the Congo.[9]

In his many defenses of his Congo mission, Leopold did not advertise the blessings he had himself received. Congo profits bought him a 1,500-ton steam-powered yacht and an estate on the French Riviera.[10]

But any crusade against Belgian atrocities in the Congo was hard to get going when neutral observers did not know which side to believe. At this point, a whistleblower inside the Congo trading system changed the contest.

E. D. Morel was born in Paris on July 10, 1873, to a French father and English mother. His mother sent him to England for schooling after the death of his father. At the age of eighteen, he joined the Liverpool shipping firm of Elder Dempster as a clerk. Elder Dempster ships carried ivory and rubber exports from the Congo and goods from Europe back to the Congo. As he learned the business, the young shipping clerk supplemented his income with articles about Africa for English newspapers.[11]

Morel was far from the usual definition of an economist. However, if economists are defined as those who discuss economic ideas, Morel passes easily. He sounded more like today's economists than many of the AEA founders. Morel had absorbed classical economics from some key mentors and his own reading.

One of the mentors was Mary Kingsley (1862–1900), another forgotten figure in the distinguished line of female economic thinkers. Kingsley was a British traveler and writer who made two remarkably adventurous trips through West Africa. She did not oppose colonial rule, and she had some insulting things to say about Africans. But at the same time, she celebrated African traders: "The journeys these bush traders make are often remarkable, and they deserve great credit for the courage and enterprise they display." Like other liberal thinkers of this era, Kingsley wanted only a minimal colonial state that just facilitated commerce.[12]

Kingsley denounced the missionaries who for the sake of their fundraising painted "a distorted portrait of the African" as a "child" who needed saving. She thought that "the evil worked by what we must call the missionary party is almost incalculable." She rejected this philanthropic mindset: "I confess I am not an enthusiast on civilising the African." The missionaries had a regrettable influence over the statesmen who made colonial policy. As she wrote to a Black editor in Liberia: "The stay-at-home statesmen think that Africans are all awful savages or silly children—people who can only be dealt with on a reformatory penitentiary line. This view you know is not mine." Sadly, Kingsley died in 1900 before the Congo campaign took off. Before her death, she had defended Morel when he started to get into trouble with his employer, Elder Dempster.[13]

Morel cited Kingsley's "silly children" quote in a 1911 book on his later visit to Nigeria. He dedicated the book to Mary Kingsley, "WHO POINTED THE WAY."[14]

The 1911 book illustrates his own economic thinking, and how it was similar to Kingsley's. He traveled four hundred miles up the Niger in 1911, consulting with Indigenous leaders. Nigerian entrepreneurs impressed him with their thriving cocoa and oil palm industries. The philanthropic impulses of European missionaries impressed him less. They could see Nigerians only as "black with sin, black with lust, black with cruelty." The missionaries saw Nigerians as waiting for Western salvation. In contrast, Morel's image of the prototypical Nigerian was as "an active, hard-working individual," who was also "a keen business man and a born trader." Nigerians responded to market incentives just as Europeans did. As he described in another book later in 1920, the Ashanti farmers of the Gold Coast (Ghana) had shown similar initiative in capturing 30 percent of the world market for cocoa. Morel rejected the stereotype of the "incurable sloth of the aboriginal inhabitants" perpetrated by postclassical economists. Nigerians and Ghanaians had shown how hard they worked when the British let them work for themselves. This view of innate equality of economic agents went back to Smith. But Morel had a much rosier view of British colonizers than Smith had.[15]

Back at the beginning of the twentieth century, Morel as unofficial economist had begun analyzing the Congo trade. The Congo commerce did not seem to fit economic predictions. The ivory and rubber exports from the Congo should have generated income for the Congolese, some of which they would normally spend on imports from Europe. Examining commercial statistics and the Elder Dempster shipping manifests from the Congo to Antwerp, Morel indeed found the ivory and rubber cargoes. However, the Elder Dempster ships going back from Antwerp to Congo carried little besides rifles and ammunition for Congo Free State soldiers. The trade between Congo and Belgium was not really a trade. The Belgians were getting ivory and rubber; the Congolese were getting almost nothing. Why were the Congolese giving something for nothing? The rifles and ammunition were a clue that violence might be a factor. At this point, Morel started reading the atrocity reports of the missionaries.[16]

Morel now raised his concerns with his boss at Elder Dempster, Sir Alfred Jones. Although Elder Dempster got a lot of revenue from their customer King Leopold, Jones did discuss Morel's findings with the king—who as usual promised to investigate and make changes. Not convinced, Morel persisted. Officials in Liverpool and Antwerp began to ostracize Morel, combined with hints of lucrative promotions to other positions that did not involve the Congo. Morel discovered the usual treatment of whistleblowers who refuse to shut up.

Morel kept escalating his personal campaign. On July 28, 1900, he published his first critical article in the English press on the Congo. He was working himself out of a good job at Elder Dempster—and into an uncertain future as a journalist working on a scandal that few British cared about. Finally, in February 1901, Morel left Elder Dempster. He asked himself: What chance did an obscure twenty-seven-year-old ex-clerk, semitrained economist, and inexperienced journalist have against King Leopold? As Morel later remembered saying at that moment, "The odds were heavy."[17]

But Morel and his allies were ready three years later to launch the Congo Reform Association (CRA), one of the biggest Anglo-American human rights campaigns since the abolition of slavery. In the same critical year of 1904, an American Congo Reform Association emerged as well. American veterans of the Anti-Imperialist League on the Philippines now signed up to combat the evils of imperialism in the Congo.

The liberal side once again had some literary celebrities on its side. Mark Twain agreed to redeploy his satirical firepower from the Blessings of Civilization business in the Philippines to the same business in the Congo Free State. Joseph Conrad supplied a nonfictional attack to supplement *Heart of Darkness*. Conrad rejected Leopold's justification of violence based on Congolese backwardness: "Barbarism per se is no crime deserving of a heavy visitation." Morel published Conrad's letter in 1905.[18]

Morel focused on economics as the best way to understand Leopold's violence in the Congo. An Irish inventor had come up with an inflatable rubber tire for bicycles in 1888. Other industrial uses, such as insulation for electric and telegraph wires, also fueled a sharp increase in global demand for rubber. Congo had an abundance of wild rubber vines, but climbing up into the rainforest to extract the sap was tedious and dangerous work. The buyers had to pay the Congolese rubber harvesters a high price to induce a large supply.[19]

However, to achieve high profits, Leopold wanted to get rubber from Congolese producers at a price far below the world price. To achieve this, he surrounded the natives with a web of overlapping economic controls. His own trading monopoly would buy the rubber from producers in the Congo at a very low price. The Congolese could not sell to any other domestic buyer besides the monopoly. They could not sell the rubber to any other Europeans because Leopold banned other Europeans from importing rubber from the Congo (violating the free trade pledge Leopold had made in Berlin that had inspired the name Congo Free State). The Congolese could not use their land for something else besides rubber because he nationalized their lands for the Congo Free State. He did not allow them even to use their own labor for something else besides rubber production.

The normal outcome of severe price controls on a good such as rubber is a collapse in supply, because suppliers don't want to supply much at low prices. Leopold's taunt that the Congo natives did not want to work was true in a different way than he intended. Of course, the Congolese didn't want to work if you didn't pay them.

A supply shortage of rubber would not generate large profits for Leopold. The only way to get a large supply was to use violence. The more severe the economic controls, the worse the violence had to be. They must deliver their quotas of rubber (creatively labeled as an in-kind tax payment) or else face death. Forced labor was the key.

Severe economic controls usually generate black markets. Producers want to smuggle their products to a black-market operator who can pay a better price. The black-market operator would be willing to pay a better price for rubber because he could resell it at the much higher world price. Only state violence could protect the profits by threatening black-market operators with jail or worse.

Morel focused on the Congo economics of violence in his first book analyzing the Congo in 1902. "Gross oppression, violence, and every form of tyranny and outrage" must follow from such extreme controls over the economy. An economy based on compulsion brings violence, Morel said, compared to an economy based on voluntary exchange. King Leopold opted for violence because of the "theory that the Negro will not work and must be compelled to do so." Morel again rejected the British and American economists' idea of innate racial tendencies toward laziness. He thought the natives would work for themselves when the buyers paid them a more attractive price for their output.[20]

The defenders of Leopold's Congo realized that the theory of Black people's innate laziness was central to the case for compulsory labor, again reviving the theory of benevolent slavery. Worried about British pressure on him to reform his Congo rule, Leopold had hired a London publicist named Demetrius Boulger, who in 1903 published a pamphlet explaining that "THE CONGO STATE IS NOT A SLAVE STATE." Boulger wondered how "the black race can be made to work without pressure or compulsion." "If Mr. Morel has some golden rule for making the negroes work voluntarily," Boulger taunted, "he should not keep it secret." Morel had not actually kept it a secret that workers respond to wages in a free-labor market.[21]

In the United States, an obscure social scientist emerged to affirm the classical economics case against forced labor in the Congo. Paul Reinsch, professor of political science at the University of Wisconsin, has attracted little attention from later historians of the Congo controversy. Although Reinsch was a political scientist, his arguments were more on the economists' side of the unclear boundary between disciplines. He was a prototype of the roving development economist, debating policy on Congo and the Philippines, participating in conferences in Latin America, and late in his career serving as ambassador to China.[22]

Reinsch was not opposed to colonization. He had supported American colonization in the Philippines. He had some insulting things to say about Filipinos and Africans, and he did not envision political equality for them. His first book on colonialism in 1900 celebrated "the great work of civilizing and developing the world." Reinsch's favorable views on colonialism were all too typical of the liberals of the late nineteenth century.[23]

But Reinsch in his analysis of colonialism went in a different direction from the Commons and Ely theories of native racial tendencies toward laziness. He doubted the colonizers' claim of benevolent compulsion of the lazy natives. He denounced violence and population removal. He observed that "the promised civilization often consists in a speedy eradication of the savages from the face of the earth." Reinsch echoed what the Cherokee preacher David Brown had said about whites: "Most of these races would be happier if they had never seen their civilizers."[24]

In 1904, the same year as the founding of the Congo Reform Association in Britain and America, Reinsch published a blast on the Congo. King Leopold's Congo Free State had let loose "bloodthirsty" Indigenous troops to force the Congolese to deliver rubber, which was supposed "to initiate them into the beatitude of civilized life." The troops proved how much beatitude they had spread by collecting the smoked and dried hands of their victims.

Like Morel, Reinsch saw the violence as part of an economic system. The Congo Free State forced rubber producers to sell their production to its "huge trade monopoly" at five cents a pound when the world price was one dollar a pound. King Leopold had outlawed all other traders that could have offered a competitive price to rubber producers. His laws treated these other traders like criminals receiving stolen goods. Leopold had violated his 1885 Berlin commitment to free trade. The Belgians' "savage levies" on the Congolese made them as bad as slave traders.[25]

The next year, Reinsch published his magnum opus, *Colonial Administration*. Reinsch was deeply conflicted about colonial rule. Like many other thinkers confronting poverty in the Rest, he could not accept doing nothing. He could not accept that "we should let all these alien societies alone, and allow them to develop unhindered." We in the West had become "responsible for the destiny of great multitudes of people," and now "this responsibility cannot practically be avoided." Reinsch did see a positive side to European colonization. It could bring peace to Africa and India. It could bring good health care and sanitation. It could build railways and roads. It could train the natives in industrial and agricultural technologies and skills. It could bring trading stations and prevent the natives from levying their own transit fees on this trade. Therefore a "civilizing colonial policy will also improve the general conditions of life."

But material progress did not justify violence. Reinsch again described the Congo system as nothing but a "slave trade" economy, which the Belgians "carried on covertly under the name of contract labor." Land expropriation, price controls, and slavery spread "terror throughout the native population along the Congo."

Reinsch argued that the main Congo problem was a lack of justice, which would include respect for property rights, and freedom to work and to trade. Non-Western peoples in general "desire justice rather than benevolent interference." Justice required that the Congolese must be allowed "freely to choose their Employers," at a type of work and wages "to which they freely consent." Reinsch reiterated yet again: "In colonial affairs, we are in need more of the sense of justice than of benevolence." He quoted an Arab proverb: "One day of justice is better than seventy years of good wishes." More than a century after Adam Smith, the classical tradition continued—justice was still the key to economics.

In the end, Reinsch almost rejected colonial civilizing by force. Like a good liberal skeptic, he asked, If our civilized ways are so great, why do we have to force others to take them? He said, "The only true civilizing influence is example freely followed." For example, Japan's successful trajectory was happening because she "is of her free will imitating our institutions and methods." If the European model was superior, it "will be gladly and spontaneously imitated by other races." Only in that scenario, Reinsch said, could "the Western nations" then "hope to exert a powerful civilizing influence." We should allow non-Western peoples the "same freedom of economic development" we Western people had been lucky to have for ourselves. Reinsch stated the ideal of national self-determination but could not quite reach it.[26]

Having not rejected colonialism, the liberal thinkers also showed limited interest in hearing from the Congolese what they thought about Leopold's Free State. On one hand, E. D. Morel realized that testimony from Congolese victims was effective in gaining Western support for the campaign against Leopold. On the other hand, Morel and the other reformers gave little or no role to the Congolese beyond being victims. Even the testimony was filtered through Western eyes.

Morel's 1904 book, *King Leopold's Rule in Africa*, gave numerous statements from missionaries quoting local witnesses to atrocities, accompanied by shocking photographs. It is refreshing to hear something from the Congolese. For example, the prominent missionaries and campaigners John and Alice Harris documented a case of a man named Nsala from Wala in the Nsongo District in 1904. Nsala told John and Alice that native soldiers had attacked his village and killed his wife, Bongingangoa, his five-year-old daughter, Boali, and a ten-year-old boy, Esanga. According to his testimony, the cannibal soldiers ate the remains of the victims. Alice Harris staged a photograph of Nsala looking at a severed hand and foot, which was all that remains of his daughter, Boali. Alice Harris's photographs made up a "Congo Atrocity Lantern Lecture" that was featured in Congo Reform Association lecture tours of the UK and US. It was no doubt effective in shocking the British and American publics into desirable support for Congo reform. From modern perspectives on "poverty porn," it is also a demeaning portrayal of Nsala for the sake of the cause. It perpetrated stereotypes about Africans being cannibals.[27]

By fair means or foul, campaigners for economic reforms and human rights in the Congo eventually got too much publicity for the British and American governments to ignore. The turning point on the Congo came in the United States on December 9, 1906, when a dissatisfied lobbyist revealed Leopold's bribe to a Senate Foreign Relations Committee staff member to get them on his side. The American Congo Reform Association had already mobilized public opinion against Leopold, but the new revelation finally tipped the balance in the US. Atrocities against the Congolese were one thing, but the king's intervention in the American political system was more than the Theodore Roosevelt administration could tolerate. The US notified the British that they would cooperate on forcing reforms on Leopold.

Leopold saw that he had lost the battle with the Congo Reform Association. On December 13, 1906, Leopold agreed to give up his personal rule over the Congo, turning it over to be a formal colony of the Belgian government. The Belgian Chamber of Representatives voted to annex the Congo.[28]

The annexation took place two years later on November 15, 1908. The following year, on October 28, 1909, the Belgian Colonial Minister Jules Renkin finally announced major economic reforms.[29]

The reforms allowed local people to gather rubber on their own and sell it to whatever private traders they wished at market prices. By 1917, there were over a thousand private traders operating in the Congo, offering local people better prices for rubber compared to Leopold's draconian price controls. The (partial) end of forced labor yielded higher wages in the free-labor market. Workers could simply leave any employer that did not pay them the market wage. The number of potential employers expanded as Renkin finally did allow free trade in the Congo for other Europeans. These reforms eliminated many of the extreme controls on markets that Morel and Reinsch had identified as the roots of the atrocities. The Belgians replaced these controls with a head tax. The tax was more moderate than the old levies of rubber that had forced the Congolese to spend one-third to two-thirds of their time working for Leopold.[30]

A British vice-consul reported in 1911 that "natives who, little more than a year ago, were spending from ten to twenty days monthly in an exhausted forest searching for rubber . . . are now left in peace to gain in their own way the money for the payment of the tax which is levied by the government." By 1912, a representative of the Congo Reform Association visited the Congo and reported to the CRA that he found no evidence of atrocities committed by the new colonial regime. On June 16, 1913, the Congo Reform Association held a final meeting in London to celebrate its triumph—"the native of the Congo is once more a free man"—and abolish itself.[31]

It was a little too good to be true. To Morel's disappointment, the Belgians' reforms were missing one crucial piece. They did not include recognition of land rights of the Congolese. The Belgians treated lands owned collectively by villages as vacant lands that defaulted to colonial state ownership. The colony made money off these through state-run plantations or by selling them for private plantations. For example, it sold tracts of land to Lever Brothers (forerunner of today's Unilever) that together amounted to one-fourth the size of Belgium. Morel did not have support from the British government on recognizing land rights for the locals, because that would challenge British colonial practice as well. "The Native question is not so simple as he thinks," the British foreign secretary commented on Morel. "We do not, in our own Colonies, say that all the land and produce of the soil belongs to the Natives."[32]

Even on the central issue of forced labor, the reforms fell far short of freedom. Morel noted in 1912 that the Belgians still allowed forced labor for three types of employers: the military, state-run plantations, and any private company that could claim it produced general benefits for the colony (such as railroads). When Renkin claimed he had eliminated forced labor for these purposes by 1911, he was lying.

Then World War I broke out, and things got even worse. After 1914, the Belgians dropped any pretense of not using forced labor. They resorted to massive drafts of porters for military expeditions. The gold mines also drafted workers to provide needed revenues. Forced labor recruiters went back to the old days, taking hostages and going on manhunts for escapees. The violence was not on the same scale as Leopold's, but it cast doubts on whether Congo reform was really a success.[33]

The problem, of course, was that colonial occupation of the Congo had not ended. Both Morel and Reinsch deployed lots of skepticism about colonialism but were not quite skeptical enough. Neither Morel nor Reinsch had seen any option for the Congo other than turning it over to Belgian government rule that they hoped would be more benevolent than Leopold's. To use today's language, they advocated economic freedom for the Congolese, but they did not advocate for political freedom.

The persistence of forced labor in the Congo was a disturbing portent. The progress against forced labor of the classical liberal period stalled during the postclassical period in the second half of the nineteenth century and the first half of the twentieth century.

The Treaty of Versailles after World War I also failed to condemn forced labor, and it continued in the Belgian Congo and elsewhere in colonial Africa up through World War II. This would be fatefully exploited by a hyperviolent anti-Western thinker.

14

Lenin vs. Wilson

In 1899, a Russian economist named V. Ilin published a book entitled *The Development of Capitalism in Russia.* He used phrases that made him sound a lot like a development economist. Drawing on ideas from Adam Smith, he celebrated how Russian "manufacture is very rapidly growing into large-scale machine industry," not to mention how "commercial intercourse with the rest of the world" was raising the Russians' "standard of living." The growth of commerce inside Russia, along with "enormous technical progress," also contributed to the momentous "economic development of Russia." However, V. Ilin also worried about the "negative and gloomy sides of capitalism." The latter worry featured more heavily in his subsequent work. V. Ilin was a pseudonym. His real name was Vladimir Ilyich Ulyanov, but he is better known by a later pseudonym: Vladimir Lenin. The advent of Leninism was to be the greatest crisis for liberalism since the heyday of benevolent slavery.[1]

Lenin would engage in a fateful debate with the West over colonialism. Lenin noted the rise of anti-colonial resistance around the world. There was an explosion of protest after the end of World War I by nationalist leaders like Ho Chi Minh of Vietnam, Sa'd Zaghlul of Egypt, Bal Gangadhar Tilak from India, and the African American leader William Monroe Trotter. Lenin celebrated those who fought against "the exploitation of an increasing number of small or weak nations by an extremely small group of the richest or most powerful nations." Western double standards on freedom played into the hands of Vladimir Lenin as he sought converts in the Rest.

At this point, he used the magic word—colonized peoples wanted nothing less than the right of "self-determination." In the critical years from 1917 to 1920, Lenin would challenge the White Man's Burden with a hyperviolent ideal of self-determination for the peoples of the Rest.[2]

Lenin also knew about the debate on forced labor under colonialism. He referred to supposedly benevolent whites training "the Negro to habits of industry," which he sarcastically noted was "not without coercion of course." Yet Lenin was hypocritical about forced labor, which he perpetrated in the Soviet Union itself and recommended to other revolutionaries elsewhere.[3]

Woodrow Wilson led the Western response to Lenin. Wilson could have won the debate on free labor except for his own lack of interest in free labor in the colonies. Wilson offered much inspirational rhetoric on self-determination but failed to go from rhetoric to action. In the end, Wilson failed to renounce either colonialism or forced labor after World War I. This would discredit the West and enhance the appeal of Leninism in the Rest.

As the debate emerged at the end of World War I on colonialism and forced labor, there would be four options for possible reforms.

First: reject neither colonialism nor forced labor. The less-than-successful campaign against abuses in the Congo had left the colonial status quo close to this point. Liberals like the Congo campaigner E. D. Morel kept denouncing this colonial violence, during and after World War I. Wilson had to consider whether to side with the liberals to reject such a status quo.

Second: reject colonialism but not forced labor. This was where Lenin headed. He rejected the first option of forced labor based on whites' superiority but wanted forced labor based on the revolutionaries' superiority. Native despotism could still turn out to be more appealing than white despotism.

Third: reject forced labor but not colonialism. This is where the liberals of this period usually wound up. Some of Wilson's advisors would recommend that he go with this option.

Fourth: reject both colonialism and forced labor. This was the liberal Promised Land, which had been somewhat hesitantly previewed by Adam Smith long ago. The liberals never quite arrived here in these years.

Lenin began the debate forcefully in his classic *Imperialism, the Highest Stage of Capitalism*. He had written it in 1916 in exile in Switzerland. He would publish it in Russia right before the Bolshevik Revolution in 1917. Lenin cited the American debate over Filipino independence to illustrate his own views on colonialism. Lenin documented the betrayal of Aguinaldo and denounced the "criminal" American military occupation in Manila.[4]

Wilson around the turn of the twentieth century was, like Lenin, writing about the Philippines. Wilson had gotten his PhD at Johns Hopkins as a student of Richard T. Ely, the founder of the American Economic Association who had so forcefully rejected the valuing of consent by classical economics. Ely listed Wilson himself as one of those whom he had consulted on starting the AEA in 1885. In 1890, Princeton appointed Wilson to the chair of jurisprudence and political economy. With disciplinary boundaries still slippery, Wilson later identified as a political scientist.[5]

In writing about the Philippines in 1900 and 1901, Wilson had rejected the Anti-Imperialist League's call for independence. He saw league members as traitors, on the side of the Filipino rebels. While he favored independence for the Filipinos eventually, they were not ready and so needed their American occupiers in the meantime. "We must govern," and "they must obey." Wilson said, "They are children and we are men in these deep matters of government and justice." Self-government did not bring blessings but rather "a curse, to undeveloped peoples, still in the childhood of their political growth." Consent of the governed was not relevant for such "politically undeveloped races." We must impose our adult wisdom by force, teaching them that they "must first love order and instinctively yield to it."

It was up to us to decide "when our work there is done and they are ready" for independence. Wilson had anticipated the we-and-they mindset that he would bring to the Versailles treaty negotiations eighteen years later in Paris in 1919.[6]

Also relevant for the later debate were Wilson's views on race at home in America. In an 1893 history of the Civil War era, Wilson cited an 1844 portrayal of benevolent slavery: "The greater part of the slave-owners were humane in the treatment of their slaves." They were "sincerely interested in the physical well-being of their dependents."

Wilson was partly just engaging in the empirical debate on whether slave owners had treated slaves well. Yet he indicated some esteem for the "masters who had the sensibility and breeding of gentlemen," where "the dignity and responsibility of ownership were apt to produce a noble and gracious type of manhood." Wilson admired the "patriarchal" relationships of such noble gentlemen to their slaves.[7]

Lenin also was not an advocate for free labor. Back in 1902, he had commented, "Under the banner of free labor, the toilers were robbed." The proletariat should not want to go back to "free trade" and "free competition," he said in 1917. Lenin had the exact opposite view to economic liberals like Morel, for whom free labor and free trade prevented violent exploitation as in the Congo. Lenin agreed with what was now a diverse assortment of AEA founders, acolytes of the Congo Free State, and socialists that free trade belonged only to a "bygone era." Lenin went a little further than these others in insisting that free labor and free trade always led to violent exploitation. The only way to move forward was to end capitalist markets altogether.[8]

To get rid of markets, Lenin offered violence against capitalists. The exploited would conquer the exploiters, both within and across nations. The proletariat's mission was "to crush, to smash to atoms, to wipe off the face of the earth the bourgeois." It was a sort of eugenics in reverse. The soon-to-be-famous "dictatorship of the proletariat" would suppress the "freedom of the oppressors, the exploiters, the capitalists." Lenin said such dictatorship "must crush them in order to free humanity from wage-slavery; their resistance must be broken by force."[9]

Lenin would also use force against Russian workers and peasants to promote communism, creating a new kind of forced labor at home. After taking power, Lenin published on January 16, 1918, a "Declaration of the Rights of the Toiling and Exploited Masses." Contrary to the promise of rights, the declaration announced a policy of "universal labor conscription" within Russia. To control both capitalists and workers, Lenin nationalized factories and banks and abolished private ownership of land. He deployed Red Army terror to enforce all of this.[10]

On May 13, 1918, the Bolsheviks announced more details of an economic system based on forced labor for Russian peasants. The decree cosigned by Lenin announced a "food dictatorship" with price controls on grain (making far more drastic the price controls that the tsar had imposed during World War I). In an extreme version of a policy combination some developing countries repeated decades later, the government printed money that fueled extreme inflation while keeping nominal food prices constant. The Bolsheviks compelled peasants to sell their grain at these punitively low prices. Lenin deployed armed troops to vanquish any peasant resistance. Anyone who failed to hand over their grain, or even who made home brew out of their own grain, were "enemies of the nation." The punishment for such enemies was confiscation of all their belongings, a ten-year prison term, and forced labor on public works. Compelling peasants to work to produce grain almost for free was already forced labor.[11]

The targets of the violence in 1918 were "kulaks," a largely fictitious class of rich peasant capitalists. The term *kulak* was so ill defined as to make virtually all grain farmers into such targets. But the armed detachments did not actually collect much food. According to the government's figures, the food brigades gathered only 570,000 tons out of a harvest of forty-nine million tons.[12]

As violence failed to produce food, Lenin resorted to more violence. On August 6, 1918, Lenin called for "merciless extermination of the traitors" who resisted grain requisitions. The Bolsheviks should just shoot them on the spot. In a telegram to provincial Bolsheviks on August 11, 1918, Lenin exhorted them to "hang (hang without fail, so that the people see) no fewer than 100 of the notorious kulaks, the rich and the bloodsuckers." In a postscript, he recommended that they "find tougher people."[13]

In the global debate, Wilson could have attacked Lenin here at his most vulnerable, on Lenin's embrace of extreme violence against his own peasants and workers. Wilson's ability to do so depended partly on whether the West could finally renounce forced labor in its own colonies in favor of free labor. Lonely liberals like the Congo campaigner E. D. Morel appealed to Wilson to embrace such freedoms. But it depended also on how much anti-colonial leaders in the Rest prioritized free labor over self-determination.

Lenin could claim leadership of the anti-colonial crusade by spelling out who was who in the world of exploiters and exploited. He suggested that "countries must be divided into three main types."

First were the "advanced capitalist countries"—Western Europe and the US. Second were less advanced Eastern Europe and Russia. Lenin was aware of the condescension of Western European peoples toward Eastern Europeans and Russians. Third were semicolonial places like Turkey, Iran, and China, and colonial territories in Asia and Africa.

A Three Worlds scheme had surfaced, four decades before the first generation of post–World War II development economists supposedly invented it. Lenin's First and Second Worlds were close to the later breakdown between capitalist and communist blocs, while his third category was close to what was later labeled the Third World.

It was the task of the oppressed proletariat in the Second World to merge their struggle with that of the Third World for self-determination. Together they would overthrow the oppressors in the First World. They would achieve "the unconditional and immediate liberation of the colonies."

The struggle of the Second World proletariat and the Third World nationalists would provoke revolution in the First World itself, Lenin predicted, and so complete the global progress out of capitalism into socialism.

Lenin's crucial innovation was to invert the West's racial hierarchy on global progress. Instead of the First World developing the Third through colonialism, it was the Third World developing the First through revolution.[14]

In his Swiss exile early in 1917, Lenin wrote another book later recognized as a communist classic, *The State and Revolution*. Lenin here conjured up another inversion, building on Marx. Within advanced capitalist countries, the oppressed proletariat should overthrow the bourgeois oppressors. The lower class were the agents of progress, not the self-appointed saviors in the upper class.

The proletariat included non-whites. Lenin overturned the West's view of superior whites within each advanced nation bringing progress to inferior non-whites like Black people. For Lenin, the proletarian non-whites were superior to the bourgeois whites. As for the proletarian whites that the AEA founders had dismissed as white trash, they also were superior to the bourgeois whites. Lenin offered non-whites and lower-class whites in the West another attractive reversal of who was saving whom.

Lenin acted quickly on colonialism after the revolution. On November 8, 1917, the day after the Bolsheviks took power, they announced their vision of a "democratic peace" that would renounce all annexations of territory by the warring powers during World War I.

The Bolsheviks in the decree went even further. They defined unjust annexations retroactively to include all the West's colonial conquests. The Bolsheviks explicitly rejected the Development Right of Conquest for colonial powers. The "backwardness of the nation forcibly annexed" never justified the forcible annexation.[15]

Lenin authored another declaration on January 3, 1918, using the charmed word *self-determination* in his peace proposals for World War I. A "democratic peace between the nations" required "the free self-determination of nations."[16]

This was powerful stuff. With the US now in the war and the outcome still uncertain, Wilson sought to counter Lenin's propaganda offensive. The British ambassador to the US had a meeting with Wilson on January 4, 1918, and reported to his government that Wilson felt he must respond to the Bolshevik appeal to the non-Western world. Four days later, Wilson announced in a speech to Congress his "Fourteen Points" to guide the peace negotiation.[17]

In point five, Wilson offered "a free, open-minded, and absolutely impartial adjustment of all colonial Claims." In determining who should be ruling whom, he would acknowledge "the interests of the populations concerned." These interests "must have equal weight" with the claims of the colonial power. It did not quite match Lenin's call for colonial self-determination, but at least it offered to consider the interests of the colonial subjects.

In a follow-up speech known as the "Four Points" to Congress on February 11, 1918, Wilson suddenly got closer to Lenin's position: "Peoples are not to be handed about from one sovereignty to another by an international conference." He wanted to respect "national aspirations." He insisted, "Peoples may now be dominated and governed only by their own consent." He now embraced the term *self-determination*, which should be an "imperative principle of actions." He predicted his own unhappy future when he said that statesmen ignore self-determination only "at their peril."[18]

Wilson had actually embraced the word *self-determination* and collective consent of the governed. After the armistice on November 11, 1918, the ideas of self-determination and colonialism would compete in the postwar treaty negotiations.

The first draft of the treaty that Wilson composed in Paris, dated January 10, 1919, called for "territorial readjustments" reflecting "racial conditions and aspirations," following "the principle of self-determination." For territories and colonies previously belonging to the defeated powers—Austria-Hungary, Turkey, and Germany—Wilson declared his proposed League of Nations would be the "trustee" to decide their fate. The principles the league should follow for these decisions were a ban on annexations, self-determination, and "the consent of the governed."[19]

It was an appealing message to the non-Western world. Wilson challenged here the colonizers' claims that colonial peoples were unfit to choose their form of government. Wilson contradicted his own procolonial rhetoric on the Philippines from nearly two decades earlier. Was this propaganda or a real commitment?

It took only twenty days to get the answers. A January 30 meeting of the victorious Allies in Paris discussed a draft that forgot to mention the word *self-determination*. The British were not enthusiasts for self-determination in their own colonies or anyone else's. The British Prime Minister David Lloyd George said at the Versailles meeting that they could hardly offer independence to those that were "cannibal colonies, where people were eating each other."[20]

The January 30 draft suggested that the need to decide the future of Germany's and Turkey's former territories was an opportunity. The Allies could strengthen their worldwide justification for their colonial rule. The justification invoked development. These territories were "inhabited by peoples not yet able to stand by themselves under the strenuous conditions of the modern world," said the draft. Now the peace treaty would apply to them the general principle that "the well-being and development of such peoples form a sacred trust of civilization."

For peoples not yet able to stand by themselves, the draft read, their "tutelage" should be "entrusted to advanced nations." The advanced nations would act as "mandatories on behalf of the League of Nations." The mandatories would be required to file annual reports with the League of Nations in which they evaluated themselves on their tutelage of their subjects.

The former Ottoman territories in the Middle East (such as Syria and Iraq) would get recognition of independence someday, but only after they got "advice and assistance" from the advanced nations until they were "able to stand alone." The proposed treaty would turn over the peoples in former German colonies in Africa and the

Pacific islands to the advanced nations with no mention of future independence.

The January 30 draft had thus eliminated all of Wilson's soaring language on self-determination and consent of the governed. The Allies approved the draft in the January 30 meeting, and this wording would be almost exactly the final text in the League of Nations covenant within the Treaty of Versailles. Wilson's supposed commitment to self-determination had quickly evaporated.[21]

Further negotiations did not change the outcome for the covenant but gave an indication of the troubles ahead. The Japanese delegate Baron Makino warned the negotiators on April 11 that the Wilsonian ideals had "quickened the common feeling of different peoples scattered over the five continents." Wilson had created new aspirations. The non-white majority of the human race deeply resented the "wrongs of racial discrimination." The Japanese had their own grievances as targets of racist immigration restrictions in the US. Baron Makino proposed that the treaty include an explicit endorsement of "the principle of the equality of Nations and the just treatment of their nationals." There was a majority vote for Baron Makino's proposal, but Wilson declared that it had failed because the vote was not unanimous.[22]

Unfortunately for Wilson, his language on self-determination had already been broadcast around the world. An American propaganda effort called the Committee on Public Information (CPI) spread Wilson's speeches. CPI records show direct or indirect dissemination of Wilson's messages to Australasia, Canada, Central America, China, Egypt, England, France, Greece, India, Italy, Japan, Liberia, Mexico, the Netherlands, Persia, Russia, Scandinavia, South Africa, South America, Spain, and Switzerland.[23]

The US propaganda effort worked a little bit too well. By the time of the Versailles treaty negotiations in Paris in 1919, Wilson had been flooded with petitions from anti-colonial advocates around the world looking for recognition for their own people's self-determination.

For example, a twenty-eight-year-old Vietnamese would-be activist named Nguyen Ai Quoc was in Paris in 1919. He had paid for his passage from Vietnam to France working as a cook's assistant on board the ship. He signed a petition coauthored with other Vietnamese on "Claims of the People of Annam [Vietnam]" on June 18, 1919. He circulated it to national delegations, including the Americans. The petition demanded political autonomy (not quite independence) for Vietnam. Nguyen Ai Quoc sought a personal meeting with Wilson, and according to some sources bought a formal suit for the occasion.

The US delegation acknowledged receipt of the letter and said they would bring it to Wilson's attention. No further communication was forthcoming, and the meeting never happened. Nguyen Ai Quoc said bitterly a decade later that Wilson's "Song of Freedom" had deceived many. The nonmeeting took on more significance in retrospect because Nguyen Ai Quoc later became the leader of Vietnam. He became better known by another pseudonym as Ho Chi Minh.[24]

As Erez Manela has argued, nonmeetings in Paris are an unusual indicator of Wilson's effect on the colonial debate. He had raised hopes among anti-colonial leaders in the Rest that led to requests for a meeting, then dashed hopes by not meeting, then decided to perpetuate colonial rule anyway.

Around the same time as Ho was pressing Vietnamese demands, Egyptian nationalists appealed to Wilson to overturn the protectorate that Britain had declared over Egypt at the beginning of World War I. The nationalist leader Sa'd Zaghlul wrote on April 22, 1919, to Wilson of how the American president had inspired the Egyptian people to press their claims for independence from British protection.

Britain had already solicitously responded to Zaghlul's appeals for self-determination by deporting him to Malta on March 9. When searching him for weapons, the British found on him only a press clipping on Wilson's Fourteen Points—a different kind of weapon. The arrest helped provoke violent clashes between Egyptians and British soldiers in which eight hundred Egyptians and sixty British died. The British foreign secretary referred to the nationalists as "paid agents" of "Bolshevists."

Attempting to stem the violence, the British released Zaghlul, and he arrived in France on April 19, 1919. His April 22 letter to Wilson requested a meeting. Wilson's secretary, Gilbert Close, told Zaghlul that he would bring the letter to Wilson's attention. After a meeting still failed to happen, Zaghlul wrote to Wilson on June 6 to affirm the Egyptian's faith in the Fourteen Points. By now, he noted despairingly, the peace conference had announced a decision on Egypt's status. Gilbert Close wrote back with another artful non-response: He wanted "to express regret that the President's time has been so completely taken up that he has not had an opportunity to make an appointment to see you."

Again, on June 18, 1919, Zaghlul wrote to the man he called "the Exponent of International Right and Justice," sensibly communicating that "we do not feel that you can form a judgment on the Egyptian situation without giving a hearing to the Egyptians themselves." Wilson was indeed busy, but maybe he should not have decided Egypt's fate without consulting an actual Egyptian. Referring to the token acknowledgments from Wilson's private secretary to previous communications, Zaghlul imagined rather desperately: "We believe you purposely left open the possibility of a future audience with us, and we respectfully request that this be granted us as soon as possible." Perhaps having learned that the previous nonresponses still gave too much encouragement, this time neither Wilson nor his secretary answered at all. Zaghlul then released publicly the whole correspondence.[25]

An almost identical nondialogue occurred on India. The Indian activist Bal Gangadhar Tilak on January 2, 1919, appealed to Wilson to support Indian self-rule. His letter called Wilson "the author of the great principle of self-determination."

Wilson's secretary, Gilbert Close, wrote Tilak back twelve days later with another masterpiece of evasion:

> I am instructed by President Wilson, to acknowledge your letter and express to you his high appreciation of your kind thought of him and to assure that the matter of

self-determination for India is a question which will be taken up in due time by the proper authorities.[26]

Tilak's appeals to Wilson for self-determination took on greater urgency in the spring of 1919. The British rulers in India passed a new law on March 21, 1919, called the Anarchical and Revolutionary Crimes Act, giving the British increased powers to detain Indian anti-colonial activists without trial. Mohandas Gandhi launched a campaign of nonviolent resistance to the new laws, saying it violated Indians' "God-given rights." On April 13, 1919, General Reginald Dyer gave orders for British soldiers to fire upon a throng of protesters against the new laws. The protesters had crowded into a walled compound in the city of Amritsar in Punjab. According to official accounts, 379 people died in the massacre. The true number was probably much higher. Gandhi did not just blame Dyer. "We do not want to punish Dyer," he said. "We want to change the system that produced Dyer."[27]

The petitions to Wilson had shown how little interest leaders like Tilak, Zaghlul, and Ho Chi Minh had in colonizers developing them for their own good. But now all the nonmeetings had confirmed the nonrecognition of any self-determination for colonial subjects.

Another nonresponse happened closer to home. The African American leader William Monroe Trotter had convened a meeting in New York of his National Equal Rights League (NERL) in December 1918. The 250 attendees included the later-to-be-famous activist Marcus Garvey. The meeting called for Wilson to add a Fifteenth Point to his Fourteen Points, the "elimination of civil, political, and judicial distinctions based on race or color in all nations for the new era of freedom everywhere." The demand applied to all countries where there was any discrimination or denial of political rights based on race. The NERL noted that four hundred thousand African American soldiers had helped win the war for democracy. The meeting appealed to the Allied leaders at the peace talks to "grant self-determination and rights without discrimination to all of the darker nations."

The NERL dispatched Trotter to Paris to present the appeal. The State Department refused to give the "subversive" a passport, so the Harvard-educated leader smuggled himself to Paris as a cook on a freighter. After all these delays, he finally arrived in Paris on May 7, 1919, to find that Wilson and the other victorious powers had ignored the NERL petitions for equality for Black people at home and abroad. He fired off a letter to protest "this awful violation of the war promises of the entente allies." Less than a month after Wilson's veto of the Japanese proposal on racial equality, Trotter pleaded with the allies to add his own declaration of racial equality to the treaty.

A secretary on the American delegation wrote Trotter back on May 16 to confirm that a petition from the NERL had been earlier received by cablegram back on March 24, but he made no comment on the petition. Getting nowhere, on June 21 just before the signing of the treaty, Trotter sent a final jeremiad to Wilson and leaders of Britain, France, Italy, and Japan. He illustrated the lack of equal rights for Black people by describing a recent lynching in Georgia of a pregnant woman named Mary Turner. The lynchers had hung her by the heels from a tree, cut open her belly, and stomped on the baby's head. Trotter proclaimed, "Imagine not that with such a scandal on humanity untouched your peace is just or will endure."[28]

As if Wilson had not already offended enough non-white people back home, the veteran American Indian activist Zitkala-Ša (now using her married name, Gertrude Bonnin) issued an editorial appeal in the winter of 1919. She noted, "The Red man asks for a very simple thing—citizenship in the land that was once his own—America," and wondered, "Who shall represent his cause at the World's Peace Conference?"[29]

A treaty provision prohibited the new states of Poland and Czechoslovakia from discriminating against their own minorities, as defined by race, religion, or language. This just highlighted the failure of Trotter and Zitkala-Ša to get Wilson's attention on discrimination against the Black and American Indian minority in America. Minority rights were only for white minorities. Observance of minority rights was required only of second-class Eastern European states.[30]

Wilson's genius was to keep finding new people to offend. The final language in the treaty also awarded China's Shantung Peninsula, formerly controlled by Germany, to Japan.

In 1913, Wilson had appointed Paul Reinsch, the classical liberal advocate for free labor during the Congo debate, as ambassador to China. By early 1919, Ambassador Reinsch was quick to see the significance of the treaty negotiations for the Chinese. On January 6, 1919, he dispatched a plea to Wilson in Paris. The president of China had repeatedly quoted Wilson's speeches on the American president's commitment to universal self-determination. Whether Wilson really honored this principle against Japan's claim to Shantung, Reinsch pleaded, would determine whether the ideal of free development would triumph in China.

Like an evangelist offering the sinner a choice of salvation or damnation, Reinsch sketched out two alternatives for Wilson. If the "Liberal powers" rejected the "enslavement of China" by the Japanese militarists in Shantung, then "the natural propensity of the Chinese to follow liberal inclinations would guide this vast country towards free government." If Wilson handed Shantung to Japan, he would tragically disillusion China on the ideals of equal freedom. Reinsch proclaimed that "the consequence of such disillusionment" on China's "moral and political development would be disastrous." The results would be tragic for Americans as well. Reinsch remarkably anticipated how things would look a century later: "Instead of looking across the Pacific towards a Chinese nation sympathetic with our ideals, [we] would be confronted with a vast materialistic military organization under ruthless control."[31]

The reformist Chinese intellectual Liang Qichao, who had promoted China's entry into the war on the side of the Allies, issued his own Cassandra prophecy after the Shantung decision: "No well-informed man can have any doubt that it will profoundly modify the history of the Asiatic continent, if not that of the whole world." Having been in Paris during the peace negotiations, Liang registered the intense disillusionment of the Chinese delegation with the West. Now, Liang said, if "driven to desperation [China] attempts something hopeless, those who have helped to decide her fate cannot escape a part of the responsibility."[32]

When news of Wilson's decision to hand Shantung over to Japan reached China on May 4, 1919, it touched off a wave of student demonstrations. The demonstrations were a turning point in the growth of anti-Western Chinese nationalism. Reinsch sympathized with the students but could offer them nothing as far as any changes in Wilson's policies toward China. On June 7, Ambassador Reinsch announced his resignation to Wilson in an angry letter. He lamented how "the great opportunity which has been held out to us by the Chinese people to assist in the development of education and free institutions will be gone beyond recall" because of Wilson's Shantung decision.[33]

As if to confirm Liang's and Reinsch's prophecies for China, a twenty-five-year-old Mao Zedong commented on Wilson's treaty decisions in 1919. Not yet a follower of the Bolsheviks, Mao surveyed the British military repression in India and other betrayals of Wilson's promises: "So much for national self-determination! I think it is really shameless!" Mao almost felt sorry for the former idealist Wilson. "Poor Wilson!" he wrote in July 1919. Mao joined the Communist Party in China that was founded two years later.[34]

The leader of the anti-treaty forces in the US, Henry Cabot Lodge, held Senate hearings in August and September 1919, and he invited critics of the treaty on self-determination. Now there was an opportunity for revenge on the hapless Wilson for all his nonmeetings and nonresponses.

The Egyptian anti-colonial leader, Zaghlul, arranged for an American lawyer named Joseph Folk to testify on his behalf at the Senate hearings, since only American citizens were allowed to appear before Congress. Folk, in his testimony on August 25, 1919, told the story of Zaghlul's arrival in Paris to find that recognition of British rule in Egypt was already in the treaty text. Then Folk related how Zaghlul and associates "asked to see President Wilson, but he could not see them." They asked "in the name of self-determination," Folk related, that the senators not approve the treaty provision that confirmed British colonial rule in Egypt.[35]

On August 28, William Monroe Trotter testified at the hearings and gleefully submitted to the senators all his unanswered petitions to Wilson from December 1918 to June 1919. In his testimony, Trotter wondered why Wilson had put a demand in the treaty that Poland respect equal rights for its minorities, but showed no interest in the demands of Black Americans for the same equal rights. He now asked the senators to amend the treaty with a declaration that "all citizens of the members of the league who belong to racial or religious minorities . . . shall enjoy the same treatment and same security in law and in fact as all persons of the majority race or religion."[36]

Next up before the Senate was an Irish American leader, Dudley Field Malone, whom Indian anti-colonial leaders had arranged to speak for them (again, since only Americans could testify). Malone related the story of Tilak appealing to the peace conference for Indian self-determination, an appeal that "received no reply." The British government had shown no interest whatsoever in Indian self-rule. If the Senate approved the league covenant, Malone said, it would break the hearts of 350 million people in India who wanted only democracy for themselves. Other heartbroken nonindependent peoples would include the Irish, Malone gratuitously added. Malone declared that he as an American could not support rushing through the Senate such a League of Nations design without hearing from "the people of every nation" affected by it. Malone's denial of support for the treaty was a major threat given the political power of Irish Americans. Tilak, watching in Paris, was delighted that the Senate had heard Indians' plea for self-determination, and he planned to follow up with more petitions to the League of Nations.[37]

Other witnesses deplored the treaty's mistreatment of China by giving the Shantung Peninsula to Japan, a sentiment that Lodge shared. Lodge tactically used these protests as part of his overall strategy to get the treaty rejected. While the rejection of the treaty is usually seen as the work of evil isolationists in the US, it has been mostly overlooked how Black leaders and anti-colonial activists also wanted to repudiate the Versailles settlement.[38]

Lenin could hardly believe his luck in getting an opponent with such a talent for self-sabotage. Wilson's Treaty of Versailles was "the heaviest blow the capitalists and imperialists of those luckless victor countries could possibly have struck at themselves," he told a congress in Moscow of "the Peoples of the East" on November 22, 1919. Lenin again identified Russia as an exploited nation on the border between Europe and Asia, between the West and the Rest. Russia had the credentials to lead the Rest's campaign against the West's imperialism.[39]

As if that weren't enough, Wilson boosted Lenin's credentials even more by deploying a minor American intervention into the Soviet Union itself. Wilson decided on the shambolic incursion into northwestern Russia and Siberia in collaboration with British and French forces in the summer of 1918, supposedly to protect Russia against Germany before the end of the war. It evolved into a lame attempt to support the anti-Bolshevik side in the Russian civil war. Five thousand American troops collaborated with the British and French in occupying Russia's Arctic ports of Murmansk and Archangel in August 1918. An American force of 145 officers and 4,805 men arrived in Siberia on September 2, 1918.[40]

With his less-than-perfect grasp of self-determination, Wilson declared the intervention was not really intervention because it was "in the interest of what the Russian people themselves desire." Accomplishing nothing, the token American attempt to save Russia did not last long. The last units of the American force in northwestern Russia had left by June 8, 1919. The Siberian expedition lingered a little longer, but the last American soldiers had left by April 1, 1920.[41]

Nevertheless, Lenin could now offer "the Peoples of the East" his own experience fighting the imperialists. "The struggle of the Soviet Republic," as Lenin referred to his resistance to the minor Western intervention, would lead the way in the global struggle "against the forces of united imperialism—of Germany, France, Britain and the USA."

Lenin said that Western claims of benevolent colonialism did not fool him and his fellow Peoples of the East. When Wilson and his allies "talk of handing out mandates for colonies," they were really handing out "mandates for spoliation and plunder" to the tiny minority of white exploiters. Now the Eastern peoples were "awakening," said Lenin. They would no longer be passive "objects of the enrichment of others." The Peoples of the East would now determine the "destiny of the whole world."[42]

Lenin had already deployed the new Communist International (Comintern) to mobilize opposition of colonial subjects to their colonizers. The founding Comintern congress met in Moscow on March 6, 1919, as the Versailles treaty text was reaching its final form in Paris. The congress noted that the great powers in Paris made all decisions in closed-door meetings, in contrast to the nonmeetings with many representatives of the rest of the world. Despite Wilson's supposed commitment to the "principle of the self-determination of peoples," the principle was already "trampled underfoot." The powers had denied independence to India and were handing over German colonies to new colonizers. The Comintern declaimed that "the revolutionary proletariats of all countries of the world must wage a resolute struggle against the Wilsonian notion of a 'League of Nations' and protest against entry into this union of plunder, exploitation and imperialist counter-revolution."[43]

The forced-labor debate had meanwhile languished. Wilson did not seize the opportunity to denounce Lenin's own embrace of forced labor for his own people under communism. It would have been hard to do so, because the other colonial powers failed to renounce forced labor during the critical years of 1918 to 1920.

As noted in the chapter on the Congo, forced labor in Africa became even more prevalent during World War I. The British, French, and Belgians fought the Germans in the African theater, with both sides conscripting natives into their armies to fight each other. The Europeans' forced labor and requisitions of food supplies from Africans left starvation in its wake, including in the Belgian Congo. It was a sad postscript to the campaign against forced labor in the Congo.

Some Versailles treaty negotiators at first considered banning forced labor in the colonies. In late 1918, a British peace proposal initially had some language prohibiting forced labor. An advisor to Wilson named George Beer and an advisor to British Prime Minister Lloyd George named P. H. Kerr had collaborated on this draft for the negotiations. In December 1918, they and some other like-minded advisors published a manifesto called "Windows of Freedom." The draft had a clause that would "prohibit forced labor in any shape or form." The British delegation put a ban on "slavery and forced labor" in their proposal for the covenant of the League of Nations in Paris on January 24, 1919.[44]

But by January 30 in Versailles, the same close-to-final draft that omitted the word *self-determination* also omitted the ban on forced labor. A "prohibition of abuses" banned "the slave trade" but not forced labor. The former was associated with Arabs and African chiefs; the latter was associated with colonial powers such as the Belgians and Germans. Perhaps the colonial powers did not want free labor principles to constrain them.[45]

Wilson's own drafts of the treaty text had never had any language banning forced labor. He and his international propaganda efforts had paid little or no attention to the issue.

The issue lingered in the background. There was a low-profile victory after the treaty signing, when officials inserted clauses against forced labor into each of the mandates in Africa and the Pacific. However, this was only after league officials also watered down the definition of forced labor. They still allowed forced labor for "essential public works and services." Later discussions at the League of Nations after the war suggested that forced labor for the natives was not really forced labor if they were only forced to work for their own good.[46]

Versailles's failure on forced labor was costly. A 1929 survey of practices in colonial Africa found forced labor in French

Cameroon, British Tanganyika, the Belgian Congo, and the Portuguese colonies.[47]

The mandates system gave the Belgians a chance to extend their toxic Congolese practices to the former German territory of Ruanda-Urundi (today's Rwanda and Burundi). The Belgians would indeed practice forced labor once again in Ruanda-Urundi, which contributed to a famine in Burundi in 1925 and 1926 and another one in Rwanda from 1928 to 1930. When World War II came along, the Belgians in the Congo resorted to forced labor for porters and rubber collectors all over again.[48]

Meanwhile, Wilson's failure to endorse either political or economic freedom in the colonies opened him to Lenin's mockery. In a revised edition of his book *Imperialism, the Highest Stage of Capitalism*, Lenin included a new foreword dated July 6, 1920. Lenin said Wilson's "brutal and despicable Treaty of Versailles" revealed the hypocrisy of the West. The West could not stick to its own values like "private property based on the labor of the small proprietor, free competition, [and] democracy." Versailles exposed the "civilizing enterprise" of the supposedly "advanced" countries as nothing more than "oppressing a thousand million people (in the colonies and semi-colonies)," Lenin taunted.[49]

Lenin was an all-too-effective skeptic on Western pretensions of being saviors of the Rest, making him an appealing alternative for anti-colonial leaders. The West had failed to counter him on both colonization and forced labor.

This was a tragedy, as the communist saviors were busy showing how they were even worse than the colonial ones. The brutal agricultural policies had caused harvests to fall. The consequence was famine, which arrived when a drought in mid-1921 reduced the harvest even further. Some thirty-three million people were on the verge of starvation. Peasants were eating grass, weeds, and rodents.

US Secretary of Commerce Herbert Hoover mobilized a huge international famine relief effort in response to Russian appeals. By the end of 1921, charity organizations like the Red Cross had shipped enough food to feed eleven million people.[50]

Like the Congo campaign and like some future aid efforts, the famine relief effort used some degrading images of those being helped. One of the most famous of today's NGOs—Save the Children—was involved in the famine relief efforts in Russia, having just been founded the previous year. As if the problem of Western condescension toward Russia wasn't bad enough, Save the Children used a posed photograph of emaciated children in its newsletter, just in time for the Christmas 1921 giving season, accompanied by some even worse poetry.[51]

The capitalists had to bail out Lenin's anti-capitalism. Lenin somewhat admitted defeat when he backed off the extreme agricultural coercion in 1921, but it would return a few years later in Stalin's forced collectivization that provoked an even bigger famine in Ukraine.

Yet apparently some anti-colonial leaders cared more about Lenin's message of self-determination than they cared about famine and violence. Native tyranny was still better to them than colonial tyranny. Someone gave Ho Chi Minh a copy of Lenin's anti-colonial writings in July 1920. Ho was converted to the Bolshevik vision: "This is what we need, this is the path to our liberation." A young Jawaharlal Nehru in 1919 doubted reports of Lenin's atrocities. "Horrible excesses are ascribed to the Bolshevists in Russia," Nehru acknowledged. "But if this is so then it is difficult to imagine how millions of human beings should prefer this terror and degradation and should voluntarily labour to bring it into existence." The Chinese nationalist leader Sun Yat-sen also overlooked the Bolshevik violence when he paid tribute to Lenin: "You, great man that you are, will live on in the memories of the oppressed people through the centuries."[52]

Wilson no longer inspired such tributes from anti-colonial leaders. Wilson had failed to include his own earlier language on self-determination and consent of the governed in the Treaty of Versailles. He had failed to embrace Japanese and African American proposals of racial equality. He had failed to assert any principle of free labor in Africa despite the appeals of Western liberals like Morel. He had failed to consult the Vietnamese and the Egyptians and the

Chinese and the Indians before deciding their fate. The bumbling former idealist had wound up with a settlement in 1919 that, far from competing with the Bolsheviks, had managed to offend almost every nation and race in the Rest, with fateful consequences that are still toxic a century later.

The continuance of colonialism and forced labor in the interwar period would create a propaganda gift for another hyperviolent leader, who would embarrass the West further into reconsidering liberal values.

15

Reductio ad Hitlerum

The year 1941 was the nadir of human liberty. The Nazis occupied most of Europe. The psychopathic Stalin ruled the USSR. Colonial powers occupied most of Asia and Africa. There were only eight liberal democracies left in the world, and five of these were denying democratic rights to non-white peoples at home or colonizing them abroad. There did not seem much hope of defeating fascism, communism, and colonialism anytime soon.[1]

In John Maynard Keynes's famous 1936 quote that ideas "are more powerful than is commonly understood," he also asserted that "madmen in authority" were "slaves of some defunct economist." The top-ranked madman in authority, Adolf Hitler, does seem like a slave to some bad ideas. Hitler embarrassed the West by taking the Development Right of Conquest to extremes. Hitler applied past Western precedents on population removal, forced labor, and colonial conquest to his genocidal campaigns against Jews and Eastern Europeans.[2]

Western leaders needed to answer his claim that his conquests and forced labor, with an extra dose of genocide, were just like theirs. This put the West in a bind, as its leaders explored whether they could renounce the right to conquer but still hold on to their colonies. The British and American reaction to Hitler's ideas determined much of the debate on liberal ideals around World War II and after. The classical liberal economist Ludwig von Mises was a lonely prewar liberal critic of Hitler, and his ideas would eventually become hugely influential. The British and the Americans produced some beautiful rhetoric but had a little trouble living up to their own words.

Hitler loved the Development Right of Conquest. But it is a fallacy to argue that an idea is bad just because Hitler liked it. Vegetarianism is not bad because Hitler was a vegetarian. This fallacy is invoked so frequently that it has gotten its own sardonic name, Reductio ad Hitlerum.[3]

One of the most effective users of the Reductio ad Hitlerum fallacy was . . . Hitler. Hitler taunted the British and the Americans: Look how much I am following the same principles you follow, just taken to their logical extreme.

As Hitler set out his understanding of "the laws of human development" in *Mein Kampf* in 1925 and 1926, he embraced conquest. He saw how "vast spaces still lie uncultivated all over the surface of the globe. Those spaces are only waiting for the ploughshare." Hitler avowed, "Nature did not set those territories apart as the exclusive pastures of any one nation or race to be held unutilized in reserve for the future." Nature instead wanted to give the land to those who could make the most of it: "Such land awaits the people who have the strength to acquire it and the diligence to cultivate it."[4]

According to Hitler, the advanced Germans were justified in taking land from the backward people. Instead of colonies in Asia and Africa, Hitler saw the Promised Land as lying right next to Germany in the East. To be exact, the conquests should be of "Russia and the border States subject to her." He said that that Russians were as racially inferior as Indians and Egyptians. He should conquer them to "acquire soil for the German plough by means of the German sword and thus provide the nation with its daily bread." Hitler had already announced in 1925 and 1926 his intention to conquer Poland and Russia in the name of global progress, which was equal in Hitler's mind to German progress.[5]

Hitler at first had considered commerce as an alternative to conquest. Instead of conquering lands to feed Germans, Hitler noted, Germany could export something else to pay for food imports: "Our industry and commerce had to be organized in such a manner as to secure an increase in the exports and thus be able to support our people." However, Hitler did not want to be dependent on other peoples for sustenance. Hitler worried that other nations would cut off food imports in time of war. He wanted to make "the national subsistence more or less independent of foreign countries and thus assure the freedom and independence of the nation."[6]

Moreover, he thought that exports to other people would require conquering those people anyway. Hitler believed the British could depend on exports only because they had conquered their colonies as markets for those exports. "No nation prepared the way for its commercial conquests more brutally than England did by means of the sword." Hitler admired how the British "use political power in order to gain economic advantages."

Even free trade was a kind of economic conquest to Hitler, and it required political and military conquest. He ridiculed the classical liberal argument for peaceful commerce without violent conquest, which "was probably the most completely nonsensical stuff ever raised to the dignity of a guiding principle in the policy of a State."[7]

Hitler's dismissal of trade was linked to his antisemitism. Hitler saw "finance and trade" as the "complete monopoly" of Jews. In his potted history, "the Jew began by lending out money at usurious interest, which is a permanent trade of his." Then "the Jew" became a "middleman" in goods trade. Hitler's sick mind justified antisemitic violence as an understandable reaction to this capitalist exploitation.[8]

Hitler believed the markets in finance and goods to be a zero-sum world, not a positive-sum world of equal partners benefiting from exchanges between them. Hitler did not get free trade.

Hitler also liked the idea of population removal within Germany itself. He would not allow "defective people" to "propagate defective offspring." His plan for forced sterilization was "perhaps a barbaric measure for those unfortunates." But preventing inferior people replacing the superior ones justified "temporary pain." Hitler thus also took eugenics to an extreme.[9]

Hitler liked forced labor. He celebrated how "the Aryan" had "subjugated inferior races and turned their physical powers into organized channels under his own leadership, forcing them to follow his will and purpose." Hitler invoked the venerable benevolent-slavery idea:

> By imposing on them a useful, though hard, manner of employing their powers [the Aryan] not only spared the lives of those whom he had conquered but probably made their lives easier than these had been in the former state of so-called "freedom."[10]

Hitler was delighted to cite some American precedents. As he said in 1928, Americans "gunned down the millions of Redskins to a few hundred thousand, and now keep the modest remnant under observation in a cage."[11]

And he loved the 1924 US immigration restrictions on Asians and Eastern European Slavs and Jews as a model for Germany. He praised the US for "excluding certain races from the right to become naturalized as citizens," in which they embraced "principles similar to those on which we wish to ground the People's State."[12]

After the war began, Hitler gave even more colonial precedents for his conquests, although only intermittently. His version of the Rest lumped together Slavs and Jews with other allegedly inferior races of Native Americans, Asians, and Africans. Hitler's great lumping was much like that of Du Pont, Ledyard, and Napoleon over a century earlier. As Hitler invaded Poland in the fall of 1939, he told Joseph Goebbels, "Only force is effective with the Poles," because "Asia begins in Poland." The Nazi governor of occupied Poland, Hans Frank, in 1942 ominously referred to the Jews of Galicia as "flat-foot Indians." The equivalence of Eastern Europeans with Native Americans and Asians went back to eighteenth-century

German history. Frederick the Great of Prussia had justified his own eighteenth-century conquests of parts of Poland by likening the "slovenly Polish trash" to the Iroquois.[13]

Hitler returned to the theme of Western precedents after invading Russia in 1941. He told a German military officer to treat the natives harshly, because "Russia is our Africa, and the Russians are our Negroes." Pontificating to his mealtime companions from his headquarters, he declared in October 1941 that the German invasion of Russia repeated the same process as "the conquest of America." Shuffling a full deck of Western conquests, Hitler announced, "Our Mississippi must be the Volga, not the Niger."[14]

Or, as Hitler used another colonial analogy, "What India was for England, the territories of Russia will be for us." As the British saw the Indians, so he saw the Slavic world: "Nothing will drag it out of its indolence unless one compels the people to work." Like Thomas Carlyle on Africans, Hitler saw the Slavs as "a mass of born slaves, who feel the need of a master."

Hitler half imitated, half ridiculed the British for pretending their conquest of India was for the Indians' own good. They posed as saviors of Indian women by banning the burning of widows known as *suttee*, but they only cared about their profits from Indian workers: "The prohibition of suttee for widows . . . [was] dictated to the English by the desire not to reduce the labour-force, and perhaps also by the desire to economise wood!"

The population removal idea had reached its most horrific form. Hitler thought it so wrong that a "higher people"—the Germans—"should painfully exist on a soil too narrow for it." In contrast, Ukrainians, "which contribute nothing to civilization, occupy infinite tracts of a soil that is one of the richest in the world." The incompetence of the natives had left Ukraine a "desert" that "we shall populate." He would turn over Ukraine to a settler colony of Germans to "Europeanize" the steppe, where they would "look upon the natives as Redskins." Referring sarcastically to white trades with the Redskins, Hitler said, "We'll supply the Ukrainians with scarves, glass beads and everything that colonial peoples like." Hitler announced that he would screen Ukrainians "carefully" for survival but fatally indicated that all Jews would fail the test.

Any qualms about German conquests were no more valid than qualms about Canada, Hitler said, where "we don't think about the despoiled Indians." As the Ukrainians and Russians increasingly fought back against Hitler's destiny for them in 1942, Hitler noted, "The struggle we are waging there against the Partisans resembles very much the struggle in North America against the Red Indians." Hitler was a fan of the version of the Development Right of Conquest that applied to the land rather than the people. He conquered Ukraine to develop the land, not the Ukrainians.[15]

To Hitler, the idea of equality was a Jewish trick to keep the Aryans from coming out on top. The "cunning Jew" had a "theory with which he wants to infect the public, namely that all men are equal."[16]

It was embarrassing how few liberals there were left to give a rejoinder to Hitler, after the decline of the liberal emphasis on consent described in the previous chapters. Hitler's most consistent liberal critic in the interwar generation revived Smith's critique of colonial conquests. This was the Austrian economist Ludwig von Mises, a fervent advocate for free markets. Mises had little influence at the time, but the views he represented would have huge influence later on in boosting the tradition of promarket economic thinking in the twentieth century. These thinkers would be known by various (not exactly equivalent) labels as Austrians, classical liberals, the Mont Pelerin Society, the Chicago school, and libertarians. Outside of those who embraced those labels was a much larger group of market-friendly neoclassical economists who would share many of Mises's views. But all that lay far in the future.

Mises was born in 1881 in what is now Lviv, Ukraine, which was then part of the Austro-Hungarian Empire. He came from a Jewish noble family. His family moved to Vienna soon after his birth. He became a well-known economist and anti-fascist critic in Vienna. Mises fled Vienna in 1934 because of the rise of the Austrian Nazis. He became a professor in Geneva, then had to flee again as the war began. In 1940, Mises just barely escaped Europe in time after a perilous journey across France, Spain, and Portugal, to catch a ship bound for New York. He spent the rest of his career in New York, as a teacher at New York University.[17]

His 1927 book *Liberalism* (much later republished to a wider audience in 1962) had a long discussion of colonialism, along with denunciations of fascism and communism. The Nazis ordered Mises's publisher to destroy all copies of the book after Hitler came to power.[18]

Mises recalled the horrors of the Belgian Congo as documented by the Congo reformers. He noted that Americans had "waged a war of extermination against the original inhabitants of the land." He hated the idea that conquest made it possible "for primitive peoples to share in the blessings of European civilization." Such civilizing was intrinsically violent. His fierce language echoed that of Smith:

> No chapter of history is steeped further in blood than the history of colonialism. Blood was shed uselessly and senselessly. Flourishing lands were laid waste; whole peoples destroyed and exterminated. All this can in no way be extenuated or justified.

The colonizers' "sanguinary cruelty rivals the despotic system of the Bolsheviks." Mises embraced the ideal of self-determination. Mises asserted "the right of the inhabitants of every territory to decide on the state to which they wish to belong." Liberalism rejected what he explicitly called "the right of conquest."

In the end, despite some contradictory instincts, Mises went further than almost all other Western economists of his own and the previous generation did—he called for an end to colonialism. European colonies "since the age of the great discoveries stand in the sharpest contrast to all the principles of liberalism."

The liberal economist Mises reached a similar destination as the illiberal anti-colonial activists in the end: "The final goal must continue to be the complete liberation of the colonies from the despotic rule under which they live today."[19]

Mises was a consistent liberal on the treatment of despised groups (to one of which he belonged). He had been a critic in 1919 of US immigration restrictions targeting, among others, "Czechs, Japanese, Chinese."[20] He criticized the semicolonial regime of the West in China, in which "foreign armies and navies," using "violent methods," imposed capitalism at gunpoint. This coerced commerce was a good way to discredit the liberal values underlying markets, Mises lamented.[21]

Mises also denounced eugenics. He contrasted his beloved laissez-faire with the Nazi eugenics program that targeted the allegedly unfit. The Führer "aimed at abolishing *laisser-faire* not only in the production of material goods, but no less in the production of men." Mises believed that the Western eugenicists deserved for Hitler to discredit them: "It is vain for the champions of eugenics to protest that they did not mean what the Nazis executed."[22]

Again, Mises repeated the classical defense of laissez-faire against its enemies—eugenics, slavery, concentration camps, and colonialism. This did not necessarily decide the debate on laissez-faire versus much milder state interventions, although Mises probably wanted it to.

Although far from embracing the liberalism of Mises for non-Western peoples, the Western Allies needed to reject Hitler's claims that his conquests were just like theirs. A key moment came in August 1941. Franklin D. Roosevelt and Winston Churchill secretly met aboard a British warship anchored in Placentia Bay off the coast of Newfoundland. Hitler had already defeated France and invaded Russia. Roosevelt and Churchill agreed on a joint statement of only four hundred words, released by telegram to a surprised world at 9 a.m. on August 14, 1941. It became known as the Atlantic Charter, and it would play a key role during the war and afterward in the clash of free ideals with fascism, colonialism, and communism.[23]

The Allies renounced conquests—at least new ones. They promised "no territorial changes that do not accord with the freely expressed wishes of the people concerned." The same people had the right "to choose the form of government under which they will live." Roosevelt and Churchill declared, "They wish to see sovereign rights and self-government restored to those who have been forcibly deprived of them."

The charter had a vision that all states should have equal access to global trade. All nations should cooperate to promote "economic advancement."

The charter said its promises of freedom applied to "all the men in all the lands," applying within nations as well as across nations.[24]

It was a breathtaking vision of liberal ideals, seemingly rejecting all at once fascism, colonialism, and communism. It embraced self-government, the consent of the governed, freedom to trade, and equal rights for everyone.

It was not quite what it seemed. Winston Churchill realized he may have gotten a little carried away with his own eloquence. He was still a big enthusiast for the British Empire, so he quickly tried to backtrack on the Charter's universal promises. Speaking to Parliament three weeks later on September 9, 1941, Churchill limited the application of the self-government ideal. Churchill said he and Roosevelt "had in mind, primarily, the restoration of the sovereignty, self-government and national life of the States and nations of Europe now under the Nazi yoke." They did not have in mind the "separate problem" of what to do with colonial peoples "which owe allegiance to the British Crown."[25]

Nice try. Many leaders of colonial peoples had already taken the charter to mean exactly what it said. An up-and-coming Black lawyer in South Africa named Nelson Mandela said the Atlantic Charter inspired him to create a charter for the African National Congress fighting against apartheid. Mandela emphasized dignity as what mattered most. As Mandela later recalled his feelings at the time: "The Atlantic Charter of 1941, signed by Roosevelt and Churchill, reaffirmed faith in the dignity of each human being."[26]

Nelson Mandela invoked the idea of dignity that had played such an important role in liberal ideals. He would describe the battle against apartheid as driven by a quest for dignity as a central human need. "Africans have a highly developed sense of dignity," he explained. Under apartheid, "the lack of human dignity experienced by Africans is the direct result of the policy of white supremacy." Apologists for apartheid had often pointed out that Black South Africans were on average materially better off than most other Africans were. To Mandela, this accurate empirical statement was beside the point. The apologists failed to recognize Black people's nonmaterial need for dignity, which the apologists could only address with "equal political rights."

After Mandela began his campaign of resistance to apartheid, he celebrated "the dignity that comes from not having succumbed to oppression and fear." Upon his incarceration in a South African prison in 1964, Mandela declared, "Any man or institution that tries to rob me of my dignity will lose because I will not part with it at any price or under any pressure." After his release from prison thirty years later, he would celebrate the end of apartheid in 1994 as "a common victory for justice, for peace, for human dignity." He described the animating spirit of his life as a "desire for the freedom of my people to live their lives with dignity and self-respect."[27]

To Mandela, the Atlantic Charter had also affirmed the liberal ideal of reciprocity. If Europeans were fighting for their rights against Nazis, they should respect non-Europeans fighting for their rights against Europeans. Therefore, Mandela hoped South African whites and their regime would understand "the principles they were fighting for in Europe were the same ones we were advocating at home."[28]

Mohandas Gandhi also appealed to the reciprocity implied by the Atlantic Charter. Writing Roosevelt on July 1, 1942, Gandhi told him that "the Allied declaration that [they] are fighting to make the world safe for freedom of the individual and for democracy sounds hollow." Britain still fought to hold on to empire in India and Africa, Gandhi reminded FDR, while "America has the Negro problem in her own home."

Meanwhile, Madame Chiang Kai-shek toured the US in 1943 to gain support for her husband's fight against the Japanese. She invoked the Atlantic Charter as a contradiction of the insulting US ban on Chinese immigration.[29]

The appeals for reciprocity inspired action. On September 2, 1945, Ho Chi Minh addressed a gathering in Hanoi's Ba Đình Square. The veteran of the failed attempts at self-determination in Paris in 1919, by now a longtime communist, hoped for a better outcome this time. He declared independence for Vietnam from French colonial rule, quoting the American Declaration of Independence and the 1791 French Declaration of the Rights of Man and of the Citizen. He now expected that the victorious Allies, having "acknowledged the principles of self-determination and equality of nations, will not refuse to acknowledge the independence of Vietnam."[30] But the US sided with the French instead of Ho.

Despite the promises of self-determination and equal rights in the Atlantic Charter, both the US and the UK fatally hesitated about ending colonialism at the end of the war. Their reluctance did further damage to the cause of promoting liberal ideals.

The West's wording of the UN Charter in 1945 still had language on colonial territories almost identical to that of the League of Nations covenant twenty-six years earlier. Some advanced countries should administer "territories whose peoples have not yet attained a full measure of self-government." These colonial rulers "accept as a sacred trust" an obligation to promote "the well-being of the inhabitants of these territories." These rulers' goal was allegedly the "political, economic, social, and educational advancement" of their colonial subjects. They only had a vague commitment to "protection against abuses," which meant the colonial rulers protected subjects against . . . the colonial rulers.

The UN Charter acknowledged only another vague commitment to eventual "self-government." The colonizer promised colonial subjects only "to assist them in the progressive development of their free political institutions." The old idea that some people were too backward for freedom still survived. Rights for peoples depended on each people's "varying stages of advancement." The charter saw a colonial system barely different from the League of Nations mandate system.[31]

Meanwhile, the other World War II victor, the Soviet Union, oversaw a rapid spread of communism through Russian conquest and/or backing of local Communist Parties. It helped that Stalin could continue the Leninist legacy of support for national self-determination, while the West had failed to end colonialism. He was surprisingly successful in getting anti-colonial activists to overlook his own violation of self-determination in Eastern Europe.

The other momentous development was the triumph of communism in China. Mao Zedong celebrated the birth of the People's Republic of China in 1949 with a reference to China's semicolonial history: "Ours will no longer be a nation subject to insult and humiliation. We have stood up." Mao foresaw how China could appeal to the anti-colonial movement elsewhere: "Our revolution has won the sympathy and acclaim of the people of all countries. We have friends all over the world."[32]

The Development Right of Conquest was still alive in the West. But Hitler's demonic twist on the advanced nations' right to colonize backward ones had finally provoked some other liberal thinkers to renounce any such right. The liberals would have to contend with the illiberalism of anti-colonial movements that was partly a reaction to the West's failure to recognize self-determination.

PART IV

THE AMBIVALENT ADVANCE OF FREEDOM, 1945–PRESENT

The great and terrible war which has now ended was a war made possible by the denial of the democratic principles of the dignity, equality and mutual respect of men, and by the propagation, in their place, through ignorance and prejudice, of the doctrine of the inequality of men and races.

Constitution of the United Nations Educational, Scientific, and Cultural Organization, 1945

16

The Fall of Colonialism and the Invention of the Third World

After the nadir of liberty during World War II, an age began of victories for the right to consent to your own development. The fall of colonialism and the rise of country self-development were a breakthrough for national self-determination. A resurgence in the classical ideal of individual freedom was led by political philosophers like Isaiah Berlin and economists like Milton Friedman. Berlin also saw citizens of independent states as preferring local autocrats to the colonial ones that did not respect the equal dignity of the Rest. The end of colonialism signified a rejection of the Development Right of Conquest by the West.

The end of eugenics after World War II, the termination of anti–Eastern European national quotas, the rise of women's rights, and the rejection of segregation for Black people were a gigantic reversal of the policies of the previous illiberal century.

In the middle of all this, the idea of Third World development was invented, with momentous consequences. The Asian-African Conference in Bandung, Indonesia, in April 1955 was the origin of the term *Third World*. The phrase was not pejorative, nor did it have roots in colonialism; it just referred to the conference's search for a nonaligned third way in the Cold War between the First World of the West and the Second World of the communist bloc in Eastern Europe. The conference embraced the new notion of Third World development. The Third World was undecided between the capitalist and communist approaches to development offered by the First and Second Worlds. Bandung's aura only grew over time with later retrospectives that celebrated the Third World leaders present in Bandung, such as Mao, Kwame Nkrumah, Jomo Kenyatta, Ho Chi Minh, and Fidel Castro.

Every sentence in the previous paragraph is wrong. But all of these assertions were made in later descriptions of Bandung, as well as in conventional histories of the development idea. What the Bandung participants had in common was not Cold War neutrality, or a self-image as Third World, but opposition to colonialism and racism.[1]

The Bandung conference symbolized the great victories over colonialism and racism that were happening and continued to happen throughout the 1950s and 1960s. The worst forms of the West's coercion and paternalism in the Rest were going down to defeat. The ideal of collective self-determination for the peoples of the Rest replaced the West's open espousal of its own ethnic superiority to develop those peoples. Bandung really symbolized the rejection of the Development Right of Conquest. These victories dramatically reversed the trend of coercion displacing consent in the previous period.

Yet the victory was not as complete as it could have been. The West's identification with colonialism had already weakened the liberal side. The myth of the invention of Third World development shows how such development was blind from the beginning to the colonial roots of the Third World concept, which as we have seen went back two centuries. The postcolonial rulers suppressed political and economic freedom as much as the colonial rulers had, even if their populations seemed to prefer native autocrats to foreign ones. All this would contribute to an anti-liberal consensus in the mainstream of development thought. The West shifted from its own colonial autocracy to supporting postcolonial autocracy in the name of progress.

Although there were huge advances away from the bad old policies of the colonial era, postcolonial states and development agencies had still not fully renounced them.

A lonely liberal named Carlos Romulo at Bandung unsuccessfully protested, as later did Isaiah Berlin. It would take more rounds of debates on liberalism for it to advance further.

The phrase *Third World* had already been invented three years earlier by a French demographer named Alfred Sauvy, but it was not used in Bandung in 1955. Sauvy himself in 1952 did use the term as referring to parts of the world not in the capitalist or communist spheres, but he also equated it to the phrase "underdeveloped countries." Sauvy did have in mind colonial attitudes toward the Third World, as he defined it also as the part of the world that was "ignored, exploited, despised." As a demographer, Sauvy worried most about explosive population growth in the Third World leading to catastrophic revolution. He asked his readers: "Do not you hear on the Côte d'Azur, the shouts that reach us from the other end of the Mediterranean, from Egypt or Tunisia?" Third World population growth would mean "pressure constantly increases in the human boiler," which required some kind of First World action to "prevent the explosion."[2]

The *Third World* term did not take off until the 1960s and did not become widespread until the 1970s and 1980s. Sauvy himself did not use his own term in a book he published in 1961. The label "underdeveloped countries" was to him like the old language of "barbarians, infidels, savages, natives, coloured men." The new term still had the "implication of superiority."

The concerns about Third World population growth were similar, he said, to the "yellow peril" idea. This was an echo of the eugenics favored in the late nineteenth and early twentieth centuries, which sought to reduce the population of allegedly inferior groups. Massive efforts to reduce Third World population growth would be part of the new development orthodoxy.[3]

Meanwhile, back in Bandung, neither Mao, nor Nkrumah, nor Kenyatta, nor Ho Chi Minh, nor Fidel Castro actually attended the

Asian-African Conference in Bandung, Indonesia, in April 1955. Fidel Castro's absence may be explained by the fact that he was not yet in power in Cuba, or possibly that he was in the Isle of Pines prison at the time of Bandung, or possibly that Cuba is not in Asia or Africa.[4]

The supposed neutrality of all countries participating in Bandung is also a myth. Most of the twenty-nine states there had decisively aligned themselves with either the West or the Soviets. Only three to ten of the states were neutral, depending on how strictly you define neutral. In fact, Bandung is more notable for the sharp debate among the Asian and African leaders on communism than for any supposed Third Way between communism and capitalism.[5]

The host of the conference was Sukarno, who had been president of Indonesia since its independence from the Dutch in 1949. Speaking to the African and Asian delegates at the opening of the conference, Sukarno affirmed the reaction to past Western humiliation. Sukarno said we are united "by a common detestation of colonialism in whatever form it appears. We are united by a common detestation of racialism." We have been "the voiceless ones in the world," Sukarno said. "We have been the un-regarded, the peoples for whom decisions were made by others whose interests were paramount, the peoples who lived in poverty and humiliation." Sukarno showed a demand for dignity and respect in the Rest.

Asserting equality with the West, the conference communiqué therefore denounced "the subjection of peoples to alien subjugation, domination and exploitation" and called on the Western colonial powers to "grant freedom and independence to such peoples."[6]

The UN Charter in 1945 had asserted "faith in fundamental human rights, in the dignity and worth of the human person, in the equal rights of men and women and of nations large and small." This was before listing development as a separate objective, "to promote social progress and better standards of life in larger freedom," which still insisted on freedom as part of what defined progress. As the Universal Declaration of Human Rights avowed in 1948, "All human beings are born free and equal in dignity and rights."[7]

The Bandung leaders stressed development as an objective. They recognized "the urgency of promoting economic development in the Asian-African region." But such development efforts were not going to violate national self-determination as in the past; they had to be consistent with "respect for national sovereignty."[8]

Many of the participants at Bandung had a notably anti-liberal approach to attaining equal dignity. Zhou Enlai, Mao's deputy, was there to represent Communist China. Zhou was unapologetic in offering communism as a template, claiming China's first five-year plan (echoing Stalin's famous five-year plans) was the best path toward industrialization. "We Communists do not hide the fact that we believe in communism and that we consider the socialist system a good system," Zhou said in Bandung.[9]

Even though many delegates rejected communism, Zhou was still able to find "common ground" with them "in doing away with the sufferings and calamities under colonialism." Zhou could also counterpose China to the West in recognizing "equality of races." The West's past commitment to racial colonialism was the gift that kept on giving for communist propagandists.[10]

The most liberal thinker at Bandung was the Filipino diplomat Carlos Romulo. Romulo's life had prepared him well to be a spokesman for liberalism for the Rest. Romulo was born in 1899 during the US war of conquest of the Philippines. His father fought alongside Aguinaldo for Filipino independence. American soldiers seeking his father's location waterboarded his grandfather to reveal it. A formative experience in his teenage years was going to the Manila Army and Navy Club to meet an American friend, only to be turned away by the Filipino busboy enforcing the club's whites-only rule.

But Romulo saw also a more favorable side of America. The colonial effort brought American teachers to the Philippines. Romulo remembered how these teachers in his high school identified the Filipino struggle for independence from America with American heroes like Washington, Jefferson, and Lincoln.

Romulo later studied for an MA at Columbia University. He was involved in the successful 1934 fight for the US Congress to pass the Tydings–McDuffie Act for Filipino independence; it promised independence on July 4, 1946. During World War II, Romulo joined the US Army as the press officer for General Douglas MacArthur. The army eventually promoted Romulo to brigadier general. He was one of the seventy-five thousand Filipinos who fought on the American side against the Japanese during the doomed fight at Bataan in 1942, after which the Japanese occupied the islands. He returned to the Philippines in 1944 to wade ashore with MacArthur in the reconquest of the islands.[11]

General Romulo was head of the Filipino delegation to the United Nations founding conference in San Francisco in 1945. He proclaimed on the Allied triumph, "This is a victory for the whole world, not for one race, one nation, or one leader, but for all men." He recounted how during his wartime tours he heard much of "the flame of hope that swept the Far East when the Atlantic Charter was made known to the world." Eastern peoples, he said, asked whether the Charter was "for one race and not for them too?" Romulo argued in 1945, mostly unsuccessfully, for the UN Charter to recognize independence for colonies.[12]

Having embraced liberal values against colonialism, Romulo in 1955 at Bandung also argued for opposition "to every form of domination, subjugation, or the exploitation of peoples," which to him included communism. He noted that the intention of communists to subvert and subjugate noncommunist states was "the explicit declaration of international communism." He noted the 1950 Chinese attack on South Korea and quoted Chinese officials on their aim to sponsor armed rebellions in other Asian countries. He was appalled that "Communists see violence as the sole means of achieving social reform." The communists believed "the way to justice is through murder," "the way to freedom is through tyranny," and "the way to plenty for the people is through the confiscation of all they own by the state." Having fought colonial tyranny, he later said, why should Asians "now accept willingly Communist totalitarianism"?[13]

In Bandung in 1955, Romulo concurred with Sukarno in his speech to the conference: "All of us here are concerned with the matter of racial equality." Romulo declared, "There has not been and there is not a Western colonial regime, which has not imposed, to a greater or lesser degree, on the people it ruled the doctrine of their own racial inferiority." The West "have yet to learn," Romulo lamented, "how deeply this issue cuts and how profoundly it unites non-Western peoples who may disagree on all sorts of questions." Romulo himself had felt, as a teenager at the Manila Army and Navy Club, the "searing experience of being demeaned in our own lands, of being systematically relegated to subject status," while the "Western white man assumed that his superiority lay in his very bones, in the color of his skin."

Romulo said racism was the "driving force in the development of the nationalist movements in our many lands." Independence was to regain "a status of simple manhood"; it was worth great sacrifice to attain it.

Now, Romulo said, economic development was indeed an imperative, but he rejected both colonial paternalism and communist violence. We need "to be free to seek our own way," he said. It was up to "the peoples of Asia and Africa" how they "go about the business of transforming their lives and their societies."

However critical of Western racism, General Romulo appreciated the long-standing Western liberal tradition of equality and anti-imperialism. "This kind of racist attitude has been the practice not of all white men, but only of some," Romulo declared, and "it flies in the face of their own profoundest religious beliefs and political goals and aspirations." Romulo asked the delegates to remember that "this white world which has fostered racism" had also done better things. "Western political thought has given us all so many of our basic ideas of political freedom, justice, and equity."[14]

Three years after Bandung, a Western political thinker appeared sharing Romulo's ideals of freedom, justice, and equity for the Rest. Isaiah Berlin gave his inaugural lecture as Chichele professor of social and political theory at Oxford in 1958. The lecture became Berlin's most influential essay, "Two Concepts of Liberty," and it set out ideas he continued to expound for the rest of his life.

Berlin traced two strands of thought that went from the eighteenth-century Enlightenment to twentieth-century events. The first strand emphasized individuals' rights to choose for themselves. The second strand saw enlightened philosophers choosing for individuals because philosophers knew what was best. It was Smith versus Condorcet again.

The "scientific experts" in the second strand "believe that all political and moral problems can be turned into technological ones." The experts knew best what was the technologically right answer and so must treat everyone else "as if they were incapable of choices." The experts must choose for them.

The problem was that any ruler could claim to be the rational expert imposing solutions by force. Hence, that argument was "used by every dictator, inquisitor and bully who seeks for moral justification for his conduct."

Most dangerous was the concept of liberty implied by the expert-force idea. The liberal branch of the Enlightenment said that liberty just meant individuals choosing for themselves. The not-so-liberal Enlightenment branch said liberty was not about individuals actually choosing anything. It was freedom to have what was in their own interests.

Therefore, in this anti-liberal view, the philosopher elites were not really violating my right to choose, because they were imposing what I should have chosen anyway. To Berlin, it was a "monstrous impersonation" to equate what I should have chosen with what I actually choose. The elites could argue "that I may be coerced for my own good which I am too blind to see," but it is even worse for them to say because it is what I really wanted that "I am not being coerced."

Escalating the danger even more was the Enlightenment belief that "there is a final solution," Berlin said. This belief saw no trade-offs, no competing goals, no intractable problems; the experts could solve everything:

> There was one true solution to any problem, as opposed to the many false ones, and that the truth could be discovered

> by a rational thinker, and demonstrated so clearly that all other rational men could not but accept it.

With this kind of not-very-liberal liberty, totalitarian regimes might justify unlimited violence to impose the right solution. Berlin traced the embrace of a compulsory final solution back to Condorcet's utopian faith in agents of progress at the end of the eighteenth century.[15]

Berlin's own life experience made him a well-qualified observer of these ideologies. Berlin was born ten years after Romulo in 1909 in Riga, in what is now Latvia and was then in the Russian Empire. His Jewish family fled Riga in 1915 to escape antisemitic violence. By 1917, they were in Petrograd, where the eight-year-old Isaac witnessed the Bolshevik Revolution. He later recalled a vivid memory of the Bolsheviks taking away an old policeman to be executed.

Not willing to live under the Bolsheviks in Petrograd or the antisemites in Riga, the Berlins immigrated to London in 1921. They belonged to the intersection of two disliked groups—Jews and Eastern Europeans—that had flooded into the UK since the late nineteenth century. This dislike had triggered efforts in Britain at restricting immigration (as also in America at around the same time). Berlin later ruefully described the American immigration quota system as distinguishing "classy countries" in northwestern Europe from Eastern European countries—including Russia—that had "no class at all."[16]

Berlin was also aware of debates on the British White Man's Burden. As a student and later a professor at Oxford, Berlin encountered the group of British thinkers that had earlier helped draft the paternalist colonial decrees of the Treaty of Versailles. Berlin later remembered them as "quasi-intellectual imperialist ideologists."[17]

Berlin served during World War II as a British diplomat in the United States. British government policy sadly forced him to downplay the early reports of the Holocaust to evade pressure for admitting Jewish refugees to Palestine. Meanwhile in his old hometown of Riga, the Nazis and their Latvian collaborators murdered most of

Riga's forty thousand Jewish men, women, and children from 1941 to 1944. Soviet troops recaptured Latvia in October 1944, after which the Soviets subjected Riga to their own brand of tyranny.[18]

Berlin in his writings seldom referred to the Holocaust. A rare exception was in a letter to the American diplomat George Kennan in 1951, later titled for publication as "On Human Dignity." He described to Kennan a "really unutterable kind of horror." Nazi troopers had told the men, women, and children they loaded "into trains bound for gas chambers" that "they were going to emigrate to some happier place." For Berlin, this demonic deception had also illustrated the bankruptcy of far more sincere claims of coercing people for their own good. Like Kant, he denied any right to use other men for our own purposes, "purposes which these men, if they realized what we were doing, might reject." On this, all the ideologies were guilty. The Russian Revolution, the colonial White Man's Burdens, the Nazi pursuit of perfect German-ness were all guilty. It appalled Berlin that anyone would think that "only the victors deserve to be heard" on what is progress, that "the victims are not allowed to testify" on what they think of this alleged progress. He would spend the rest of his life speaking for the victims.[19]

Berlin saw the Enlightenment thinkers that rejected laissez-faire wholesale as a threat to liberty. Citing the nineteenth-century utopian socialist Comte Henri de Saint-Simon in a 1952 lecture, Berlin noted "his cries that individual liberty is dangerous and must be suppressed." Saint-Simon according to Berlin therefore rejected "laissez–faire," the idea of "the divine Smith," because it "leads to absolute chaos." Utopian socialists believed in economic planning: "It is quite impossible to get anything done unless we plan things, direct things from the center." Some planners thought ominously that labor "must be compulsory if necessary" to fulfill the plan, Berlin noted. Forced labor went together with planning.

The dangers to liberty arose even more when planners had only "concrete" measures of progress, just aiming at "satisfying the greatest number of needs." With objective progress, planners didn't need to consult anyone on what they actually wanted. The heirs of Condorcet, the opponents of Smith, the supposed satisfiers of the greatest number of human needs, were the planners "who ignore or despise what men are and what they live by."[20]

However, Berlin certainly did not embrace the free market with the same fervor as Ludwig von Mises. He did not share the slippery-slope notion of Friedrich Hayek, in which even a milder degree of state direction was still the "road to serfdom." Berlin in 1952 thought that economic planning could take "mild and humane forms in the case of, for example, the American New Deal, or the post-war socialist State in England." But planning could also take "violent, ruthless, brutal, fanatical forms in the case of directively planned Fascist and Communist societies." There was a continuum of compulsion; nobody should equate New Dealers with Nazis; everyone should be judged on a continuum on how much violence they were willing to endorse.[21]

Berlin's vision of liberty led him to reject colonialism as well as fascism and communism. Men and women did not want only the material benefits that colonizers supposedly brought. Men and women also wanted others to recognize them as human beings, who were entitled to choose their own paths according to their own purposes.

From the viewpoint of a colonial subject, Berlin elaborated, the lack of recognition could be both individual and collective. "I may feel unfree in the sense of not being recognized as a self-governing individual human being; but I may feel it also as a member of an unrecognized or insufficiently respected group." To those who did not understand my need for recognition, it seemed "an unintelligible paradox" that I would prefer to be "misgoverned by some member of my own oppressed class or race" to being "well and tolerantly treated" by a white ruler.

The British Empire had seen their African subjects as children and themselves as schoolmasters. Berlin declared for himself, "I object to paternalism, I mean, ultimately, I think, what I object to is being treated like a schoolboy." Respecting the principle of reciprocity, he therefore recognized Africans' rights to not be treated like schoolboys.[22]

Berlin averred that the demand in African and Asian nations was for "equality of status." Berlin's use of *status* was similar to how Smith and Kant had used *dignity*. "A lot of persons coming to them with, for example, offers of help, or offers of aid" did NOT meet this demand for status. The demand was NOT met when we "give them quite different things, such as economic prosperity or other blessings."[23]

Berlin thought that the history of the West humiliating the Rest was partly to blame for the partial failure of liberal ideals to spread from the West to the Rest. If the Russians "had not been treated as a barbarous mass by the West in the 19th century," if the Chinese had not been "humiliated by opium wars," they might not have been so tempted by communism, which "promised them to inherit the earth." They found appealing ideas under which they would be "victors over the very people who . . . despised them and mocked them and looked down upon them."[24]

Romulo and Berlin represented a lucid moment on both collective and individual agency—the right to choose for yourself. Such a moment had not happened for over a century. And clarity on freedom of choice was often lost afterward.

Nevertheless, as with other times in the history of liberal ideas, the liberals seemed to lose the intellectual argument but then turned out to win on what actually happened. They had recognized the demand for self-determination as a value in itself.

The vast majority of former colonies gained independence in the 1950s and 1960s. The number of independent states particularly surged in the early 1960s.

The long struggle of self-determination against the Development Right of Conquest had finally yielded a great victory. After the grim centuries of conquest, slavery, and colonialism, the new nations now had far more power to accept or reject others' plans for their development. This would help make possible the more benevolent development efforts of the latter half of the twentieth century.

In this story, however, victories are often only partial triumphs. Self-determination of nations often masked violent suppression of self-determination for minorities. According to a later accounting in 2006, forty-seven states were perpetrating violence against seventy-two ethnic groups around the world. The violence included forced resettlement, torture, systematic killings, ethnic cleansing, reprisal killings, and military campaigns against rebels. There were also some violent movements among the minority groups themselves. Well-known examples of such minority groups included Palestinians, Darfuris, Uyghurs, Rohingya, and Tutsis. It was an echo of the population removals of the colonial era.[25]

Most of the new postcolonial governments were far from embracing liberal values. The postcolonial autocrats rejected economic freedom as well as political freedom. To Kwame Nkrumah in newly independent Ghana, the colonialists had demonstrated capitalism was inevitably tied to colonial exploitation. He rejected the capitalism of the colonizers who "took our lands, our lives, our resources and our dignity. Without exception, they left us nothing but our resentment."[26]

W. E. B. Du Bois, who had announced in 1903 that the problem of the twentieth century was the problem of the color line, now was a proponent of communism. The ninety-year-old Du Bois wrote a speech to be read to an All-African Peoples Conference hosted by Kwame Nkrumah in Accra in 1958. He thought the collective quest for African dignity required the sacrifice of individual liberty: "Give up individual rights for the needs of Mother Africa." Du Bois saw the best way to pursue the quest as socialism:

> Africa, awake! Put on the beautiful robes of Pan-African socialism. You have nothing to lose but your chains! You have a continent to regain! You have freedom and human dignity to attain![27]

The socialism and violence of postcolonial states were a major setback for liberals like Carlos Romulo and Isaiah Berlin. Isaiah

Berlin had captured the tension between collective and individual freedom, between national self-determination and freedom from postcolonial tyranny, between the dignity of the group and the dignity of the individual. Berlin saw even more bravely that these values were not necessarily reconcilable. The question still unresolved was, How could a liberal version of development meet the demand for self-determination of groups as well as of individuals?

Emphasizing only material development solved none of these problems. The development economists in the 1960s would have to confront whether to support Soviet-type planning or economic freedom, whether to support autocracy or democracy, and whether to support nationalism or minority rights. They would have to confront whether to militarily and financially support autocratic allies to fight communism or to support freedom from Western intervention.

17

Vietnam and the Illiberal Development Mainstream

In early 1961, President John F. Kennedy launched a new age of development. In his inaugural speech on January 20, 1961, he addressed the "people in the huts and villages of half the globe struggling to break the bonds of mass misery." He assured them that "we pledge our best efforts to help them help themselves, for whatever period is required."[1]

The events of 1961 would look forward to today's development effort, but they also looked back on the history of colonial approaches to development. The "we" and "they" language of Kennedy and his development advisors would show how paternalism survived its near-death experience at the end of colonialism. The new forms of Western intervention were certainly not as bad as those in the colonial era, nor did they reverse the triumph for national self-determination. But Kennedy and one important development economist that advised him alienated anti-colonial leaders further with more subtle violations of collective self-determination. The Development Right of Conquest appeared in new forms (albeit milder, and not advocating full conquest) in US military intervention in the name of development in Vietnam, as it later would appear again in Afghanistan. Kennedy and his advisors displayed little sympathy for national dignity as a goal, and how this goal might be violated by Western intervention. The problematic legacy of all this continues to reverberate in the present.

Kennedy's language was close to that of President Harry S. Truman, who had launched the US foreign aid program twelve years earlier in his inauguration speech in 1949:

> We must embark on a bold new program for making the benefits of our scientific advances and industrial progress available for the improvement and growth of underdeveloped areas. More than half the people of the world are living in conditions approaching misery.

Truman had declared: "For the first time in history, humanity possesses the knowledge and skill to relieve suffering of these people." Humanity (i.e., Americans) sharply increased aid to these people in the late 1950s, with enthusiastic support from then-Senator John F. Kennedy. As president, Kennedy would ratchet aid up still further in 1961. It was not an accident that the aid surged as the US and the Soviets competed to woo the (partly mythological) nonaligned Third World.[2]

Western self-interest still shaped the development idea. Kennedy's enthusiasm for development partially reflected the escalation of the Cold War in Vietnam in the late 1950s and early 1960s. Vietnam was not typical of aid efforts, but it was central to the debate on coercion versus consent in a crucial period for development. It reinforced the anti-liberal mainstream among the new generation of development economists, continuing the setback for liberals seen for Carlos Romulo, Isaiah Berlin, and others.

The new development mainstream was a lot closer to Condorcet than to Adam Smith. The exclusive focus on increasing material income was partly to blame for all this. State-sponsored planning and forced investment were OK if they raised GDP, which most development economists of that era thought they did. So the mainstream had some tolerance for Soviet-style development that included some direct and indirect forms of forced labor.

Among the most important development economists of the era was Walt Whitman Rostow, best known for having invented the phrase "self-sustained growth." In Rostow's 1960 best-selling book *The Stages of Economic Growth*, he described societies moving from the stage of long-standing historical stagnation into this "self-sustained growth." He used the metaphor of a plane taking off—with aid supplying the extra jet fuel to get the plane off the ground.[3]

Rostow in *The Stages of Economic Growth* had embraced a simple model already exposited by another development economist, Nobel laureate Sir Arthur Lewis, that saw economic growth as determined by investment. If the stock of machinery and equipment determined production, they reasoned, then investment in new machinery and equipment would make production grow.

If investment became high enough to fuel growth in gross domestic product that exceeded population growth, there would be positive economic growth per capita—the takeoff. When investment was not high enough, there was no economic growth per capita and the economy remained stuck in the stage of traditional stagnation.[4]

Investment could become high enough for takeoff through aid. The less-developed people could not afford to save enough to finance the necessary investment. Nor did they have access to private international lending to finance this investment. The way out was Western aid to finance investment in poor countries.[5]

As the aid recipient country's income increased with an aid-financed takeoff, it would be able to afford more saving of its own to finance investment. Eventually its saving would be high enough, and its investment financed by its own saving high enough, to sustain growth without aid. The country had now entered its stage of "self-sustained growth," and it no longer needed aid. Rostow's model (based on Lewis's model) caught on as the standard development model. It was still in use when this author started working at the World Bank twenty-five years later in 1985.[6]

Two months after his inauguration, on March 22, 1961, Kennedy ushered in the new age of development in front of Congress. He saw a historic opportunity for aid from the Western developed nations to create a "Decade of Development" in Latin America, Africa, the Middle East, and Asia. Foreign aid would help launch developing countries into "a stage of self-sustained growth," after which they would no longer need aid. Kennedy proposed a new agency to consolidate all previous US government aid efforts, which on November 3, 1961, would become the United States Agency for International Development (USAID).[7]

Kennedy's language in his aid speech of March 22, 1961, sounded a lot like Rostow's, possibly because Rostow wrote the key parts of the aid speech of March 22, 1961. Rostow had laid it all out for Kennedy in a memo on March 2 suggesting an Economic Development Decade, in which foreign aid would launch by 1970 at least "half of the peoples of the underdeveloped areas into self-sustained growth and off the dole." Kennedy could thus reassure Congress that high aid spending would be temporary—always an appealing message.[8]

In another memo on March 13, Rostow had given Kennedy his own model's calculations on how to attain a growth rate of 2 percent per capita in the underdeveloped areas. He calculated the investment rate necessary to generate enough economic growth to exceed population growth by 2 percentage points. Then he calculated how much saving there was in developing countries, which was not enough to finance the required investment. The difference between the target investment rate and available saving had to be filled with foreign aid, so now Rostow knew how much aid was necessary for takeoff. After subtracting the amount available from other Western donors, Rostow could then give the necessary amount of US foreign aid that the president should request from Congress.[9]

Perhaps feeling a little bombarded by Rostow memos, Kennedy in his aid speech did not include Rostow's nerdy details. But at least Kennedy could assure Congress that he based his proposed foreign aid amounts on scientific computations. These gave him "the rock-bottom minimum of funds necessary to do the job" of achieving Third World development.[10]

Kennedy offered an inspiring vision of an escape from poverty, but his idea of development still showed some traces of its colonial precedents. Kennedy in his March 22 aid message to Congress said that "many of these less-developed nations are on the threshold of" being able "to stand permanently on their own feet." On the threshold, but not quite able yet. The language recalled the colonial mandates of the 1919 Treaty of Versailles for the "peoples not yet able to stand by themselves under the strenuous conditions of the modern world."[11]

Rostow said in a speech in 1963 that the development of nations was like the development of an individual from childhood to adulthood, recycling that venerable metaphor from the colonial era. Nations in the "childhood" of development should imitate the adult developed nations.[12]

Rostow rarely used such explicit language of paternalism. But, he later confessed to his own self-image as a savior to the Third World. In a 1984 retrospective, Rostow compared his 1961 self to "missionaries from Western societies who went out to distant and often obscure places," in order "to promulgate the faith." However, he said he kept quiet about his feelings so as not to offend "proud, aspiring, highly nationalistic developing nations."[13]

In the aid speech, Kennedy showed his own paternalism. He insisted that an aid recipient government must increase the country's own saving rate, as well as adopt donor-recommended policies like tax reform. The donors needed to tell the recipients what their own development requires. Kennedy thus announced that "our aid should be conditioned on the recipients' ability and willingness to take the steps necessary" to achieve takeoff.[14]

Kennedy was contradicting himself. He said aid would appeal to the Third World because it gave them what they want. But the aid had to be conditioned on them wanting what they were supposed to already want.

To be sure, Kennedy in his 1961 speech said aid was to respect the "national integrity and independence" of new nations emerging from colonialism. But the commitment to independence was not quite what it seemed. The main and only threat to independence of the new nations that Kennedy mentioned was "Communist pressure," including external military attack and internal subversion.

Western aid was to assist postcolonial nations "to maintain their independence" against communist pressure. Communist pressure was certainly a threat to national self-determination, but it was not the only one. Kennedy failed to recognize the West's military interventions as also a threat to the Rest's self-determination. Kennedy's definition of "independent" was "non-Communist."

Aid was as much to end communism as it was to end poverty. Kennedy in his aid speech denied that his new aid program would be "based merely on reaction to communist threats." In another passage, he felt the need to deny again that his only motivation for aid was "negatively to fight Communism." He then spent the rest of the speech appealing for Congressional support for aid to react to communist threats and negatively to fight communism.[15]

To be fair to Kennedy and Rostow, communist subversion of developing nations was a major threat to freedom worldwide. And communists really did violate national self-determination in Eastern Europe and elsewhere. US economic and military support to vulnerable noncommunist nations could be seen as just aiding their self-defense.

All of these tensions over aid show up in 1961 with America's defense of South Vietnam against communist takeover by North Vietnam. Rostow was the development economist who tried the most to resolve such tensions.

Rostow applied the paternalistic idea of conditions to South Vietnam in a memo to Kennedy on May 10, 1961. We had the right way to develop South Vietnam, Rostow told Kennedy, but the corrupt South Vietnamese dictator Ngô Đình Diệm did not listen. Rostow lamented, "We have pressed for a long time on Diem, without notable success." Rostow wanted to raise the government's tax revenue to finance a crash program that included wells, schools, health clinics, irrigation canals, and roads. As Americans defined development, Americans wanted Vietnamese development more than the Vietnamese did.

So Rostow had to force our development on Diệm. "We have still to find the technique for bringing our great bargaining power to bear on leaders of client states to do things they ought to do but don't want to do." If Diệm still did not want what he was supposed to want, Rostow entertained the idea of a military coup to get rid of him. Rostow hoped that some young army generals might be willing to go along with what "we want in Viet-Nam but have been unable to get from Diem."[16]

Aid was also supposed to get developing nations to embrace the Free World model of development instead of the communist model. Yet paradoxically, Rostow was surprisingly positive about the communist model of development. In *The Stages of Economic Growth*, Rostow described how the victory of the Communists in China in 1949 had begun China's takeoff.[17]

Rostow was likewise positive about Soviet development achievements. The three decades after Stalin launched his brutal five-year plans in 1928 showed "a pace of industrial growth unique in modern experience, held at forced draught by a system of state controls." Both Stalin and Mao forced the population's consumption down to low levels to create the savings to finance high rates of investment to drive high growth. Stalin also used the forced labor of over ten million workers. Takeoff seemingly for Rostow was always desirable. The takeoff did not care whether it was forced or voluntary.[18]

Rostow suffered from the old confusion of positive and normative economics. He positively predicted investment raised economic growth, which may have been true. He used this positive prediction to reach a normative conclusion that more investment was always desirable.

With the Soviet development model producing growth, Rostow felt the West was on the defensive in offering a free development model to the Third World. He would try to persuade the underdeveloped nations, rather plaintively, that "Communism is by no means the only form of effective state organization" that can launch a takeoff.[19]

Communism had already proved itself as a way to achieve takeoffs. Democracy had to prove that it also could achieve takeoffs in Asia, the Middle East, and Africa, Rostow said. This was where Western aid came to the rescue by helping noncommunist leaders to achieve high rates of investment for a takeoff, thereby showing the feasibility of "democratic development." Yet Rostow's democratic development did not involve much democracy.[20]

Rostow thought economic growth would and should satisfy nationalist leaders. He tried to persuade leaders to "focus their minds on the tasks of development." All that mattered was to "launch themselves into self-sustained growth." The postcolonial leaders must resist "the temptations to press nationalism in other directions."[21]

Rostow in *The Stages of Economic Growth* said the battle was between those postcolonial leaders who wanted "to assert power and dignity on the world scene," and those who wanted only to "modernize the economy." The first direction for nationalism was "to right real or believed past humiliations suffered on the world scene"; the second was to simply achieve higher GDP per capita.

Rostow was unusual for his generation of development economists in even mentioning the goal of dignity. Rostow knew that national leaders and citizens might have nonmaterial goals like independence from humiliating foreign control in addition to the development goal. For Rostow, only material development was an acceptable national goal. Perhaps it was not up to him to decide.[22]

The Act for International Development, passed in September 1961, likewise mentioned dignity. While it focused US policy on "aiding peoples of less developed friendly countries of the world to develop their resources and improve their living standards," it also wanted them "to realize their aspirations for justice, education, dignity, and respect as individual human beings."[23]

The dignity goal lost to the development goal. John F. Kennedy also believed that development should trump self-determination.

When he addressed the United Nations on September 25, 1961, on the Decade of Development program, Kennedy said, "Political sovereignty is but a mockery without the means of meeting poverty and literacy and disease." "Self-determination is but a slogan" without meeting this poverty, he repeated. Rather than allow self-determination to divert them, underdeveloped nations should get excited instead by "the United Nations' existing efforts in promoting economic growth." These efforts "can be expanded and coordinated," he enthused. Poor nations should get excited by "technical assistance and pilot projects." They should get excited instead by America's aid effort in which it shared "its capital and its technology to help others help themselves."[24]

Rostow did not shy away from using force to fight both poverty and communism. From October 15 to November 3, 1961, Rostow visited South Vietnam as part of a fact-finding mission dispatched by Kennedy. The mission's report on US economic aid to Diệm suggested supporting a village development program called "agrovilles."[25]

The mission's recommendation of agrovilles in 1961 was a little puzzling because they had already failed. In 1959, Diệm and his brother and principal adviser Ngô Đình Nhu had begun the agrovilles program in the Mekong Delta to resettle peasants tempted by communism into model villages. The government would drain the land and provide canals, roads, and new houses. As it turned out, the government forced the peasants themselves to build the canals and roads at low wages or no wages. The farmers had to buy the land for the model village from the government. The funds for new houses to replace those the peasants had lost in the resettlement were insufficient. As an observer of one agroville reported, the model village was bare land without shade trees and the peasants were now up to six kilometers away from their rice fields.

A domestic opposition group to Diệm protested how this plan forced peasants "to leave their work and go far from their homes and fields, separated from their parents, wives and children . . . to construct beautiful but useless agrovilles." Diệm showed his commitment to democracy by arresting most of the group in 1960.

Given peasant resistance to beautiful but useless model villages, however, the government in the end constructed only twenty-three agrovilles. Diệm had given up on the agroville scheme altogether by 1961.[26]

But a surge in Viet Cong activity in 1961 still required a counterinsurgency strategy. The agrovilles vaguely resembled what the British had done in a successful counterinsurgency campaign in Malaysia. But American advisers could hardly advocate the failed agroville program. Therefore, they gave a new name—"strategic hamlets"—to a virtually identical program of forced resettlement into model villages. The old colonial policy of population removal was still alive in the new age of development.[27]

Diệm's brother, Nhu, justified the program's compulsion as necessary by citing Rostow's *Stages of Economic Growth* on the need to put an end to traditional society as a precondition for takeoff. A US government official in 1962 saw Nhu's strategic hamlets as analogous to China's brutal Great Leap Forward. Nevertheless, the official said, the US should support them because of the "Rostowian premise that an agricultural revolution must precede any industrial revolution." Rostow himself in 1962 envisioned the guerrilla war turning in the US's favor "if the hamlet program, and all it stands for, takes hold."[28]

In March 1962, the American and Vietnamese militaries began a program called "Operation Sunrise" in an area to the north of Saigon with heavy Viet Cong activity. Six hundred government soldiers moved peasants into a strategic hamlet called Ben Tuong. The army told potential settlers they would get a school, schoolbooks, a clinic, medical supplies, a market, water wells, and a defense force to protect them. Seventy families volunteered for resettlement, but another 135 families needed extra persuasion at gunpoint. The army burned their old houses. In Ben Tuong, the government gave the seventy volunteer families land to build their own houses. The government gave the 135 nonvolunteer families a barracks on the edge of the village. There was a concrete administration building and a clinic, but the peasants had to construct themselves the rest of what the government promised them.

The promise of a local market did not work out. The hamlet was so far from the nearest market town that the peasants would have to pay an unaffordable $2.85 per person for a one-way motor pedicab ride to reach the market. The US government gave each family $21 as compensation for lost property, but the government subtracted the cost of the new houses from this amount, leaving them with about enough for two pedicab rides—$5.57 each.

The settlers in Ben Tuong consisted primarily of the very young and very old. The prime-age adults went into hiding to escape the blessings of American development. Even using force, the army had only managed to move 7 percent of the local district population into Ben Tuong.[29]

A young woman in the strategic hamlet told a visiting *New York Times* reporter that the troops burned the villagers' two tons worth of rice stores. A banner in Ben Tuong told the settlers whose villages the government troops had just destroyed that "we will root out all the Viet Cong who destroy our villages."[30]

Two Rand Corporation consultants visited strategic hamlets from January to April 1962. They noted the hamlets forced villagers into communal labor, which had amounted to forty-five to ninety days of labor in three months, with a five-day break for the New Year holiday. The Rand consultants saw the coercive program as losing instead of winning hearts and minds. Forced labor had been a much-hated feature of the French colonial regime in Vietnam.[31]

The South Vietnamese army controlled who could enter and leave the model village, which they surrounded with a barbed wire fence. Some observers likened the strategic hamlet to a detention center. The army forced the prisoners to pay for their own barbed wire.[32]

Yet the supporters of strategic hamlets saw a rosier picture. The US Information Service gave the settlers a free weekly paper called *Toward the Good Life*. The paper explained to the settlers that Operation Sunrise had moved them to Ben Tuong both to defeat the Viet Cong and to raise rural living standards. The paper acknowledged that "in some cases, they are being required to move."[33]

US Defense Secretary Robert S. McNamara visited a strategic hamlet during his lightning trip to Vietnam on May 11, 1962. He saw "nothing but progress and hope for the future."[34]

A South Vietnamese government report on the strategic hamlet program in 1963 offered even more hope for the future. The report announced the US will fund the following goods for families in the strategic hamlets: (1) fertilizer, increasing rice yields by 250 percent, (2) hundreds of new schoolrooms, (3) insect and rodent control, increasing rice yields even more, (4) new crop varieties, quadrupling sweet potato yields, (5) motorized boats, quintupling catches by fishermen, (6) rural dispensaries for thousands of hamlets, and (7) better pigs, raising incomes of hundreds of thousands of families.[35]

On February 4, 1963, the US Army chief of staff, General Earle G. Wheeler, deployed the venerable gerund defense in defense of the strategic hamlets after leading a survey mission to review them. The tide was "turning in our favor," Wheeler said. The military measures "are providing increasing opportunities for political and economic growth. And the Government is starting to take advantage of these opportunities. The Government is beginning to reach the people." More gerunds followed: "The Agency for International Development is assisting these officials in achieving their expectations for a better life," and "the Government of Vietnam is showing [the peasant] both promise and progress, and he is responding encouragingly."[36]

The gerunds did not succeed very long in hiding the unpopularity of the hamlets. As early as October 16, 1962, Rostow's own deputy was informing him that in Central Vietnam, the strategic hamlets were "mostly pure façade." The villagers saw no benefit for themselves in the program, and it failed to reduce Viet Cong attacks. A US government report noted that by August 1963, it was already clear that the strategic hamlet program had "largely ceased to progress." Strategic hamlets produced only successful counterattacks by the Viet Cong. Despite all the supposed success of Operation Sunrise, the Viet Cong captured the model village of Ben Tuong on August 20, 1963.[37]

The dawning realization of these failures caused US support for Diệm to weaken further. The coup Rostow had explored back in 1961 finally happened. Disgruntled military officers overthrew and murdered Diệm and his brother Nhu on November 1–2, 1963, with US support. The new government halted the construction of strategic hamlets.[38]

To be fair, strategic hamlets were probably the worst example of US development efforts in Vietnam. But like other extremes in this history of development violence, they illustrate the most coercive side of development that liberals wanted to eliminate on moral grounds. Even then, Rostow's variety of violence-for-your-own-good was certainly not as extreme as that of previous generations of thinkers. But he pursued development to achieve military victory, and he justified the pursuit of military victory as necessary for development. In the end, he achieved neither development nor victory.

How did Rostow evaluate his own role in the age of development? In 1984, the World Bank held a conference celebrating the Pioneers in Development, the first generation of development economists. The World Bank included Rostow as one of the Pioneers.

Rostow in 1984 made clear he "has no regrets." He said his ideas "hold up reasonably well in retrospect." He did acknowledge that "disruptive external expressions of nationalism proved harder to avoid than we would have hoped, notably in South Asia and Africa." He did not mention Vietnam.[39]

Although the US attempt to develop Vietnam ended after the fall of Saigon in 1975, Rostow's development ideas had a more lasting effect. His embrace of forced investment, his surprisingly positive view of forced development under Stalin and Mao, and his lack of interest in market solutions helped fuel an illiberal consensus in aid and development establishment. It was time for a new generation of liberals to challenge this consensus.

18

Liberal Economists Strike Back

Milton and Rose Friedman were the leading skeptics of foreign aid and development planning during Rostow's generation, reinforced by their intellectual ally P. T. Bauer. They perceived that thinkers like Rostow had shown far too much sympathy for even the most violent proponents of planning—Lenin and Stalin. Like Smith, the Friedmans and Bauer wanted voluntary commerce to replace mandatory development. Rejecting the emphasis of Rostow and other development economists on material income alone, these liberal economists wanted freedom to be an end in itself. This was the alternative vision they offered as the ideological battle with communism reached its climax.

The Friedmans and Bauer led the emergence of the modern promarket aid skeptics. They continued the free-market tradition promoted previously by Ludwig von Mises. They continued and advanced the long-standing liberal campaign against forced labor. They fought back against the triumph of illiberal views seen in the previous two chapters. Their legacy on self-determination would be ambiguous, partly explained by the perpetual liberal struggle to reconcile collective and individual self-determination. As often with liberal skeptics, they would sometimes have trouble listening to their own skepticism.

In 1938, Milton Friedman and Rose Director got married. Milton later declared that Rose was an equal partner in his public policy work. The only time she had explicit coauthorship was for their classic book *Free to Choose*. Following Milton's declaration, this chapter will cite both Milton and Rose for quotes from *Capitalism and Freedom* (where the author is given as Milton with the assistance of Rose), as well as *Free to Choose*.

Like many other key liberals in the post–World War II debate on freedom—such as Mises, Berlin, and P. T. Bauer—the Friedmans were members of a group previously targeted by anti-liberal Western thinking on immigration restrictions. They were all of Eastern European Jewish heritage. Milton was born on July 31, 1912, in Brooklyn, New York. His parents had immigrated in the 1890s from Carpatho-Ruthenia, in what was then the Austro-Hungarian Empire but later became part of the Soviet Union. Rose Director was born in Charterisk in what is now Ukraine in December 1911, brought to the US by her family just before the outbreak of World War I. Many of the relatives she left behind later died in the Holocaust.[1]

The families of Milton and Rose were thus part of the flood of Eastern European Jews coming to the US before World War I, who would after that war become the target of immigration restrictions. Milton wrote to Rose in March 1938 about his desperation to pressure the US government to admit refugees from the Nazis. He concluded it was hopeless: "I suppose we can't do much but go our own individual futile ways." The anti–Eastern European national quotas on US immigration would be repealed in the 1960s. Although they had little engagement with that policy change, the shift against prejudice may have made it easier for their views to gain acceptance more broadly.[2]

Milton and Rose were visitors at Cambridge University from 1953 to 1954, where they met P. T. Bauer. Rose noted him as among those at Cambridge who believed that "individual freedom is the prime objective of social arrangements." Milton celebrated him as the world's leading expert on foreign aid. The Friedmans were going to interact with Bauer a lot on development in the next four decades.[3]

In 1971, P. T. Bauer published his magnum opus, *Dissent on Development*, which denounced both paternalism and coercion in development policy. To begin with, the term "Third World" was "a particularly infelicitous expression." It lumped together diverse individuals in Asia, Africa, and Latin America as if they were just a blob of "malleable clay" to be shaped by aid experts. To Bauer, the aid mainstream implied "western superiority," because its views were "that without aid the underdeveloped countries could not work out their salvation, that they must follow our ways and that they cannot progress without us." Bauer disagreed "that individual Africans and Asians are invariably unenterprising," or that "individual Africans and Asians cannot or do not take a long-term view." Against this picture, he noted the success of smallholder rubber producers in Sumatra and Borneo beginning in the 1920s and 1930s. Likewise, Bauer noted the success of local producers with kola nuts in western Nigeria, coffee and cotton in East Africa, and cocoa, groundnuts, and oil palm products in West Africa. Many of these products require producers to wait for years for initial plantings to produce a crop.[4]

The intended beneficiaries of this aid were likely to resent the aid donors' "patronizing attitude," canceling out the supposed ability of Western donors to gain Third World allies against the Soviets. The aid donors increased resentment even more by trying to make the recipients "follow our ways," even "against the will of the supposed beneficiaries." Bauer rejected this on both normative and positive grounds. Morally, "the right to force people to change their values, attitudes and conduct simply in the interests of higher incomes is disputable." As Bauer had laconically phrased it earlier in his career: "The right of some people to force others to develop is not self-evident."[5]

Bauer's central critique of top-down development planning was that "it suggests that persons neither have nor should have any choice, control or responsibility in matters which affect their position and prospects." The view of a Third World peoples as "a standardized mass" was made even worse by then, making them "subject to rulers with unlimited power" whom development advisors would guide.

The development mainstream therefore "first dehumanizes people and then envisages an inhuman destiny for them." The debate over development planning was not just a debate about facts, about whether planning worked, but about how much one valued individual freedom. Bauer in another article emphasized that "the choice between policies must also depend on value judgments."[6]

But Bauer hindered his own appeal to people in Asia and Africa with his favorable view of colonial rule. He saw such rule as involving "relatively little coercion, or even interference in the lives of the great majority of the people," while establishing law and order and secure property rights. Bauer did not emphasize a demand for self-determination, although he noted colonial status was humiliating to many subjects. Bauer was susceptible to a temptation that afflicted other liberals in this history, of looking for a colonial shortcut that could drop free institutions onto another society.[7]

Although the Friedmans were influenced by Bauer, they had their own direct exposure to development efforts. Milton's first exposure to development policies came in India in 1955. The Indian government asked the Eisenhower administration for an economist to give advice on the Indian development plan. Eisenhower was eager to counter the development advisors in India who advocated Soviet-style five-year plans, so he dispatched the promarket Friedman to visit India.

The Indian government politely ignored Friedman's promarket advice, which he outlined in a memo never to be seen again. Yet Friedman would not give up so easily. A year later, he wrote how freedom in India would allow "the enormous pent-up energies of millions of intelligent and vigorous people" to be released for development. However, current development policy in India favored a centralized plan to be enforced by government control. Friedman saw the plan as "a threat to political and civil freedom."[8]

In 1958, Friedman published for the first time his overall critique of foreign aid and the mainstream aid thinkers. Again, he differed with them when he saw freedom as an end in itself. He denounced the "totalitarian" influences on development thinking. He wanted "free men" to "peaceably use their capacities, abilities, and resources." Free people should be allowed to pursue their own "aspirations," not conform to someone else's aspirations for them.

The mainstream development economists failed to notice how much planning required "the use of central force and authority to enforce conformity" with the plan. Friedman quoted a report on aid by the Center for International Studies at MIT, where Rostow was a member. The report said aid should go to countries where "national effort is being mobilized for development." The measure of this effort was how much governments were able to "capture a good fraction of increases in income for the purpose of further investment." In the Rostow view, governments should "capture" private income to meet investment targets.[9]

Friedman noted sardonically that the US failed to satisfy this capture requirement. The government who best satisfied the capture criterion would be the Soviet Union. The Soviets suppressed consumption of Soviet citizens to plow resources into the five-year plan. The Soviet plan combined forced saving, forced labor, and forced industrialization, as it had under Lenin. Friedman was continuing the venerable liberal critique of forced labor. Friedman in 1958 lamented that foreign aid wound up supporting the Communists' approach.[10]

For the rest of his career, Milton in collaboration with Rose would develop further this critique of compulsion. He applied the critique both to developing nations and to the United States.

Seeing the Friedmans only as advocates of laissez-faire misses their moral principles. They first advocated liberty. Then they arrived at policies that they saw as consistent with that liberty. Those who disagreed with these policies could have at least acknowledged—but almost never did acknowledge—the Friedmans' normative ideal of freedom.

In their advocacy for freedom, Milton and Rose reprised most of the key arguments of liberal thinkers going back to Adam Smith. Like Adam Smith, the Friedmans saw development as a spontaneous order. They were deeply doubtful about the Western experts who claimed they could plan development, when in fact "no one can predict in advance what will turn out to be the most effective use of a nation's productive resources." An economy developed like a language. There was no linguistic planner to force particular words on native speakers. An economy developed also like musical culture. Rose and Milton noted that no central planner forced the citizens of Calcutta to like the same music as the citizens of Vienna.[11]

Moreover, Milton and Rose suspected the self-interest of the Western agents of progress in the Rest. Rose got snarky during their trip to India: "We may not be helping the Indians but we're certainly creating plenty of plushy job opportunities for lower quality American so-called economists. I didn't know there were so many." She thought the Ford Foundation didn't accomplish much besides enabling "the American employees to live at a very high level" with a half dozen servants. The new class of policy experts in universities and think tanks at home was also just another special interest group, one that had been successful in getting high salaries for its own members. Rose and Milton here made an ad hominem attack on their intellectual opponents. But they also shared the classic doubts as to whether the experts themselves were really free from self-interest.[12]

The experts claimed to be superior in intelligence or education to others and therefore thought they should be in charge. The Friedmans disagreed. The elite's claims of superiority, even if true, "did not give them the right to rule others." How sad, then, that "the new class has repeatedly succeeded in imposing its views, despite widespread public objection." Both in the Third World and in the First, the Friedmans had rejected the expert right to rule that went back to Condorcet.[13]

Like Smith, Milton and Rose stressed reciprocity—you should give others the same rights you wanted to have for yourself. Those in the West who favored Soviet-style planning for India or other aid recipients "would be horrified at the idea of applying its principles at home." It was not so easy to achieve reciprocity. "Each of us feels more deeply about not having our freedom interfered with," the Friedmans lamented, "than we do about interfering with the freedom of others." Yet sometimes the freedom of others won anyway.

The Friedmans mentioned the abolition of American slavery as a triumph for reciprocity.[14]

Like some other (but not all) liberal thinkers, the Friedmans at least tentatively in 1958 recognized a collective right of nations to self-determination. This could have been a key moment in the liberal debate if anyone had listened, or if the Friedmans had emphasized it more in their later writings. Any Western effort to spread free enterprise should not be "telling other governments what to do." The governments of the West should not "force men to be free" in the Rest. At most, Western governments should offer the nations of the Rest free access to their own markets, which would "make it easier for other countries to take the path of freedom if they wish to." Free trade offered a way for nations to interact peacefully. This was close to the vision of a liberal international order based on trade and mutual respect of sovereignty. But it would be hard for free market economists—including the Friedmans—to resist telling other governments what to do.[15]

They were much more forceful on individual self-determination. More than any other Western economists of their generation, the Friedmans condemned paternalism. They rejected their anti-liberal opponents' desire that "some shall decide for others." Ordinary citizens should have the "power to control their own destiny." True liberty was "the liberty to shape one's own life," the individuals' right to pursue their "own objectives." As with Kant's idea of human dignity, the Friedmans thought people had the right to serve their "own purposes and not to be treated simply as an instrument to promote someone else's purposes." The liberal principle the Friedmans celebrated was that "every person was to be his own ruler."[16]

The right to individual self-determination applied to all races and nations. The Friedmans rejected the idea that some peoples needed paternal guidance because they were unfit to be free. Different outcomes for different peoples did not reflect inherent differences. Some people were underdeveloped, but this was usually because those people lacked freedom. Freedom would release "the energies of millions of able, active, and vigorous people."[17]

The Friedmans gave examples. Indians in India did not have good development outcomes, as Milton had noted since his 1955 trip. Observers noted the Indians' apparent "sloth and lack of enterprise." Nevertheless, Indians were dynamic entrepreneurs in other less restrictive environments, such as Great Britain. Similarly, the low development level of China "cannot be attributed to the character of the people," the Friedmans said. Just look at the success of the Chinese in Singapore, Hong Kong, and Taiwan.[18]

But the Indians and the Chinese did not have to succeed to earn freedom. Equal rights for people of any "nationality, color, religion, sex" was a core principle no matter what. The denial of rights based on ethnicity or gender was to sacrifice "the freedom of some for the advantage of others." Equal rights applied both at home and abroad.[19]

The Friedmans liked markets because they could make individual self-determination possible for all groups. Markets allowed "the freedom of individuals to pursue their own objectives." Markets made this possible as long as interactions between individuals were consensual rather than coercive. They celebrated Adam Smith's key insight: If there is a right to choose, then exchange will take place only if both parties believe they will benefit. The Friedmans continued the long liberal fight to recognize individual choice as a good thing in itself; it was the whole basis of a beneficial market economy.[20]

How could such wonderful freedom happen? Was the answer really to do nothing? Didn't liberal economists have an obligation to help defeat communism? The Friedmans faced their own crisis as they tried to answer these difficult questions during a visit to Augusto Pinochet's Chile in 1975.

On October 24, 1970, Salvador Allende had won a democratic presidential election in Chile. Allende led a bloc of parties that included socialists and Communists. The US government sought to prevent Allende's election through covert action and then destabilized his regime afterward. In June 1970, Henry Kissinger doubted Chileans were fit to be free: "I don't know why we need to stand by and watch a country go communist due to the irresponsibility of its own people."[21]

The next three years brought chaos. As president, Allende imposed price controls, which led to shortages of food and other basic goods. A survey in 1972 found that 48 percent of Chileans reported difficulty obtaining household staples.[22]

Allende's price controls were unsuccessful in stopping inflation. This was because the Allende government printed money to finance government spending. In the first eight months of 1973, inflation accelerated to 235 percent in annual terms and the economy kept contracting. Inflation was a coercive tax on individuals, seizing their wealth and turning it over to the government for its own forced development schemes. Every 100 percentage points of annual inflation lowers the purchasing power of cash and checking accounts by 50 percent. An inflation rate of 235 percent lowered the purchasing power of cash and checking accounts by 70 percent. If inflation continued at that rate for three years, the real value of money would be reduced by 97 percent. Rich people had more hedges against inflation—such as real estate or foreign assets—than poor people did, so the poor may have suffered the most from inflation.[23]

How could Chile get out of this mess? Despite the political and economic disarray, there was little popular support for the military to resolve the crisis. Surveys in 1973 showed 70 percent of Chileans opposed a coup.[24]

The military had other ideas. On September 11, 1973, General Augusto Pinochet led a coup that deposed Allende. Allende died in the coup, in what later investigations found to be suicide. Pinochet's new regime executed and tortured left-wing opponents.[25]

The Pinochet regime was unable to stop the inflation inherited from Allende. Inflation in 1974 was 505 percent, and then 374 percent in 1975. Some concerned Chileans invited foreign economists to help. Milton and Rose Friedman accepted such an invitation. On March 20, 1975, they arrived in Chile for a visit of six days.[26]

Milton understandably decided the inflation was the main problem. Milton met with Pinochet the day after his arrival for forty-five minutes. Friedman informed the Chilean leader that printing money was the cause of inflation. He proposed a "shock treatment" of quickly cutting government spending. Such cuts would eliminate the need to print money. Pinochet worried about whether the shock treatment would increase unemployment. He requested that Milton send him a letter with more detailed economic advice after his visit, and Milton agreed to do so.[27]

Milton sent Pinochet the promised letter on April 21, 1975. He gave him a simple economics lesson. Government spending was 40 percent of national income, while tax revenue was only about 30 percent of income. The government printed money to cover the budget deficit of 10 percent of national income. Ending inflation required cutting government spending to eliminate further printing of money. Friedman again recommended to Pinochet the shock treatment of a rapid cut in government spending, as well as elimination of price controls. He predicted the shock program would end inflation in a matter of months.

Milton also told Pinochet he had a second problem, which was how to promote "an effective social market economy." Chile had been sadly moving away from this goal, Milton said, because of "trends toward socialism that started 40 years ago, and reached their logical—and terrible—climax in the Allende regime." Friedman congratulated Pinochet: "You have been extremely wise in adopting the many measures you have already taken to reverse this trend."[28]

Pinochet replied to Friedman on May 16, 1975. He said Friedman's recommendations mostly coincided with the economic plan proposed by the secretary of the treasury, Jorge Cauas. Pinochet expressed to Milton his "gratitude for your personal contribution to an analysis of the economic situation of my country."[29]

Friedman's meeting and correspondence with Pinochet became the most controversial moment of his long career. In October 1975, *New York Times* columnist Anthony Lewis criticized Friedman's role in promoting "an economic policy that could not be imposed on a free society." The same month, students at the University of Chicago began protests against Friedman, even picketing outside the Friedmans' apartment.[30]

One of the most forceful critiques of Friedman came from a Chilean exile in the United States, Orlando Letelier, who was a cabinet minister under Allende. Letelier was hardly a credible witness for liberty, since he had participated in the violation of Chileans' economic freedom. On August 28, 1976, Letelier published a broadside in *The Nation*. Letelier thought, "It is curious that the man who wrote a book, *Capitalism and Freedom*," should now be involved in the authoritarian imposition of "freedom" on Chileans. The regime had to resort to executions and concentration camps, Letelier said, because they failed "to convince the majority of Chileans that their policies are reasonable and necessary." Letelier gave the classic skeptics' argument—if your advice is so great, why do you need to force us to take it?[31]

Three weeks later, a car bomb in Washington, DC, killed Letelier and his American colleague Ronni Moffitt. Pinochet's involvement was immediately suspected and later confirmed.

Less than a month later, the Nobel Committee gave the Nobel Prize in Economics to Milton Friedman. Two previous Nobel laureates immediately published a letter denouncing Friedman because of his role in Chile. Demonstrators against Friedman showed up at his award ceremony in Sweden.[32]

Friedman fought back against unfair criticism. Nobody protested when he made trips to the Soviet Union and Yugoslavia, he said. (He later noted that nobody protested in 1988 when he advised the Communist rulers of China.) In a letter to an economics professor critic on July 16, 1975 (published in *The Wall Street Journal* and in the University of Chicago student newspaper), Friedman made clear:

> I do not approve or condone the regimes in Chile, Brazil, Yugoslavia, or Russia. I had nothing to do with their establishment. I would fervently wish their replacement with free democratic societies. I do not regard visiting them as an endorsement.[33]

Moreover, Friedman noted he had actually criticized the unfree regime when he lectured at two Chilean universities during his visit. He had referred to the "military junta" as being "very far indeed from a free society," because it "denies the liberties and freedoms of the people."[34]

The episode thus gave Friedman an opportunity to restate forcefully his commitment to both political and economic freedom. Another Nobel laureate, Paul Samuelson, criticized Friedman anyway. In a 1980 lecture, Samuelson denounced what he called "the devil's fix." This evil fix was to "get rid of democracy and impose upon society the market regime." Chilean military leaders exemplified this "market fascism," advised by "University of Chicago economists who favored free markets." The leaders brutally imposed the free market solution that a democratic society would never have accepted. Even an increase in the "production index" would not vindicate such policies, Samuelson said, because violating freedoms was bad in itself. Samuelson thought this issue so important that he added a discussion of market fascism to the 1980 edition of his popular economics textbook.

Yet in the same 1980 lecture, Samuelson criticized Friedman for valuing freedom as an end in itself. Samuelson thought Friedman should have accepted "the index numbers of soaring real output" as enough to vindicate European policies of state-managed capitalism. He mocked him for asking (in Samuelson's words), "What is material prosperity to individuals who have lost their libertarian freedoms?"[35]

Friedman could not win. Samuelson ridiculed him if he treated freedom as a goal in addition to material prosperity in Western Europe. Then Samuelson denounced him if he failed to treat freedom as a goal in addition to material prosperity in Chile.

In the end, the criticism of Friedman for advising Pinochet was wildly unfair. Development economists had been advising undemocratic leaders for a couple decades before Friedman's visit to Chile and would continue to do so in the five decades after. Should economists refuse to offer advice to any leader who was not perfectly democratic? It wasn't easy to decide, but few economists then or now would accept such a constraint.

Another Nobel laureate had a more thoughtful critique of Friedman's policy role. James M. Buchanan shared Friedman's enthusiasm for laissez-faire policies. Nevertheless, Buchanan criticized Friedman in a private letter to an economist friend in March 1974, a year before Friedman's visit to Chile. Buchanan complained that Friedman "thinks and talks as if he is telling people what they should want."[36]

In a 1959 article, Buchanan got even more radical about freedom to choose. Claiming that a policy would improve some material indicator (like gross domestic product) was not enough to justify the economist's preferred policy. Such objective success did not prove that anyone had actually agreed to the policy. It was not the economist's job to tell people what they "ought to want." The economist's advice should be constrained by what people actually did want.

Buchanan sided forcefully with the definition of progress as consent and not as material improvement. The test of whether a policy change was beneficial was "not objective improvement in some measurable social aggregate," Buchanan argued, but whether there was "consensus among members of the choosing group." In his 1986 Nobel Prize lecture, Buchanan put it most succinctly: "Economists should cease proffering policy advice as if they were employed by a benevolent despot."[37] Buchanan seemed to demand almost superhuman restraint by economists when they were asked for advice, and almost nobody passed this test.

At the same time, the success of the Friedmans in offering a liberal alternative in development thinking is indisputable. The surge in global trade and the success of the export-oriented Four Asian Tigers (Hong Kong, Singapore, South Korea, and Taiwan) from the sixties through the eighties made it easier for their views to gain support. As the eighties ended, their long campaign against Soviet economics and illiberal aid economics was about to achieve an unanticipated and remarkable victory.

19

The End of History?

Beginning on November 9, 1989, a crowd of West and East Germans tore down the Berlin Wall. Eight days later, demonstrations in Prague triggered a Velvet Revolution that overthrew Czechoslovakia's Communist rulers. The longtime dissident Václav Havel was elected president on December 29, 1989. Two years later, a coup in the Soviet Union by Communist hard-liners failed in August 1991. The democratically elected president of the Russian Soviet Federative Socialist Republic, Boris Yeltsin, had led the resistance to the coup. The USSR ceased to exist on Christmas Day 1991. Soviet communism, which seemed so formidable a force to Rostow's and Friedman's generation, had collapsed with remarkable speed.[1]

The fall of the Soviets coincided with advances in individual, political, and economic freedom worldwide. The most extreme forms of autocracy, forced labor, and coercive population policies became less common. There was progress away from men coercing women. Promarket economic reforms replaced development planning in many developing countries. Many economists and leaders in Latin America, Africa, and Asia embraced these promarket reforms. It was the liberals that saw the connections between these movements from coercion to consent.

It was the greatest victory for liberal ideals in history. Many liberal thinkers in the West were filled with hope. In the summer of 1989, a political scientist named Francis Fukuyama published an article titled "The End of History?" He turned it into a book published (without the question mark) in 1992. Another thinker striking a blow for political and economic freedom would be the Nobel laureate Amartya Sen, with his hugely influential 1999 masterpiece *Development as Freedom*.[2]

Yet as always, liberal victories were far from complete and were potentially reversible. Liberal politics in the end spread much less than liberal economics. Even the economic liberalization would not proceed uncontested. The Turkish economist Dani Rodrik would lead a backlash against what he and others would call *neoliberalism*. To be clear, not even Rodrik favored a return to the more extreme economic controls of the pre-1990s period, and this backlash has so far not reversed the global shift toward market freedoms. Yet liberalism remains fragile.

As with Berlin's and Friedman's Eastern European Jewish heritage, Francis Fukuyama was yet another liberal thinker with ties to a group in the Rest previously disrespected by the West. His paternal grandfather was one of the Japanese immigrants to the West Coast who were later the target of immigration restrictions. The US government interned this same grandfather during World War II.[3]

Like previous liberal thinkers such as Smith, Mill, and Berlin, Fukuyama argued that humans had a demand for dignity and not just material development: "Men seek not just material comfort, but respect or recognition, and they believe that they are worthy of respect because they possess a certain value or dignity." Fukuyama thought that "economic interpretations of history are incomplete and unsatisfying, because man is not simply an economic animal."[4]

To Fukuyama, the end of Soviet communism demonstrated that "what truly satisfies human beings is not so much material prosperity as recognition of their status and dignity." Fukuyama believed the overthrow of Soviet communism had a lot to do with the quest for dignity after years of humiliation: "The Soviet people" had been "humiliated by their rulers." Noting the history of Western prejudice against Russians, Fukuyama said the Soviet people were still despised "by the rest of Europe." But now they had "proved everyone wrong."[5]

Likewise, Fukuyama quoted Václav Havel from a New Year's Day address to Czechoslovakia in 1990. The Communist regime had "denigrated man into a production force." To everyone's surprise, "the acquiescent, humiliated, skeptical Czechoslovak people" had suddenly overthrown the "totalitarian system in a completely decent and peaceful way."[6]

Fukuyama later saw the "demand for dignity" as linked to agency. He thought that "people wanted to be treated like adults, adults who were able to influence the governments that lorded over them." Liberals offered such values, recognizing "individuals who are equal in their freedom, that is, who have an equal degree of choice and agency in determining their collective political lives."[7]

Fukuyama noted in 1992 an impressive number of other triumphs for political liberalism. Many countries were moving from autocracy to democracy. Pinochet in Chile lost power after a democratic referendum in 1988. A democratic government took over in 1989. Elsewhere in Latin America, Fukuyama noted, military rulers had given way to democrats since the 1980s.[8]

Although authoritarian governments in Spain, South Korea, and Taiwan had achieved prosperity, he noted "prosperity was not enough." All three countries moved toward democracy. Citizens campaigned for democratic governments that would "treat them like adults rather than children, recognizing their autonomy as free individuals."[9]

In South Africa, it was the beginning of the end for apartheid. The white minority government released Nelson Mandela from jail in 1990 and began negotiations for a transition to majority rule. The essence of apartheid had been to deny the "liberal premise of universal human equality," Fukuyama noted. Now another alternative to liberalism had been defeated.[10]

The share of the world's countries that were pure autocracies (without even the pretense of elections) fell in the early 1990s, continuing a downward trend since the end of World War II. Liberal democracies were a growing share of the world's states. The intermediate categories of electoral autocracy (elections but not free and fair) and electoral democracy (free and fair elections but not guarantees of individual liberties) also became more common.[11]

Celebrating these already visible trends in 1992, Fukuyama enthused that

> the twin crises of authoritarianism and socialist central planning have left only one competitor standing in the ring as an ideology of potentially universal validity: liberal democracy, the doctrine of individual freedom and popular sovereignty.[12]

Fukuyama did not anticipate how the spread of liberal democracy would halt in the new millennium and then go into a partial reverse. Fukuyama had to (unsuccessfully) defend himself against the charge of triumphalism, announcing a liberal utopia that had ended history. He later explained that readers had misunderstood the title *The End of History*. He meant End in the sense of goal rather than termination. By History he meant the trend toward modernization or development. In other words, he was asserting that the goal of development was dignity and freedom.[13]

Fukuyama noted a surge in economic as well as political freedom. There was a shift away from the central planning approach to development that had been winning the battle during the heyday of Rostow. African socialism and Latin American statism lost favor in their most extreme variants. In Chile, the democratic rulers that succeeded Pinochet kept the promarket policies that the Friedmans had favored.

The change was most dramatic and common with the movement away from severe government controls over international trade. We can track freedom of trade using the Economic Freedom of the World data source. Their index of free trade is computed using data on tariffs, nontariff barriers (such as import quotas), black-market exchange rates relative to official exchange rates, and capital controls.[14]

By this measure, sub-Saharan Africa, South Asia, the Middle East, North Africa, and Latin America were as far from free trade as was communist Eastern Europe in the early 1980s. Controls on the market for foreign currency offered exporters an unfavorable exchange rate that killed off incentives to export. High tariffs and import quotas drove up the domestic price of imported goods. These trade penalties discouraged the specialization in which each country exported what it was best at producing and imported what it was not good at producing. State coercion enforced these punitive policies on citizens just trying to control their own economic lives, to make a living, and to afford essential goods.

In Ghana, for example, cocoa exporters were forced to sell to a government Cocoa Marketing Board at a price far below the world price of cocoa. Corrupt officials diverted some of the resultant profits of the Marketing Board to themselves. Under the regime of the dictator Jerry Rawlings in the early 1980s, cocoa producers got less than 10 percent of the world price. The inflation-adjusted price received by cocoa farmers was only about a fifth of what it had been in the early 1960s.[15] In effect, the cocoa farmers were forced to mostly work for the government instead of for themselves.

Ghanaian cocoa farmers would have liked to sell their product in neighboring Côte d'Ivoire, which had more favorable prices for producers. However, the Rawlings regime imposed the death penalty for cocoa smuggling and other acts of "economic sabotage." The regime executed thirty-three people in 1983 and 1984 for these and other alleged crimes.[16]

Both economists and human rights advocates in the 1980s often failed to see the link between punitive economic controls and human rights violations. They had failed to learn from previous history such as Leopold's Congo and Lenin's Russia. Perhaps the links were harder to see because the violence in Ghana and most other 1980s cases of economic controls were less extreme than in Congo and Russia.

In the 1990s, China, sub-Saharan Africa, South Asia, the Middle East, North Africa, and Latin America liberalized, although still stopping far short of complete free trade. For example, the leader Jerry Rawlings in Ghana liberalized the punitive policies on cocoa beginning in the second half of the 1980s.

East Asia (besides China), Western Europe, and North America were already quite liberalized in 1980 and did not have as much of a change.

The high inflation rates that Friedman had fought in Chile were also becoming less common. Friedman had seen these as a coercive tax on individuals' savings. The share of countries with annual inflation above 20 percent or even 40 percent had peaked at over 30 percent in the early 1990s, then fell sharply in the second half of the 1990s, and remained low afterward (Figure 3).

The new consensus for more economic freedom was broad. Although the freedom agenda was identified with the Right, many Democrats in the US also embraced promarket reforms. The hugely influential economist Lawrence Summers was chief economist of the World Bank in the early 1990s, treasury secretary under

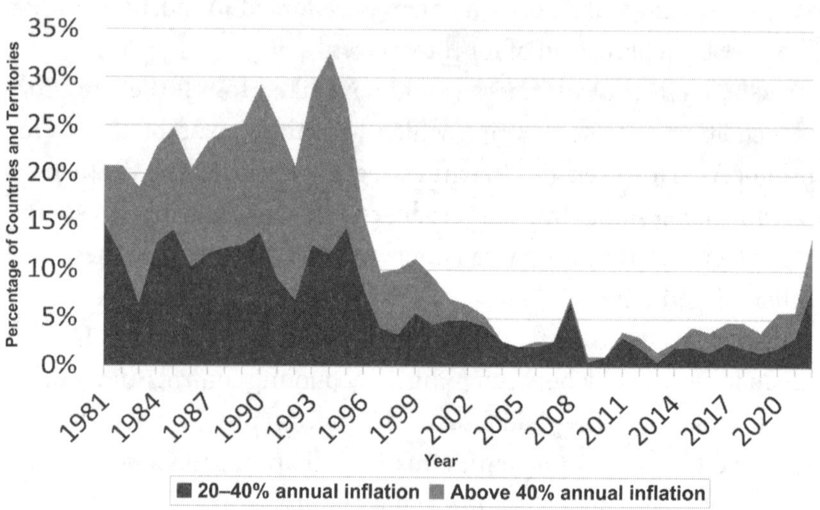

Figure 3. Share of the world's countries and territories with high inflation. Source: International Monetary Fund, World Economic Outlook Database, April 2023.

Clinton, and then director of the National Economic Council under Obama. When Milton Friedman died in 2006, he wrote an appreciation saying, "Any honest Democrat will admit that we are now all Friedmanites."[17]

Another influential economist now came along to show that left and right may not be coherent categories for the freedom debate. Nobel laureate Amartya Sen authored an influential 1999 book, *Development as Freedom*. Sen had long identified himself with the Left. Later describing his views as a graduate student at Cambridge, Sen says that he was "definitely much left of center," but he criticized the Left for how they thought that poor people didn't want freedom, that it was "a kind of bourgeois luxury, which I didn't think it was at all." Further scrambling the left-right distinctions in development, Sen acknowledged his debt to that icon of the Right in development, P. T. Bauer.[18]

Amartya Sen had helped inspire another material indicator, the Human Development Index of the United Nations Development Programme. Sen seemed to embrace both the Condorcet version of development as objective progress and the Smith vision of development as choice.

Despite his enthusiasm for the Human Development Index, Sen wanted to convince "us" thinkers and policymakers that development policies do not "require us to rank all development experiences in one linear order," based on an objective material indicator. Sen made clear "basic civil rights and political freedoms" must be available to all to participate in "the emergence of social values." We citizens must have the freedom to decide how much we value freedom.[19]

Debating this kind of deep freedom is not about whether it raises GNP per capita. "We must see a frequently asked question in the development literature to be fundamentally misdirected," Sen said. The wrong question was "Do democracy and basic political and civil rights help to promote the process of development?" The case for rights "does not have to be freshly established through their indirect contribution to the growth of GNP or to the promotion of industrialization." Sen in fact believed that there was enough evidence for freedom causing high growth of GNP, but this evidence was neither necessary nor sufficient to make the case for freedom. Instead, "these rights can be seen as being constitutive of the process of development."[20]

The phrase "these rights can be seen as being constitutive of the process of development" probably will not appear on placards in freedom marches anytime soon. Yet Sen's academic jargon could not be clearer—freedom was not only or mainly a means to development; freedom *was* development.

Sen took on all of economics, which "has tended to move away from focusing on the value of freedoms to that of utilities, incomes and wealth." This shift has led "to an underappreciation of the full role of the market mechanism." Sen saw humans as valuing agency for its own sake, and not just as a means to get to our preferred economic outcome. He offered the thought experiment in which I compare a basket of goods that I have chosen to the exact same basket chosen for me by somebody else. If it is the same goods, how could my well-being be any different? But Sen saw us as having preferences that are not only about material goods, but are about the process of decision-making itself. Even if my master always says yes to my requests to consume my favorite goods, I object to having to ask the master for permission in the first place.[21]

Sen also discussed the case for freedom relative to the centuries-long debate on forced labor and population removal.

On forced labor, Sen gave the classic example of the intrinsic desire for freedom that has already appeared several times in this book. According to some modern historians, Sen noted, slaves in the American South may actually have had material incomes and life expectancies higher than urban workers in the North. "And yet slaves did run away," Sen laconically noted. Sen had repeated again the classical skeptics' argument—if you slave owners are so good for them, why do they flee your benevolence?[22]

Labor bondage still existed in some places in Asia and Africa, Sen noted. "Upper-caste landowners in one of the most backward parts of India (viz., Bihar) are terrorizing—through selective murder and rape—the families of laborers 'tied' to their lands."[23]

But the forced labor cases that Sen noted were becoming rarer, and it was even rarer to defend it in the name of progress. The share of countries or colonies where the state accepted forced labor had dwindled to almost nobody in the decades since World War II.

Sen's discussion of population removal gives another hugely important example of coercion in modern development. Population policies such as China's one-child policy and India's sterilization policies in the mid-1970s under Indira Gandhi sought to engineer population by force.[24]

In China during the early 1980s, the one-child policy was led by a major general named Qian Xinzhong. With Malthusian fears about high population growth causing poverty, the government forbade couples to have more than one child. Under Qian, the policy involved putting IUDs in women who already had one child, sterilizing parents that had two children, and aborting disallowed pregnancies.[25]

As the historian Matthew Connelly shows in a classic book, this attempt to force poor people to have fewer children was in many ways the heir to the population-replacement ideas of the nineteenth and early twentieth centuries. It is recognizably similar to how post-classical economists in that era embraced eugenics to limit childbearing of lower-class whites and banned immigration by less-developed groups. In all these cases, the aim was to limit poverty by preemptively limiting the poor from appearing within developed societies or even anywhere in the Rest where they could be a threat to the West.

Indira Gandhi led compulsory sterilization efforts in India. Some voices in the Western development establishment defended her. World Bank President Robert McNamara in a 1977 speech at MIT explained that when "population pressures become too great, nations will be driven to more coercive methods." McNamara thought that Gandhi's coercion was necessary to prevent even greater coercion from overpopulation-induced revolutions: "Neither can any government afford to let population pressures grow so dangerously large that social frustrations finally erupt into irrational violence and civil disintegration. That would be coercion of a very different order."[26]

The United Nations Fund for Population Activities in 1983 gave its first Population Award to Indira Gandhi and Qian Xinzhong. The UN Secretary-General Javier Pérez de Cuéllar praised the awardees: "Considering the fact that China and India contain over 40 per cent of humanity, we must all record our deep appreciation of the way in which their governments have marshaled the resources necessary to implement population policies on a massive scale."[27]

For Sen, the forcible-population-control examples allowed an illustrative test of the claim that "poor people are not really bothered by coercion." But Sen postulated that the "people who suffer most from these coercive measures—who are brutally forced to do things they do not want to do—are often among the poorest and least privileged in the society."

Sen did not usually relate the debate on coercion to colonial history. *Development as Freedom* does have one evocative description of the insulting British views of Indians' reproductive behavior. He quoted Churchill that Indians breed "like rabbits," and that Indians were "the beastliest people in the world, next to the Germans."[28]

As bad as China's and India's forced sterilizations and abortions were, the good news was that there were few imitators elsewhere. The Indian and Chinese population policies were a good example for liberal thinkers like Sen on the evils of coercion, but forced controls over women's fertility decisions were also becoming less common. Even China relaxed its policy over time. In 2016, the Chinese government announced an end to the one-child policy. The regime now permitted couples to have two children. Couples no longer had to ask the state for permission to have another child.[29]

Sen also broke through about women's right to consent. He noted how the violence against parents for population control was in particular violence against women. Such policies to Sen violated "women's exercise of reproductive freedom."[30]

The usual emphasis in development was on "statistical predictions" that "female education and female employment opportunity would reduce fertility rates and the frequency of childbearing," Sen noted. To Sen, however, the value of "women's enhanced freedom" was not as a means to something else like lower population growth, but as an end in itself.[31]

Here was another breakthrough in the 1990s for the idea of consent. Even the development thinkers that showed little interest in the idea of individual freedom were now ready to accept women's freedom as an end in itself. A UN-sponsored World Conference on Women in Beijing in 1995 had already achieved a key turning point for women's rights in development. It did not reflect an abrupt change in legal rights for women around the world, but a response to the gradual change that was already happening (Figure 4).[32]

The declaration adopted by the Beijing conference was full of the language of coercion versus consent for women. Like two centuries of liberal thinkers beginning with Adam Smith, the conference saw rape as the most evocative example of how consent had to be an end in itself. Rape was mentioned twenty-six times in the declaration. Forced sex included "trafficking in women," "forced prostitution,"

Figure 4. Fraction of countries with nondiscriminatory rights for women. Source: World Bank, Women, Business & the Law, 2023.

"sexual harassment," "marital rape," "forced marriages," and "systematic rape of women in war."[33]

The declaration drew the crucial link between sexual coercion and women's dignity. "Sexual harassment" in the workplace "is an affront to a worker's dignity." Sexual violence against women was "humiliating and degrading." It was "incompatible with the dignity and the worth of the human person."[34]

The campaign for women almost accidentally promoted economic freedom, because women's rights mean equal economic freedom for women. The movement toward women's rights in the Beijing declaration also involved equal economic and legal rights that were progressively being realized in Figure 4. The Beijing conference insisted that women need equality on "the right to inheritance and to ownership of land and other property."[35]

Like Sen, the Beijing delegates saw the link between coercive population policies and women's rights. They recognized "the right of all women to control . . . their own fertility."[36]

UN declarations are often seen by many (including this author) as full of meaningless promises rarely kept. The worst violators of human rights shamelessly sign declarations on human rights. With the Beijing declaration, one could wonder whether the promises of legal reform would be kept, and whether even laws on the books would be enforced.

But the 1995 declaration is notable because it was so rare to discuss coercion versus consent in even the most toothless declarations by the UN and other development establishment actors. Women's rights were not only critical in themselves but were an opening to discuss universal rights to consent.

Yet the victory of liberalism was far from complete. In particular, liberal economic ideas were far less than universally triumphant.

The first problem was the struggle that liberals had long faced—how to reconcile self-determination with economic freedom. The US Treasury, the World Bank, and the International Monetary Fund may have agreed on promarket reforms by 1992, and indeed this agreement had already been labeled the Washington Consensus by the economist John Williamson in 1989. But the name Washington Consensus revealed a little too much about how the consensus was imposed from Washington. Low- and middle-income countries could get badly needed loans from the World Bank and IMF only if they agreed to reforms decreed by Bank and Fund staff. The fatal combination of foreign advisors with some coercion would keep discrediting promarket recommendations made by the World Bank and the International Monetary Fund in the 1990s, especially for Africa, Latin America, and Russia.

The second problem was that the promarket economic reforms were thought to be desirable only if there were immediate material gains. Most observers thought the reforms based on the consensus at first did not have much impact on economic growth. Anti-globalization protests that exploded in the late 1990s saw liberalized commerce as worsening material poverty and inequality. This seemed enough of a basis to reject it.

By 2006, the Turkish economist Dani Rodrik declared, "The Washington Consensus has not produced the desired results. . . . Nobody really believes in the Washington Consensus anymore." Rodrik said, "The debate now is not whether the Washington Consensus is dead or alive, but over what will replace it."[37]

As time went on, there was more evidence of growth turnarounds and poverty reduction correlated with movements away from extreme state controls. But the emphasis on material results alone—on both sides of the debate—neglected Sen's and others' arguments for freedom as an end in itself.[38]

Another obituary appeared a decade later for the Consensus already reported dead in the previous obituary. Nobel laureate Joseph Stiglitz announced again in 2016 that the Washington Consensus, now known as neoliberalism, "is dead in both developing and developed countries." And then again in 2023, a speech by Biden administration National Security Adviser Jake Sullivan led to a media headline: "The Biden Administration Just Declared the Death of Neoliberalism." Three deaths seems a little excessive even for someone you really want to be dead.[39]

Actually, the association of liberal reforms with a Washington-imposed Consensus did not turn out to be fatal. In the end, many of the promarket reforms in the Rest were led or advocated by home-grown reformers, such as Ngozi Okonjo-Iweala and Charles Soludo in Nigeria, Yegor Gaidar and Anatoly Chubais in Russia, Leszek Balcerowicz in Poland, Václav Klaus in Czechoslovakia, Simeon Djankov in Bulgaria, Hernando de Soto and Mario Vargas Llosa in Peru, a large number of Indian economists, and many other Latin American economists. Political leaders were often reformers themselves, like those in China and India, many other Asian countries, and many Latin American, Eastern European, and African countries.[40]

As of 2022, globalization was not reversed. The movement toward freer trade was associated with big increases in exports from low- and middle-income countries. Over the last four decades, these exports increased tenfold in inflation-adjusted terms, to about $10 trillion in 2022.

There are many other consensual interactions between the West and the Rest. One is the movement of students from illiberal societies to get education in liberal societies. Even enemies of the United States like Iran and Russia send students to the US. Many students from illiberal societies seek liberal education.

Another way to dramatize consensual interactions between the West and the Rest is by airline routes between countries: Africa had 161 million airline passengers in 2023, while the Asia-Pacific Region had 1.4 billion. Every international flight reflects people voluntarily going to another place (at least temporarily) and people in that place voluntarily receiving them.[41]

The fierce debate on the growth effects of liberal reforms partly missed the point of liberals like Fukuyama and Sen. As throughout this history, the material gains from freedom were neither necessary nor sufficient to justify freedom. The demand for agency and dignity was something deeper than experts quarreling about material effects of liberal policies.

On December 17, 2010, in the small town of Sidi Bouzid, Tunisia, twenty-six-year-old Mohamed Bouazizi poured paint thinner over himself and set himself on fire. He would die from his burns three weeks later. Bouazizi was a vendor selling apples, pears, bananas, oranges, and dates on the street. On the morning of December 17, a forty-five-year-old municipal police officer named Faida Hamdy seized Bouazizi's fruit and his electronic scale in lieu of a fine for selling without a permit. When he resisted, she slapped him. Two of her colleagues beat him. He went to the municipal building and asked for his property back, was denied and beaten some more. "Why are you doing this to me?" witnesses reported that he said. "I just want to work." His mother, Mannoubia, later said: "We are poor people in Sidi Bouzid. We don't have money but we have our dignity, and his dignity was taken away with that slap." She said that "Mohammed did what he did for the sake of his dignity." His brother, Salem, said Mohamed's message from martyring himself was "that the poor also have the right to buy and sell."

Bouazizi's action triggered a revolt in Tunisia that drove the seventy-four-year-old dictator Zine el-Abidine Ben Ali into exile in mid-January 2011. Posters pictured Mohamed Bouazizi as "the spark of the uprising of dignity."[42]

The revolt spread throughout the Arab world. What became known as the Arab Spring failed to achieve democratic rule or economic freedom, but it did show something about the aspirations of citizens. For liberals like Francis Fukuyama or Hernando de Soto, Mohamed Bouazizi illustrated the aspiration for democratic and economic rights, which represented a demand for dignity.[43]

This story does not prove that violations of economic rights caused the Arab Spring. Many activists with many different agendas cited the story. Even the facts of what happened on December 17, 2010, are disputed.[44]

The story is simply a reminder that state controls over the economy, such as onerous licensing requirements for vendors, already involve some state coercion of individuals. The Tunisian state took away Bouazizi's agency on what to sell and to whom. It took away its customers' agency on what to buy and whom to buy it from. It prevented the mutual realization of self-interest of Bouazizi and his customers through a consensual exchange. State regulations give an opening to state officials to harass individuals. Some harassment could be worse in corrupt and authoritarian regimes.

The liberal asks not only what the effect of policy on poverty is, but also how many slaps are involved. Inequality is not only about material incomes, but also about who gets to slap whom.

Bouazizi's story is also a reminder that the usual image of state intervention as taking from the rich to give to the poor is also not necessarily accurate. States may take from the poor to give to richer corrupt officials. This may be humiliating to the poor; it may violate their dignity.

Inequality of dignity matters as well as inequality of incomes. The modern anti-market backlash against inequality failed to recognize how the liberal campaign was itself achieving greater equality. This kind of equality was not about equality of outcomes but about equality of rights. The right to consent to your own progress had been often denied on the basis of race, class, or gender. Now that was less common. The heirs to the liberal tradition could see the moral connections between the end of eugenics after World War II, the end of anti-Asian and anti–Eastern European national immigration quotas in the US, the end of legal segregation for Black people, the fall of Soviet communism, the spread of democracy, the end of apartheid, the movement away from forced labor and coercive population policies, the progress toward equal rights for women, the movement away from paternalistic development planning, and promarket economic reforms.

Adam Smith's prophesied movement of "nations into some sort of respect for the rights of one another" had been partially fulfilled. The relation of the West to the Rest, previously based on coercion, was now based mainly on consent. The Development Right of Conquest had indeed been mostly replaced by commerce. People in the Rest now had more freedom than ever to choose: what occupations to enter, what products to sell and to whom, what products they wanted to buy and from whom, whether to remit money from abroad to back home, where to get an education, and whether to accept investments from abroad.

The trend toward freedom is neither inexorable nor irreversible. As of this writing, new threats to freedom have emerged with proposed increases in US tariffs and possible restrictions on foreign students. It's a little premature to declare the attainment of a liberal paradise. It probably will always be premature. No utopias were available, but ruling out some forms of Western coercion in the name of progress had been a good start.

Epilogue

Development in Search of Dignity

> The extreme poor are robbed of their dignity and their agency. They are made to understand that they should be grateful for help, even when they don't particularly want it.
>
> —Abhijit V. Banerjee and Esther Duflo, *Good Economics for Hard Times*

In 2012, some writers in Africa and in the African diaspora reacted to an aid effort in Uganda. The Nigerian American writer Teju Cole thought this aid effort neglected "the agency of the people of Uganda in their own lives." It failed to notice that "a great deal of work had been done, and continues to be done, by Ugandans to improve their own country." Cole thought that "those who are being helped ought to be consulted over the matters that concern them." As Ugandan social entrepreneur T. M. S. Ruge said about the Ugandan aid recipients, aid should respect "their agency to determine the course of their future." He protested about how much "they become bit players in their own story."[1]

The quest for agency is everywhere and nowhere in the business of development aid. As elsewhere in this book, the demand for dignity tends to be most visible in extreme cases that illustrate again that material aid is not enough by itself. The Ugandan aid to which

Cole and Ruge reacted was an extreme in its pure ludicrousness. Other similar extremes in Africa generated protests and some effort on the part of aid organizations to reform themselves. More serious issues of consent, self-determination, and equality arose with Western military interventions in Uganda and in Afghanistan. Evil actors like Vladimir Putin could exploit the backlash against such interventions for his anti-liberal crusade. Neither the case of Uganda nor that of Afghanistan was typical of the aid mainstream, where academics and aid policymakers struggled to address paternalism. The aid critics themselves disagreed on whether to condemn all aid or only the most extreme violations of dignity.

Cole and Ruge were protesting a YouTube video called *KONY 2012*, posted on March 12, 2012, which has since had 103 million views. An American NGO called Invisible Children in the video advocated Western intervention to capture an evil warlord named Joseph Kony in Uganda, who for many years had been kidnapping children to make them into child soldiers. It featured the voice of a former child abductee of Kony named Jacob Acaye, whom the filmmaker Jason Russell interviewed as a child. As an adult, Acaye went on speaking tours of the US and after the video release testified before Congress.[2]

The Kony 2012 campaign sought to make Kony's atrocities so famous in the US that Americans would demand action. The desired action would be the US government sending military forces to capture Kony. The video quotes George Clooney saying, "I want indicted war criminals to enjoy the same level of celebrity as me." Previous awareness raising by Invisible Children was so successful that the Obama administration sent one hundred US military advisers into Central Africa in October 2011. The Kony 2012 video aimed to raise awareness even further so as to ensure continued support for the US intervention.[3]

Even the filmmaker's five-year-old son is asked for his opinion in the video. Teju Cole wondered, "How would that little boy come to understand that others have autonomy; that their right to life is not exclusive of a right to self-respect?"[4]

In sardonic posts on Twitter, Cole lambasted those he saw as would-be saviors: "From Sachs to Kristof to Invisible Children to TED, the fastest growth industry in the US is the White Savior Industrial Complex." Cole was criticizing the American humanitarian crusader Nicholas Kristof, who in turn dismissed Cole's critique as representing only "middle-class educated Africans." They may be uncomfortable with white saviors, Kristof said. "To me though," Kristof explained, "it seems even more uncomfortable to think that we as white Americans should not intervene in a humanitarian disaster because the victims are of a different skin color." Kristof elucidated: "If I were a Congolese villager, I would welcome these uncertain efforts over the sneering scorn of do-nothing armchair cynics."[5]

Cole did not claim to speak for all Africans. "There are other middle-class educated Africans who see this matter differently from me," he noted. To imply homogenous African opinion would also be stereotypical. Real people "sometimes disagree with each other," Cole said. Indeed, he could have pointed out that there are many Africans who work for aid agencies and Western NGOs.[6]

Cole saw Kristof's problem as the same one that has recurred in this history: the exclusive focus on material need. "All he sees is hungry mouths," Cole said. "All he sees is need."[7]

The Cole–Kristof debate recalls Amartya Sen's discussion. Sen noted that policymakers often take self-respect to be "a rather 'genteel' concern." But Sen insisted otherwise, quoting the philosopher John Rawls. "Self-respect" is "perhaps the most important primary good" for "a theory of justice as fairness." The word *self-respect* had also been used by Harriet Jacobs, Frederick Douglass, Nelson Mandela, and Mahmood Mamdani.[8]

It is easy to mock viral videos featuring the aid thinking of George Clooney. The jokes write themselves. More serious development people treated Kony 2012 as comic relief if they mentioned it at all. Certainly, a YouTube video is a less serious matter than conquest in the name of development. This incident is practically begging for the cliché that history repeats itself first as tragedy, then as farce.[9]

Yet the demeaning portrayals of aid recipients are not a trivial issue. The modern struggle over what became known as "poverty porn" is thought to go back to Ethiopia famine relief in 1984. But this book has shown it really goes back to Winthrop's Massachusetts, the abolitionists, the Congo reformers, and Russia famine relief campaigns.

For Ethiopia famine relief, a group of musicians, including such celebrities as Bono, produced a "Live Aid" concert in 1985 to raise funds for famine victims. Their 1984 song "Do They Know It's Christmas?" became a huge hit. The cover of the subsequent album portrayed the contrast between happy British children and emaciated African children with flies on their eyes. The lyrics of the song featured a "we" and "they": "We can spread a smile of joy" to places "where nothing ever grows, no rain nor rivers flow," where it is doubtful whether "they know it's Christmas time at all."[10]

The Live Aid organizers were so impressed with their own concert that they brought it back for the twentieth anniversary in 2005 to raise funds for African aid. They brought "Do They Know It's Christmas?" back again for the thirtieth anniversary in 2014 to raise funds to fight Ebola. In 2024, the fortieth-anniversary rerelease of the song was mercifully low-key.

The British Zambian aid critic Dambisa Moyo was a little dismayed in 2009 that elected officials in Africa were less heavily represented in determining development aid policy than Bono. Moyo said that "to the bewilderment and chagrin of many an African," aid policy has "been left to musicians who reside outside Africa." She seeks an alternative to the one "in which Africans are viewed as children, unable to develop on their own or grow without being shown how or made to." Moyo had celebrated independence from colonial rule, which she said had given Africans "a deep sense of dignity" and "self-respect."[11]

Likewise, the Senegalese entrepreneur Magatte Wade wrote in 2014 that the "Do They Know It's Christmas?" images have consequences for what could have been more dignified relationships with Africans. She described her conversation with a venture capitalist about funding for her enterprise:

> "Don't we need to be digging wells and creating schools for poor children?" he asked. For him, "helping Africa" could only mean providing charity for the poor, pathetic African children he had seen in hundreds of NGO marketing campaigns.[12]

Wade reports that her advocacy for dignity and not just material aid has only selective appeal:

> Whenever I speak about the dignity and respect Africans deserve to the African audience in the United States or abroad, I receive standing ovations. It's because they too feel the pain and disrespect of these stereotypes that hurt Africa's future. Conversely, when I say the same thing to Euro-American audiences I get blank stares asking me *what about the wells?*[13]

Some Western NGOs realized there was a problem of poverty porn. The General Assembly of the Liaison Committee of Development NGOs to the European Communities in 1989 adopted a "Code of Conduct: Images and Messages Relating to the Third World." It launched a movement to "respect the individual subjectivity, dignity, identity, culture and volition of those portrayed."[14] This followed upon a 1987 review of the images in Ethiopia that found "there were no instances of ordinary Africans being able to speak for themselves."[15]

The NGOs kept trying to get poverty porn under control. In 2006, another organization of European NGOs (CONCORD) agreed on another code of principles. The code asked NGOs to "avoid images and messages that potentially stereotype, sensationalise or discriminate against people," and to show images that "respect human dignity." It required NGOs to ask permission to take someone's picture to be in an aid brochure. The CONCORD code said NGOs should give those they portrayed an "opportunity to communicate their stories themselves."[16]

Dóchas, the Irish Association of Non-Governmental Development Organisations, developed an eloquent guide on how to follow the CONCORD code of conduct. The 2023 version includes "regarding people as active, valuable and capable agents of change in their own lives." It asks NGOs to abolish the "we" and the "they": "Try not to generalise diverse groups of people under the terms 'they' or 'these people.'" It demands informed consent by those featured in NGO stories, photographs, or videos.[17]

By 2021, *The New York Times* editorial board had come to embrace the cause of respectful aid. It quoted the Haiti-born consultant Marie-Rose Romain Murphy and Somalia-born NGO executive Degan Ali:

> The first step is to immediately cease the marketing of people in the Global South as passive "beneficiaries" of aid who need "white saviors."[18]

The World Bank also became more sensitive to depictions of developing countries, so much so that it stopped using the label "developing countries." As Daniel Gerszon Mahler, Alaka Holla, and Umar Serajuddin argued in a 2024 World Bank blog post, even the word "development" is problematic. They see it as a metaphor referring to the process by which children mature, which raises obvious concerns of "paternalism and patronization." They quote another article by Themrise Khan, Seye Abimbola, Catherine Kyobutungi, and Madhukar Pai complaining that development language creates "a false hierarchy among nations."[19]

To be fair, it would be difficult to have no acceptable words to analyze world poverty and to make aid and trade decisions. Some developing country governments continue to refer to themselves as developing countries, including China.[20]

And few of those of us who work on development are innocent of paternalistic imagery. Books on development as well as aid reports often feature children on the covers. The Kenyan political scientist

Ken Opalo wrote a critique of a picture of a child on one of my own books:

> Can we all promise never to fall into the temptation to include anonymous African children . . . on the cover of books on poverty and development? . . . Were the boy's parents or guardians consulted? Do they even know that their kid is on the cover of Easterly's book?[21]

Aid images may not seem to be such an important issue, and it's not clear that policing language would be a big help. But aid images can also be a tell on attitudes behind more serious efforts, such as military interventions.

Another commentator on Kony 2012 was the Ugandan academic Mahmood Mamdani, who is a professor at Columbia and executive director of the Makerere Institute of Social Research in Uganda. The beginning of this book quoted Mamdani asserting his own dignity as a refugee in a British camp in 1972.[22]

Mamdani in 2012 noted that Kony 2012 celebrated the US intervention on the side of the Ugandan government of Yoweri Museveni. Museveni had initiated a counterinsurgency campaign in the north of Uganda back in 1986. In 1996, the government army targeted Acholi districts in the north with civilian massacres and the burning down of entire villages, forcing much of the rural Acholi population into refugee camps. The government called the camps "protected villages," but Mamdani sees them as concentration camps run by government soldiers. Excess mortality in the camps ran about one thousand deaths per week. This was the situation exploited by the Acholi rebel Joseph Kony and the Lord's Resistance Army (LRA).[23]

Mamdani argues that not coincidentally Museveni was a US ally in the war on terror, contributing troops to the fight against al-Shabaab in Somalia. He has had good relations with the US since he took power in 1986. Since that date, Museveni has received foreign aid of $50.3 billion in today's dollars.[24]

Uganda was a small-scale military intervention. Other interventions in the name of progress were on a larger scale. As in Uganda in 2012 (or Massachusetts in 1629), images of the desperate poor asking to be rescued justified military interventions that happened for other reasons.

When George W. Bush announced that the US military and its allies had entered Afghanistan on October 7, 2001, he depicted the effort as partly intended to rescue desperate Afghans: "We'll also drop food, medicine and supplies to the starving and suffering men and women and children of Afghanistan." One could certainly see the US war on the Taliban as self-defense after September 11, 2001. The debate would be on whether it was also justified as a war for development.[25]

Little more than a month later, First Lady Laura Bush gave a radio address featuring the same images. She was launching "a world-wide effort to focus on the brutality against women and children by" Al-Qaeda and the Taliban. As the US-led forces were defeating the Taliban, she said, "the people of Afghanistan—especially women—are rejoicing."

As John Winthrop imagined an Indian saying "come over and help us" nearly four centuries ago, Laura Bush imagined generic Afghan women rejoicing about the arrival of US soldiers.

Mrs. Bush uses the venerable language of the civilizing mission: "Civilized people throughout the world are speaking out in horror," because "our hearts break for the women and children in Afghanistan."[26]

Women's rights in Afghanistan were certainly a great cause and have tragically been violated again since the Taliban victory in 2021. As always, the question is not are they fit to go uninvaded, but are we fit to invade? As so often in this history, it was the evil forces who could capitalize on perceived violations of national self-determination, which helped the Taliban to eventually win the twenty-year war.

Systematic statistical evidence shows that US foreign aid, as well as aid from other Western donors, shifted after 2001 to countries with wars and terrorism, like Afghanistan and Uganda. Phrases like "nation building" and fixing "failed states" became more common after 9/11.[27]

Partly this was motivated by an admirable empathy for the victims of war, as with Kony 2012. But Mamdani argued it reflected the self-interest of the US and other Western donors in having the war on terror decide who gets aid. Some of the aid goes to the incumbent governments' armies, and part of the aid may also be captured by warlords.[28]

Mamdani argued that Western military intervention in the name of development violates the equality guidelines of a liberal international order. He perceives a self-appointed role for rich countries to intervene in poor countries, while of course rejecting any reciprocal intervention of poor countries in rich countries.

In 1899, Chicago Professor J. Laurence Laughlin had quoted Lincoln to express his dislike for American conquest of the Philippines: "I hate it because it deprives our republican example of its just influence in the world—enables the enemies of free institutions, with plausibility, to taunt us as hypocrites."[29]

In recent years, the leading enemy of free institutions taunting the West as hypocrites has been Vladimir Putin. On July 28, 2023, Vladimir Putin hosted seventeen African heads of state at a Russia-Africa summit in Saint Petersburg. Almost a year and a half after his invasion of Ukraine, Putin was getting some support within Africa against the West. American officials noted a decline in attendance from a prewar Russia-Africa summit in 2019 that had forty-three African heads of state. But that previous summit happened after Putin had already occupied parts of Ukraine in 2014. Fifteen African governments had abstained from a March 2022 UN resolution condemning Putin's new invasion of Ukraine, while two had voted against it. Africa was the region most deeply divided by the Ukraine war.[30]

Putin cynically tried to use past Western military interventions to excuse his own sadistic violence. Putin wooed African leaders to recognize him as one of the global leaders against what he and the African governments both called neocolonialism. In a speech to the African leaders, Putin highlighted the West's hypocritical denunciation of the Ukraine invasion as violating the UN Charter while the West forgot it had its own military interventions in Iraq, Libya, and Syria. "If they actually want someone to observe the UN Charter as well as other norms of international law," Putin said, "they should themselves take the effort to fulfil them."[31]

Ugandan leader Yoweri Museveni was one of those convinced by Putin's arguments. He explained his gratitude to Putin for convening the forum. Looking to history, he noted how "the relationship between the Soviet Union and Africa was crucial for the liberation of Africa."[32] But Museveni had used anti-colonialism to excuse his own violent denial of self-determination to Acholis.

Putin himself insistently appeals to history, citing everything from Sweden's intervention in Russia in the seventeenth century to Western-supported shock therapy in the 1990s. "They treated us like a colony," Putin said bitterly about the 1990s. Echoing a theme going back to Catherine the Great and Tolstoy, Putin complains how the West divides up the world into the "so-called civilized countries" and "the rest" who are "barbarians and savages." He complains that it is the West who decides "who is not worthy" of the "right to self-determination."[33]

The Russian tyrant's own hypocrisy is shown by noting that some of these assertions of self-determination came in a ceremony annexing four Ukrainian regions to Russia. Ukraine had its own struggle for dignity through self-determination, but it was a struggle against Russia rather than against the West. Indeed, a decade earlier Ukrainian demonstrators had overthrown a pro-Russian Ukrainian president, Viktor Yanukovych, in what became known as the Revolution of Dignity. Significantly, the trigger for the revolt in November 2013 was Yanukovych's decision not to sign an association agreement with the European Union. The agreement would have included movement toward a free trade area with the EU, as well as "respect for democratic principles, rule of law, good governance, human rights and fundamental freedoms." The new pro-Western government of Ukraine signed the agreement in 2014.[34]

Ukraine's approach to dignity was an attempt at a positive-sum game of liberal values—individual freedom and consent of the governed at home, voluntary international trade, and mutual respect of sovereignty with other nations. The murderous Putin's approach to dignity was a zero-sum game, bolstering Russia's national dignity by taking away Ukraine's. It came after centuries of the West's own zero-sum game of coercion of people in the Rest in the name of progress.

Sadly, Putin was able to exploit this history to justify his own tyranny at home and abroad, just as Lenin and Hitler had justified their violence by citing Western hypocrisy on liberal values. It was not that easy to keep getting shamed by psychotic tyrants, but Western leaders did their best.

Away from the extremes of poverty porn and military interventions, the mainstream development field started to acknowledge a demand for agency and dignity in aid. The best examples are the economics Nobel laureates Abhijit Banerjee and Esther Duflo, who see agency and dignity as urgent because aid efforts too often deny it (as reflected in their quote in the epigraph to this chapter).[35]

Crucially, Banerjee and Duflo see the poor as "entitled to be seen for who they are and to not be defined by the difficulties besieging them." The poor have a life; they are not just made up of desperate needs.[36]

But Banerjee and Duflo are conflicted. They think that aid policy often forces agency on the poor whether they want it or not: "The poor are being handed the responsibility for making things better for themselves, largely without being asked whether this is what they want."[37]

The attempts of aid organizations to promote agency is revealing, Duflo says in a related lecture. One education project in India created village education committees (VECs) for the intended beneficiaries to participate in running the program. But her follow-up research (together with coauthors) found that "very few parents knew that a VEC even existed, and even fewer, what the VEC should or could do. Perhaps most impressively, one quarter of the VEC members did not even know they were on the VEC." Duflo concluded that poor parents may care about education "but may have no energy left to figure out exactly how to work the system."[38]

But who should have the agency to decide who gets agency? Although a democratic process could balance agency and paternalism, Duflo notes this democratic consent is not available in poor countries with authoritarian systems. The lack of democratic consent is a valid issue, Duflo acknowledges, but "is not one that should stop us from getting started." Until democracy arrives, Duflo says we (I'm not sure who "we" is) should focus on the most obvious material needs and let evidence be the guide for how we do development: "A number of outcomes (avoiding infant mortality for example) should be uncontroversially desirable, and there is a fair amount of scientific evidence for how to achieve them." To Duflo in the end, material progress is enough without waiting for consent. This is probably the consensus view in the development mainstream. It is the same old tension between progress as defined objectively by scientists versus progress defined by the choices of its intended beneficiaries.[39]

Another revealing moment in today's aid-paternalism debate passed almost unnoticed. In New York City from September 25 to September 27, 2015, there was a United Nations summit. More than 150 world leaders showed up, and even Pope Francis gave a speech. The leaders announced a dramatic commitment to end world poverty, as measured by percentage of the world's population living on less than $1.90 a day. They set the date to reach zero poverty as 2030, as part of what became known as the Sustainable Development Goals (SDGs). The SDGs' focus on material poverty seems to represent business as usual.[40]

But there is another much-less-noticed feature of the SDGs that is relevant to the nonmaterial need to consent to your own progress. The 2015 agenda also had a nonmaterial target as one of its numerous goals. It declares, "We recognize that each country has primary responsibility for its own economic and social development."

Target 17.15 was to "respect each country's policy space and leadership to establish and implement policies for poverty eradication and sustainable development." You can see why this jargon-ridden goal did not shake the aid world. Many readers (including me) have dismissed words like these as meaningless buzzwords. But in writing down this history of paternalism and coercion, I have changed my mind. Even buzzwords on nations determining their own development are a radical change from colonizers forcing their own ideas of development on others. Having one supposedly superior group conquer another for the good of the latter was a type of patronizing violence now almost universally rejected (except perhaps for Afghanistan). The SDGs are clear elsewhere about national self-determination as an end in itself. The leaders who signed the document agreed on "the need to respect the territorial integrity and political independence of States."[41]

Of course, collective self-determination and nonintervention hardly assure liberal values by themselves. Having a national dictator decree what development is also denies citizens the right to consent to their own progress. But at least the coercion of one set of actors—colonial developers in the past and Western aid agencies today—has been ruled out of bounds. The liberals have often been oblivious to this as one of the triumphs of the liberal idea of the right to consent, while the anti-liberals have been even more unlikely to give any credit to liberal ideas for this.

What are the liberal alternatives to the most paternalistic parts of aid? Moyo and Wade are in the liberal tradition started by Adam Smith of seeing market relationships as an alternative to paternalist relationships. Moyo wants "trade, FDI, the capital markets, remittances, micro-finance and savings" to replace aid. An investor from the West funding an entrepreneur from the Rest is a relationship between equals who freely choose to participate, she notes, in which each side expects to benefit.[42]

As Wade had written in 2012, "I prefer the humanity of a tough business person in a negotiation in which he or she is trying to make a deal." Dignity is why she wants trade and not aid: "I want to be engaged in relationships with people who believe that I'm worth struggling with, not just pitying." For Wade, for Westerners to see Africans only as objects of charity and not as equal trading partners is humiliating. For her, markets feature the dignity of individual consent and self-determination.[43]

Moyo and Wade are the only African and diaspora intellectuals quoted in this chapter seeing markets as the leading alternative to aid. As often happened with the liberal intellectuals in this book, Moyo and Wade seem to represent an extreme minority and yet are closer than the majority to what actually happened. Figure 5 shows how market-based flows—remittances from migrants, foreign direct investment, and export revenues—have dwarfed foreign aid inflows in low- and middle-income countries. The ratio reached fifty-one times as much in 2021. If the market-based flows were a 5'8" person, aid would be only 1.3" tall. Most poor people are already making their own choices rather than having academic evidence on aid determine those choices.

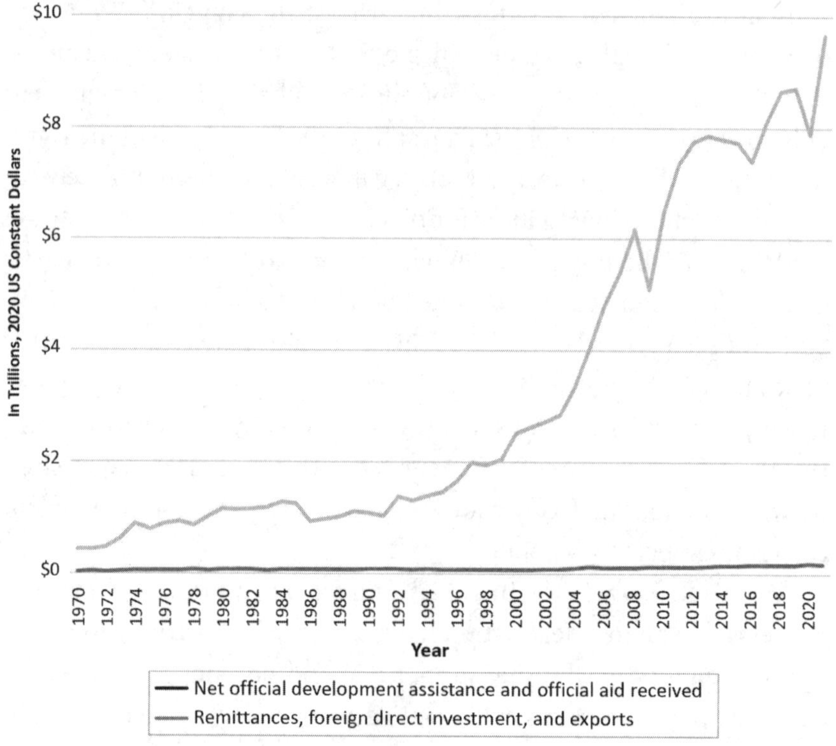

Figure 5. Aid versus market-based flows for low- and middle-income countries. Source: World Bank World Development Indicators.

The role of international markets is less pronounced for sub-Saharan Africa, but market-based flows in Africa today are still nine times larger than foreign aid inflows (Figure 6).

The much-stereotyped "African" of aid campaigns is more likely to be producing his or her own income through markets than receiving charity. They are making their own choices in trade rather than having choices made for them. Trade is already replacing aid. In Ethiopia, the land of helpless victims portrayed in Live Aid concerts, commerce thrives on a large scale in 2022. Ethiopians export coffee to Germany, cut flowers to the Netherlands, and clothing to the US. They choose to import machinery from the UK, pharmaceuticals from Belgium, and cereals from the US.[44]

The aid debate was not quite as important as it seemed to its participants. The endpoint of four centuries of struggle over liberal values in development was not the debate on whether aid should feature Village Education Committees. The "we" in the West was obsessed with our aid to the Rest, either positively or negatively. Maybe we need to get over ourselves a little bit.

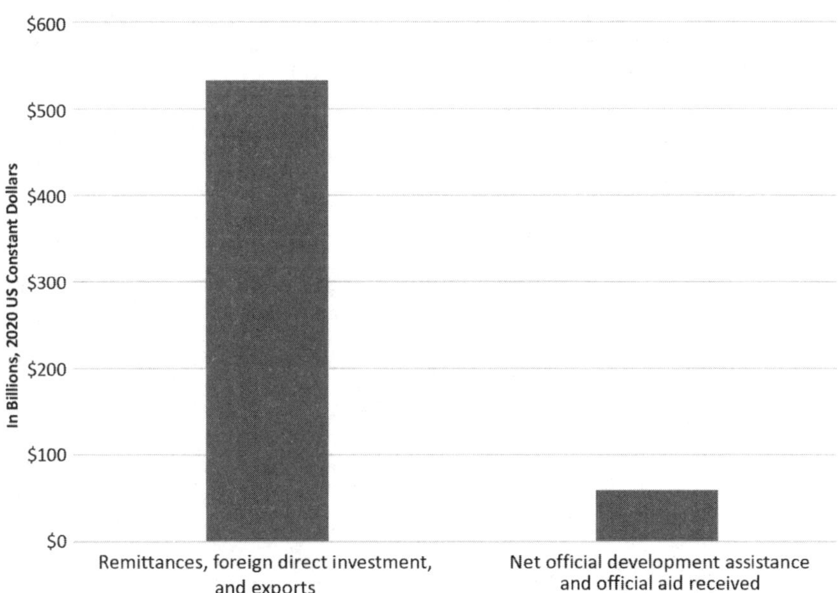

Figure 6. Market-based versus aid inflows for sub-Saharan Africa, 2021. Source: World Bank World Development Indicators.

More important was how aid addressed the threats to liberal values as represented by figures like Putin. Does aid at its worst unintentionally boost the illiberal cause? The answer will depend on how much development aid can reject paternalism. It will depend on whether development aid can reject the hierarchy of the developers and those to be developed.

Development is not something that we do to them. Liberal development is a we without a them. Liberal trade has a we and no them. Liberal democracy has a "we the people" and no them. Freedom includes everyone in the we, in which we exchange with each other on the basis of consent, self-determination, and equality, in which everyone has a right to agency and dignity.

Whether everyone will finally be included in freedom's "we" will determine the fate of freedom. It will determine whether, in the words of Lincoln, "we shall nobly save, or meanly lose, the last best, hope of earth."

Acknowledgments

I have accumulated large debts of gratitude to many people (in no particular order).

I am deeply grateful to longtime colleagues from whom I have learned much over many years and who also gave comments on this manuscript: Ross Levine, Maria Carkovic, Lant Pritchett, Yaw Nyarko, Chris Blattman, Charles Calomiris, Ian Vasquez, Stephen Haber, Deirdre McCloskey, David Levy, Peter Boettke, Dennis Whittle, Michael Clemens, Moussa Blimpo, Hippolyte Fofack, Emmanuel Jimenez, and Angus Deaton.

I was also fortunate to get comments from NYU colleagues and students: Jonathan Morduch, Kevin Davis, Martin Rotemberg, Peter Henry, Pranabes Dutta, Youn Baek, and Aya Jibet.

I benefited enormously from comments from some of the authors whose work I covered in the book: Guillaume Ansart, Dean Pavlakis, Robert Vitalis, Elizabeth Borgwardt, Joshua Cherniss, David Ekbladh, Steven Lukes, Erez Manela, Colin Calloway, and Nils Gilman.

Some of the comments came in through a workshop held at the NYU Development Research Institute. I am grateful for the support of DRI codirectors Rajeev Dehejia and Yaw Nyarko for this, as well as for funding from the Thomas W. Smith Foundation.

For historical trade data, I am grateful to Yueling Huang for research assistance.

I got wonderful feedback from audiences at places where I gave lectures using material from the book: Ohio University (especially Julia Paxton and Cortney Rodet), Medical Benevolence Foundation (Andy Mayo and Patrick Coughlin), Acton Institute (Caleb Whitmer and Michael Matheson Miller), King's College London (Bryan Cheang and Mark Pennington), the Alamos Alliance (Roberto

Salinas Léon and Phil Gramm), and Fordham University's Graduate Program in International Political Economy and Development (Henry Schwalbenberg, Genevieve Connell, and Frederic Bomba).

I am deeply grateful to the team at Basic for their guidance and support, above all the publisher Lara Heimert, as well as (in alphabetical order) Katherine Beitner, Jessica Breen, Susan Gollnick, Joseph Gunther, Michael Kaler, Kristen Kim, Angela Messina, Liz Morris, Brianne Oliva, Naomi Tomlin, and Michelle Welsh-Horst.

I want to profusely thank my agent Andrew Wylie for helping make my career as an author even possible, now more than ever.

For many conversations and much emotional encouragement, I am grateful to my kids and stepchildren and their partners Rachel, Frank, Genevieve, Caleb, Grace, Wesley, Luke, and Dana; to my sister Patricia; and to my brother John.

By far I owe the biggest debt of gratitude to my wife, Lizzie, whose commentary and support made all the difference.

A Note on Sources

It has been possible to cover the broad range of thinkers, topics, and events in this book due only to the superb secondary literature. These sources have helped guide me to the most important texts, quotes, events, and facts in the primary sources, which I could then expand by further reading them. The notes record citations of both the secondary and primary sources. Where I present the analysis of the secondary sources, I note this at the beginning of each chapter's notes and/or in the relevant subsection of the chapters.

Bibliography

Abouzeid, Rania. "Bouazizi: The Man Who Set Himself and Tunisia on Fire." *Time*, January 21, 2011. https://content.time.com/time/magazine/article/0,9171,2044723,00.html.

Adams, Charles Francis, ed. *Memoirs of John Quincy Adams, Comprising Portions from His Diary from 1795 to 1848*. Vol. 1. Philadelphia: J. B. Lippincott, 1875. https://archive.org/details/memoirsofjohnqui04adamuoft/.

Adams, John Quincy. *Diary*. 51 vols. Primary Source Cooperative at the Massachusetts Historical Society. Accessed May 17, 2025. Editorial Statement at www.primarysourcecoop.org/jqa/about; vol. 28 [5 August 1809 to 31 July 1813] at www.masshist.org/jqadiaries/php/diaries#28.

Adams, John Quincy. *An Address, Celebrating the Anniversary of Independence*. Cambridge, MA: Hilliard and Metcalf, 1821.

Adams, John Quincy. *Writings of John Quincy Adams*. Edited by Worthington Chauncey Ford. Vol. 7, *1820–1823*. Macmillan, 1917. https://archive.org/details/writingsofjohnqu0007wort/.

Ali, Degan, and Marie-Rose Romain Murphy. "Black Lives Matter Is Also a Reckoning for Foreign Aid and International NGOs." OpenDemocracy, July 19, 2020. www.opendemocracy.net/en/transformation/black-lives-matter-also-reckoning-foreign-aid-and-international-ngos.

American Sociological Association. "William G. Sumner." Updated July 20, 2023. www.asanet.org/william-g-sumner.

Amnesty International. "Ghana: Political Imprisonment and the Death Penalty." December 19, 1991. www.amnesty.org/en/wp-content/uploads/2021/06/afr280031991en.pdf.

Anderson, Rufus. *Memoir of Catharine Brown*. Boston: Crocker and Brewster, 1828.

Ansart, Guillaume, ed. *Condorcet: Writings on the United States*. Penn State University Press, 2012. Kindle.

Arcand, Jean-Louis, David Sylvan, Anastasia Aladysheva, and Elena Gadjanova. "Guns, Germs, and Slaves: An Alternative View of the Colonial Origins of Comparative Development." Preprint, October 2021. www.jeanlouisarcand.com/publication/arcand-2021/arcand-2021.pdf.

Arezki, Rabah, Youssouf Camara, Patrick Imam, and Roland Kpodar. "Foreign Aid and Conflicts: The Effects of 9/11 on Donor Behavior." Working Paper No. 2025/016. International Monetary Fund, January 17, 2025. www.imf.org/en/Publications/WP/Issues/2025/01/17/Foreign-Aid-and-Conflicts-The-Effects-of-9-11-on-Donor-Behavior-560273.

Associated Press. "Putin Woos African Leaders at a Summit in Russia with Promises of Expanding Trade and Other Ties." July 28, 2023. https://apnews.com/article/russia-africa-summit-putin-food-grain-00408e40403c3c30f89371a474bb4f9d.

Bain, David Haward. *Sitting in Darkness: Americans in the Philippines*. Houghton Mifflin, 1984.

Ball, Terence, and Antis Loizides. "James Mill." In *Stanford Encyclopedia of Philosophy*, edited by Edward N. Zalta and Uri Nodelman. Stanford University, 1995–. Fall 2024 ed. https://plato.stanford.edu/archives/fall2024/entries/james-mill/.

Banerjee, Abhijit V., and Esther Duflo. "Mandated Empowerment." *Annals of the New York Academy of Sciences* 1136 (2008): 333–341.

Banerjee, Abhijit V., and Esther Duflo. *Good Economics for Hard Times*. PublicAffairs, 2019. Kindle.

Barber, William J. *British Economic Thought and India, 1600–1858: A Study in the History of Development Economics*. Clarendon Press, 1975.

Bashford, Alison, and Joyce E. Chaplin. *The New Worlds of Thomas Robert Malthus: Rereading the Principle of Population*. Princeton University Press, 2016. Kindle.

Bateman, Merrill J., Alexander Meeraus, David M. Newbery, William Asenso Okyere, and Gerald T. O'Mara. "Ghana's Cocoa Pricing Policy." Working Paper No. 429. Agricultural and Rural Development Department, World Bank, June 1990.

Bauer, P. T. *Economic Analysis and Policy in Underdeveloped Countries*. Duke University Press, 1957.

Bauer, P. T. *Dissent on Development*. Harvard University Press, 1976.

Bauer, P. T. "N. H. Stern on Substance and Method in Development Economics." *Journal of Development Economics* 2 (1975): 387–405.

Bayly, C. A. "The Boxer Uprising and India Globalizing Myths." In *The Boxers, China, and the World*, edited by Robert Bickers and R. G. Tiedemann. Rowman & Littlefield, 2007.

Beaumont, Peter. "Mohammed Bouazizi: The Dutiful Son Whose Death Changed Tunisia's Fate." *Guardian*, January 20, 2011. www.theguardian.com/world/2011/jan/20/tunisian-fruit-seller-mohammed-bouazizi.

Behnke, Camille. "Putin Searches for More Friends at Africa Summit but Low Turnout Dampens Bid for Influence." *NBC News*, July 29, 2023. www.nbcnews.com/news/world/putin-searches-friends-africa-summit-low-turnout-dampens-bid-influence-rcna96599.

"Beijing Declaration and Platform for Action." United Nations, 1995. www.un.org/womenwatch/daw/beijing/pdf/BDPfA%20E.pdf.

Berg, A. Scott. *Wilson*. Penguin, 2013. Kindle.

Bergès, Sandrine. *Sophie de Grouchy's "Letters on Sympathy": A Critical Engagement with Adam Smith's "The Theory of Moral Sentiments."* Oxford University Press, 2019. https://doi.org/10.1093/oso/9780190637088.001.0001.

Berlin, Isaiah. *Conversations for Tomorrow*. Televised discussion with J. B. Priestley and A. J. Ayer. Recorded on March 26, 1964, and broadcast on BBC television April 25, 1964. Isaiah Berlin Virtual Library.

Berlin, Isaiah. "Four Lectures on Russian Historicism: The Russian Obsession with History and Historicism." Totem Park, University of British Columbia, March

2, 1971. Isaiah Berlin Virtual Library. https://berlin.wolf.ox.ac.uk/published_works/singles/bib297.pdf.

Berlin, Isaiah. *Freedom and Its Betrayal: Six Enemies of Human Liberty*. Updated Edition. Edited by Henry Hardy. Princeton University Press, 2002. Kindle.

Berlin, Isaiah. "A Letter to George Kennan: On Human Dignity." *New Republic*, January 28, 2002.

Berlin, Isaiah. Manuscript D, "Two Concepts of Liberty." Text delivered to the Clarendon Press [published in *Four Essays* in 1969]. Isaiah Berlin Virtual Library. http://berlin.wolf.ox.ac.uk/published_works/tcl.

Berlin, Isaiah. "National Superiority and Inferiority." Talk and discussion. Home Service, 1958. Isaiah Berlin Virtual Library. https://berlin.wolf.ox.ac.uk/lists/broadcasts/national.pdf.

Berlin, Isaiah. Original dictation (A), "Two Concepts of Liberty." 1958, Isaiah Berlin Virtual Library. http://berlin.wolf.ox.ac.uk/published_works/tcl.

Berlin, Isaiah. *Russian Thinkers*. Edited by Henry Hardy and Aileen Kelly. Penguin, 2013. Kindle.

Berlin, Isaiah. *The Sense of Reality: Studies in Ideas and Their Consequences*. Edited by Henry Hardy. Farrar, Straus and Giroux, 1996.

Bermeo, Nancy G. *Ordinary People in Extraordinary Times: The Citizenry and the Breakdown of Democracy*. Princeton University Press, 2003. Kindle.

Bigart, Homer. "McNamara Terms Saigon Aid Ample." *New York Times*, May 12, 1962.

Bigart, Homer. "US Helps Vietnam in Test of Strategy Against Guerrillas." *New York Times*, March 29, 1962. https://timesmachine.nytimes.com/timesmachine/1962/03/29/83221129.html.

Bigart, Homer. "US Prints Paper for Vietnamese." *New York Times*, April 4, 1962.

Bigart, Homer. "Vietnam Village Builds and Hopes." *New York Times*, April 8, 1962.

Blackbourn, David. "The Conquest of Nature and the Mystique of the Eastern Frontier in Germany." In *Germans, Poland, and Colonial Expansion to the East*, edited by Robert L. Nelson. Palgrave Macmillan, 2009.

Blassingame, John W., and John R. McKivigan, eds. *The Frederick Douglass Papers*. Series One, vol. 4, *1864–1880*. Yale University Press, 1991.

Blight, David W. *Frederick Douglass: Prophet of Freedom*. Simon & Schuster, 2018. Kindle.

Boettke, Peter J. *The Struggle for a Better World*. Mercatus Center at George Mason University, 2021. Kindle.

Boot, Max. *The Savage Wars of Peace: Small Wars and the Rise of American Power*. Basic Books, 2002. Kindle.

Boulger, Demetrius C. *The Congo State Is Not a Slave State: A Reply to Mr. E. D. Morel's Pamphlet Entitled "The Congo Slave State."* Sampson Low, Marston, 1903.

Borgwardt, Elizabeth. *A New Deal for the World: America's Vision for Human Rights*. Harvard University Press, 2005. Kindle.

Boyd, Willis D. "The Île a Vache Colonization Venture, 1862–1864." *The Americas* 16, no. 1 (1959): 45–62. www.jstor.org/stable/979258.

Bradley, Mark Philip. *Imagining Vietnam and America: The Making of Postcolonial Vietnam, 1919–1950*. University of North Carolina Press, 2000. Kindle.

Braidwood, Stephen J. *Black Poor and White Philanthropists: London's Blacks and the*

Foundation of the Sierra Leone Settlement 1786–1791. Liverpool University Press, 1994. https://doi.org/10.5949/UPO9781846317293.

Brands, H. W. *Bound to Empire: The United States and the Philippines*. Oxford University Press, 1992. Kindle.

Bremer, Francis J. *John Winthrop: America's Forgotten Founding Father*. Oxford University Press, 2003. Kindle.

"British Economic Association," *Economic Journal* 1 (1891): 2–8.

Brown, Albert G. *Speeches, Messages, and Other Writings*. Jas B. Smith, 1859.

Brown, David. "Cherokees." *Missionary Herald* 21, no. 11 (November 1825): 354–355.

Brown, David. Letter to editors of the Richmond *Family Visitor*. In *American Missionary Register* 6, no. 7 (July 1825): 220–221.

Brown, Vincent. *Tacky's Revolt: The Story of an Atlantic Slave War*. Harvard University Press, 2020. Kindle.

Buccola, Nicholas. *The Political Thought of Frederick Douglass*. New York University Press, 2012. Kindle.

Buchanan, James M. "The Constitution of Economic Policy." Prize Lecture to the memory of Alfred Nobel, December 8, 1986. www.nobelprize.org/prizes/economic-sciences/1986/buchanan/lecture/.

Buchanan, James M. "Positive Economics, Welfare Economics, and Political Economy." *Journal of Law and Economics* 2 (October 1959): 124–138. www.jstor.org/stable/724934.

Burin, Eric. *Slavery and the Peculiar Solution: A History of the American Colonization Society*. University Press of Florida, 2005.

Burnard, Trevor. *Jamaica in the Age of Revolution*. University of Pennsylvania Press, 2020. Kindle.

Burrows, Guy, and Henry M. Stanley. *The Land of the Pigmies*. Thomas Y. Crowell, 1898. https://archive.org/stream/cu31924028653271/cu31924028653271_djvu.txt.

Bush, George W. "Presidential Address to the Nation." White House, Office of the Press Secretary, October 7, 2001. https://georgewbush-whitehouse.archives.gov/news/releases/2001/10/20011007-8.html.

Bush, Laura. "Radio Address by Mrs. Bush." Office of the First Lady. Crawford, Texas, November 17, 2001. https://georgewbush-whitehouse.archives.gov/news/releases/2001/11/20011117.html.

Calloway, Colin G. *The Indian World of George Washington*. Oxford University Press, 2018. Kindle.

Capaldi, Nicholas. *John Stuart Mill: A Biography*. Cambridge University Press, 2004. Kindle.

Carlyle, Thomas. *Latter-Day Pamphlets*. 1850. Public Domain Books, Kindle.

[Carlyle, Thomas]. "Occasional Discourse on the Negro Question." *Fraser's Magazine for Town and Country* 40 (December 1849): 670–679. www.efm.bris.ac.uk/het/carlyle/occasion.htm.

Carlyle, Thomas. *Past and Present*. HardPress, 2017. Kindle. Originally published in London in 1872 by Chapman and Hall.

Carlyle, Thomas. *Reminiscences by Thomas Carlyle*. Edited by Charles Eliot Norton. London: Macmillan, 1887.

Carlyle, Thomas. "Thomas Carlyle to Dr. Carlyle [brother]," May 4, 1859. In vol. 2 of *New Letters of Thomas Carlyle*, edited by Alexander Carlyle. London: John Lane, 1904.

Carretta, Vincent. Introduction to *Thoughts and Sentiments on the Evil of Slavery*, by Quobna Ottobah Cugoano. Penguin Classics, 1999.

Carretta, Vincent, ed. *Unchained Voices: An Anthology of Black Authors in the English-Speaking World of the Eighteenth Century*. University Press of Kentucky, 2004. Kindle.

Cass, Lewis. "Removal of the Indians." *North American Review*, January 1830.

Catton, Philip E. "Counter-Insurgency and Nation Building: The Strategic Hamlet Programme in South Vietnam, 1961–1963." *International History Review* 21, no. 4 (1999): 918–940. www.jstor.org/stable/40109167.

Center for International Studies. "The Objectives of United States Economic Assistance Programs." 85th Congress, 1st Session. Document 52, July 1957. US Government Printing Office, 1957. Pages 57–58.

Centre for the Study of the Legacies of British Slavery. "Gilbert Francklyn: Profile & Legacies Summary, 1733–1799." www.ucl.ac.uk/lbs/person/view/2146632169.

Cherniss, Joshua L. "'A Cautious, Sober Love Affair with Humanity': Humanism in the Thought of Isaiah Berlin." Senior essay in political science, Yale University, 2002. Isaiah Berlin Virtual Library. https://berlin.wolf.ox.ac.uk/writings_on_ib/cherniss.pdf.

Child, Lydia Maria. "An Appeal for the Indians." *National Anti-Slavery Standard*, 1868.

Child, Lydia Maria. *An Appeal in Favor of That Class of Americans Called Africans*. New York: John S. Taylor, 1836. Public Domain Books, Kindle.

Child, Lydia Maria. *The First Settlers of New-England: Or, Conquest of the Pequods, Narragansets, and Pokanokets, as Related by a Mother to Her Children*. Boston: Munroe and Francis, 1829.

Child, Lydia Maria. *Hobomok and Other Writings on Indians*. Edited and with an Introduction by Carolyn L. Karcher. Rutgers University Press, 1986. Kindle.

Cirium Aviation Analytics. "New Cirium Report and Data Shows Strong Growth in International Flying to and from Africa." Accessed May 19, 2025. www.cirium.com/thoughtcloud/cirium-report-data-strong-growth-international-flying-to-from-africa.

Clarkson, Thomas. *Essay on the Slavery and Commerce of the Human Species, Particularly the African*. Philadelphia: Joseph Crukshank, 1787.

Clarkson, Thomas. *The History of the Abolition of the African Slave-Trade*. 2 vols. Published online by Liberty Fund. Originally published in 1808.

Claudio, Lisandro E. "The Anti-Communist Third World: Carlos Romulo and the Other Bandung." *Southeast Asian Studies* 4, no. 1 (2015): 125–156.

Cole, Teju. *Known and Strange Things*. Random House, 2016. Kindle.

Cole, Teju. "The White-Savior Industrial Complex." *Atlantic*, March 21, 2012. www.theatlantic.com/international/archive/2012/03/the-white-savior-industrial-complex/254843/.

Comin, Diego, William Easterly, and Erick Gong. "Was the Wealth of Nations Determined in 1000 BC?" *American Economic Journal: Macroeconomics* 2, no. 3 (2010): 65–97.

Commissioner of Indian Affairs. *Annual Report of the Commissioner of Indian Affairs to the Secretary of the Interior for the Year 1872*. US Government Printing Office, 1872. https://archive.org/details/usindianaffairs72usdorich.

Commons, John R. "Economic Effects of Immigration." Part 3, in *Reports of the Industrial Commission on Immigration*. 57th Congress, House of Representatives, 1st Session, No. 181. Volume XV of the Commission's Reports. US Government Printing Office, 1901.

Commons, John R. *Races and Immigrants in America*. Macmillan, 1907. Kindle.

CONCORD (European NGO Confederation for Relief and Development). Code of Conduct on Images and Messages, 2006. https://concordeurope.org/2012/09/27/code-of-conduct-on-images-and-messages/.

Connelly, Matthew. *Fatal Misconception: The Struggle to Control World Population*. The Belknap Press of Harvard University Press, 2008. Kindle.

Conrad, Joseph. *Heart of Darkness*. Digireads.com, 2015. Kindle.

Constant, Benjamin. *Constant: Political Writings*. Edited and translated by Biancamaria Fontana. Cambridge University Press, 1988. Kindle.

Coppedge, Michael, John Gerring, Carl Henrik Knutsen, et al. "V-Dem Codebook v13." Varieties of Democracy (V-Dem), 2023. www.v-dem.net/documents/24/codebook_v13.pdf.

Coyne, Christopher J. *In Search of Monsters to Destroy: The Folly of American Empire and the Paths to Peace*. Independent Institute, 2022. Kindle.

Cozzens, Peter. *Tecumseh and the Prophet: The Shawnee Brothers Who Defied a Nation*. Knopf Doubleday, 2020. Kindle.

C-SPAN. *Uganda's Joseph Kony and the Lord's Resistance Party*. April 24, 2012.

Cugoano, Quobna Ottobah. *Thoughts and Sentiments on the Evil of Slavery*. Edited by Vincent Carretta. Penguin Classics, 1999.

Cullinane, M. *Liberty and American Anti-Imperialism: 1898–1909*. Palgrave Macmillan, 2012.

Dalrymple, William. *The Anarchy: The East India Company, Corporate Violence, and the Pillage of an Empire*. Bloomsbury Publishing, 2019. Kindle.

Davies, Wyre. "Doubt over Tunisian 'Martyr' Who Triggered Revolution." *BBC*, June 17, 2011. www.bbc.com/news/world-middle-east-13800493.

de Soto, Hernando. "The Real Mohamed Bouazizi." *Foreign Policy*, December 16, 2011. https://foreignpolicy.com/2011/12/16/the-real-mohamed-bouazizi/.

Dóchas, the Irish Association of Non-Governmental Development Organisations. *The Dóchas Guide to Ethical Communications 2023*. Dóchas, 2023. www.dochas.ie/resources/communications-pe/ethical-communications/.

Dodd, Haldane. "Supporting Economic & Social Development." Air Transport Action Group, 2024. Accessed May 19, 2025. https://atag.org/industry-topics/supporting-economic-social-development.

Donnell, John C., and Gerald C. Hickey. "The Vietnamese 'Strategic Hamlets': A Preliminary Report." US Air Force, Project Rand Research Memorandum. RM-3208-ARPA, September 1962. www.rand.org/content/dam/rand/pubs/research_memoranda/2006/RM3208.pdf.

Douglass, Frederick. "Henry Clay." *The North Star*, 1848, 4–8. Manuscript/mixed material. Accessed May 17, 2025. www.loc.gov/item/mss1187900365/.

Douglass, Frederick. *The Life and Times of Frederick Douglass*. Start Publishing, 2012. Kindle.

Douglass, Frederick. *My Bondage and My Freedom*. Digireads.com Classics, 2011. Kindle.

Douglass, Frederick. *Narrative of the Life of Frederick Douglass*. Dover Publications, 1995. Kindle.

Drescher, Seymour. *The Mighty Experiment: Free Labor Versus Slavery in British Emancipation*. Oxford University Press, 2002. Kindle.

Dubnov, Arie M. *Isaiah Berlin: The Journey of a Jewish Liberal*. Palgrave Macmillan, 2012. Kindle.

Du Bois, W. E. B. "The Relation of the Negroes to the Whites in the South." *Annals of the American Academy of Political and Social Science* 18 (July 1901): 121–140. www.jstor.org/stable/1009886.

Du Bois, W. E. B. *The World and Africa and Color and Democracy*. Oxford University Press, 2007. Kindle.

Du Bois, W. E. B. *The Souls of Black Folk: Essays and Sketches*. University of Massachusetts Press, 2018. Kindle.

Duflo, Esther. "Human Values and the Design of the Fight Against Poverty." Tanner Lectures, May 2012. www.povertyactionlab.org/sites/default/files/documents/TannerLectures_EstherDuflo_draft.pdf.

Duiker, William J. *Ho Chi Minh: A Life*. Hachette Books, 2000. Kindle.

Easterly, William. *The Elusive Quest for Growth: Economists' Adventures and Misadventures in the Tropics*. MIT Press, 2001.

Easterly, William. "The Paradox of Aid and Donor Self-Interest." In *Handbook of Aid and Development*, edited by Raj Desai, Shantayanan Devarajan, and Jennifer Tobin. Elgar, 2024.

Easterly, William. "Progress by Consent: Adam Smith as Development Economist." *Review of Austrian Economics* 34, no. 2 (2021): 179–201.

Easterly, William. "In Search of Reforms for Growth: New Stylized Facts on Policy and Growth Outcomes." Working Paper No. 26318. National Bureau of Economic Research, 2019. www.nber.org/papers/w26318.

Easterly, William, and Laura Freschi. "Why the World Bank Supports Tyrants: The Gerund Defense." *Aid Watch* (blog). June 8, 2010. www.nyudri.org/aidwatcharchive/2010/06/why-the-world-bank-supports-tyrants-the-gerund-defense.

Easterly, William, and Ross Levine. "The European Origins of Economic Development." *Journal of Economic Growth* 21 (2016): 225–257. https://doi.org/10.1007/s10887-016-9130-y.

Eastley, Aaron. "Conrad, *The Times*, and Some Explorers." *Conradiana* 44, no. 2/3 (2012): 91–125. www.jstor.org/stable/24643269.

Ebenstein, Lanny. *Milton Friedman: A Biography*. St. Martin's, 2007. Kindle.

The Editors of Encyclopaedia Britannica. "Salvador Allende." Britannica.com. Accessed May 18, 2025. www.britannica.com/biography/Salvador-Allende.

Edmunds, R. David. *The Shawnee Prophet*. University of Nebraska Press, 1983. Kindle.

Edwards, Sebastian, and Leonidas Montes. "Milton Friedman in Chile: Shock Therapy, Economic Freedom, and Exchange Rates." *Journal of the History of Economic Thought* 42, no. 1 (2020): 105–132. https://doi.org/10.1017/S1053837219000397.

Egyptian Delegation to the Peace Conference. "Collection of Official Correspondence from November 11, 1918, to July 14, 1919; Twelve Appendices Containing Verbatim Transcriptions of Official Egyptian Reports, Correspondence, Depositions of Victims and Eye-Witness, and Photographs of Atrocities Committed by British Troops in Egypt." Paris, The Delegation, 1919. Accessed May 17, 2025. https://babel.hathitrust.org/cgi/pt?id=coo1.ark:/13960/t83j41k9b&seq=5.

Ekbladh, David. *The Great American Mission: Modernization and the Construction of an American World Order*. Princeton University Press, 2010. Kindle.

Ely, Richard T. "The American Economic Association 1885–1909." *American Economic Association Quarterly* 11, no. 1, 3rd series (1910): 47–111. www.jstor.org/stable/3000023.

Ely, Richard T. "Fraternalism vs. Paternalism in Government." *Century* 55, no. 5 (1898): 780–784.

Ely, Richard T. "Pauperism in the United States." *North American Review* 152, no. 413 (1891): 395–409. www.jstor.org/stable/25102157.

Ely, Richard T. "Report of the Organization of the American Economic Association." *Publications of the American Economic Association* 1, no. 1 (1886): 5–32. www.jstor.org/stable/2485628.

Ely, Richard T. *Studies in the Evolution of Industrial Society*. Chautauqua Press, 1903.

Embassy of Indonesia. *Report on Indonesia* 6, no. 9 (June 1955): 8–31.

Equiano, Olaudah. *The Interesting Narrative and Other Writings*. Edited and introduced by Vincent Carretta. Penguin, 2003. Kindle.

Ethridge, Robbie. *Creek Country: The Creek Indians and Their World*. University of North Carolina Press, 2003. Kindle.

EU-Ukraine Association Agreement. "Quick Guide to the Association Agreement." December 7, 2015. www.eeas.europa.eu/sites/default/files/071215_eu-ukraine_association_agreement.pdf.

Evarts, Jeremiah. "An Article on the Removal of the Indians." *North American Review* 31, no. 69 (1830): 396–442.

Evarts, Jeremiah. *Essays on the Present Crisis in the Condition of the American Indians*. Boston: Perkins and Marvin, 1829.

Fahim, Kareem. "Slap to a Man's Pride Set Off Tumult in Tunisia." *New York Times*, January 21, 2011. www.nytimes.com/2011/01/22/world/africa/22sidi.html.

Fall, Bernard. *The Two Vietnams: A Political and Military Analysis*. Taylor & Francis, 1984. Kindle.

Farrant, Andrew. "Advising the 'Devil' or 'Preaching' to the Public? The Controversy over Milton Friedman's 1975 Visit to Chile." In *Research in the History of Economic Thought and Methodology*, vol. 38A, edited by Luca Fiorito, Scott Scheall, and Carlos Eduardo Suprinyak. Emerald, 2020. Kindle.

Faust, Drew Gilpin. *James Henry Hammond and the Old South: A Design for Mastery*. Louisiana State University Press, 1982. Kindle.

Fehrenbach, Heide, and Davide Rodogno. "'A Horrific Photo of a Drowned Syrian Child': Humanitarian Photography and NGO Media Strategies in Historical Perspective." *International Review of the Red Cross* 97, no. 900 (2015): 1121–1155.

Figes, Orlando. *The Crimean War: A History*. Metropolitan Books, 2010.

First Congress of the Communist International. "The International Situation and the Policy of the Entente." Translated by Alix Holt and Barbara Holland. March 6, 1919. Marxists Internet Archive. www.marxists.org/history/international/comintern/1st-congress/international.htm.

Fisher, Marc. "In Tunisia, Act of One Fruit Vendor Sparks Wave of Revolution Through Arab World." *Washington Post*, March 26, 2011. www.washingtonpost.com/world/in-tunisia-act-of-one-fruit-vendor-sparks-wave-of-revolution-through-arab-world/2011/03/16/AFjfsueB_story.html.

Fitzpatrick, John C., ed. "Speech to Indian Chiefs." Philadelphia, November 29, 1796. In *The Writings of George Washington from the Original Manuscript Sources, 1745–1799*. Vol. 35. US Government Printing Office, 1931. https://archive.org/details/writingsofgeorge35wash/page/n11/mode/2up.

Fitzpatrick, John C., ed. "Talk to the Cherokee Nation." Philadelphia, August 29, 1796. In *The Writings of George Washington from the Original Manuscript Sources, 1745–1799*. Vol. 35. US Government Printing Office, 1931. https://archive.org/details/writingsofgeorge35wash/page/n11/mode/2up.

Floyd, John. "Letters of John Floyd, 1813–1838." *Georgia Historical Quarterly* 33, no. 3 (1949): 228–269.

Fogel, Robert William, and Stanley L. Engerman. *Time on the Cross: The Economics of American Negro Slavery*. Little, Brown and Company, 1974.

Foglesong, David S. *America's Secret War Against Bolshevism: US Intervention in the Russian Civil War, 1917–1920*. University of North Carolina Press, 1995. Kindle.

Folk, Joseph. Statement in Treaty of Peace with Germany Hearing Before the Committee on Foreign Relations. United States Senate, 66th Congress. US Government Printing Office, 1919.

Foner, Eric. *The Fiery Trial: Abraham Lincoln and American Slavery*. W. W. Norton, 2020. Kindle.

Foner, Philip S., ed. *The Life and Writings of Frederick Douglass*. 5 vols. International Publishers, 1950.

Fontana, Biancamaria. Introduction to *Constant: Political Writings*. Cambridge University Press, 1988. Kindle.

Foot, Rosemary. "Remembering the Past to Secure the Present: Versailles Legacies in a Resurgent China." *International Affairs* 95, no. 1 (2019): 143–160. https://doi.org/10.1093/ia/iiy211.

Foreign Assistance Act of 1961, Pub. L. No. 87–195, 75 Stat. (1961). U.S.C. www.govinfo.gov/content/pkg/STATUTE-75/pdf/STATUTE-75-Pg424-2.pdf#page=1.

Founders Online. "From George Washington to Lafayette, 11 August 1790." National Archives. https://founders.archives.gov/documents/Washington/05-06-02-0112.

Founders Online. "From James Madison to Hobohoilthle, [6 November] 1809." National Archives. https://founders.archives.gov/documents/Madison/03-02-02-0072.

Founders Online. "From Thomas Jefferson to Benjamin Hawkins, 18 February 1803." National Archives. https://founders.archives.gov/documents/Jefferson/01-39-02-0456.

Founders Online. "From Thomas Jefferson to Henry Dearborn, 28 August 1807." National Archives. https://founders.archives.gov/documents/Jefferson/99-01-02-6267.

Founders Online. "Thomas Jefferson to David Bailie Warden, 29 December 1813." National Archives. https://founders.archives.gov/documents/Jefferson/03-07-02-0046.

Founders Online. "Thomas Jefferson to Jared Sparks, February 4, 1824." National Archives. https://founders.archives.gov/documents/Jefferson/98-01-02-4020.

Founders Online. "Thomas Jefferson to John Lynch, 21 January 1811." National Archives. https://founders.archives.gov/documents/Jefferson/03-03-02-0243.

Founders Online. "To George Washington from Henry Knox, 7 July 1789." National Archives. https://founders.archives.gov/documents/Washington/05-03-02-0067.

Founders Online. "To James Madison from Hobohoilthle, 29 September 1809." National Archives. https://founders.archives.gov/documents/Madison/03-04-02-0656.

Founders Online. "To Thomas Jefferson from Benjamin Hawkins, 14 June 1786." National Archives. https://founders.archives.gov/documents/Jefferson/01-09-02-0536.

Founders Online. "To Thomas Jefferson from Benjamin Hawkins, 23 January 1800." National Archives. https://founders.archives.gov/documents/Jefferson/01-31-02-0285.

Founders Online. "To Thomas Jefferson from Benjamin Hawkins, 12 July 1800." National Archives. https://founders.archives.gov/documents/Jefferson/01-32-02-0035.

Founders Online. "To Thomas Jefferson from Benjamin Hawkins, 1 March 1801." National Archives. https://founders.archives.gov/documents/Jefferson/01-33-02-0093.

Founders Online. "To Thomas Jefferson from Benjamin Hawkins, 11 July 1803." National Archives. https://founders.archives.gov/documents/Jefferson/01-41-02-0005.

Founders Online. "II. First Annual Message to Congress, 8 December 1801." National Archives. https://founders.archives.gov/documents/Jefferson/01-36-02-0034-0003.

Fox Bourne, H. R. *Civilisation in Congoland: A Story of International Wrong-Doing.* P. S. King & Son, 1903.

Fox-Genovese, Elizabeth. *Within the Plantation Household: Black and White Women of the Old South.* University of North Carolina Press, 1988. Kindle.

Francklyn, Gilbert. *Observations Occasioned by the Attempts Made in England to Effect the Abolition of the Slave Trade.* London: Logographic, 1789.

Fraser Institute. "Economic Freedom of the World: 2022 Annual Report." www.fraserinstitute.org/studies/economic-freedom-of-the-world-2022-annual-report.

Friedman, Milton. *Foreign Economic Aid: Means and Objectives.* Hoover Institution, Stanford University, 1995.

Friedman, Milton. "The Fragility of Freedom." *Encounter*, November 1976.

Friedman, Milton. "The Indian Alternative." *Encounter*, January 1957. www.unz.com/print/Encounter-1957jan-00071.

Friedman, Milton, and Rose Friedman. *Free to Choose: A Personal Statement*. HMH Books, 1980. Kindle.

Friedman, Milton, and Rose Friedman. *Two Lucky People: Memoirs*. University of Chicago Press, 2000.

Friedman, Milton, with the assistance of Rose D. Friedman. *Capitalism and Freedom*. 40th Anniversary ed. University of Chicago Press, 2002. Kindle.

Fryer, Peter. *Staying Power: The History of Black People in Britain*. Pluto, 2018. Kindle.

Fukuyama, Francis. "Americans Are Not Very Good at Nation-Building." Interview by Stephen Moss. *Guardian*, May 23, 2011. www.theguardian.com/books/2011/may/23/francis-fukuyama-americans-not-good-nation-building.

Fukuyama, Francis. "The End of History?" *The National Interest*, no. 16 (1989): 3–18. www.jstor.org/stable/24027184.

Fukuyama, Francis. *The End of History and the Last Man*. Free Press, 2006. Kindle.

Fukuyama, Francis. *Identity: The Demand for Dignity and the Politics of Resentment*. Farrar, Straus and Giroux, 2018.

Furstenberg, Barbara Jean. "The Scholar and Public Policy: An Analysis of the Thought of Paul S. Reinsch." Master's thesis, University of Wisconsin, 1964.

Galvin, William Francis. "The History of the Arms and Great Seal of the Commonwealth of Massachusetts." Secretary of the Commonwealth of Massachusetts. Accessed December 27, 2021. www.sec.state.ma.us/pre/presea/sealhis.htm.

Garrison, William Lloyd. *Thoughts on African Colonization*. 1832. Public Domain Books, Kindle.

General Act of the Berlin Conference on West Africa. February 26, 1885. https://loveman.sdsu.edu/docs/1885GeneralActBerlinConference.pdf.

General Assembly of the Liaison Committee of Development NGOs to the European Communities, 1989. *Code of Conduct: Images and Messages Relating to the Third World*.

Gernes, Todd S. "Poetic Justice: Sarah Forten, Eliza Earle, and the Paradox of Intellectual Property." *New England Quarterly* 71, no. 2 (1998): 229–265. www.jstor.org/stable/366504.

Gerszon Mahler, Daniel, Alaka Holla, and Umar Serajuddin. "Time to Stop Referring to the 'Developing World.'" *Data Blog*, World Bank, January 23, 2024. https://blogs.worldbank.org/en/opendata/time-stop-referring-developing-world.

Gilman, Nils. *Mandarins of the Future: Modernization Theory in Cold War America*. Johns Hopkins University Press, 2003. Kindle.

GlobalSecurity.org. "Uganda–US Relations." www.globalsecurity.org/military/world/uganda/forrel-us.htm.

Green, Michael D. *The Politics of Indian Removal: Creek Government and Society in Crisis*. University of Nebraska Press, 1982.

Guelzo, Allen C. *Fateful Lightning: A New History of the Civil War and Reconstruction*. Oxford University Press, 2012. Kindle.

Guelzo, Allen C. *Lincoln's Emancipation Proclamation: The End of Slavery in America*. Simon & Schuster, 2004. Kindle.

Guettel, Jens-Uwe. *German Expansionism, Imperial Liberalism, and the United States, 1776–1945*. Cambridge University Press, 2012. Kindle.

Guyatt, Nicholas. "The Adams Doctrine and an 'Empire of States.'" *Diplomatic History* 47, no. 5 (2023). https://academic.oup.com/dh/article/47/5/823/7232512.

Guyatt, Nicholas. *Bind Us Apart: How Enlightened Americans Invented Racial Segregation*. Basic Books, 2016. Kindle.

Halberstam, David. *The Best and the Brightest*. Random House, 2001. Kindle.

Halbert, H. S., and T. H. Ball. *The Creek War of 1813 and 1814*. Montgomery, AL: White, Woodruff & Fowler, 1895.

Hämäläinen, Pekka. *Indigenous Continent: The Epic Contest for North America*. Liveright, 2022. Kindle.

Hammond, James Henry. *Letters on Southern Slavery: Addressed to Thomas Clarkson, the English Abolitionist*. Silver Bluff, SC: January 28 and March 24, 1845.

Harris, Abram L. *Race, Radicalism, and Reform: Selected Papers*. Edited by William Darity Jr. Routledge, 2017.

Harris, Alice. Congo Atrocity Lantern Lecture. Accessed November 28, 2023. http://antislavery.nottingham.ac.uk/items/show/2093.

Harris, Robert L. "Early Black Benevolent Societies, 1780–1830." *Massachusetts Review* 20, no. 3 (1979): 603–625.

Harvey, David Allen. "Slavery on the Balance Sheet: Pierre-Samuel Du Pont de Nemours and the Physiocratic Case for Free Labor." *Journal of the Western Society for French History* 42 (2014): 75–87.

Haveman, Christopher D. *Rivers of Sand: Creek Indian Emigration, Relocation, and Ethnic Cleansing in the American South*. University of Nebraska Press, 2016.

Hawkins, Benjamin. *Creek Confederacy and a Sketch of the Creek Country*. Georgia Historical Society, 1848. Kindle.

Hawkins, Benjamin. *Letters of Benjamin Hawkins, 1796–1806*. Georgia Historical Society, 1916.

Hawkins, Benjamin. "A Sketch of the Present State of the Objects Under the Charge of the Principal Agent for Indian Affairs South of the Ohio." Appended to Thomas Jefferson, "Report to Congress," December 8, 1801. In *American State Papers, Indian Affairs, Class II, Vol. 1*, 647–648. US Congress. Compiled by Walter Lowrie and Matthew St. Clair Clarke. Washington: Gales and Seaton, 1832.

Hay, Stephen N. "Rabindranath Tagore in America." *American Quarterly* 14, no. 3 (1962): 439–463. www.jstor.org/stable/2710456.

Heavner, Theodore. "Memorandum from the Deputy Director of the Vietnam Working Group (Heavner) to the Director (Wood)." Washington, August 3, 1962. In *Foreign Relations of the United States, 1961–1963, Volume II, Vietnam, 1962*, edited by John P. Glennon, David M. Baehler, and Charles S. Sampson; general editor Glenn W. LaFantasie. US Government Printing Office, 1990. Kindle. Locations 13556–13573. https://history.state.gov/historicaldocuments/frus1961-63v02/d257.

Heimert, Alan, and Andrew Delbanco, eds. *The Puritans in America: A Narrative Anthology*. Harvard University Press, 1985. Kindle.

Herman, Arthur. *1917: Lenin, Wilson, and the Birth of the New World Disorder*. Harper, 2017. Kindle.

History of Economic Thought. "James Laurence Laughlin, 1850–1933." Accessed May 19, 2025. www.hetwebsite.net/het/profiles/laughlin.htm.

"History of the Founding of the American Economic Association." *Journal of Economic Issues* 20, no. 2 (1986): i–iii. www.jstor.org/stable/4225708.

Hitler, Adolf. *Hitler's Table Talk, 1941–1944: His Private Conversations*. Translated by Norman Cameron and R. H. Stevens. Enigma Books, 2000.

Hitler, Adolf. *Mein Kampf*. Translated by James Murphy. London: Hurst and Blackett, 1939. Kindle.

Ho Chi Minh, *Selected Works*. Vol. 3. Hanoi: Foreign Languages Publishing House, 1960–62. Pages 17–21. http://historymatters.gmu.edu/d/5139.

Hochschild, Adam. *Bury the Chains: Prophets and Rebels in the Fight to Free an Empire's Slaves*. Houghton Mifflin Harcourt, 2020. Kindle.

Hochschild, Adam. *King Leopold's Ghost: A Story of Greed, Terror, and Heroism in Colonial Africa*. 2nd Mariner Books Edition. HarperCollins 2020. Kindle.

Holloway, Kerrie, with Francesca Grandi. "Dignity in Displacement: A Review of the Literature." Working Paper. Overseas Development Institute, Humanitarian Policy Group, June 2018. https://odi.org/en/publications/dignity-in-displacement-a-review-of-the-literature/.

Hoxie, Frederick, E. *A Final Promise: The Campaign to Assimilate the Indians, 1880–1920*. University of Nebraska Press, 1984.

Hülsmann, Jörg Guido. *Mises: The Last Knight of Liberalism*. Ludwig von Mises Institute, 2007.

Human Rights Watch. "Ghana: Revolutionary Injustice—Abuse of the Legal System Under the PNDC Government." January 31, 1992. www.hrw.org/report/1992/01/31/ghana-revolutionary-injustice/abuse-legal-system-under-pndc-government.

Human Rights Watch. "Who Is Joseph Kony? Questions and Answers on the Lord's Resistance Army." March 2012. www.hrw.org/sites/default/files/related_material/Kony%20QA%203%2021%202012.pdf.

Ignatieff, Michael. *Isaiah Berlin: A Life*. Henry Holt, 1999.

Invisible Children. "KONY 2012." Posted March 5, 2012. YouTube, 29:58. https://youtu.be/Y4MnpzG5Sqc?si=qBbIDmLxRAhDLDvr.

Ireland, Alleyne. "On the Need for a Scientific Study of Colonial Administration." *Proceedings of the American Political Science Association* 3, Third Annual Meeting (1906): 210–221. www.jstor.org/stable/3038548.

Ireland, Alleyne. *Tropical Colonization: An Introduction to the Study of the Subject*. New York: Macmillan, 1899.

Isenberg, Nancy. *White Trash: The 400-Year Untold History of Class in America*. Penguin, 2016. Kindle.

Jacobs, Harriet. *Incidents in the Life of a Slave Girl*. Grapevine Books, 2022. Kindle.

Jacobs, Margaret D. "Maternal Colonialism: White Women and Indigenous Child

Removal in the American West and Australia, 1880–1940." *Western Historical Quarterly* 36, no. 4 (2005): 453–476. www.jstor.org/stable/25443236.

Jasanoff, Maya. *The Dawn Watch: Joseph Conrad in a Global World*. Penguin, 2018. Kindle.

Jefferson, Thomas. "Fifth Annual Message." December 3, 1805. https://millercenter.org/the-presidency/presidential-speeches/december-3-1805-fifth-annual-message.

Jefferson, Thomas. "First Annual Message to Congress." December 8, 1801. Avalon Project, Yale Law School. https://avalon.law.yale.edu/19th_century/jeffmes1.asp.

Jefferson, Thomas. *Notes on the State of Virginia*. Digireads.com, 2010. Kindle.

Jefferson, Thomas. "Second Inaugural Address." March 4, 1805. Avalon Project, Yale Law School. https://avalon.law.yale.edu/19th_century/jefinau2.asp.

Jenks, Jeremiah W., Charles S. Hamlin, Edwin R. A. Seligman, and Albert Shaw. "Report of the Committee on Colonies." *Publications of the American Economic Association* 1, no. 3, 3rd series, Essays on Colonial Finance (1900): 17–20. www.jstor.org/stable/2485788.

John F. Kennedy Presidential Library and Museum. Historic Speeches. "Address to the United Nations General Assembly." September 25, 1961. www.jfklibrary.org/learn/about-jfk/historic-speeches/address-to-the-united-nations-general-assembly.

Johnson, Robert H. "Memorandum from Robert H. Johnson of the Policy Planning Staff to the Counselor of the Department of State (Rostow) [The Situation in Central Vietnam]." October 16, 1962. In *Foreign Relations of the United States, 1961–1963, Volume II, Vietnam, 1962*, edited by John P. Glennon, David M. Baehler, and Charles S. Sampson; general editor Glenn W. LaFantasie. US Government Printing Office, 1990. Locations 16494–16498. https://history.state.gov/historicaldocuments/frus1961-63v02/d303.

Jones, Gregg. *Honor in the Dust: Theodore Roosevelt, War in the Philippines, and the Rise and Fall of America's Imperial Dream*. Penguin, 2012. Kindle.

Kahin, George McTurnan. *The Asian-African Conference: Bandung Indonesia, April 1955*. Cornell University Press, 1956.

Kakel, C. *The American West and the Nazi East: A Comparative and Interpretive Perspective*. Palgrave Macmillan, 2011. Kindle.

Kant, Immanuel. *Anthropology, History, and Education*. Edited by Robert B. Louden and Günter Zöller. Cambridge University Press, 2007.

Kant, Immanuel. *Kant: Political Writings*. Translated by H. B. Nisbet. Cambridge University Press, 1991. Kindle.

Kant, Immanuel. *Practical Philosophy*. Translated and edited by Mary J. Gregor. Cambridge University Press, 1996. Kindle.

Kappler, Charles J., ed. "Treaty with the Creeks: 1790." In *Indian Affairs: Laws and Treaties*. Vol. 2, *Treaties*. US Government Printing Office, 1904. https://avalon.law.yale.edu/18th_century/cre1790.asp.

Karcher, Carolyn L. *The First Woman in the Republic: A Cultural Biography of Lydia Maria Child*. Duke University Press, 1994. Kindle.

Karcher, Carolyn L. Introduction to *Hobomok and Other Writings on Indians*, by Lydia Maria Child. Rutgers University Press, 1986. Kindle.

Karnow, Stanley. *In Our Image: America's Empire in the Philippines*. Random House, 1989. Kindle.

Kennedy, John F. "Administration of Foreign Assistance and Related Functions." Executive Order 10973, White House, November 3, 1961. www.thecre.com/fedlaw/legal20/eo10973.htm.

Kennedy, John F. "Conference on India and the United States." Washington, DC, May 4, 1959. Papers of John F. Kennedy. Pre-Presidential Papers. Senate Files, Box 903, John F. Kennedy Presidential Library. www.jfklibrary.org/archives/other-resources/john-f-kennedy-speeches/india-and-the-us-conference-washington-dc-19590504.

Kennedy, John F. "Inaugural Address." January 20, 1961. National Archives. www.archives.gov/milestone-documents/president-john-f-kennedys-inaugural-address.

Kennedy, John F. "The New Dimensions of American Foreign Policy." Remarks at University of Pennsylvania, Philadelphia, Pennsylvania, November 1, 1957. John F. Kennedy Presidential Library. www.jfklibrary.org/archives/other-resources/john-f-kennedy-speeches/university-of-pennsylvania-19571101.

Kennedy, John F. "Special Message to Congress on Foreign Aid." March 22, 1961. www.presidency.ucsb.edu/documents/special-message-the-congress-foreign-aid-1.

Kershaw, Ian. *Hitler: 1936–1945; Nemesis*. W. W. Norton, 2000. Kindle.

Keynes, John Maynard. "Obituary for Mary Paley Marshall (1850–1944)." *Economic Journal*, June–September 1944, 268–284.

Keynes, John Maynard. *The General Theory of Employment, Interest, and Money*. Palgrave Macmillan, 2018.

Khan, Themrise, Seye Abimbola, Catherine Kyobutungi, and Madhukar Pai. "How We Classify Countries and People—and Why It Matters." *BMJ Global Health* 7, no. 6 (2022). https://gh.bmj.com/content/7/6/e009704.

Kiernan, Victor. *The Lords of Human Kind: European Attitudes to Other Cultures in the Imperial Age*. Zed Books, 2015. Kindle.

Kingsley, Mary H. *Travels in West Africa: Congo Français, Corisco, and Cameroons* (eBook prepared by Les Bowler, St. Ives, Dorset), 1897.

Kingsley, Mary H. *West African Studies*. 3rd ed. Taylor and Francis, 1964.

Kipling, Rudyard. *Kipling: Poems*. Knopf Doubleday, 2007. Kindle.

Korsgaard, Christine M, ed. *Kant: Groundwork of the Metaphysics of Morals*. Cambridge University Press, 2012. Kindle.

Kotkin, Stephen. *Stalin: Paradoxes of Power, 1878–1928*. Penguin, 2014. Kindle.

Kremlin. "Meeting with Heads of African Delegations on Ukrainian Agenda [transcript]." Saint Petersburg, Russia, July 28, 2023. http://en.kremlin.ru/events/president/transcripts/71835.

Kremlin. "Meeting with President of Uganda Yoweri Kaguta Museveni [transcript]." Saint Petersburg, July 27, 2023. http://en.kremlin.ru/events/president/transcripts/71823.

Kristof, Nicholas. "Viral Video, Vicious Warlord." *New York Times*, March 14, 2012. www.nytimes.com/2012/03/15/opinion/kristof-viral-video-vicious-warlord.html.

Latham, Michael E. *Modernization as Ideology: American Social Science and "Nation Building" in the Kennedy Era*. University of North Carolina Press, 2000. Kindle.

Latham, Michael E. *The Right Kind of Revolution: Modernization, Development, and US Foreign Policy from the Cold War to the Present*. Cornell University Press, 2011. Kindle.

Lauren, Paul Gordon. *The Evolution of International Human Rights: Visions Seen*. University of Pennsylvania Press, 2011. Kindle.

Lauren, Paul Gordon. *Power and Prejudice: The Politics and Diplomacy of Racial Discrimination*. 2nd ed. Routledge, 2018. Kindle.

Laughlin, J. Laurence. *Patriotism and Imperialism*. Liberty Tracts no. 2. Chicago: Central Anti-Imperialist League, 1899.

Leahy, Peter Francis. "Why Did the Strategic Hamlet Program Fail?" Master's thesis, US Army Command and General Staff College, 1990.

Lee, Arthur. *An Essay in Vindication of the Continental Colonies of America, from a Censure of Mr. Adam Smith, in His Theory of Moral Sentiments. With Some Reflections on Slavery in General*. London: T. Becket and P. A. De Hondt, 1764.

Lenin, Vladimir Ilyich, "Address to the Second All-Russia Congress of Communist Organisations of the Peoples of the East." November 22, 1919. *Lenin's Collected Works*, 4th English ed. Vol. 30. Translated by George Hanna. Progress Publishers, 1965. Marxists Internet Archive. www.marxists.org/archive/lenin/works/1919/nov/22.htm.

Lenin, Vladimir Ilyich. "Declaration of Rights of the Working and Exploited People." January 3, 1918. In *Lenin's Collected Works*. Vol. 26, 423–425, edited by George Hanna; translated by Yuri Sdobnikov and George Hanna. Progress Publishers, 1972. Marxists Internet Archive. www.marxists.org/archive/lenin/works/1918/jan/03.htm.

Lenin, Vladimir Ilyich. *Essential Works of Lenin: "What Is to Be Done?" and Other Writings*. Dover Publications, 1966. Kindle.

Lenin, Vladimir Ilyich. *Imperialism: The Highest Stage of Capitalism*. Parus, 1917. Kindle.

Lenin, Vladimir Ilyich. "Report on Peace." Second All-Russia Congress of Soviets of Workers' and Soldiers' Deputies. October 26 (November 8), 1917. Marxists Internet Archive. www.marxists.org/archive/lenin/works/1917/oct/25-26/26b.htm.

Lenin, Vladimir Ilyich. "The Socialist Revolution and the Right of Nations to Self-Determination." April 1916. Marxists Internet Archive. www.marxists.org/archive/lenin/works/1916/jan/x01.htm.

Lenin, Vladimir Ilyich. "Telegram to Comrades Kuraev, Bosh, Minkin, and Other Penza Communists." August 11, 1918. Marxists Internet Archive. www.marxists.org/archive/lenin/works/1918/aug/11c.htm.

Lenin, Vladimir Ilyich. *What Is to Be Done? Burning Questions of Our Movement* [in Russian]. J.H.W. Dietz, 1902. Available in English from the Marxists Internet Archive at www.marxists.org/archive/lenin/works/1901/witbd.

Leonard, Thomas C. *Illiberal Reformers: Race, Eugenics, and American Economics in the Progressive Era*. Princeton University Press, 2016. Kindle.

Letelier, Orlando. "The 'Chicago Boys' in Chile: Economic Freedom's Awful Toll." *The Nation*, August 1976. www.thenation.com/article/archive/the-chicago-boys-in-chile-economic-freedoms-awful-toll/.

Leverkuehn, Paul. *German Military Intelligence*. Praeger, 1954.

Levitz, Eric. "The Biden Administration Just Declared the Death of Neoliberalism." Intelligencer, *New York*, May 3, 2023. https://nymag.com/intelligencer/2023/05/biden-just-declared-the-death-of-neoliberalism.html.

Levy, David M. *How the Dismal Science Got Its Name: Classical Economics and the Ur-Text of Racial Politics*. University of Michigan Press, 2002.

Levy, David M., and Sandra J. Peart. *Escape from Democracy: The Role of Experts and the Public in Economic Policy*. Cambridge University Press, 2016.

Levy, David M., and Sandra J. Peart. "Harriet Martineau: Economist as Storyteller and Traveler." *Independent Review* 28, no. 2 (2023): 193–202.

Levy, David M., and Sandra J. Peart. "Sympathy, Evolution, and *The Economist*." *Journal of Economic Behavior & Organization* 71 (2009): 29–36.

Levy, David M., and Sandra J. Peart, *Towards an Economics of Natural Equals: A Documentary History of the Early Virginia School*. Cambridge University Press, 2020.

Lewis, David Levering. *W. E. B. Du Bois, 1868–1919: Biography of a Race*. Henry Holt, 1993. Kindle.

Lewis, David Levering. *W. E. B. Du Bois, 1919–1963: The Fight for Equality and the American Century*. Henry Holt, 2000. Kindle.

Library of Congress. "La Rochefoucauld d'Enville, Louis-Alexandre, duc de, 1743–1792." https://id.loc.gov/authorities/names/no91011155.html.

Lincoln, Abraham. *Speeches and Writings*. Vol. 1, *1832–1858*. Edited by Don E. Fehrenbacher. Library of America, 1989. Kindle.

Lincoln, Abraham. *Speeches and Writings*. Vol. 2, *1859–1865*. Edited by Don E. Fehrenbacher. Library of America, 1989. Kindle.

Lindert, Peter H., and Jeffrey G. Williamson. *Unequal Gains: American Growth and Inequality Since 1700*. Princeton University Press, 2016. Kindle.

Linn, Brian McAllister. *The Philippine War, 1899–1902*. University Press of Kansas, 2000. Kindle.

Locke, John. *Two Treatises of Government and a Letter Concerning Toleration*. Digireads.com, 2009. Kindle.

Logically Fallacious. "Reductio ad Hitlerum." www.logicallyfallacious.com/logicalfallacies/Reductio-ad-Hitlerum.

Long, Edward. *The History of Jamaica*. Vol. 2. London: T. Lowndes, 1774.

López, Sixto. "Sixto Lopez to the American People." L. K. Fuller, 1900. https://catalog.hathitrust.org/Record/103233555.

Louis, Wm. Roger, and Jean Stengers. *E. D. Morel's History of the Congo Reform Movement*. Clarendon Press, 1968.

Lower, Wendy. *Nazi Empire-Building and the Holocaust in Ukraine*. University of North Carolina Press, 2005. Kindle.

Lukes, Steven, and Nadia Urbinati, eds. *Condorcet: Political Writings*. Cambridge University Press, 2012. Kindle.

Maddison Project Database (MDP). Version 2020. In Jutta Bolt and Jan Luiten van Zanden, "Maddison-Style Estimates of the Evolution of the World Economy: A New 2020 Update." Maddison-Project Working Paper WP-15, 2020.

Madison, James. "State of the Union Address." November 29, 1809. www.presidentialrhetoric.com/historicspeeches/madison/stateoftheunion.1809.html.

Malle, Silvana. *The Economic Organization of War Communism, 1918–1921*. Cambridge University Press, 2009.

Malone, Dudley Field. Statement in Treaty of Peace with Germany: Hearings Before the Committee on Foreign Relations. United States Senate, Sixty-Sixth Congress. US Government Printing Office, 1919.

Malthus, Thomas Robert. *An Essay on the Principle of Population: The 1803 Edition*. Edited by Shannon C. Stimson, Niall O'Flaherty, Deborah Valenze, E. A. Wrigley, Kenneth Binmore, and Karen O'Brien. Yale University Press, 2018. www.jstor.org/stable/j.ctv1bvnf95.

Malthus, Thomas Robert. *A Summary View of the Principle of Population*. London: J. Murray, 1830.

Mamdani, Mahmood. *From Citizen to Refugee: Uganda Asians Come to Britain*. 2nd ed. Pambazuka Press, 2011. Kindle.

Mamdani, Mahmood. "Kony: What Jason Did Not Tell the Invisible Children." *Al Jazeera*, March 13, 2012. www.aljazeera.com/opinions/2012/3/13/kony-what-jason-did-not-tell-the-invisible-children.

Mamdani, Mahmood. "Responsibility to Protect or Right to Punish?" *Journal of Intervention and State-Building* 4, no. 1 (2010): 53–67. https://doi.org/10.1080/17502970903541721.

Mandela, Nelson. *Long Walk to Freedom: The Autobiography of Nelson Mandela*. Little, Brown and Company, 1994.

Manela, Erez. *The Wilsonian Moment: Self-Determination and the International Origins of Anticolonial Nationalism*. Oxford University Press, 2007. Kindle.

Mantena, Karuna. *Alibis of Empire: Henry Maine and the Ends of Liberal Imperialism*. Princeton University Press, 2010.

Manuel, Frank E. *The Prophets of Paris*. Harvard University Press, 1962.

Manzo, Kate. "Imaging Humanitarianism: NGO Identity and the Iconography of Childhood." *Antipode* 40, no. 4 (2008): 632–657.

Mao Zedong. "The Chinese People Have Stood Up!" September 21, 1949. Opening address at the First Plenary Session of the Chinese People's Political Consultative Conference. In *Selected Works of Mao Tse-tung*. Marxists Internet Archive. www.marxists.org/reference/archive/mao/selected-works/volume-5/mswv5_01.htm.

Mao Zedong. *Mao's Road to Power: Revolutionary Writings, 1912–49*. Vol. 1, *Pre-Marxist Period, 1912–20*. Taylor and Francis, 1993. Kindle.

Marshall, Alfred. *Principles of Economics*. 8th ed. Macmillan, 1920. Kindle. Online Library of Liberty. http://oll.libertyfund.org/titles/1676.

Marshall, Alfred, and Mary Paley Marshall. *The Economics of Industry*. London: Macmillan, 1888.

Marshall, Alfred, and Royden Harrison. "Two Early Articles by Alfred Marshall." *Economic Journal* 73, no. 291 (1963): 422–430. www.jstor.org/stable/2228577.

Martin, Joel W. "Crisscrossing Projects of Sovereignty and Conversion: Cherokee Christians and New England Missionaries During the 1820s." In Joel W. Martin, and Mark A. Nicholas, eds., *Native Americans, Christianity, and the Reshaping of the American Religious Landscape*. Online ed. University of North Carolina Press, 2010. https://doi.org/10.5149/9780807899663_martin.8.

Martin, Joel W. Introduction in *Native Americans, Christianity, and the Reshaping of the American Religious Landscape*, edited by Joel W. Martin and Mark A. Nicholas. University of North Carolina Press, 2010.

Martineau, Harriet. *Harriet Martineau's Autobiography*. Vol. 1. Online Library of Liberty. Originally published by James R. Osgood & Co. in 1877. https://oll.libertyfund.org/titles/chapman-harriet-martineau-s-autobiography-vol-1.

Martineau, Harriet. *Illustrations of Political Economy, No. IV, Demerara*. London: William Clowes, 1832. Kindle.

Martineau, Harriet. *The Martyr Age of the United States of America: With an Appeal on Behalf of the Oberlin Institute in Aid of the Abolition of Slavery*. Newcastle Upon Tyne: Finlay and Charlton, 1840.

Martineau, Harriet. *Retrospect of Western Travel*. Vol. 2. London: Saunders and Otley, 1838. Online Library of Liberty. https://oll.libertyfund.org/titles/martineau-retrospect-of-western-travel-vol-2.

Martineau, Harriet. *Society in America*. 2 vols. London: Saunders and Otley, 1837. Kindle.

Marx, Karl. "The Eighteenth Brumaire of Louis Bonaparte." 1852. Marxists Internet Archive. www.marxists.org/archive/marx/works/1852/18th-brumaire/ch01.htm.

Marx, Karl. "Theses on Feuerbach." 1845. Marxists Internet Archive. www.marxists.org/archive/marx/works/1845/theses/theses.htm.

Mashantucket (Western) Pequot Tribal Nation. "About page." Accessed May 15, 2025. www.mptn-nsn.gov.

Massachusetts Historical Society. "A Copy of an Address Composed by a Cherokee Indian, Named Dewi or David Brown." *Proceedings 1871–1873*, February 1871. Google Books. https://play.google.com/books/reader?id=VD2ysKTfwi4C&pg=GBS.PA29&hl=en.

Masson, Marjorie, and J. F. Jameson. "The Odyssey of Thomas Muir." *American Historical Review* 29, no. 1 (1923): 49–72. www.jstor.org/stable/1839274.

Mayer, Arno J. *Wilson vs. Lenin: Political Origins of the New Diplomacy*. Meridian Books, 1964.

McCloskey, Deirdre N. *Why Liberalism Works: How True Liberal Values Produce a Freer, More Equal, Prosperous World for All*. Yale University Press, 2019.

McCusker, John J. "Colonial Statistics." In *Historical Statistics of the United States: Earliest Time to the Present*, edited by S. B. Carter, S. S. Gartner, M. R. Haines, Alan L. Olmstead, Richard Sutch, and Gavin Wright. Vol. 671. Cambridge University Press, 2006.

McDaniel, Antonio. "Extreme Mortality in Nineteenth-Century Africa: The Case of Liberian Immigrants." *Demography* 29 (1992): 581–594. https://doi.org/10.2307/2061853.

McDaniel, Antonio. *Swing Low, Sweet Chariot: The Mortality Cost of Colonizing Liberia in the Nineteenth Century*. University of Chicago Press, 1995.

McLean, Iain, and Fiona Hewitt, eds. *Condorcet: Foundations of Social Choice and Political Theory*. Elgar, 1994.

McMeekin, Sean. *The Russian Revolution: A New History*. Basic Books, 2017. Kindle.

McNab, David Thornton. "Herman Merivale and the British Empire, 1806–1874, with special reference to British North America, Southern Africa, and India."

PhD diss., Lancaster University, January 1978. www.research.lancs.ac.uk/portal/en/publications/herman-merivale-and-the-british-empire-18061874-with-special-reference-to-british-north-america-southern-africa-and-india(354fcfc1-66b1-4d59-b6d7-081a3c3551d1).html.

McNamara, Robert S. "Population and International Security." *International Security* 2, no. 2 (1977): 25–55.

Meek, R. L., D. D. Raphael, and Peter Stein, eds. *The Glasgow Edition of the Works and Correspondence of Adam Smith.* Vol. 5, *Lectures on Jurisprudence.* Oxford University Press, 1978. Published online, May 2014.

Mehta, Uday Singh. *Liberalism and Empire: A Study in Nineteenth-Century British Liberal Thought.* University of Chicago Press, 1999.

Merivale, Herman. *Lectures on Colonization and Colonies.* London: Longman, Green, and Roberts, 1861.

Milford, Louis LeClerc de. *A Cursory Glance at My Different Travels & My Sojourn in the Creek Nation.* Translated by Geraldine de Courcy, edited by John Francis McDermott. R. R. Donnelly & Sons, 1956.

Mill, Harriet Taylor. "Enfranchisement of Women." *Westminster and Foreign Quarterly Review, LV* (July 1851), 289–311. In John M. Robson, ed., with Introduction by Stefan Collini. *The Collected Works of John Stuart Mill, Volume XXI—Essays on Equality, Law, and Education.* University of Toronto Press, 1984. Online Library of Liberty. https://oll.libertyfund.org/titles/mill-the-collected-works-of-john-stuart-mill-volume-xxi-essays-on-equality-law-and-education.

Mill, James. Art. VI. "Publications on the Affairs of India." *Edinburgh Review* 31 (April 1810): 128–157. https://archive.org/details/sim_edinburgh-review-critical-journal_1810-04_16_31.

Mill, James. Art. VII. "Voyage aux Indes Orientales." *Edinburgh Review* 30 (January 1810): 363–384. https://archive.org/details/sim_edinburgh-review-critical-journal_1810-01_15_30.

Mill, James. "Testimony." August 25, 1831. In "Minutes of Evidence Before Select Committee on the Affairs of the East India Company," 396–397. Google Books. https://play.google.com/books/reader?id=ezdDAAAAcAAJ&pg=GBS.PA396&hl=en.

Mill, John Stuart. *The Autobiography of John Stuart Mill.* Seven Treasures Publications, 2009.

Mill, John Stuart. *Considerations on Representative Government.* 1861. In John M. Robson, ed., with Introduction by Alexander Brady. *The Collected Works of John Stuart Mill, Volume XIX—Essays on Politics and Society, Part 2.* Online Library of Liberty. https://oll.libertyfund.org/titles/robson-the-collected-works-of-john-stuart-mill-volume-xix-essays-on-politics-and-society-part-2.

Mill, John Stuart. "The Contest in America." 1862. In John M. Robson, ed., with Introduction by Stefan Collini. *The Collected Works of John Stuart Mill, Volume XXI—Essays on Equality, Law, and Education.* University of Toronto Press, 1984. Online Library of Liberty. https://oll.libertyfund.org/titles/mill-the-collected-works-of-john-stuart-mill-volume-xxi-essays-on-equality-law-and-education.

Mill, John Stuart. "Grote's Plato." 1866. In John M. Robson, ed., with Introduction by Francis Edward Sparshott. *The Collected Works of John Stuart Mill, Volume*

XI—Essays on Philosophy and the Classics. University of Toronto Press, 1978. Online Library of Liberty. https://oll.libertyfund.org/titles/mill-the-collected-works-of-john-stuart-mill-volume-xi-essays-on-philosophy-and-the-classics.

Mill, John Stuart. "The Negro Question." 1850. In John M. Robson, ed., with Introduction by Stefan Collini. *The Collected Works of John Stuart Mill, Volume XXI—Essays on Equality, Law, and Education*. University of Toronto Press, 1984. Online Library of Liberty. https://oll.libertyfund.org/titles/mill-the-collected-works-of-john-stuart-mill-volume-xxi-essays-on-equality-law-and-education.

Mill, John Stuart. *On Liberty*. Introduction by W. L. Courtney. London: Walter Scott Publishing Co., 1859. Kindle.

Mill, John Stuart. *Principles of Political Economy with Some of Their Applications to Social Philosophy*. London: Longmans, Green, Reader, and Dyer, 1871. Google Books. https://play.google.com/books/reader?id=ujAoAAAAYAAJ&pg=GBS.PA569&hl=en.

Mill, John Stuart. *The Subjection of Women*. 3rd ed. London: Longmans, Green, Reader, and Dyer, 1870. Kindle.

Mill, John Stuart. *Utilitarianism*. London: Parker, Son, and Bourn, 1863.

Miller, David Hunter. *The Drafting of the Covenant*. 2 vols. New York: G. P. Putnam's Sons, 1928.

Miller, Stuart Creighton. *Benevolent Assimilation: The American Conquest of the Philippines, 1899–1903*. Yale University Press, 1982.

Milne, David. *America's Rasputin: Walt Rostow and the Vietnam War*. Farrar, Straus and Giroux, 2008. Kindle.

Minorities at Risk Project. "Minorities at Risk Dataset." Center for International Development and Conflict Management, 2009. Retrieved from www.mar.umd.edu on February 25, 2024.

Mises, Ludwig von. *Socialism: An Economic and Sociological Analysis*. Translated by J. Kahane. Yale University Press, 1951.

Mises, Ludwig von. *Human Action: Scholar's Edition*. Ludwig von Mises Institute, 1998. Kindle.

Mises, Ludwig von. *Liberalism*. Dead Authors Society, 2018. Kindle.

Mishra, Pankaj. *From the Ruins of Empire: The Intellectuals Who Remade Asia*. Farrar, Straus and Giroux, 2012. Kindle.

Mishra, Pankaj. *Bland Fanatics: Liberals, Race, and Empire*. Farrar, Straus and Giroux, 2020. Kindle.

M'Kenney, Thomas L. *Memoirs, Official and Personal; With Sketches of Travels Among the Northern and Southern Indians; Embracing a War Excursion, and Descriptions of Scenes Along the Western Borders*. Vol. 1. 2nd ed. New York: Paine and Burgess, 1846.

Moland, Lydia. *Lydia Maria Child: A Radical American Life*. University of Chicago Press, 2022. Kindle.

Morel, E. D. *Affairs of West Africa*. William Heinemann, 1902.

Morel, E. D. *The Black Man's Burden*. B. W. Huebsch, 1920.

Morel, E. D. *King Leopold's Rule in Africa*. 1905. Kindle.

Morel, E. D. *Nigeria: Its Peoples and Its Problems*. Smith, Elder, 1911. Kindle.

Moyo, Dambisa. *Dead Aid: Why Aid Is Not Working and How There Is a Better Way for Africa*. Farrar, Straus and Giroux, 2009. Kindle.

Munroe, James Phinney. *A Life of Francis Amasa Walker*. H. Holt, 1923.

Murphy, Gretchen. *Hemispheric Imaginings: The Monroe Doctrine and Narratives of US Empire*. Duke University Press, 2005. Kindle.

Muthu, Sankar. *Enlightenment Against Empire*. Princeton University Press, 2003. Kindle.

National Park Service. "Emancipation Statue." Capitol Hill Parks. District of Columbia. Updated July 16, 2024. www.nps.gov/cahi/learn/historyculture/emancipation-statue.htm.

New York Times Editorial Board. "Foreign Aid Is Having a Reckoning." Opinion, *New York Times*, February 13, 2021. www.nytimes.com/2021/02/13/opinion/africa-foreign-aid-philanthropy.html.

Nkrumah, Kwame. *Africa Must Unite*. Praeger, 1963.

Nobel Prize Outreach. "Milton Friedman: Biographical." Accessed May 14, 2025. www.nobelprize.org/prizes/economic-sciences/1976/friedman/biographical/.

Nunn, Nathan, and Nancy Qian. "US Food Aid and Civil Conflict." *American Economic Review* 104, no. 6 (2014): 1630–1666.

Nworah, Kenneth Dike. "The Liverpool 'Sect' and British West African Policy, 1895–1915." *African Affairs* 70, no. 281 (1971): 349–364. www.jstor.org/stable/721056.

Okrent, Daniel. *The Guarded Gate: Bigotry, Eugenics and the Law That Kept Two Generations of Jews, Italians, and Other European Immigrants Out of America*. Scribner, 2019. Kindle.

Online Library of Liberty. "J Laurence Laughlin." Accessed May 19, 2025. https://oll.libertyfund.org/person/j-laurence-laughlin.

Opalo, Ken. "Who Is the African Child on the Cover of William Easterly's New Book?" Personal website, December 21, 2013. https://kenopalo.com/2013/12/21/who-is-the-african-child-on-the-cover-of-william-easterlys-new-book/.

Open Society Foundations. "Understanding Ukraine's Euromaidan Protests." Updated May 2019. www.opensocietyfoundations.org/explainers/understanding-ukraines-euromaidan-protests.

Osborne, Milton E. *Strategic Hamlets in South Vietnam: A Survey and Comparison*. Cornell University Press, 1965. www.jstor.org/stable/10.7591/j.ctv1nhkt6.7.

Painter, Nell. *The History of White People*. W. W. Norton, 2010.

Pande, Rohini, and Helena Roy. "*If You Compete with Us, We Shan't Marry You*": The (Mary Paley and) Alfred Marshall Lecture. *Journal of the European Economic Association* 19, no. 6, December 2021, 2992–3024. https://doi.org/10.1093/jeea/jvab049.

Pavlakis, Dean. *British Humanitarianism and the Congo Reform Movement, 1896–1913*. Routledge, 2015. Kindle.

Pazzanese, Christina. "Amartya Sen's Nine-Decade Journey from Colonial India to Nobel Prize and Beyond." *Harvard Gazette*, June 3, 2021. https://news.harvard.edu/gazette/story/2021/06/tracing-amartya-sens-path-from-childhood-during-the-raj-to-nobel-prize-and-beyond/.

Peart, Sandra J., and David M. Levy. "Denying Human Homogeneity: Eugenics & The Making of Post-Classical Economics." *Journal of the History of Economic Thought* 25, no. 3 (2003): 261–288. https://doi.org/10.1080/1042771032000114728.

Peart, Sandra J., and David M. Levy. "Economics and Race: A Long View." Unpublished manuscript. August 8, 2022.

Peart, Sandra J., and David M. Levy, eds. *The Street Porter and the Philosopher: Conversations on Analytical Egalitarianism*. University of Michigan Press, 2008. Kindle.

Peart, Sandra J., and David M. Levy. *The "Vanity of the Philosopher": From Equality to Hierarchy in Post-Classical Economics*. University of Michigan Press, 2005. Kindle.

Pedersen, Susan. *The Guardians: The League of Nations and the Crisis of Empire*. Oxford University Press, 2015. Kindle.

Phillipson, Nicholas. *Adam Smith: An Enlightened Life*. Yale University Press, 2010. Kindle.

Pipes, Richard. *The Russian Revolution*. Knopf Doubleday, 1990. Kindle.

Pitts, Jennifer. "Republicanism, Liberalism, and Empire in Postrevolutionary France." In *Empire and Modern Political Thought*, edited by Sankar Muthu. Cambridge University Press, 2012. Kindle.

Pitts, Jennifer. *A Turn to Empire: The Rise of Imperial Liberalism in Britain and France*. Princeton University Press, 2005. Kindle.

Pletsch, Carl E. "The Three Worlds, or the Division of Social Scientific Labor, Circa 1950–1975." *Comparative Studies in Society and History* 23, no. 4 (1981): 565–590. www.jstor.org/stable/178394.

Postlethwayt, Malachy. *The National and Private Advantages of the African Trade Considered*. 2nd ed. London: William Otridos, 1772. https://archive.org/details/bim_eighteenth-century_the-national-and-private_postlethwayt-malachy_1772.

Pound, Merritt B. *Benjamin Hawkins, Indian Agent*. University of Georgia Press, 1951.

Prados de la Escosura, L. "Lost Decades? Economic Performance in Post-Independence Latin America." *Journal of Latin America Studies* 41 (2009): 279–307. Updated data.

Prucha, Francis Paul, ed. *Cherokee Removal: The "William Penn" Essays and Other Writings*, by Jeremiah Evarts. University of Tennessee Press, 1981.

Prucha, Francis Paul. "Protest by Petition: Jeremiah Evarts and the Cherokee Indians." *Proceedings of the Massachusetts Historical Society* 97, 3rd series (1985): 42–58. www.jstor.org/stable/25080942.

Pugach, Noel H. *Paul S. Reinsch: Open Door Diplomat in Action*. KTO, 1979.

Putin, Vladimir. "Speech at Ukrainian Annexation Ceremony [transcript]." The Kremlin, October 1, 2022. Mirage News. www.miragenews.com/full-text-of-putins-speech-at-annexation-866383/.

Quinton, Amelia Stone. *The Indian's Friend*. September 1897.

Rae, John. *Life of Adam Smith*. London: Macmillan, 1895. Kindle.

Reinsch, Paul S. *An American Diplomat in China*. Page, 1922.

Reinsch, Paul S. *Colonial Administration*. Macmillan, 1905.

Reinsch, Paul S. "Colonial Autonomy, with Special Reference to the Government of the Philippine Islands." *Proceedings of the American Political Science Association* 1 (1904): 116–139. www.jstor.org/stable/3038325.

Reinsch, Paul S. "Real Conditions in the Congo Free State." *North American Review* 178, no. 567 (1904): 216–221. www.jstor.org/stable/25119525.

Reinsch, Paul S. *World Politics at the End of the Nineteenth Century*. Macmillan, 1900.

Robinson, Austin. Review of *What I Remember*, by Mary Paley Marshall. *Economic Journal* 58, no. 229 (1948): 122–124. www.jstor.org/stable/2226358.

Rodrik, Dani. "Goodbye Washington Consensus, Hello Washington Confusion?" *Journal of Economic Literature* 44 (December 2006): 969–983.

Røge, Pernille. *Economistes and the Reinvention of Empire: France in the Americas and Africa, c. 1750–1802*. Cambridge University Press, 2019. Kindle.

Rómulo, Carlos P. *I Walked with Heroes*. Verdun, 1962. Kindle.

Rómulo, Carlos P. *The Meaning of Bandung*. The University of North Carolina Press, 1956.

Rosenberg, Jonathan. "For Democracy, Not Hypocrisy: World War and Race Relations in the United States, 1914–1919." *International History Review* 21, no. 3 (1999): 592–625. www.jstor.org/stable/40109078.

Ross, Ian Simpson. *The Life of Adam Smith*. Oxford University Press, 2010. Kindle.

Rostow, W. W. "Development: The Political Economy of the Marshallian Long Period." In *Pioneers in Development*, edited by Gerald M. Meier and Dudley Seers. Oxford University Press, 1984.

Rostow, W. W. "Draft of Crucial Portion of Foreign Aid Message [memorandum to JFK]." March 13, 1961. www.jfklibrary.org/asset-viewer/archives/JFKPOF/064a/JFKPOF-064a-009.

Rostow, W. W. "The Idea of an Economic Development Decade [memorandum to JFK]." March–May 1961. www.jfklibrary.org/asset-viewer/archives/jfkpof-064a-009.

Rostow, W. W. "Letter from the Counselor of the Department of State (Rostow) to the Ambassador in Vietnam (Nolting)," September 5, 1962. In *Foreign Relations of the United States, 1961–1963, Volume I, Vietnam, 1961*, edited by Ronald D. Landa and Charles S. Sampson; general editor John P. Glennon. US Government Printing Office, 1988. Kindle Locations 14531–14543. https://history.state.gov/historicaldocuments/frus1961-63v02/d275.

Rostow, W. W. "Memorandum from the President's Deputy Special Assistant for National Security Affairs (Rostow) to the President." May 10, 1961. In *Foreign Relations of the United States, 1961–1963, Volume I, Vietnam, 1961*, edited by Ronald D. Landa and Charles S. Sampson; general editor John P. Glennon. US Government Printing Office, 1988. Kindle Locations 3601–3610. https://history.state.gov/historicaldocuments/frus1961-63v01.

Rostow, W. W. *The Stages of Economic Growth: A Non-Communist Manifesto*. Cambridge University Press, 1990. Kindle.

Rothschild, Emma. "Adam Smith in the British Empire." In *Empire and Modern Political Thought*, edited by Sankar Muthu. Cambridge University Press, 2012. Kindle.

Rothschild, Emma. "The Atlantic Worlds of David Hume." In *Soundings in Atlantic History*, edited by Bernard Bailyn and Patricia L. Denault. Harvard University Press, 2009. www.jstor.org/stable/j.ctt13x0fhm.16.

Rothschild, Emma. *Economic Sentiments: Adam Smith, Condorcet, and the Enlightenment*. Harvard University Press, 2001. Kindle.

Rubinson, Karen S. "Herodotus and the Scythians." *Expedition Magazine* 17, no. 4 (1975).

Ruge, T. M. S. "'Kony 2012' Is Not a Revolution." *New York Times*, March 14, 2012. www.nytimes.com/roomfordebate/2012/03/09/kony-2012-and-the-potential-of-social-media-activism/kony-2012-is-not-a-revolution.

Rusling, James S. "Interview with President William McKinley." *The Christian Advocate*, January 22, 1903, 17. Reprinted in Charles Sumner Olcott. *The Life of William McKinley, Volume 2*, 109–111. Houghton Mifflin, 1916. Available from *The American Yawp Reader*. www.americanyawp.com/reader/19-american-empire/william-mckinley-on-american-expansionism-1903.

Rutland, Peter. "Neoliberalism and the Russian Transition." *Review of International Political Economy* 20, no. 2 (2013): 332–362. www.jstor.org/stable/42003296.

Saillant, John. "The American Enlightenment in Africa: Jefferson's Colonizationism and Black Virginians' Migration to Liberia, 1776–1840." *Eighteenth-Century Studies* 31, no. 3, Americas (1998): 261–282.

Samuelson, Paul A. "The World Economy at Century's End." In *Human Resources, Employment and Development Volume 1: The Issues Proceedings of the Sixth World Congress of the International Economic Association*, Mexico City, 1980, edited by Shigeto Tsuru. Macmillan, 1983. https://vdoc.pub/documents/human-resources-employment-and-development-volume-1-the-issues-2lil3jo2hf8g.

Saunt, Claudio. *A New Order of Things: Property, Power, and the Transformation of the Creek Indians, 1733–1816*. Cambridge University Press, 2004. Kindle.

Saunt, Claudio. *Unworthy Republic: The Dispossession of Native Americans and the Road to Indian Territory*. W. W. Norton, 2020. Kindle.

Sauvy, Alfred. *Fertility and Survival*. Criterion Books, 1961.

Sauvy, Alfred. "Trois mondes, une planète [Three Worlds, One Planet; in French]." *L'Observateur*, no. 118 (August 1952): 14.

Schmidt, Brian C. "Paul S. Reinsch and the Study of Imperialism and Internationalism." In *Imperialism and Internationalism in the Discipline of International Relations*, edited by David Long and Brian C. Schmidt. State University of New York Press, 2005. Kindle.

Sebastiani, Silvia. *The Scottish Enlightenment*. Palgrave Macmillan, 2013.

Sebestyen, Victor. *Lenin: The Man, the Dictator, and the Master of Terror*. Knopf Doubleday, 2017. Kindle.

Sen, Amartya. *Development as Freedom*. Oxford University Press, 1999. Kindle.

Sen, Amartya. *Home in the World: A Memoir*. Liveright, 2021. Kindle.

Sherwood, Henry Noble. "The Formation of the American Colonization Society." *Journal of Negro History* 2, no. 3 (1917): 209–228. https://docsouth.unc.edu/church/sherwood/sherwood.html.

Shick, Tom W. "A Quantitative Analysis of Liberian Colonization from 1820 to 1843 with Special Reference to Mortality." *Journal of African History* 12, no. 1 (1971), 45–59. https://doi.org/10.1017/S0021853700000062.

Ségur, Philippe-Paul Comte de. *History of the Expedition to Russia, Undertaken by the Emperor Napoleon in the Year 1812*. 2 vols. A. L. Fowle, 1900.

Sharp, Granville. *Memoirs of Granville Sharp*. Edited by Prince Hoare. London: Henry Colburn, 1820.

Sharp, Granville. *Short Sketch of Temporary Regulations (Until Better Shall be Proposed) for the Intended Settlement on the Grain Coast of Africa, Near Sierra Leona*. H. Baldwin, Fleet-Street, 1786. Kindle.

Sheehan, Bernard W. *Seeds of Extinction: Jeffersonian Philanthropy and the American Indian*. Omohundro Institute and University of North Carolina Press, 1973. Kindle.

Sheehan, Neil. *A Bright Shining Lie: John Paul Vann and America in Vietnam*. Knopf Doubleday, 1988. Kindle.

Siegel, Brian. "Tales of the Tribe of Ishmael: A Research Note." *Indiana Magazine of History* 106, no. 2 (2010): 189–196. www.jstor.org/stable/10.5378/indimagahist.106.2.0189.

Sklar, Kathryn Kish. *Women's Rights Emerges Within the Antislavery Movement, 1830–1870: A Brief History with Documents*. Palgrave Macmillan, 2000.

Smith, Adam. *The Theory of Moral Sentiments*. Illustrated ed. Uplifting Publications, 2009. Kindle. Originally published in 1759.

Smith, Adam. *The Wealth of Nations*. Illustrated ed. Dolphin Books, 2008. Kindle. Originally published in 1776 by W. Strahan and T. Cadell.

Smith, Mary-Antoinette, ed. *Essays on the Slavery and Commerce of the Human Species*, by Thomas Clarkson and Quobna Ottobah Cugoano. Broadview, 2010.

"South Viet Nam: Cutting the Arc." *Time*. April 6, 1962. https://time.com/archive/6831033/south-viet-nam-cutting-the-arc/.

Spring, Gardiner. *Memoirs of the Rev. Samuel J. Mills: Late Missionary to the South Western Section of the United States, and Agent of the American Colonization Society, Deputed to Explore the Coast of Africa*. London: Francis Westley, 1820.

Starr, Frederick. "The Congo Free State and Congo Belge." *Journal of Race Development* 1, no. 4 (1911): 383–399.

Stiglitz, Joseph. "Nobel Prize–Winning Economist Stiglitz Tells Us Why 'Neoliberalism Is Dead.'" *Business Insider*, August 19, 2016. www.businessinsider.com/joseph-stiglitz-says-neoliberalism-is-dead-2016-8.

Summers, Lawrence H. "The Great Liberator." Opinion, *New York Times*, November 19, 2006. www.nytimes.com/2006/11/19/opinion/19summers.html.

Sumner, William Graham. "Conquest of the US by Spain." In *War and Other Essays*. ed. Albert Galloway Keller. Yale University Press, 1919. Online Library of Liberty. https://oll.libertyfund.org/pages/sumner-the-conquest-of-the-us-by-spain-1898.

Sutch, Richard. "National Income and Product." In *Historical Statistics of the United States: Earliest Time to the Present, Millennial Edition*, edited by Richard Sutch and Susan B. Carter. Cambridge University Press, 2006, 1800–1830. https://hsus.cambridge.org/HSUSWeb/.

Supreme Court, Dred Scott, Plaintiff in Error, v. John F.A. Sandford. December Term, 1856. Legal Information Institute. www.law.cornell.edu/supremecourt/text/60/393.

Swift, Jonathan. *Gulliver's Travels*. Dover, 1996. Kindle.

Syed, Jawad, and Faiza Ali. "The White Woman's Burden: From Colonial Civilisation to Third World Development." *Third World Quarterly* 32, no. 2 (2011): 349–365. https://doi.org/10.1080/01436597.2011.560473.

Tagore, Rabindranath. *Towards Universal Man*. Asia Publishing House, 1961.

Tai, Hue-Tam Ho, *Radicalism and the Origins of the Vietnamese Revolution*. Harvard University Press, 1992.

Taylor, Maxwell. "Letter from the President's Military Representative (Taylor) to the

President." November 3, 1961. In *Foreign Relations of the United States, 1961–1963, Volume I, Vietnam, 1961*, ed. Ronald D. Landa and Charles S. Sampson; general editor John P. Glennon. US Government Printing Office, 1988. Kindle Locations 11318–11330. https://history.state.gov/historicaldocuments/frus1961-63v01/d210.

Thies, Clifford F., and Ryan Daza. "Richard T. Ely: The Confederate Flag of the AEA?" *Econ Journal Watch* 8, no. 2 (2011): 147–156.

Thompson, Edward. *Rabindranath Tagore, Poet & Dramatist*. Oxford University Press, 1926.

Tichenor, Daniel J. *Dividing Lines: The Politics of Immigration Control in America*. Princeton University Press, 2002.

Tillery, Alvin B. "'Not One Was Willing to Go!': The Paradoxes of 'Liberia's Offerings.'" In *Between Homeland and Motherland: Africa, US Foreign Policy, and Black Leadership in America*. Cornell University Press, 2011. https://doi.org/10.7591/9780801461019-003.

Tocqueville, Alexis de. *Democracy in America*. Translated by Arthur Goldhammer. LOA series no. 147. Library of America, 2004. Kindle.

Tolstoy, Leo. *War and Peace*. Translated by Richard Pevear and Larissa Volokhonsky. Knopf Doubleday, 2007. Kindle.

Tomkins, Stephen. *The Clapham Sect: How Wilberforce's Circle Transformed Britain*. Lion Hudson, 2010. Kindle.

Tracy, Ebenezer Carter. *Memoir of the Life of Jeremiah Evarts*. HardPress, 2018. Kindle. Originally published in 1845 by Crocker and Brewster.

Trans-Atlantic Slave Trade—Database. SlaveVoyages. Accessed May 14, 2025. www.slavevoyages.org/voyage/database.

Treaty of Hartford Ending the Pequot War, 1638 [image from the Connecticut State Library]. *Venture Smith's Colonial Connecticut*. https://venturesmithcolonialct.org/library/treaty-of-hartford-1638/.

Treaty of Peace with Germany (Treaty of Versailles). Treaty and protocol signed at Versailles, June 28, 1919. HathiTrust. https://babel.hathitrust.org/cgi/pt?id=uva.x004399666&seq=57.

Trotter, William Monroe. Statement in Treaty of Peace with Germany: Hearings Before the Committee on Foreign Relations. United States Senate, Sixty-Sixth Congress. US Government Printing Office, 1919.

Truman, Harry S. "Inaugural Address." Speech delivered at the Capitol, January 20, 1949. Henry S. Truman Library and Museum. www.trumanlibrary.gov/library/public-papers/19/inaugural-address.

Tullberg, Rita McWilliams. "Alfred Marshall and the Male Priesthood of Economics." *Quaderni di storia dell'economia politica* 9, no. 2/3 (1991): 235–268. www.jstor.org/stable/43317515.

Tůma, Oldřich. "Czechoslovakia's Velvet Revolution." Wilson Center Digital Archive. Accessed May 19, 2025. https://digitalarchive.wilsoncenter.org/essays/czechoslovakias-velvet-revolution.

Tuteja, K. L. "Jallianwala Bagh: A Critical Juncture in the Indian National Movement." *Social Scientist* 25, no. 1/2 (1997): 25–61. www.jstor.org/stable/3517759.

Twain, Mark. *Great Short Works of Mark Twain*. Edited by Justin Kaplan. HarperCollins, 2006. Kindle.

UK Parliament. "War Situation." September 9, 1941. https://api.parliament.uk/historic-hansard/commons/1941/sep/09/war-situation.

Ullrich, Volker. *Hitler: Ascent, 1889–1939*. Knopf Doubleday, 2016. Kindle.

Underhill, John. *Newes from America; Or, A New and Experimentall Discoverie of New England; Containing, A Trve Relation of Their War-like Proceedings These Two Yeares Last Past, with a Figure of the Indian Fort, or Palizado*, edited by Paul Royster. DigitalCommons@University of Nebraska—Lincoln. https://digitalcommons.unl.edu/cgi/viewcontent.cgi?article=1037&context=etas.

UNESCO. The Constitution of United Nations Educational, Scientific, and Cultural Organization. Adopted in London on 16 November 1945. Updated July 24, 2024. www.unesco.org/en/legal-affairs/constitution.

United Nations. *Charter of the United Nations*. Signed in San Francisco, 1945. www.un.org/en/about-us/un-charter.

United Nations. "Transforming Our World: The 2030 Agenda for Sustainable Development." Resolution adopted by the General Assembly, September 25, 2015. https://sdgs.un.org/2030agenda.

United Nations. *United Nations Summit on Sustainable Development Informal Summary*. September 25–27, 2015, New York. https://sustainabledevelopment.un.org/content/documents/8521Informal%20Summary%20-%20UN%20Summit%20on%20Sustainable%20Development%202015.pdf.

United Nations. "The Universal Declaration of Human Rights (UDHR)." Proclaimed by the United Nations General Assembly in Paris on 10 December 1948. www.un.org/en/about-us/universal-declaration-of-human-rights.

US Census Bureau. "B19013I: 2020 Median Income in the Past 12 Months (in 2020 Inflation-Adjusted Dollars), Household Income by Race and Hispanic or Latino Origin of Householder." https://data.census.gov/table/ACSDT5Y2020.B19013I.

US Census Bureau. "My Tribal Area." Mashantucket Pequot Reservation. www.census.gov/tribal/?aianihh=2145.

US Department of State. "Address by President John F. Kennedy to the UN General Assembly [archived content]." September 25, 1961. https://2009-2017.state.gov/p/io/potusunga/207241.htm.

US Department of State. Bureau of African Affairs. "U.S. Relations with Uganda." Bilateral Relations Fact Sheet. March 18, 2022. https://2021-2025.state.gov/u-s-relations-with-uganda/.

US Department of State. Office of the Historian. "The Berlin Wall Falls and USSR Dissolves." Accessed May 19, 2025. https://history.state.gov/departmenthistory/short-history/berlinwall.

US Department of State. Office of the Historian. "Biographies of the Secretaries of State: John Quincy Adams (1767–1848)." Accessed May 19, 2025. https://history.state.gov/departmenthistory/people/adams-john-quincy.

US Department of State. Office of the Historian. "The Collapse of the Soviet Union." Accessed May 19, 2025. https://history.state.gov/milestones/1989-1992/collapse-soviet-union.

US Department of State. Office of the Historian. "The Minister in China (Reinsch) to the Acting Secretary of State [telegram]." *Papers Relating to the Foreign Relations of the United States, The Paris Peace Conference, 1919, Volume II*, edited by Joseph V. Fuller; general editor Tyler Dennett. US Government Printing Office, 1942. https://history.state.gov/historicaldocuments/frus1919Parisv02/d441.

US Philippine Commission, Jacob Gould Schurman, George Dewey, Elwell S. Otis, Charles Denby, and Dean C. Worcester. *Report of the Philippine Commission to the President.* Vols. 1–4. US Government Printing Office, 1900.

US Senate. Equal Rights Amendment. Hearing Before a Subcommittee of the Committee on the Judiciary, 70th Congress, 2nd Session. February 1, 1929. Google Books. https://play.google.com/books/reader?id=yOslAAAAMAAJ&pg=GBS.RA1-PA40&hl=en.

Varouxakis, Georgios. *Liberty Abroad: J. S. Mill on International Relations.* Cambridge University Press, 2013. Kindle.

Varouxakis, Georgios. *Mill on Nationality*. Routledge, 2002. Kindle.

Vattel, Emer de. *The Law of Nations*. Edited by Bela Kapossy and Richard Whatmore. Liberty Fund, 2008. Kindle.

Vietnam (Republic). "Viet Nam's Strategic Hamlets." Directorate General of Information, 1963. https://vietnamproject.archives.msu.edu/objects/159-547-3348/.

Vitalis, Robert. "The Midnight Ride of Kwame Nkrumah and Other Fables of Bandung (Ban-doong)." *Humanity*, June 2014. https://humanityjournal.org/issue4-2/the-midnight-ride-of-kwame-nkrumah-and-other-fables-of-bandung-ban-doong/.

Vitalis, Robert. *White World Order, Black Power Politics.* Cornell University Press, 2015. Kindle.

Wade, Magatte. "African Aid: No More 'Pity Shit.'" Africa Network, *Guardian*, October 4, 2012. www.theguardian.com/world/2012/oct/04/african-aid-no-more-pity.

Wade, Magatte. "Stop Raising Money for Relief and Start Investing in Africa." Medium, December 4, 2014. https://medium.com/@magattew/stop-raising-money-for-relief-and-start-investing-in-africa-bd5c44a75557.

Wallace, Anthony F. C. *Jefferson and the Indians: The Tragic Fate of the First Americans*. Belknap Press of Harvard University Press, 1999. Kindle.

Walker, Francis A. *The Indian Question*. Boston: James R. Osgood, 1874.

Walker, Francis A. "Restriction of Immigration." *Atlantic*, June 1896.

Wang, Feng, Baochang Gu, and Yong Cai. "The End of China's One-Child Policy." Brookings Institution, March 30, 2016. www.brookings.edu/articles/the-end-of-chinas-one-child-policy/.

Warburton, William. "Sermon VIII." In *Twelve Anniversary Sermons Preached Before the Society for the Propagation of the Gospel in Foreign Parts*. London: T.B. Sharpe, J. Hatchard & Son, 1766.

Warren, Wendy. *New England Bound: Slavery and Colonization in Early America.* Liveright, 2016. Kindle.

Washington, George. "Farewell Address." Presented in a newspaper article, 1796. https://history.state.gov/milestones/1784-1800/washington-farewell.

Washington, George. "Talk to the Cherokee Nation." Speech delivered in Philadelphia, August 29, 1796. National Archives. https://founders.archives.gov/documents/Washington/05-20-02-0388.

Washington, George. "Third Annual Message to Congress [transcript]." October 25, 1791. https://millercenter.org/the-presidency/presidential-speeches/october-25-1791-third-annual-message-congress.

Washington, Margaret. "'From Motives of Delicacy': Sexuality and Morality in the Narratives of Sojourner Truth and Harriet Jacobs." *Journal of African American History* 92 (Winter 2007): 57–73. www.jstor.org/stable/20064154.

Watrous, Stephen D., ed. *John Ledyard's Journey Through Russia and Siberia, 1787–1788: The Journal and Selected Letters.* University of Wisconsin Press, 2011. Kindle.

Watson, Ivan, and Jomana Karadsheh. "The Tunisian Fruit Seller Who Kickstarted Arab Uprising." *CNN*, March 22, 2011. www.cnn.com/2011/WORLD/meast/03/22/tunisia.bouazizi.arab.unrest/index.html.

Wein, Tom. "A Research Agenda for Dignity in International Development." Working paper, 2020. https://dignityproject.net/wp-content/uploads/2020/12/Wein-Research-Agenda-Working-Paper-041220.pdf.

Westad, Odd Arne. *The Global Cold War: Third World Interventions and the Making of Our Times.* Cambridge University Press, 2007. Kindle.

Westermann, Edward B. *Hitler's Ostkrieg and the Indian Wars: Comparing Genocide and Conquest.* University of Oklahoma Press, 2016. Kindle.

White, Jonathan W., and Scott Sandage. "What Frederick Douglass Had to Say About Monuments." *Smithsonian*, June 30, 2020. www.smithsonianmag.com/history/what-frederick-douglass-had-say-about-monuments-180975225/.

Whitman, James Q. *Hitler's American Model: The United States and the Making of Nazi Race Law.* Princeton University Press, 2017. Kindle.

Willett, Robert L. *Russian Sideshow: America's Undeclared War, 1918–1920.* Potomac Books, 2003. Kindle.

Williams, David. *Condorcet and Modernity.* Cambridge University Press, 2004.

Williams, Samuel Cole. "William Tatham, Wataugan." *Tennessee Historical Magazine* 73 (1921): 154–179.

Willoughby, W. W. "The American Political Science Association." *Political Science Quarterly* 19, no. 1 (1904): 107–111. www.jstor.org/stable/2140238.

Wilson Center Digital Archive. "Yeltsin, Boris: 1931–2007." Accessed May 19, 2025. https://digitalarchive.wilsoncenter.org/people/yeltsin-boris.

Wilson, James Grant, and John Fiske, eds. *Appleton's Cyclopedia of American Biography.* New York: D. Appleton, 1900. https://archive.org/details/appletonscyclopa01wils.

Wilson, James Grant, and John Fiske, eds. "David Brown." In *Appleton's Cyclopedia of American Biography.* Vol. 1. New York: D. Appleton, 1887.

Wilson, Woodrow. "Address to Congress: Analyzing German and Austrian Peace Utterances." Delivered to a Joint Session of Congress, February 11, 1918. https://history.state.gov/historicaldocuments/frus1918Supp01v01/d59.

Wilson, Woodrow. "Democracy and Efficiency." *Atlantic*, March 1901. www.theatlantic.com/magazine/archive/1901/03/democracy-and-efficiency/520041/.

Wilson, Woodrow. *Division and Reunion: 1829–1889*. 5th ed. New York: Longmans, Green & Co., 1894.

Wilson, Woodrow. "Fourteen Points [transcript]." Address to the Joint Session of Congress, January 8, 1918. National Archives. www.archives.gov/milestone-documents/president-woodrow-wilsons-14-points.

Wilson, Woodrow. "The Ideals of America." *Atlantic*, December 1902. www.theatlantic.com/magazine/archive/1902/12/the-ideals-of-america/376192/.

Winch, Donald. *Classical Political Economy and Colonies*. G. Bell and Sons, 1965.

"Windows of Freedom." *The Round Table: A Quarterly Review of the Politics of the British Empire* 9, no. 33 (1918): 1–47.

Winthrop, John. "Generall Considerations for the Plantation in New England, with an Answer to Several Objections." Higginson Copy, 1629. Winthrop Papers Digital Edition, Massachusetts Historical Society, 2021. www.masshist.org/publications/winthrop/index.php/view/PWF02d07.

Winthrop, John. *A Journal of the Transactions and Occurrences in the Settlement of Massachusetts and the Other New England Colonies*. New Haven, CT: Babcock and Company, 1790.

Winthrop, John. Letter to William Bradford, May 25, 1637. www.masshist.org/publications/winthrop/index.php/view/PWF03d358.

Winthrop, John. "Reasons for the Plantation in New England." c. 1628. The Winthrop Society, 2022. www.winthropsociety.com/copy-of-the-officers.

Winthrop, John. "Reasons to Be Considered, and Objections with Answers." First Draft, 1629. Winthrop Papers Digital Edition, Massachusetts Historical Society, 2021. www.masshist.org/publications/winthrop/index.php/view/PWF02d079.

Winthrop, John. "Reasons to Be Considered for Justifying the Undertakers of the Intended Plantation in New England and for Encouraging Such Whose Hearts God Shall Move to Join with Them in It." In *The Puritans in America: A Narrative Anthology*, edited by Alan Heimert and Andrew Delbanco. Harvard University Press, 1985. Kindle.

Wisconsin Historical Society. "Historical Essay: Reinsch, Paul Samuel 1869–1923." N.d. https://wisconsinhistory.org/Records/Article/CS12261.

Wolff, Larry. *Inventing Eastern Europe: The Map of Civilization on the Mind of the Enlightenment*. Stanford University Press, 1994.

Wood, Allen. General introduction in *Practical Philosophy*, by Immanuel Kant. Translated and Edited by Mary J. Gregor. Cambridge University Press, 1996. Kindle.

Woods, Randall Bennett. *John Quincy Adams: A Man for the Whole People*. Penguin, 2024. Kindle.

Woolsey, Theodore S. *The Government of Dependencies in the Foreign Policy of the United States: Political and Commercial Addresses and Discussion at the Annual Meeting of the American Academy of Political and Social Science, April 7–8, 1899*. Kraus Reprint Company, 1970.

World Bank Group. Women, Business & the Law. https://wbl.worldbank.org/en/wbl.

World Trade Organization. "Who Are the Developing Countries in the WTO?" N.d. www.wto.org/english/tratop_e/devel_e/d1who_e.htm.

Wright, J. Leitch Jr. *Creeks and Seminoles: Destruction and Regeneration of the Muscogulge People*. University of Nebraska Press, 1986.
Wright, Richard. *The Colour Curtain: A Report on the Bandung Conference*. Dennis Dobson, 1956.
Van der Gaag, Nikki, and Cathy Nash. *Images of Africa: The UK Report*. Oxfam, 1987.
Yang, Lin. "China: We're Still a Developing Nation. US Lawmakers: No Way." *Voice of America*, April 8, 2023. www.voanews.com/a/china-we-re-still-a-developing-nation-us-lawmakers-no-way/7041814.html.
Yarema, Allan. *The American Colonization Society: An Avenue to Freedom?* University Press of America, 2006.
Zasloff, Joseph J. "Rural Resettlement in South Viet Nam: The Agroville Program." *Pacific Affairs* 35, no. 4 (1962–1963): 327–340. www.jstor.org/stable/2753142.
Ziltener, Patrick, Daniel Künzler, and André Walter. "Measuring the Impacts of Colonialism: A New Data Set for the Countries of Africa and Asia." *Journal of World-Systems Research* 23 (2017): 156–190. https://doi.org/10.5195/jwsr.2017.683.
Zitkala-Ša. *American Indian Stories, Legends, and Other Writings*. Penguin, 2003. Kindle.
Zitkala-Ša. "An Indian Teacher Among Indians." *Atlantic*, March 1900. www.theatlantic.com/magazine/archive/1900/03/an-indian-teacher-among-indians/636832/.
Zurcher, Christoph. "What Do We (Not) Know About Development Aid and Violence? A Systematic Review." *World Development* 98 (2017): 506–522.

Notes

Preface

Sumner, "Conquest of the US by Spain."

1. Mamdani, *From Citizen to Refugee*, 96–104. See his biography at https://anthropology.columbia.edu/content/mahmood-mamdani and https://codesria.org/pr-mahmood-mamdani-1998-2002/.
2. Yaw Nyarko, transcript of remarks in private conference, May 20, 2022, 2:57:56, used with permission.
3. Mamdani, *From Citizen to Refugee*, 91.

Chapter 1: Our Conquest of Them for Their Own Good

1. Heimert and Delbanco, *Puritans in America*, 70–71; Bremer, *John Winthrop*, 157–158; for seal, see Galvin, "History of Arms."
2. See different versions of Winthrop's justifications in Winthrop, "Reasons for the Plantation in New England"; Bremer, *John Winthrop*, 37; Winthrop, "Reasons to Be Considered"; Winthrop, "Generall Considerations"; Winthrop, "Justifying the Undertakers," 71–73.
3. Winthrop, "Reasons to Be Considered."
4. Winthrop, "Reasons to Be Considered"; Winthrop, "Generall Considerations."
5. For Pequot population and the effect of introduced disease, see Hämäläinen, *Indigenous Continent*, 76–79; for Winthrop's view, see Winthrop, "Reasons to Be Considered"; Winthrop, "Generall Considerations."
6. For the alliance with the Mohegans and Narragansetts, and Pequot deaths at Mistick, see Hämäläinen, *Indigenous Continent*, 79–80; Underhill, *Newes from America* (London, 1638), 35; Winthrop, *Journal*, 222. For English treatment of the Pequot after the war, see Winthrop, *Journal*, 226–227. For Winthrop on Mononotto, see Bremer, *John Winthrop*, 272–274; Winthrop, letter to Bradford.
7. For sending the Pequots into slavery, see Winthrop, *Journal*, 228–229. For the return exchange, see Warren, *New England Bound*, 16; Winthrop, *Journal*, 263–264.
8. Hämäläinen, *Indigenous Continent*, 86–87; Treaty of Hartford.
9. Sources for data are Maddison Project for 1650–1790; McCusker, "Colonial Statistics" for 1790–1870; Sutch, "National Income and Product" for 1800–1830; and Prados de la Escosura, "Lost Decades?" for updated data.
10. Smith, *Wealth of Nations*, Locations 8912–8914.

11. US Census Bureau, "B19013I: 2020 Median Income"; for historical incomes, see Maddison Project Database, regional data; for technology, see Comin et al., "Wealth of Nations in 1000 BC." The ratio of median household incomes is not equal to the ratio of average per capita incomes but does give an order of magnitude.

12. Information from Mashantucket Pequot Tribal Nation, "About Page," and US Census, "My Tribal Area."

13. For his Spanish critique, see Smith, *Wealth of Nations*, Locations 8860–8866; for the generalized critique, see Smith, *Wealth of Nations*, Locations 7016–7023.

14. Smith, *Wealth of Nations*, Locations 7016–7023, 8901.

15. Smith, *Wealth of Nations*, Locations 233–239.

16. Smith, *Wealth of Nations*, Location 10492.

17. Smith, *Theory of Moral Sentiments*, 86–87, 224.

18. Smith, *Wealth of Nations*, Locations 10498–10499.

19. Smith, *Wealth of Nations*, Locations 9940–9946.

20. The concept of equality in liberalism is inspired in part by what Peart and Levy in *"Vanity of the Philosopher,"* 132, describe as "Smith's deep analytical egalitarianism," and in the subtitle as "From 'Equality' to 'Hierarchy.'" See also Peart and Levy, *Street Porter and the Philosopher*; Levy, *How the Dismal Science Got Its Name*. This book was heavily influenced by their work. See also McCloskey, *Why Liberalism Works*, 9–10, for stressing the liberal values of "equality of status" of peoples "not to be pushed or bossed around without their voluntarily given consent or contract." And see Boettke, *The Struggle for a Better World*, 2, 288, on liberalism as "equal treatment of equals," which fought coercion of groups like women, Black people, and American Indians in the US.

21. Indigenous mortality statistics from Arcand et al., "Guns, Germs, and Slaves."

PART I: TWO KINDS OF PROGRESS

Lukes and Urbinati, *Condorcet*.

Chapter 2: The Expert and the Economist

This chapter draws heavily on the following secondary sources: Pitts, *A Turn to Empire*; Muthu, *Enlightenment Against Empire*; Sebastiani, *Scottish Enlightenment*; Rothschild, *Economic Sentiments*; Ross, *Life of Adam Smith*; Phillipson, *Adam Smith*; Lukes and Urbinati, *Condorcet*; Ansart, *Condorcet*; Manuel, *The Prophets of Paris*; McLean and Hewitt, *Condorcet;* Bergès, "Family, Gender, and Progress"; Winch, *Classical Political Economy and Colonies*; Williams, *Condorcet and Modernity*; Barber, *British Economic Thought and India*; Mehta, *Liberalism and Empire.*

1. Lukes and Urbinati, *Condorcet*, 7.

2. Lukes and Urbinati, *Condorcet*, 126, 136–137, 145–146.

3. For "vegetating in the infant condition," "infancy of the human race," and "condition of apathy," see Lukes and Urbinati, *Condorcet*, 123, 27, 15.

4. Ansart, *Condorcet*, 88–89.

5. For Lespinasse inviting Condorcet to salon, see Ansart, *Condorcet*, 119, and Lukes and Urbinati, *Political Writings*, editors' introduction; for her advice to Condorcet, see McLean and Hewitt, *Condorcet*, xvi, and Williams, *Condorcet and Modernity*, 12; for the salon's observation of his behavior, see Lukes and Urbinati, *Political Writings*, editors' introduction, and Rothschild, *Economic Sentiments*, 206.

6. For Amélie Suard, see Williams, *Condorcet and Modernity*, 13; for Madame de Meulan, see Manuel, *Prophets of Paris*, 57.

7. For their marriage day, see McLean and Hewitt, *Condorcet*, xxix; for the Venus of the Lyceum, see Bergès, *Sophie de Grouchy*, 6.

8. For the timing of his radical views, see Lukes and Urbinati, *Condorcet*, Location 632; for his invocation of the reciprocity principle, see Lukes and Urbinati, *Condorcet*, 156.

9. For Condorcet attracting the duchess's interest, see McLean and Hewitt, *Condorcet*, xxxiii; for her role among the Physiocrats, see Ross, *Life of Adam Smith*, 221; for the duke's age, see Library of Congress, "La Rochefoucauld d'Enville; for the duke and Condorcet's friendship, see McLean and Hewitt, *Condorcet*, xxvi–xxvii.

10. For the duchess meeting Smith, see Rae, *Life of Adam Smith*, Locations 2743–3273, 4868; for Smith's temporary residence, see Ross, *Life of Adam Smith*, 222–223; for Smith's participation in the salon and bad French, see Ross, *Life of Adam Smith*, Location 411; for the duchess learning English, see Rae, *Life of Adam Smith*, Locations 2743–3273.

11. For Smith owning Condorcet's book, see Rothschild, *Economic Sentiments*, 82; for Condorcet's Sketch, see Lukes and Urbinati, *Condorcet*, 95.

12. Bergès, *Sophie de Grouchy*, 23.

13. For "greedy and barbarous men" and Condorcet's prescription for a reversal, see Lukes and Urbinati, *Condorcet*, 74–75.

14. Lukes and Urbinati, *Condorcet*, 2.

15. Lukes and Urbinati, *Condorcet*, 127–129.

16. Ansart, *Condorcet*, 77.

17. Lukes and Urbinati, *Condorcet*, 127.

18. Lukes and Urbinati, *Condorcet*, 127–129.

19. Lukes and Urbinati, *Condorcet*, 7.

20. For "the means to individual welfare," "the real advantages that should result," and the normative words, see Lukes and Urbinati, *Condorcet*, 127–129.

21. Lukes and Urbinati, *Condorcet*, 129.

22. Lukes and Urbinati, *Condorcet*, 129.

23. Lukes and Urbinati, *Condorcet*, 147.

24. Lukes and Urbinati, *Condorcet*, 139–140; Berlin, Manuscript D, 49.

25. Ansart, *Condorcet*, 35, 96, 88.

26. Lukes and Urbinati, *Condorcet*, 129–130.

27. This exposition of Smith's critique draws on Pitts, *A Turn to Empire*.

28. Adam Smith, *Wealth of Nations*, Location 6708, 7055, and 10512.

29. Smith, *Wealth of Nations*, Location 6997.

30. Smith, *Wealth of Nations*, Location 8868.
31. Smith, *Wealth of Nations*, Location 9945.
32. Smith, *Wealth of Nations*, Locations 8959–8963, 8976–8979, and 9032–9036.
33. Smith, *Wealth of Nations*, Location 9202.
34. Easterly, "Progress by Consent."
35. Smith, *Wealth of Nations*, Locations 12180–12183.
36. Smith, *Wealth of Nations*, Locations 10951–10958.
37. Smith, *Wealth of Nations*, Locations 233–239.
38. Smith, *Wealth of Nations*, Locations 7133–7136.
39. For Smith doubting the merchants' claims, see Smith, *Wealth of Nations*, Locations 7133–7136.
40. For Smith's impartial spectator, see Adam Smith, *Theory of Moral Sentiments*, 86–87.
41. Smith, *Theory of Moral Sentiments*, 170.
42. Smith, *Theory of Moral Sentiments*, 303.
43. Smith, *Theory of Moral Sentiments*, 137–138.
44. Smith, *Wealth of Nations*, Locations 10196–10199.
45. Dalrymple, *The Anarchy*, 259–267.
46. Smith, *Wealth of Nations*, Locations 8286–8290, 1123–1132, and 10119–10124.
47. Smith, *Wealth of Nations*, Locations 11976–11979, 12043–12046.
48. Smith, *Wealth of Nations*, Locations 10177–10179.
49. For Mickle's criticism, see Rothschild, "Adam Smith in the British Empire," 193–194.
50. Smith, *Wealth of Nations*, Locations 9780–9793.
51. Smith, *Wealth of Nations*, Locations 217–220.
52. Pitts, *A Turn to Empire*, 32.
53. Smith, *Theory of Moral Sentiments*, 189.
54. Smith, *Theory of Moral Sentiments*, 240.
55. Smith, *Theory of Moral Sentiments*, 240–242.
56. For his criticism of the Physiocrats, see Smith, *Wealth of Nations*, Locations 10737–10744.
57. Lukes and Urbinati, *Condorcet*, 183.
58. Lukes and Urbinati, *Condorcet*, 181–182.
59. Lukes and Urbinati, *Condorcet*, 137.
60. Lukes and Urbinati, *Condorcet*, 188–189.
61. McLean and Hewitt, *Condorcet*, xxxv–xxxvi.
62. McLean and Hewitt, *Condorcet*, xxxiii.
63. McLean and Hewitt, *Condorcet*, xxxvi.
64. McLean and Hewitt, *Condorcet*, xxxiii.
65. McLean and Hewitt, *Condorcet*, lxxxii.
66. Ansart, *Condorcet*, 19–20.
67. For the letter, see Ansart, *Condorcet*, 19–20; for the Sketch's examination of revolutions, see Lukes and Urbinati, *Condorcet*, 103–104.

68. Lukes and Urbinati, *Condorcet*, 192–193.
69. Lukes and Urbinati, *Condorcet*, 195.
70. Lukes and Urbinati, *Condorcet*, Locations 350–358.
71. Bergès, *Sophie de Grouchy*, 269.
72. Bergès, *Sophie de Grouchy*, 267, 270, 278–281.
73. Lukes and Urbinati, *Condorcet*, Location 487.
74. McLean and Hewitt, *Condorcet*, xl–xlii.
75. Lukes and Urbinati, *Condorcet*, 147.
76. Karl Marx, "Theses on Feuerbach."

Chapter 3: The Demand for Dignity

1. I especially noticed the modern identification of a demand for dignity when I discovered the work of Wein, "A Research Agenda"; my discovery of Kant's writings on dignity is thanks mainly to the marvelous work by Muthu, *Enlightenment Against Empire*, whose exposition I set out in this chapter.
2. United Nations, "Universal Declaration of Human Rights."
3. For the two separate passions, see Smith, *Theory of Moral Sentiments*, 251–252, 275–276, 278; for "what chiefly enrages us," see Smith, *Theory of Moral Sentiments*, 112–113.
4. Korsgaard, *Kant: Groundwork*, Location 206.
5. Kant, *Practical Philosophy*, 417–418; Muthu, *Enlightenment Against Empire*, 198.
6. Kant, *Practical Philosophy*, 557; Muthu, *Enlightenment Against Empire*, 129–130.
7. Korsgaard, *Kant: Groundwork*, 40–41.
8. Korsgaard, *Kant: Groundwork*, 33–34.
9. Korsgaard, *Kant: Groundwork*, 35–42.
10. Korsgaard, *Kant: Groundwork*, 42.
11. Korsgaard, *Kant: Groundwork*, 46–47; Muthu, *Enlightenment Against Empire*, 139.
12. Korsgaard, *Kant: Groundwork*, 47–48.
13. Quoted in Wood, general introduction, Location 253.
14. Kant, *Political Writings*, 133.
15. Kant, *Practical Philosophy*, 393–394.
16. Muthu, *Enlightenment Against Empire*, 157.
17. Quoted in Muthu, *Enlightenment Against Empire*, 184; original at Kant, *Anthropology, History, and Education*, 59.
18. Kant, *Anthropology, History, and Education*, 50.
19. Muthu, *Enlightenment Against Empire*, 184.
20. Muthu, *Enlightenment Against Empire*, 196; Kant, *Practical Philosophy*, 328–331.
21. Kant, *Practical Philosophy*, 489–490.

PART II: LIBERALS DOUBT EMPIRE, 1776–1865

Clarkson, *History*.

Chapter 4: Smith and Allies Challenge the Slave Trade

This chapter draws extensively on the following secondary sources: Hochschild, *Bury the Chains*; Drescher, *Mighty Experiment*; Carretta, *Thoughts and Sentiments*; Carretta, *Unchained Voices*; Peart and Levy, *Street Porter and the Philosopher.*

1. Trans-Atlantic Slave Trade Database, sum of embarked slaves by flag, broad regions of disembarkation; number of embarked slaves by flag, specific regions disembarkation.
2. Brown, *Tacky's Revolt*, 1.
3. Brown, *Tacky's Revolt*, 35, 147.
4. Burnard, *Jamaica in the Age of Revolution*, 119; Brown, *Tacky's Revolt*, 159, 183; Burnard, *Jamaica*, 31.
5. The time of lecture is suggested by the editors on page 19 of Meek et al., *Lectures on Jurisprudence*; Meek et al., *Lectures on Jurisprudence*, Wednesday, February 16, 1763, 183–184.
6. Meek et al., *Lectures on Jurisprudence*, Tuesday, February 15, 1763, 181.
7. Ross, *The Life of Adam Smith*, 28; Phillipson, *Adam Smith*, 122.
8. Ross, *Life of Adam Smith*, 121–122.
9. Smith, *The Wealth of Nations*, Location 6201.
10. Adam Smith, *Theory of Moral Sentiments*, 172.
11. Meek et al., *Lectures on Jurisprudence*, Friday, January 21, 1763, 128–129.
12. Meek et al., *Lectures on Jurisprudence*, 146.
13. Meek et al., *Lectures on Jurisprudence*, 143–144.
14. Meek et al., *Lectures on Jurisprudence*, 178–179.
15. Meek et al., *Lectures on Jurisprudence*, 146.
16. Smith, *Wealth of Nations*, Locations 1531–1537.
17. Smith, *Wealth of Nations*, Locations 1905–1910.
18. Smith, *Theory of Moral Sentiments*, 288.
19. Smith, *Theory of Moral Sentiments*, 211–212.
20. Rothschild, "Atlantic Worlds of David Hume"; Lee, *Essay in Vindication.*
21. Drescher, *Mighty Experiment*, 12; Postlethwayt, *National and Private Advantages*, 4–5; Postlethwayt's biography is available at www.hetwebsite.net/het/profiles/postlethwayt.htm.
22. Burnard, *Jamaica*, 70–71; Long, *History of Jamaica*, 271, 399–400, 502.
23. See Fogel and Engerman, *Time on the Cross.*
24. Drescher, *Mighty Experiment*, 31; Smith, *Wealth of Nations*, Locations 15199–15207.
25. Smith, *Wealth of Nations*, Locations 15199–15207.
26. Warburton, *Sermons*, 138.
27. The narrative in the remainder of this chapter closely follows that in Hochschild, *Bury the Chains*, Location 87 and following. See also Carretta introduction in Cugoano, *Thoughts and Sentiments*, 185; Clarkson, *History*, Location 2258; for Clarkson rejoinder, see Clarkson, *Essay*, 141.
28. Clarkson, *History*, vol. 1, Locations 2606–2610, 2653–2655.
29. Hochschild, *Bury the Chains*, Location 2017.
30. This paragraph summarizes points made by Hochschild, *Bury the Chains*,

Location 2017; image is at https://oll.libertyfund.org/page/images-of-the-british-abolitionist-movement.

31. Equiano, *Interesting Narrative*; for the success of the book, see Hochschild, *Bury the Chains*, Locations 2042, 3822, 2508, 2565.

32. Hochschild, *Bury the Chains*, 2493.

33. Equiano, *Interesting Narrative*, 318.

34. For Clarkson's letter, see Hochschild, *Bury the Chains*, Location 2493; for subscriber list, see Equiano, *Interesting Narrative*, 318; Clarkson, *History*.

35. Carretta, *Unchained Voices*, 10.

36. Hochschild, *Bury the Chains*, Location 2042; on Cugoano's quotations of Clarkson, see Carretta's editor introduction in Cugoano, *Thoughts and Sentiments*, Location 255, and Clarkson citations in Cugoano, *Thoughts and Sentiments*, 168–169; for subscribers' names, see Cugoano, *Thoughts and Sentiments*, 147; for the printer and lack of support, see Cugoano, *Thoughts and Sentiments*, 153.

37. Carretta's introduction in Cugoano, *Thoughts and Sentiments*, Locations 69–84; Cugoano, *Thoughts and Sentiments*, 8.

38. Cugoano, *Thoughts and Sentiments*, 12.

39. Carretta's introduction in Cugoano, *Thoughts and Sentiments*, Locations 72–168; Hochschild, *Bury the Chains*, Location 2047; Cugoano, *Thoughts and Sentiments*, 8.

40. Cugoano, *Thoughts and Sentiments*, 22–23.

41. Carretta's introduction in Cugoano, *Thoughts and Sentiments*, Location 362; Cugoano, *Thoughts and Sentiments*, 17.

42. Carretta's introduction in Cugoano, *Thoughts and Sentiments*, Location 362; Cugoano, *Thoughts and Sentiments*, 17, 15.

43. Cugoano, *Thoughts and Sentiments*, 98, 100.

44. Cugoano, *Thoughts and Sentiments*, 141.

45. Carretta's introduction in Cugoano, *Thoughts and Sentiments*, Locations 270 and 24; Hochschild, *Bury the Chains*, Location 2061.

46. Hochschild, *Bury the Chains*, Location 2435.

47. Hochschild, *Bury the Chains*, Location 2898; Clarkson, *History*, vol. 2, Location 1934.

48. Clarkson, *History*, vol. 2, Locations 2154–2159.

49. Hochschild, *Bury the Chains*, Location 4675.

50. Clarkson, *History*, vol. 2, Locations 4597–4602.

51. Rothschild, *Economic Sentiments*, 56; Masson and Jameson, "Odyssey of Thomas Muir."

52. Rothschild, *Economic Sentiments*, 57–58.

53. Ross, *Life of Adam Smith*, 434–436.

54. Rothschild, *Economic Sentiments*, 58–59.

55. Thanks to David Levy for suggesting this genealogy of influence from Smith.

Chapter 5: The West Invents the Rest

The Eastern European part of this chapter exposits the work of Wolff, *Inventing Eastern Europe*. The Sierra Leone part draws heavily on Braidwood, *Black Poor and White Philanthropists*. Other important secondary sources were Røge, *Economistes*; Harvey, "Slavery on the Balance Sheet"; Fryer, *Staying Power*; Drescher, *Mighty Experiment*; Comin et al., "Wealth of Nations in 1000 BC."

1. Comin et al., "Wealth of Nations in 1000 BC."
2. Since revised and updated: Maddison Project Database, regional data.
3. Harvey, "Slavery on the Balance Sheet," 83.
4. Røge, *Economistes*, 99.
5. Lukes and Urbinati, *Condorcet*, 127–128.
6. Lukes and Urbinati, *Condorcet*, editors' introduction, xxvii.
7. Lukes and Urbinati, *Condorcet*, 153.
8. For Du Pont on India, see Harvey, "Slavery on the Balance Sheet," 77; for Du Pont on Mauritius, see Wolff, *Inventing Eastern Europe*, 271; for Du Pont on the US, see Bashford and Chaplin, *New Worlds of Thomas Robert Malthus*, 255–256.
9. Wolff, *Inventing Eastern Europe*, 269–271.
10. Wolff, *Inventing Eastern Europe*, 222–223, 266–267.
11. Wolff, *Inventing Eastern Europe*, 19, 22.
12. Wolff, *Inventing Eastern Europe*, 11, 285–290, 310–315, 360; Rubinson, "Herodotus and the Scythians."
13. Wolff, *Inventing Eastern Europe*, 343–350; Watrous, *John Ledyard's Journey*, 3–4.
14. Tomkins, *Clapham Sect*, 21–23.
15. Watrous, *John Ledyard's Journey*, 4–5.
16. Wolff, *Inventing Eastern Europe*, 343–354; Watrous, Ledyard, *John Ledyard's Journey*, 6–12.
17. This section and following exposits the Ledyard narrative and quotations of Wolff, *Inventing Eastern Europe*, 343–354, while taking and expanding the original quotes from Watrous, *John Ledyard's Journey*, 124.
18. Watrous, *John Ledyard's Journey*, 144, 195, 180.
19. Watrous, *John Ledyard's Journey*, 127, 145.
20. Watrous, *John Ledyard's Journey*, 194.
21. Wolff, *Inventing Eastern Europe*, 346; Watrous, *John Ledyard's Journey*, 156–157.
22. Watrous, *John Ledyard's Journey*, 204, 229.
23. Watrous, *John Ledyard's Journey*, 45.
24. Watrous, *John Ledyard's Journey*, 223, 211.
25. Watrous, *John Ledyard's Journey*, 252–253, 30–31.
26. Røge, *Economistes*, 185, 226–227. The evidence for the 1774 memo is based on later recollections, and no such memo has been found in the archives.
27. Braidwood, *Black Poor*, 2–6, chap. 2.
28. Braidwood, *Black Poor*, 10, chap. 2, and footnote 76.
29. Braidwood, *Black Poor*, 6–10, chap. 2; Sharp, *Memoirs*, 266.
30. Sharp, *Short Sketch*, Locations 784–792.
31. Braidwood, *Black Poor*, 7, 9–10, chap. 2.
32. For the committee's response, see Fryer, *Staying Power*, 199–200; for the House of Commons, see Braidwood, *Black Poor*, 14, chap. 2.

33. Carretta, editor's introduction in Cugoano, *Thoughts and Sentiments*, Location 72; Braidwood, *Black Poor*, 30, chap. 2; Equiano, *Interesting Narrative*, 299, Location 6248; Braidwood, *Black Poor*, 13–14, chap. 4; seventy of the whites were wives of Black settlers.

34. Cugoano, *Thoughts and Sentiments*, 104–106; Braidwood, *Black Poor*, 19, chap. 3.

35. Braidwood, *Black Poor*, 16, chap. 3.

36. Cugoano, *Thoughts and Sentiments*, 362, 104–106.

37. Equiano, *Interesting Narrative*, 228; Location 4455; 327. Braidwood notes that there were conflicting reports in the newspapers on whether there was settler discontent.

38. Braidwood, *Black Poor*, 16, chap. 3.

39. Braidwood, *Black Poor*, 3, chap. 5.

40. Braidwood, *Black Poor*, 5, chap. 5.

41. Braidwood, *Black Poor*, 12–14, chap 5.

42. Braidwood, *Black Poor*, 17, chap. 5.

43. Centre for the Study of the Legacies of British Slavery, "Gilbert Francklyn"; Braidwood, *Black Poor*, 11, chap. 6, and Francklyn, *Observations*, xii-xiii.

44. Braidwood, *Black Poor*, 11, chap. 6.

45. Ségur, *History of Expedition*, vol. 1, 50.

46. Ségur, *History of Expedition*, vol. 2, 133.

47. Ségur, *History of Expedition*, vol. 2, 15.

48. For Napoleon and the officer's views on Russia, see Ségur, *History of Expedition*, vol. 1, 50, vol. 2, 153; for Ségur's, see vol. 2, 15, 370–371.

49. Wolff, *Inventing Eastern Europe*, 363; Ségur, *History of Expedition*, vol. 2, 42.

50. Figes, *The Crimean War*, 9, 225; I follow Wolff on looking at both Ségur's and Tolstoy's versions.

51. Wolff, *Inventing Eastern Europe*, 373; Tolstoy, *War and Peace*, Locations 14512, 20614.

52. Wolff, *Inventing Eastern Europe*, 374; Tolstoy, *War and Peace*, Locations 27573, 27703, 27997.

Chapter 6: Benjamin Constant Critiques Conquest

This chapter draws heavily on and partly exposits the section "Constant and the Distrust of Empire" in Pitts, *A Turn to Empire*. It also draws heavily on Fontana, introduction, and on Rothschild, *Economic Sentiments*.

1. Fontana, introduction, Locations 409–414.
2. Fontana, introduction, Locations 96–98, 104–106, 208–212.
3. Pitts, *Turn to Empire*, 176–177; Constant, *Political Writings*, Locations 4536–4541.
4. Constant, *Political Writings*, Locations 840–844; Pitts, *A Turn to Empire*, 176.
5. Pitts, *A Turn to Empire*, 173–174; Constant, *Political Writings*, Locations 754–757, 781–783.
6. Pitts, *A Turn to Empire*, 180.
7. Pitts, *A Turn to Empire*, 317.
8. Pitts, *A Turn to Empire*, 239.

9. Mill, review of *Missionaire*; Mill, review of four books; for joining the East India Company, see Ball and Loizides, "James Mill."

10. Quoted by Winch, *Classical Political Economy*, 163; original in Mill, review of four books, 154.

11. Partially quoted by Winch, *Classical Political Economy*, 164; James Mill, Testimony.

12. Constant, *Political Writings*, Locations 3690–3691.

13. Constant, *Political Writings*, Locations 3714–3720.

14. Constant, *Political Writings*, Locations 3720–3725, 3741–3745.

15. Constant, *Political Writings*, Locations 3720–3725, 3745–3746.

16. Constant, *Political Writings*, Locations 3750–3777.

17. Constant, *Political Writings*, Locations 3946–3950.

18. Pitts, *A Turn to Empire*, 173.

19. Pitts, *A Turn to Empire*, 179.

20. Pitts, *A Turn to Empire*, 182–183.

21. Pitts, *A Turn to Empire*, 206.

22. Pitts, *A Turn to Empire*, 221–222, 224; also see Pitts, "Republicanism," 284.

23. Pitts, "Republicanism," 275–276.

24. Washington's Farewell Address.

25. For Adams, see US Department of State, Adams biography; Adams, *Diary*, vol. 28, September 24, September 29–30, October 27, 1812; Woods, *John Quincy Adams*, 290 and following. For Adams and Constant, see Adams, *Diary*, vol. 29, February 15, 1815; May 4, 1815; February 18, 1816.

26. Adams, *An Address*, 22–23. For a discussion of the quote as applied to modern policy debates, see Coyne, *In Search of Monsters*. In 2019, a think tank named the Quincy Institute for Responsible Statecraft was established in Washington, DC, to advocate for the principles John Quincy Adams outlined in this speech.

27. Adams, *An Address*, 31–32.

28. Adams, *An Address*, 29.

29. Guyatt, "Adams Doctrine"; Adams, *An Address*, 12.

30. Adams to Everett partially quoted in Murphy, *Hemispheric Imaginings*, 53–54; for other quotes, see Adams, *Writings*, 200–201, 206.

31. Guyatt, "Adams Doctrine"; Murphy, *Hemispheric Imaginings*, 69–70; Adams, *An Address*, 8, 12.

Chapter 7: The Civilizing Plan for the Creek Indians

This chapter draws heavily on Calloway, *Indian World of George Washington*; Wallace, *Jefferson and the Indians*; Sheehan, *Seeds of Extinction*; Wright, *Creeks and Seminoles*; Green, *The Politics of Indian Removal;* Ethridge, *Creek Country*; Saunt, *A New Order of Things* and *Unworthy Republic*; Haveman, *Rivers of Sand*; Bashford and Chaplin, *New Worlds of Thomas Robert Malthus*.

1. Sheehan, *Seeds of Extinction*, 142.

2. For Hawkins, see Wallace, *Jefferson and the Indians*, Locations 2347–2353; for the Plan of Civilization, see Founders Online, "Benjamin Hawkins to Thomas Jefferson," July 11, 1803.

3. Bashford and Chaplin, *New Worlds of Malthus*, 234–235.

4. Locke, *Two Treatises of Government*, 81–83.

5. Calloway, *Indian World of Washington*, 325; Vattel, *Law of Nations*, Locations 4509, 3027.

6. Kiernan, *Lords of Human Kind*, 20; Jonathan Swift, *Gulliver's Travels*, 181, 197.

7. Wallace, *Jefferson and the Indians*, Locations 3790–3796, 2492–2496; Williams, "William Tatham, Wataugan."

8. Wallace, *Jefferson and the Indians*, Location 2057; Calloway, *Indian World of Washington*, 331; Founders Online, "Henry Knox to George Washington."

9. Calloway, *Indian World of Washington*, 340; Washington, "Third Annual Message to Congress."

10. For the treaty, see Calloway, *Indian World of Washington*, 469; Kappler, "Treaty with the Creeks." For Washington to Lafayette, see Calloway, *Indian World of Washington*, 371; Founders Online, "George Washington to Lafayette, August 11, 1790."

11. Calloway, *Indian World of Washington*, 459; Fitzpatrick, "Speech to Indian Chiefs," 300.

12. Washington, "Talk to the Cherokee Nation"; Fitzpatrick, "Talk to the Cherokee Nation," 193.

13. Pound, *Benjamin Hawkins*, 4. Hawkins was born in North Carolina on August 15, 1754. Calloway, *Indian World of Washington*, 468; Wallace, *Jefferson and the Indians*, Locations 2347–2353.

14. Wallace, *Jefferson and the Indians*, Locations 1832–1833, 2020–2025; Founders Online, "Benjamin Hawkins to Thomas Jefferson, June 14, 1786."

15. Founders Online, "Benjamin Hawkins to Thomas Jefferson, January 23, 1800"; Calloway, *Indian World of Washington*, 475; Founders Online, "Benjamin Hawkins to Thomas Jefferson, July 12, 1800."

16. Founders Online, "Benjamin Hawkins to Thomas Jefferson, March 1, 1801."

17. Hawkins, "A Sketch"; Wallace, *Jefferson and the Indians*, Locations 2570–2575.

18. Jefferson, "First Annual Message to Congress, December 8, 1801."

19. Founders Online, "Thomas Jefferson to Benjamin Hawkins, February 18, 1803."

20. Founders Online, "Hawkins to Jefferson, July 11, 1803."

21. Calloway, *Indian World of Washington*, 470; Ethridge, *Creek Country*, 15, 19.

22. Milford, *A Cursory Glance*, xix–xxvii, 49–51.

23. Founders Online, "Hawkins to Jefferson, January 23, 1800"; Wallace, *Jefferson and the Indians*, Location 2531; Jefferson, "First Annual Message."

24. Easterly and Freschi, "Why the World Bank Supports Tyrants."

25. Wallace, *Jefferson and the Indians*, Location 3486; Jefferson, "Fifth Annual Message."

26. Madison, "State of the Union Address."

27. Quoted in Bashford and Chaplin, *New Worlds of Malthus*, 255–256.

28. Founders Online, "Hawkins to Jefferson, January 23, 1800"; Hawkins, *Creek Confederacy.*

29. Hawkins, *Creek Confederacy*, 43–44.

30. Ethridge, *Creek Country*, 13, 20, 21; Calloway, *Indian World of Washington*, 475, Location 10684.

31. Wallace, *Jefferson and the Indians*, Locations 3790–3796; 176, Williams, "William Tatham, Wataugan."

32. Hawkins, *Creek Confederacy*, 26–27.

33. Saunt, *New Order of Things*, 179; Hawkins, *Letters*, 239–241.

34. For Hawkins on Tame King, see Hawkins, *Creek Confederacy*, 26–27.

35. Hawkins, *Letters*, 417, Colonel Hawkins to the Secretary of War Fort Wilkinson, May 8, 1802; Saunt, *New Order of Things*, 182.

36. Hawkins, *Creek Confederacy*, 26–27; Wallace, *Jefferson and the Indians*, Locations 3783–3787; Calloway, *Indian World of Washington*, 473; Saunt, *New Order of Things*, 1, 179.

37. For Tame King's statement, see Saunt, *New Order of Things*, 220; for Jefferson's reaction, see Wallace, *Jefferson and the Indians*, Locations 3810–3814; Thomas Jefferson, "Second Inaugural Address."

38. On the two brothers, see Wallace, *Jefferson and the Indians*, Locations 3848–3850. On the widespread story that the mother of Tenskwatawa and Tecumseh was Creek, see Ethridge, *Creek Country*, 238–239; Wallace, *Jefferson and the Indians*, Locations 3950–3952; Edmunds, *Shawnee Prophet*, Locations 501–508. Another author says their father and mother were Shawnee but grew up among the Creeks: Cozzens, *Tecumseh and the Prophet*, 21.

39. Wallace, *Jefferson and the Indians*, Locations 3917–3918, 3954–3956; Founders Online, "Thomas Jefferson to Henry Dearborn, August 28, 1807."

40. Saunt, *New Order of Things*, 215; Founders Online, "Hobohoilthle to James Madison, September 29, 1809."

41. Founders Online, "James Madison to Hobohoilthle, November 6, 1809."

42. Ethridge, *Creek Country*, 238–239; Cozzens, *Tecumseh and the Prophet*, 359–362; Wallace, *Jefferson and the Indians*, Locations 3820–3824.

43. Saunt, *New Order of Things*, 265; Ethridge, *Creek Country*, 240.

44. Calloway, *Indian World of Washington*, 475, Location 10684; Wright Jr., *Creeks and Seminoles*, 175; Halbert and Ball, *The Creek War of 1813 and 1814*, 235, 273; Floyd, "Letters," 235.

45. Ethridge, *Creek Country*, 20–21, 240–241.

46. Sheehan, *Seeds of Extinction*, 244; Founders Online, "Thomas Jefferson to David Bailie Warden, December 29, 1813."

47. Sheehan, *Seeds of Extinction*, 251–252.

48. Sheehan, *Seeds of Extinction*, 264.

Chapter 8: The Liberal Fight Against Indian Removal

1. Saunt, *Unworthy Republic*, 63–64; Cass, "Removal."

2. Saunt, *Unworthy Republic*, 64–65; Sheehan, *Seeds of Extinction*, 143; Tracy, *Jeremiah Evarts*, Locations 7426–7437.

3. Tracy, *Jeremiah Evarts*, Locations 9038–9041.

4. Tracy, *Jeremiah Evarts*, Locations 9038–9041, 9233–9246, 9330–9333, 9645–9651.

5. Evarts, *Essays on the Present Crisis*, 55; Sheehan, *Seeds of Extinction*, 143.

6. Sheehan, *Seeds of Extinction*, 60.

7. Child, *Hobomok*, Locations 3245–3246.

8. Karcher, *First Woman*, Locations 812, 41–44; Moland, *Lydia Maria Child*, 36.

9. Child, *First Settlers*, iii; Karcher, *First Woman*, 96–97.

10. Child, *First Settlers*, vi.

11. Child, *First Settlers*, 254.

12. On women's rights, see Karcher, *First Woman*, 399–400; on rejecting paternalism toward "heathens," see Child, *Hobomok*, Locations 3237–3240; Child, "An Appeal for the Indians." In the next sentence, she gives an example of missionaries to the Delaware Indians, making clear that she had Indians in mind when she used the word "heathens."

13. Child, *First Settlers*, 244–246.

14. Child, *First Settlers*, 259–260.

15. Child, *First Settlers*, 259–260.

16. For birth, see James Grant Wilson and John Fiske, eds., *Appletons' Cyclopedia of American Biography*, 397–398; for education, see Anderson, *Memoir of Catharine Brown*, 24–28, 41–43, 45; for campaigning, see Martin, Introduction, 1, 2, 4; Martin, "Crisscrossing Projects," 67–69; Saunt, *Unworthy Republic*, 60–61. These last three sources were the source of many of the quotes below; I also expand and give the original sources below.

17. Martin, "Crisscrossing Projects," 67–69.

18. Brown's tour itinerary comes from the map at the beginning of Martin and Nicholas, *Native Americans*. For the preserved speech, see Martin, "Crisscrossing Projects," 86.

19. Massachusetts Historical Society, "A Copy of an Address," 36–37.

20. Brown, "Cherokees," 354–355; letter later quoted in M'Kenney, *Memoirs*, 36–40.

21. M'Kenney, *Memoirs*, 36, 38.

22. Saunt, *Unworthy Republic*, 60–61; and Massachusetts Historical Society, "A Copy of an Address," 30–35.

23. Saunt, *Unworthy Republic*, 60–61. For original, see Brown, letter in *American Missionary Register*, 221.

24. Brown, letter in *American Missionary Register*, 220.

25. M'Kenney, *Memoirs*, 36; Martin, "Crisscrossing Projects," 83.

26. For death of Evarts, see Tracy, *Jeremiah Evarts*, Locations 11459–11460; for collapse of movement, see Prucha, "Protest by Petition," 57; for Trail of Tears, see Saunt, *Unworthy Republic*, 65.

27. Evarts, "Removal of the Indians," 400–401.

28. Evarts, "Removal of the Indians," 400, 402, 416; Prucha, *Cherokee Removal*, 216–217.

29. Evarts, "Removal of the Indians," 402.

30. Evarts, "Removal of the Indians," 400, 402, 416.

31. Malthus, *Essay on Principle of Population*, 15; quoted and discussed in Bashford and Chaplin, *New Worlds of Malthus*, 114.

32. Malthus, *Essay on Principle of Population*, 13, 15.

33. Bashford and Chaplin, *New Worlds of Malthus*, 84–85.

34. Quoted and discussed in Bashford and Chaplin, *New Worlds of Malthus*, 203; original from Malthus, *Summary View*, 28–29.

35. Malthus, *Essay on Principle of Population*, 15; quoted and discussed in Bashford and Chaplin, *New Worlds of Malthus*, 9, 86–87.

36. See variable Euro Share in appendix of Easterly and Levine, "European Origins." The dataset does not include the British mandate of Palestine because of inadequate data. The source of the "killed" data is Arcand et al., "Guns, Germs, and Slaves."

37. Algerian data from Easterly and Levine, "European Origins."

38. Pitts, *A Turn to Empire*, 326.

39. Algerian dataset from Easterly and Levine, "European Origins"; for Tocqueville, see Pitts, *A Turn to Empire*, 217.

40. Merivale, *Lectures on Colonization*, 514; McNab, "Herman Merivale and the British Empire."

41. Tocqueville, *Democracy in America*, 390–391.

42. Tocqueville, *Democracy in America*, 391, quoted in Sheehan, *Seeds of Extinction*, 279.

Chapter 9: What Shall We Do for Black Progress?

This chapter draws heavily upon Guyatt, *Bind Us Apart*; Yarema, *The American Colonization Society*; Burin, *Slavery and the Peculiar Solution*; Tillery, "Not One Was Willing to Go!"; Guelzo, *Lincoln's Emancipation Proclamation*; Levy, *How the Dismal Science Got Its Name*; Blight, *Frederick Douglass*; Foner, *The Fiery Trial*; Capaldi, *John Stuart Mill*; Mantena, *Alibis of Empire*; Varouxakis, *Mill on Nationality* and *Liberty Abroad*; McDaniel, *Swing Low, Sweet Chariot*; Shick, "Quantitative Analysis"; Boyd, "Île a Vache"; Gernes, "Poetic Justice"; Sklar, *Women's Rights Emerges*.

1. Jefferson, *Notes on Virginia*, 97–98.

2. Jefferson, *Notes on Virginia*, 94; Founders Online, "Thomas Jefferson to John Lynch, January 21, 1811."

3. Saillant, "American Enlightenment in Africa"; Founders Online, "From Jefferson to Jared Sparks, February 4, 1824."

4. Quoted in Lincoln, *Speeches and Writings*, vol. 1, 271.

5. Guyatt, *Bind Us Apart*, 264–265; Burin, *Slavery and the Peculiar Solution*, 13.

6. Yarema, *American Colonization Society*, 16, 18, 19, 25; Burin, *Slavery and the Peculiar Solution*, 17, 32; Guyatt, *Bind Us Apart*, 266–267.

7. Sherwood, "Formation of the American Colonization Society," 226.

8. Yarema, *American Colonization Society*, 36; Gardiner Spring, *Memoirs of the Rev. Samuel J. Mills*, 114, 131.

9. Guelzo, *Fateful Lightning*, 56, 58.

10. Burin, *Slavery and the Peculiar Solution*, 13; Yarema, *American Colonization Society*, 36.

11. Yarema, *American Colonization Society*, 38–39; Shick, "Quantitative Analysis."

12. Yarema, *American Colonization Society*, 39–42.

13. Burin, *Slavery and the Peculiar Solution*, 151–152.

14. McDaniel, "Extreme Mortality in Nineteenth-Century Africa," 583, 590; Saillant, "American Enlightenment in Africa."

15. McDaniel, *Swing Low, Sweet Chariot*, 153; Saillant, "American Enlightenment in Africa."

16. Shick, "Quantitative Analysis," 45; Burin, *Slavery and the Peculiar Solution*, 24–25, and Table 2 covering 1820–1860; Yarema, *American Colonization Society*, 72, 17.

17. Harris, "Early Black Benevolent Societies," 609–610; Guyatt, *Bind Us Apart*, 259–263; Tillery, "Not One Was Willing to Go!," 16, 17; Garrison, *Thoughts on African Colonization*, 222, 224.

18. Sklar, *Women's Rights Emerges*, 98–99.

19. Garrison, *Thoughts on African Colonization*, 291, 293, 299.

20. Quoted in Nicholas Guyatt, "Adams Doctrine"; Adams, *Memoirs of John Quincy Adams*, 293, 354.

21. Martineau, *Illustrations of Political Economy*, Locations 505–508.

22. Martineau, *Illustrations of Political Economy*, Locations 1581–1588.

23. Harriet Martineau, *Retrospect of Western Travel*, 8.

24. Yarema, *American Colonization Society*, 55; Garrison, *Thoughts on African Colonization*, 216, 228.

25. Guelzo, *Fateful Lightning*, 61–62.

26. Smith, *Essays on Slavery*, 41–43, 385–386.

27. Hammond, *Letters on Southern Slavery*, 3, 11, 15, 17, 20.

28. Carlyle, *Latter-Day Pamphlets*, 14; see discussion of Carlyle and Mill debate in Levy, *How the Dismal Science Got Its Name*.

29. Carlyle, *Latter-Day Pamphlets*, 20–21.

30. Carlyle, *Past and Present*, Location 3287.

31. Carlyle, *Latter-Day Pamphlets*, Location 647.

32. Mill, *Principles of Political Economy*, 282.

33. Mill, *Representative Government*, Locations 291–300.

34. Mill, *Subjection of Women*, Locations 7449–7459.

35. Mill, "Enfranchisement of Women," Locations 10461–10467.

36. Mill, *Autobiography*, 99–102.

37. Quoted in Levy and Peart, "Sympathy, Evolution"; original in Mill, "Grote's Plato," Locations 10727–10734.

38. Capaldi, *John Stuart Mill*, Locations 3799–3802, 2519–2523; Mill, *Utilitarianism*, 12–14.

39. Capaldi, *John Stuart Mill*, Locations 3451–3455; Mill, *Principles of Political Economy*, 569.

40. Mill, "The Negro Question," Locations 3654–3668; Carlyle's reply in 1850 to Mill, from Carlyle, *Latter-Day Pamphlets*, 23. Levy's *Dismal Science* argues it is a reply to Mill.

41. Carlyle, "Occasional Discourse"; Carlyle, *Latter-Day Pamphlets*, 14.

42. Capaldi, *John Stuart Mill*, Location 4234; Carlyle, letter to Dr. Carlyle, *New Letters*, 196.

43. Carlyle, "Occasional Discourse"; I am indebted to Levy, *How the Dismal Science Got Its Name*, for this overall point and for supporting quotes.

44. Carlyle, "Occasional Discourse." See Levy, *How the Dismal Science Got Its Name*, on the history of the phrase *dismal science*.

45. Peart and Levy, "Economics and Race," 16; Carlyle, *Reminiscences*, 177.

46. Levy, *How the Dismal Science Got Its Name*; Levy and Peart, "Sympathy, Evolution."

47. Mill, "The Negro Question," Locations 3799–3810.

48. Martineau, *Society in America*, vol. 1, Locations 2053–2114.

49. Martineau, *Society in America*, vol. 2, Location 1741.

50. Hammond, *Letters on Southern Slavery*, 8–10; Faust, *James Henry Hammond*, 314–315.

51. Hammond, *Letters on Southern Slavery*, 8–10, 15.

52. Martineau, *Retrospect of Western Travel*, vol. 2, 44; Martineau, *Society in America*, vol. 2, Locations 1571, 1815.

53. Fox-Genovese, *Within the Plantation Household*, 392.

54. Karcher, *First Woman*, 182; Child, *An Appeal*, 120–121; Moland, *Lydia Maria Child*, 109–110; Martineau, *Martyr Age*, 8.

55. Child, *An Appeal*, 253, quoted in Karcher, *First Woman*, 188.

56. Washington, "From Motives of Delicacy," 57, 60; Karcher, *First Woman*, 435–437.

57. Jacobs, *Incidents*, 32–33.

58. Jacobs, *Incidents*, 67.

59. Jacobs, *Incidents*, 33–34.

60. Jacobs, *Incidents*, 156; Brown, *Speeches, Messages, and Other Writings*, 162.

61. Jacobs, *Incidents*, 238.

62. Jacobs, *Incidents*, 63, 67–69.

63. Jacobs, *Incidents*, 67.

64. Blight, *Frederick Douglass*, 59–60, 262; Douglass, *My Bondage and My Freedom*, 91.

65. Blight, *Frederick Douglass*, 202–205.

66. Douglass, *My Bondage and My Freedom*, 165.

67. Douglass, *Life and Times of Frederick Douglass*, 642–644; Blight, *Frederick Douglass*, 196–197.

68. Foner, *Life and Writings of Frederick Douglass*, vol. 1, 320–321; Blight, *Frederick Douglass*, 196–197.

69. "To deprive her of this right," quoted in Buccola, *Political Thought of Frederick Douglass*, 69–70; expanded original from Foner, *Life and Writings of Frederick Douglass*, vol. 4, 232, 237.

70. Blight, *Frederick Douglass*, 13–17; Douglass, *My Bondage and My Freedom*, 30–31, 19–20; Douglass, *Narrative of the Life*, 48–49; quoted in Buccola, *Political Thought of Frederick Douglass*, 27–28.

71. Douglass, "Henry Clay," 4–6.

72. Douglass, "The American Colonization Society," speech in Faneuil Hall, May 31, 1849, in Foner, *The Life and Writings of Frederick Douglass*, vol. 1, 387–389.

73. Frederick Douglass, "To Henry Clay," in Foner, *The Life and Writings of Frederick Douglass*, vol. 1, 284, 288; Douglass, "Henry Clay," 2.

74. Lincoln, *Speeches and Writings*, vol. 1, 270–271.

75. Lincoln, *Speeches and Writings*, vol. 1, 271; Lincoln, *Speeches and Writings*, vol. 2, Locations 5727–5733.

76. Lincoln, *Speeches and Writings*, vol. 1, 316.

77. Lincoln, *Speeches and Writings*, vol. 1, 402.

78. Supreme Court, *Dred Scott*, 36.

79. Lincoln, *Speeches and Writings*, vol. 1, 685–686.

80. Lincoln, *Speeches and Writings*, vol. 1, 582.

81. Guelzo, *Fateful Lightning*, 281–282, 294–295.

82. Mill, "Contest in America," Locations 4896–4898.

83. Guelzo, *Fateful Lightning*, 298–299.

84. Foner, *Fiery Trial*, 184–186.

85. Foner, *Fiery Trial*, 200–201.

86. Lincoln, *Speeches and Writings*, vol. 2, 341; Burin, *Slavery*, 162.

87. Foner, *Fiery Trial*, 222–226.

88. Lincoln, *Speeches and Writings*, vol. 2, 355–356; Foner, *Fiery Trial*, 184–186; Boyd, "Île a Vache," 47.

89. Lincoln, *Speeches and Writings*, vol. 2, 368; Foner, *Fiery Trial*, 222–226.

90. Foner, *Fiery Trial*, 233–234.

91. Foner, *Fiery Trial*, 237–238; Lincoln, *Speeches and Writings*, vol. 2, 395, 411–415.

92. Burin, *Slavery*, 164; Foner, *Fiery Trial*, 239–240; 47–49, Boyd, "Île a Vache."

93. Boyd, "Île a Vache," 50, 52–53, 55–56; Foner, *Fiery Trial*, 259–260; Lincoln, *Speeches and Writings*, vol. 2, Locations 8972–8978; Burin, *Slavery*, 165.

Chapter 10: The Victory of the Man Without a Plan

This chapter draws heavily on Blight, *Frederick Douglass*.

1. Quoted in Blight, *Frederick Douglass*, 425–427. Expanded quotes from Foner, *Life and Writings of Frederick Douglass*, vol. 3, 188–191.

2. Quoted in Blight, *Frederick Douglass*, 425–427. Expanded quotes from Foner, *Life and Writings of Frederick Douglass*, vol. 3, 212, 217–218.

3. Foner, *Life and Writings of Frederick Douglass*, vol. 3, 188–191.

4. Foner, *Life and Writings of Frederick Douglass*, vol. 3, 188–191.

5. Quoted in Blight, *Frederick Douglass*, 425–427. Expanded quote from Foner, *Life and Writings of Frederick Douglass*, vol. 3, 188–191.

6. Quoted in Blight, *Frederick Douglass*, 425–427. Expanded quote from Foner, *Life and Writings of Frederick Douglass*, vol. 3, 222.

7. Foner, *Life and Writings of Frederick Douglass*, vol. 3, 188–191.

8. Foner, *Life and Writings of Frederick Douglass*, vol. 3, 188–191.

9. Foner, *Life and Writings of Frederick Douglass*, vol. 3, 348–349.

10. Blight, *Frederick Douglass*, 557–558; Blassingame and McKivigan, *Frederick Douglass Papers*, vol. 4, 420.

11. Blassingame and McKivigan, *Frederick Douglass Papers*, vol. 4, 421–422.
12. Blassingame and McKivigan, *Frederick Douglass Papers*, vol. 4, 418–420.
13. Foner, *Life and Writings of Frederick Douglass*, vol. 4, 309–331.
14. For the modern controversy over this statue, see Blight, *Frederick Douglass*, 2–3; National Park Service, "Emancipation Statue"; White and Sandage, "Frederick Douglass About Monuments."
15. White and Sandage, "Frederick Douglass About Monuments."
16. Quoted in Blight, *Frederick Douglass*, 557–558; Blassingame and McKivigan, *Frederick Douglass Papers*, vol. 4, 421.
17. Blassingame and McKivigan, *Frederick Douglass Papers*, vol. 4, 419–420.
18. Blassingame and McKivigan, *Frederick Douglass Papers*, vol. 4, 420.
19. Buccola, *Political Thought of Frederick Douglass*, 166–167.

Part III: The Regress of Liberty, 1865–1945
Ely, "Fraternalism vs. Paternalism."

Chapter 11: How Economists Forgot Consent
This chapter draws heavily on Leonard, *Illiberal Reformers*; Peart and Levy, "*Vanity of the Philosopher*" and "Denying Human Homogeneity." See also Isenberg, *White Trash*; Hoxie, *A Final Promise*; Harris, *Race, Radicalism, and Reform*; Painter, *History of White People*.

1. Marshall quoted in Tullberg, "Alfred Marshall"; the original quote had a typo: "postponed" instead of "proposed." From *Bee-Hive* of April 18, 1874, as reprinted in Marshall and Harrison, "Two Early Articles by Alfred Marshall."
2. Commons, *Races and Immigrants in America*, Locations 2970–2971.
3. Marshall and Harrison, "Two Early Articles by Marshall."
4. Marshall and Harrison, "Two Early Articles by Marshall."
5. "Alfred Marshall, 1842–1924," 4.
6. Marshall and Harrison, "Two Early Articles by Marshall."
7. Lindert and Williamson, *Unequal Gains*.
8. Ely, "The American Economic Association"; Leonard, *Illiberal Reformers*, 12–13; "History of the Founding of the American Economic Association"; Furstenberg, *Scholar and Public Policy*, 13.
9. Ely, "Pauperism in the United States," 409.
10. Ely, "Report," 6–7, 16, 19, 20.
11. Ely, "Report," 16–17; Ely, "The American Economic Association," 64.
12. Ely, "The American Economic Association," 15, 19.
13. "History of the Founding of the American Economic Association," i–iii.
14. Ely, "The American Economic Association," 62–64.
15. Ely, "The American Economic Association," 91.
16. Quoted in Peart and Levy, "*Vanity of the Philosopher*," 77; original in Marshall, *Principles of Economics*, Locations 9651–9665.
17. Marshall, *Principles of Economics*, Locations 7457–7469.
18. Peart and Levy, "*Vanity of the Philosopher*," 77; Marshall, *Principles of Economics*, Locations 12592–12595.

19. Marshall and Marshall, *Economics of Industry*, 28, 37.

20. Mill, "The Negro Question," 465.

21. Marshall and Marshall, *Economics of Industry*, 31.

22. Marshall, *Principles of Economics*, Locations 3195–3202.

23. Levy and Peart, "Harriet Martineau," 197.

24. Marshall, *Principles of Economics*, Location 17412.

25. Martineau, *Autobiography*, Locations 2305–2312.

26. Quoted in Pande and Roy, "If You Compete with Us," 3001, on which this and the following paragraph are based. They cite as source for the quote Tullberg, "Alfred Marshall."

27. Keynes, "Obituary for Mary Paley Marshall," 268, 274–275; Robinson, review of *What I Remember*, 122–124.

28. Ely, *Studies in the Evolution of Industrial Society*, 138–139.

29. Quoted in Thies and Daza, "Richard T. Ely," 151; original from Ely, "Fraternalism vs. Paternalism in Government," 781.

30. Ely, "Pauperism," 395–409; Siegel, "Tales of the Tribe of Ishmael," 192–193, 196; Peart and Levy, *"Vanity of the Philosopher,"* 112; Painter, *History of White People*, 260–263.

31. Isenberg, *White Trash*, 135–137, 179; Ely, "Pauperism in the United States," 395–409.

32. Ely, *Studies in Evolution*, 173–175.

33. Munroe, *Francis Amasa Walker*, 127, 208, 269.

34. Walker, *The Indian Question*, 17, 24, 34, 36, 44–45, 48–51, 53–55, 57–58, 62, 79–82.

35. Commissioner of Indian Affairs, *Annual Report*, 9, 36.

36. Quinton, *The Indian's Friend*, 10; quoted Jacobs, "Maternal Colonialism," 469; see also Syed and Ali, "The White Woman's Burden," 349–365.

37. Jacobs, "Maternal Colonialism," 470; Zitkala-Ša, *American Indian Stories*, Locations 158–197.

38. Zitkala-Ša, "An Indian Teacher Among Indians."

39. Zitkala-Ša, *American Indian Stories*, 188–189.

40. Walker, "Restriction of Immigration"; quoted in Leonard, *Illiberal Reformers*, 144; also in Okrent, *The Guarded Gate*, 60.

41. See the great discussion in Okrent, *Guarded Gate*, 343.

42. Leonard, *Illiberal Reformers*, 10–11, 31. This book has been a guide to many of the economists featured in this chapter. Commons became president in 1917; see www.aeaweb.org/about-aea/leadership/officers/past-officers/presidents.

43. Commons, *Races and Immigrants in America*, Locations 1858–1861.

44. Commons, *Races and Immigrants in America*, Locations 907–915.

45. Commons, *Races and Immigrants in America*, Locations 583–598, 226–229.

46. Commons, *Races and Immigrants in America*, Locations 1677–1679, 1887–1892.

47. Commons, *Races and Immigrants in America*, Locations 301–357.

48. Isenberg, *White Trash*, 135; Commons, *Races and Immigrants in America*, Locations 1679–1681, 2708–2713, 2767–2770.

49. Commons approvingly quoted a witness using the words "carelessness, ill temper, and unreliability" before a commission investigating immigration policy in 1901 in Commons, *Economic Effects of Immigration*, 314; quoted in Tichenor, *Dividing Lines*, Location 2480; also quoted in Leonard, *Illiberal Reformers*, 175. On Roosevelt, see Commons, *Races and Immigrants in America*, Locations 2643–2644.

50. Leonard, *Illiberal Reformers*, 169, 185; US Senate, Equal Rights Amendment hearing.

Chapter 12: America in the Philippines and the New Colonial Expansion

This chapter draws on Karnow, *In Our Image*; Cullinane, *Liberty and American Anti-Imperialism*; Boot, *Savage Wars of Peace*; Brands, *Bound to Empire*; Miller, *"Benevolent Assimilation"*; Bain, *Sitting in Darkness*; Jones, *Honor in the Dust*; Linn, *Philippine War, 1899–1902*; Lewis, *W. E. B. Du Bois*; Vitalis, *White World Order*; Mishra, *From the Ruins of Empire* and *Bland Fanatics*.

1. American Sociological Association, "William G. Sumner"; Karnow, *In Our Image*, 27.

2. US Philippine Commission, *Report*, vol. 1; Sumner, "Conquest of the US by Spain," Locations 139–151.

3. Sumner, *War and Other Essays*, Locations 2918–2924.

4. Ziltener et al., *Measuring the Impacts of Colonialism*.

5. Mill, *On Liberty*, 6.

6. Mill, *On Liberty*, 6–7.

7. Mishra, *Bland Fanatics*, 87–88.

8. Mill, *Considerations on Representative Government*, 267, 366.

9. Vitalis, *White World Order*, 42; original in American Economic Association, *Essays in Colonial Finance* (Macmillan, 1900), 17–20.

10. "About Us," AAPSS; Theodore S. Woolsey, *Government of Dependencies*, 3, 11–14.

11. Ireland, *Tropical Colonization*, 156, 224. Ireland is quoting a British colonial expert on Black people's "lazy backwardness."

12. Ireland, "On the Need," 210–221; See also Vitalis, *White World Order*, 29–30, 44.

13. Kipling, *Kipling: Poems*, 96–98.

14. "Rudyard Kipling"; Mishra, *From the Ruins of Empire*, 225; Thompson, *Rabindranath Tagore*, 190; Bayly, *The Boxer Uprising*, 148–149.

15. On their Nobel Prizes, see "Rudyard Kipling," Nobel Foundation, www.nobelprize.org/prizes/literature/1907/kipling/facts/; "Nobel Prize in Literature 1913," Nobel Foundation, www.nobelprize.org/prizes/literature/1913/summary/. On Tagore's speech, see Isaiah Berlin, *Sense of Reality*, 262; original in Tagore, *Towards Universal Man*, 117; Hay, "Rabindranath Tagore in America," 444, letter of Tagore to Harriet Monroe, December 31, 1913.

16. Mishra, *From the Ruins of Empire*, 242; Hay, "Rabindranath Tagore in America," 457–458.

17. Boot, *Savage Wars of Peace*, 104; Cullinane, *Liberty and American Anti-Imperialism*, 26–27.

18. Boot, *Savage Wars of Peace*, 104; Cullinane, *Liberty and American Anti-Imperialism*, 20–21, 130–131; original letter at López, "Sixto Lopez to the American People," 12, from a letter dated August 8, 1900.

19. Brands, *Bound to Empire*, 25–26; Cullinane, *Liberty and American Anti-Imperialism*, 27; Rusling, Interview with President McKinley; Hay, "Rabindranath Tagore in America," 137.

20. Cullinane, *Liberty and American Anti-Imperialism*, 27.

21. Sumner, "Conquest of the US by Spain," Locations 242–256.

22. Sumner, "Conquest of the US by Spain," Location 207.

23. For the lynching, which occurred on February 22, 1898, see "1898 Postmaster Lynching," Smithsonian National Postal Museum, https://postalmuseum.si.edu/exhibition/behind-the-badge-case-histories-assaults-and-murders/1898-postmaster-lynching. For Sumner's question, see Sumner, "Conquest of the US by Spain," Locations 521–529.

24. Sumner, "Conquest of the US by Spain," Location 208.

25. Sumner, "Conquest of the US by Spain," Locations 252–260.

26. Sumner, "Conquest of the US by Spain," Locations 139–265.

27. Boot, *Savage Wars of Peace*, 106; Cullinane, *Liberty and American Anti-Imperialism*, 22; Karnow, *In Our Image*, 185–186.

28. Karnow, *In Our Image*, 28; Brands, *Bound to Empire*, 51.

29. US Philippine Commission, *Report*, vols. 1, 3.

30. US Philippine Commission, *Report*, vol. 1, 1–6, 118, 121.

31. Brands, *Bound to Empire*, 63, Location 1428.

32. Miller, *"Benevolent Assimilation,"* Locations 2049–2053; Brands, *Bound to Empire*, 69; Karnow, *In Our Image*, 239–244, 276–278, 293–294, 312–313; Boot, *Savage Wars of Peace*, 114–115, Locations 2647–2652.

33. Karnow, *In Our Image*, 223–224.

34. Karnow, *In Our Image*, 253–256; Boot, *Savage Wars of Peace*, 116, Location 2677; Linn, *The Philippine War*, 220, Location 4619.

35. Boot, *Savage Wars of Peace*, 119–120, 122, Location 2738; Cullinane, *Liberty and American Anti-Imperialism*, 120–121; Karnow, *In Our Image*, 270–272; Jones, *Honor in the Dust*, 219, 235, 265–266.

36. Boot, *Savage Wars of Peace*, 123, Location 2835; Karnow, *In Our Image*, 266–267.

37. Twain, *Great Short Works*, 205–211, 214.

38. Du Bois, "Relation of the Negroes," 121.

39. Du Bois, *Souls of Black Folk*, Locations 2317–2326.

40. Du Bois, *Souls of Black Folk*, Location 500.

41. Karnow, *In Our Image*, 274–275; Boot, *Savage Wars of Peace*, 123–125.

42. "J Laurence Laughlin"; "James Laurence Laughlin, 1850–1933."

43. Laughlin, *Patriotism and Imperialism*, 13, 15, 16.

Chapter 13: Leopold's Congo and the Revival of Benevolent Slavery

This chapter draws heavily on Hochschild, *King Leopold's Ghost*; also on Pavlakis, *British Humanitarianism*; Jasanoff, *Dawn Watch*; Schmidt, "Paul S. Reinsch."

1. Hochschild, *King Leopold's Ghost*, 44; Starr, "Congo Free State," 384–385.

2. Hochschild, *King Leopold's Ghost*, 44; Starr, "Congo Free State," 388; General Act of the Berlin Conference on West Africa.

3. Hochschild, *King Leopold's Ghost*, 147; Jasanoff, *Dawn Watch*, 201–202; Conrad, *Heart of Darkness*, 13, 21, 30, 62–64.

4. Jasanoff, *Dawn Watch*, 203–204; Conrad, *Heart of Darkness*, 66, 73–74.

5. Hochschild, *King Leopold's Ghost*, 147; Conrad, *Heart of Darkness*, 63, 72.

6. Hochschild, *King Leopold's Ghost*, 148–149; Eastley, "Conrad," 94, 96, 101.

7. Hochschild, *King Leopold's Ghost*, 165; Fox Bourne, *Civilisation in Congoland*, 202, 210–214, 222–224.

8. Fox Bourne, *Civilisation in Congoland*, 202–204.

9. Burrows and Stanley, *The Land of the Pigmies*, 285–288.

10. Hochschild, *King Leopold's Ghost*, 223–224.

11. Louis and Stengers, *Morel's History*, ix; Hochschild, *King Leopold's Ghost*, 177–178.

12. Kingsley, *Travels in West Africa*, 273.

13. Kingsley, *Travels in West Africa*, 273, 310–311; Mary Kingsley, *West African Studies*, xvi; Nworah, "The Liverpool 'Sect,'" 361.

14. Morel, *Nigeria*, viii.

15. Morel, *Nigeria*, Locations 600, 1006; Morel, *Black Man's Burden*, 166, 182–183, 187.

16. Louis and Stengers, *E. D. Morel's History*, 36–37; Hochschild, *King Leopold's Ghost*, 180.

17. Louis and Stengers, *E. D. Morel's History*, 45–46, 48–49; Hochschild, *King Leopold's Ghost*, 186; Pavlakis, *British Humanitarianism*, 44. This account is based on Morel's later memoir (published much later by Louis and Stengers). Other accounts dispute Morel's dramatization of the breach with Sir Alfred Jones and Elder Dempster: Pavlakis, *British Humanitarianism*, 44; Morel, *E. D. Morel's History*, 262–264.

18. Hochschild, *King Leopold's Ghost*, 207; Cullinane, *Liberty and American Anti-Imperialism*, 163–164, 167–169; Pavlakis, *British Humanitarianism*, 166; Jasanoff, *Dawn Watch*, 211–213; Morel, *King Leopold's Rule in Africa*, Location 6863.

19. Jasanoff, *Dawn Watch*, 208–210; Hochschild, *King Leopold's Ghost*, 158–159.

20. Morel, *Affairs of West Africa*, 177, 342, 352.

21. Boulger, *Congo State Is Not a Slave State*, 3; Hochschild, *King Leopold's Ghost*, 238.

22. Wisconsin Historical Society, "Historical Essay: Reinsch."

23. Reinsch, "Colonial Autonomy," 116–139; Schmidt, "Paul S. Reinsch," Locations 999–1001; Vitalis, *White World Order*, 49–50.

24. Reinsch, *World Politics*, 20, 43, 360; Schmidt, "Paul S. Reinsch," Locations 940–943.

25. Reinsch, "Real Conditions in the Congo Free State," 219–221.

26. Reinsch, *Colonial Administration*, 12, 13, 23, 24, 30, 31, 35, 44, 69–73, 343–345, 360–362, 366–367, 379, 404–405.

27. Morel, *King Leopold's Rule*, photo on page 144, description on pages 444–445; Harris, Congo Atrocity Lantern Lecture.

28. Pavlakis, *British Humanitarianism*, 166–167, 253–254; Hochschild, *King Leopold's Ghost*, 248–249.

29. Pavlakis, *British Humanitarianism*, 76, 221, 229–230.

30. On free trade finally entering the Congo, see Pavlakis, *British Humanitarianism*, 242–243.

31. For the vice-consul, see Pavlakis, *British Humanitarianism*, 237–238; for the final meeting, see Louis and Stenger, *E. D. Morel's History*, 206.

32. Pavlakis, *British Humanitarianism*, 242–243; Hochschild, *King Leopold's Ghost*, 272.

33. Pavlakis, *British Humanitarianism*, 239–241.

Chapter 14: Lenin vs. Wilson

The title of this chapter is borrowed from Mayer, *Wilson vs. Lenin*. The chapter draws heavily on and exposits the analysis of Manela, *Wilsonian Moment*, and draws as well on Vitalis, *White World Order*; Berg, *Wilson*; Pedersen, *The Guardians*; Sebestyen, *Lenin*; Pipes, *The Russian Revolution*; Herman, *1917*.

1. Lenin, *Essential Works*, 11, 13, 28–29, 38, 42, 45–47.

2. Lenin, *Essential Works*, 264–267.

3. Lenin, *Essential Works*, 250.

4. Sebestyen, *Lenin*, 240; Lenin, *Essential Works*, 177, 254–256.

5. Leonard, *Illiberal Reformers*, 12–13; Ely, "Report of the Organization of the American Economic Association," 7; Berg, *Wilson*, 114; Willoughby, "The American Political Science Association," 110.

6. Wilson, "Ideals of America"; Wilson, "Democracy and Efficiency"; Manela, *Wilsonian Moment*, 28–30.

7. Peart and Levy, "Economics and Race," 60; original in Wilson, *Division and Reunion*, 125–126.

8. Lenin, "What Is to Be Done?," Location 3411; Lenin, *Essential Works*, 257.

9. Lenin, *Essential Works*, 337–338, 347.

10. Pipes, *The Russian Revolution*, Location 17293; Lenin, "Declaration of Rights."

11. Kotkin, *Stalin*, 298–300; Malle, *Economic Organization of War Communism*, 360.

12. Pipes, *The Russian Revolution*, Location 18912, 19269; Sebestyen, *Lenin*, 393–397.

13. Pipes, *The Russian Revolution*, Location 19102; Sebestyen, *Lenin*, 393–397; Lenin, Telegram.

14. Mayer, *Wilson vs. Lenin*, 299; Lenin, "Socialist Revolution."

15. Mayer, *Wilson vs. Lenin*, 262–265; Lenin, "Report on Peace."

16. Lenin, "Declaration of Rights."

17. Berg, *Wilson*, 468–469.

18. Manela, *Wilsonian Moment*, 40–42; Wilson, "Fourteen Points," 1918; Wilson, "Address to Congress."

19. Miller, *Drafting of the Covenant*, vol. 2, document 7: Wilson's Second Draft or First Paris Draft, January 10, 1919, 70, 87.

20. Miller, *Drafting of the Covenant*, vol. 2, 195.

21. Miller, *Drafting of the Covenant*, vol. 2, 108–110.

22. Miller, *Drafting of the Covenant*, vol. 2, 387–391.

23. Manela, *Wilsonian Moment*, 47–51.

24. Manela, *Wilsonian Moment*, 3–4; Tai, *Radicalism*, 67–70; Bradley, *Imagining Vietnam and America*, 10–11; Duiker, *Ho Chi Minh*, 98–102.

25. This section exposits the narrative and analysis of Manela, *Wilsonian Moment*, 141–147, 151–152; Egyptian delegation to the peace conference, collection of official correspondence, 53, 55, 58–61.

26. Manela, *Wilsonian Moment*, 163, 166.

27. Manela, *Wilsonian Moment*, 168–170; Tuteja, "Jallianwala Bagh," 25, 41.

28. Manela, *Wilsonian Moment*, 34; Lewis, *W. E. B. Du Bois*, 59–60; Trotter, Statement, 679–681, 684–685, 687–691; Rosenberg, "For Democracy, Not Hypocrisy," 592–593.

29. Zitkala-Ša, *American Indian Stories*, 192.

30. Treaty of Peace with Germany, Articles 86 and 93.

31. Manela, *Wilsonian Moment*, 111–112; Pugach, *Paul S. Reinsch*; US Department of State, "The Minister in China (Reinsch)."

32. Manela, *Wilsonian Moment*, 190; Mishra, *From the Ruins of Empire*, 180, 207–208.

33. Reinsch, *An American Diplomat in China*, 358, 361, 364; Manela, *Wilsonian Moment*, 186–189.

34. Manela, *Wilsonian Moment*, 194–195; Mao, *Mao's Road to Power*, xxi, 335, 337–338.

35. Folk, Statement, 651–652, 673.

36. Trotter, Statement, 680–681, 684.

37. Malone, Statement, 750–752, 754; Manela, *Wilsonian Moment*, 172–173.

38. Manela, *Wilsonian Moment*, 172–173, 194; Berg, *Wilson*, 615–616, 627, 652–653.

39. Lenin, Address to Second All-Russia Congress.

40. McMeekin, *The Russian Revolution*, 283; Foglesong, *America's Secret War*, Location 4794; Willett, *Russian Sideshow*, Locations 3546, 3690.

41. Foglesong, *America's Secret War*, Location 4373; Willett, *Russian Sideshow*, Locations 3078, 5287.

42. Lenin, Address to Second All-Russia Congress.

43. First Congress of the Communist International, "The International Situation."

44. "Windows of Freedom," 25–29, 35; Miller, *Drafting of the Covenant*, vol. 1, 106.

45. Miller, *Drafting of the Covenant*, vol. 1, 110.

46. This section on forced labor exposits the analysis of Pedersen, *The Guardians*, 233, 237–239, 251–252.

47. Pedersen, *The Guardians*, 238–239.

48. Pedersen, *The Guardians*, 244; Pavlakis, *British Humanitarianism*, 242.

49. Lenin, *Imperialism*, 4–7, 10.

50. McMeekin, *The Russian Revolution*, 321–324.

51. Fehrenbach and Rodogno, "'Horrific Photo,'" 1138.

52. Duiker, *Ho Chi Minh*, Location 1393; Nehru quoted in Westad, *Global Cold War*, Location 1819; Lenin, *Imperialism*, Location 356.

Chapter 15: Reductio ad Hitlerum

This chapter draws heavily on Borgwardt, *A New Deal*; Whitman, *Hitler's American Model*; Westermann, *Hitler's Ostkrieg*; Kakel, *American West and the Nazi East*.

1. The eight liberal democracies included five colonial powers or countries with unequal rights at home (defined as also including policy toward Indigenous inhabitants): Australia, Canada, New Zealand, the United Kingdom, and the United States. The other three were Costa Rica, Sweden, and Switzerland. See "Political Regime, 1941," Our World in Data, https://ourworldindata.org/grapher/political-regime-updated2016?time=1941.

2. Keynes, *General Theory*, 340.

3. Logically Fallacious, "Reductio ad Hitlerum."

4. The first volume of *Mein Kampf* appeared on July 18, 1925, and the second volume on December 11, 1926. See Ullrich, *Hitler: Ascent*, 175.

5. Hitler, *Mein Kampf*, 66–71, 131, 135, 185–186, 273–275.

6. Hitler, *Mein Kampf*, 68–69.

7. Hitler, *Mein Kampf*, 71.

8. Hitler, *Mein Kampf*, 135.

9. Hitler, *Mein Kampf*, 113.

10. Hitler, *Mein Kampf*, 129.

11. Hitler, *Mein Kampf*, 125; Whitman, *Hitler's American Model*, 9–10; Kakel, *American West and Nazi East*, 1–2.

12. Hitler, *Mein Kampf*, 189–190.

13. Kershaw, *Hitler: Nemesis*, Location 5813; Blackbourn, "Conquest of Nature," 160; Guettel, *German Expansionism*, Locations 3750–3756; Whitman, *Hitler's American Model*, 115–116; Lower, *Nazi Empire-Building*, 3, 19–20.

14. Leverkuehn, *German Military Intelligence*, Location 2488; Kershaw, *Hitler: Nemesis*, Location 9814; Westermann, *Hitler's Ostkrieg*, 3.

15. Kakel, *American West and Nazi East*, 1–2; Hitler, *Hitler's Table Talk*, 23–24, 31, 33–34, 37–38, 68–69, 198–199, 621.

16. Hitler, *Mein Kampf*, 185–186.

17. I am grateful to Peter Boettke for alerting me to Mises's writings on colonialism. See Hülsmann, *Mises*, 3, 678, 683–684, 753–757, 795–796.

18. Hülsmann, *Mises*, 561–562.

19. Mises, *Liberalism*, Locations 1866, 2019, 2130, 2136, 2138, 2144, 2147, 2151–2152, 2162, 2175, 2182–2201, 2203, 2141.

20. Hülsmann, *Mises*, 299–300, 305–306.

21. Hülsmann, *Mises*, 299–300, 305–306; Mises, *Human Action*, Location 16403.

22. Mises, *Socialism*, 13–14, 440–441, 581–582.

23. Borgwardt, *A New Deal*, 1, 4–6.
24. Text of the Atlantic Charter given in Borgwardt, *A New Deal*, 303–304.
25. This section exposits and expands upon Borgwardt, *A New Deal*, 4–5, 29–30; UK Parliament, "War Situation."
26. Quoted in Borgwardt, *A New Deal*, 29.
27. Mandela, *Long Walk to Freedom*, 10, 367–368, 391, 620–621, 624.
28. Quoted in Borgwardt, *A New Deal*, 29.
29. Lauren, *Power and Prejudice*, Locations 3699, 3714–3715.
30. Latham, *Right Kind of Revolution*, 27; Ho Chi Minh, *Selected Works*, 17–21.
31. United Nations, *Declaration Regarding Non-Self-Governing Territories*.
32. Mao, "Chinese People Have Stood Up!"

PART IV: THE AMBIVALENT ADVANCE OF FREEDOM, 1945–PRESENT

UNESCO, Constitution of United Nations.

Chapter 16: The Fall of Colonialism and the Invention of the Third World

This chapter draws upon Vitalis, "Midnight Ride"; Dubnov, *Isaiah Berlin*; Ignatieff, *Isaiah Berlin*; Cherniss, "'Cautious, Sober Love Affair'"; Lauren, *Power and Prejudice* and *Evolution of International Human Rights*.

1. Vitalis, "Midnight Ride."
2. Sauvy, "Trois mondes"; see also Pletsch, "The Three Worlds," 590.
3. Sauvy, *Fertility and Survival*, 7–8.
4. Vitalis, "Midnight Ride."
5. Vitalis, "Midnight Ride."
6. Embassy of Indonesia, *Report on Indonesia*, 8, 11, 12, 28–31; Lauren, *Power and Prejudice*, Location 5333.
7. United Nations, *Charter of the United Nations*; United Nations, "UDHR."
8. Embassy of Indonesia, *Report on Indonesia*, 28.
9. Embassy of Indonesia, *Report on Indonesia*, 17.
10. Quoted in Foot, "Remembering the Past," 154; expanded quotation and originals in Kahin, *The Asian-African Conference*, 52, 60.
11. Romulo, *I Walked with Heroes*, Locations 170, 179, 453, 711, 1502–1507, 2356, 3135, 3586, 3626, 3766; 133–134; Claudio, "Anti-Communist Third World," 125–156.
12. Lauren, *Power and Prejudice*, Location 4208; Lauren, *Evolution of International Human Rights*, 181.
13. Claudio, "Anti-Communist Third World," 141–146; Romulo, *The Meaning of Bandung*, 81–83, 86.
14. Embassy of Indonesia, *Report on Indonesia*, 8, 11, 12, 24, 28–31; Wright, *The Colour Curtain*, 132; Lauren, *Power and Prejudice*, Locations 5333–5354, 5366.
15. Berlin, Original dictation (A), "Two Concepts of Liberty," 16–17, 23, 25, 28, 34; Berlin, Manuscript D, "Two Concepts of Liberty," 1, 15, 18, 49.
16. Dubnov, *Isaiah Berlin*, 19, 22, 29–30, 35–36, 38–39; Berlin, "National Superiority and Inferiority," 4.

17. Dubnov, *Isaiah Berlin*, 116.

18. Dubnov, *Isaiah Berlin*, 172–173; "Riga," Holocaust Encylopedia, United States Holocaust Memorial Museum, accessed July 26, 2021, https://encyclopedia.ushmm.org/content/en/article/riga.

19. Cherniss, "'Cautious, Sober Love Affair,'" 19; Berlin, "A Letter to George Kennan," 24, 26.

20. Berlin, *Freedom and Its Betrayal*, 113, 115–116, 124, 133–136, 139; Berlin, *Russian Thinkers*, Locations 6052–6063.

21. Berlin, *Freedom and Its Betrayal*, 113, 115–116, 124, 133–136, 139.

22. Berlin, *Conversations for Tomorrow*, 10, 14; Cherniss, "'Cautious, Sober Love Affair,'" 30.

23. Berlin, "National Superiority and Inferiority," 5–6, 12.

24. Berlin, *Four Lectures on Russian Historicism*, 114.

25. Derived from "Minorities at Risk Dataset."

26. Quoted in Bauer, *Dissent on Development*, 151; original in Nkrumah, *Africa Must Unite*, 13.

27. Lauren, *Evolution of Human Rights*, 363; Du Bois, *The World and Africa*, 330, 334, 335.

Chapter 17: Vietnam and the Illiberal Development Mainstream

This chapter draws upon Latham, *Right Kind of Revolution*; Milne, *America's Rasputin*; Latham, *Modernization as Ideology*; Fall, *Two Vietnams*; Ekbladh, *Great American Mission*; Gilman, *Mandarins of the Future*.

1. Latham, *Right Kind of Revolution*, 7; Kennedy, "Inaugural Address."

2. Truman, "Inaugural Address"; Kennedy, "New Dimensions of American Foreign Policy"; Kennedy, "Conference on India and the United States."

3. Rostow, *Stages of Economic Growth*, 144.

4. Rostow, *Stages of Economic Growth*, 19–21.

5. Rostow, *Stages of Economic Growth*, 142–144.

6. Rostow, *Stages of Economic Growth*, 58.

7. Latham, *Right Kind of Revolution*, 57; Kennedy, Special Message to the Congress on Foreign Aid; Kennedy, Administration of Foreign Assistance and Related Functions.

8. Milne, *America's Rasputin*, 78–79; Latham, *Modernization as Ideology*, 69; Rostow, "The Idea of an Economic Development Decade."

9. Rostow, "Draft of Crucial Portion of Foreign Aid Message."

10. Kennedy, Special Message on Aid.

11. Kennedy, Special Message on Aid; Milne, *America's Rasputin*, 78–79; Treaty of Peace with Germany, 56.

12. Latham, *Modernization as Ideology*, 92.

13. W W. Rostow, "Development," 240.

14. Kennedy, Special Message on Aid.

15. Kennedy, Special Message on Aid.

16. Rostow, "Memorandum to the President," May 10, 1961.

17. Rostow, *Stages of Economic Growth*, 36, 45–47.

18. Rostow, *Stages of Economic Growth*, 93, 98–99, 102–105.
19. Rostow, *Stages of Economic Growth*, 163–164.
20. Rostow, *Stages of Economic Growth*, 166–167, 163–164.
21. Rostow, *Stages of Economic Growth*, 144.
22. Rostow, *Stages of Economic Growth*, 8, 26, 29, 58, 113.
23. Foreign Assistance Act of 1961.
24. US Department of State, "Address by President John F. Kennedy."
25. Taylor, "Letter to the President," Locations 11318–11330.
26. Latham, *Modernization as Ideology*, 170–171; Milne, *America's Rasputin*, 105–106; Catton, "Counter-Insurgency and Nation Building," 935; Osborne, *Strategic Hamlets in South Viet-Nam*, 21, 23, 25.
27. Milne, *America's Rasputin*, 105–106; Zasloff, "Rural Resettlement in South Viet Nam," 327–340.
28. Milne, *America's Rasputin*, 105–106; Catton, "Counter-Insurgency and Nation Building," 935; Heavner, "Memorandum to the Director"; Rostow, "Letter to the Ambassador in Vietnam."
29. Latham, *Modernization as Ideology*, 180–185; Latham, *Right Kind of Revolution*, 140–141; Leahy, "Why Did the Strategic Hamlet Program Fail?," 98–101; Fall, *Two Vietnams*, 377, 380; Osborne, *Strategic Hamlets*, 37; Homer Bigart, "Vietnam Village Builds and Hopes," 3.
30. Bigart, "US Helps Vietnam," 1, 3.
31. Donnell and Hickey, *Vietnamese "Strategic Hamlets,"* iii, vii, 10–11, 13–14.
32. Latham, *Right Kind of Revolution*, 140–141; Fall, *Two Vietnams*, 380; Donnell and Hickey, *Vietnamese "Strategic Hamlets,"* iii, vii, 10–11, 13–14.
33. Osborne, *Strategic Hamlets*, 37–44; Bigart, "US Prints Paper for Vietnamese."
34. Bigart, "McNamara Terms Saigon Aid Ample."
35. Vietnam (Republic), Viet Nam's Strategic Hamlets, 10–11.
36. Osborne, *Strategic Hamlets*, 43; Vietnam (Republic), "Viet Nam's Strategic Hamlets," 27–28.
37. Milne, *America's Rasputin*, 106–107; Johnson, "Memo [Situation in Central Vietnam]," Locations 16494–16498; Fall, *Two Vietnams*, 377, 382; Ekbladh, *The Great American Mission*, 202.
38. Halberstam, *The Best and the Brightest*, 328–331; Sheehan, *A Bright Shining Lie*, 369–371; Osborne, *Strategic Hamlets*, 30, 40.
39. Rostow, "Development: Political Economy," 245, 249, 258.

Chapter 18: Liberal Economists Strike Back

This chapter draws on Ebenstein, *Milton Friedman*; Bermeo, *Ordinary People*; Edwards and Montes, "Milton Friedman in Chile"; Levy and Peart, *Escape from Democracy* and *Towards an Economics*.

1. Friedman and Friedman, *Two Lucky People*, xxi, 3, 4.
2. Ebenstein, *Milton Friedman*, 5–6; Nobel Prize Outreach, "Milton Friedman"; Friedman and Friedman, *Two Lucky People*, 77.
3. Friedman and Friedman, *Two Lucky People*, 242, 244.

4. Bauer, *Dissent on Development*, 24–25, 106, 128, 43–44.

5. Bauer, *Dissent on Development*, 24–25, 106, 128, 200–202; Bauer, *Economic Analysis*, 113, 114, 122.

6. Bauer, *Dissent on Development*, 221; Bauer, "N. H. Stern on Substance and Method," 388, 397.

7. Bauer, *Dissent on Development*, 149, 153.

8. Friedman and Friedman, *Two Lucky People*, 257, 268; Friedman, *The Indian Alternative*, 71–73.

9. The report quoted by Friedman is Center for International Studies, "Objectives of US Economic Assistance Programs," 57–58.

10. Friedman, *Foreign Economic Aid*, 4–5, 11–14.

11. Friedman, *Foreign Economic Aid*, 11; Friedman and Friedman, *Free to Choose*, 25.

12. Friedman and Friedman, *Two Lucky People*, 308, 314; Friedman and Friedman, *Free to Choose*, 141, 301.

13. Friedman and Friedman, *Free to Choose*, 129, 301.

14. Friedman, *Foreign Economic Aid*, 14; Friedman and Friedman, *Free to Choose*, 299.

15. Friedman, *Foreign Economic Aid*, 14–15; Friedman and Friedman, *Free to Choose*, 51.

16. Friedman and Friedman, *Capitalism and Freedom*, 33; Friedman and Friedman, *Free to Choose*, 54, 128, 129.

17. Friedman, *Foreign Economic Aid*, 12.

18. Friedman and Friedman, *Free to Choose*, 60; Friedman and Friedman, *Two Lucky People*, 533.

19. Friedman and Friedman, *Free to Choose*, 132, 134.

20. Friedman and Friedman, *Free to Choose*, 1, 13.

21. Quoted in Bermeo, *Ordinary People*, 138.

22. Bermeo, *Ordinary People*, 157.

23. Britannica, "Salvador Allende"; Bermeo, *Ordinary People*, 157.

24. Bermeo, *Ordinary People*, 166.

25. "The Allende Years and the Pinochet Coup, 1969–1973," Office of the Historian, US State Department, https://history.state.gov/milestones/1969-1976/allende.

26. Inflation in Chile, World Bank World Development Indicators.

27. Dates are given as March 19–27, including travel time, in Farrant, "Advising the 'Devil,'" Location 3629. Milton's own account is given in Friedman and Friedman, *Two Lucky People*, 399–400; more precise dates are in Edwards and Montes, "Milton Friedman in Chile," 110.

28. Friedman and Friedman, *Two Lucky People*, 591–593.

29. Friedman and Friedman, *Two Lucky People*, 594.

30. Edwards and Montes, "Milton Friedman in Chile," 115.

31. Letelier, "The 'Chicago Boys' in Chile."

32. Edwards and Montes, "Milton Friedman in Chile," 117–118.

33. Friedman and Friedman, *Two Lucky People*, 595–596.

34. Edwards and Montes, "Milton Friedman in Chile," 114–116; Milton Friedman, *The Fragility of Freedom*, 8–14.

35. Paul A. Samuelson, "World Economy at Century's End," 67, 75–76.

36. Quoted in Boettke, *The Struggle for a Better World*, 145.

37. James M. Buchanan, "Positive Economics"; Buchanan, "The Constitution of Economic Policy."

Chapter 19: The End of History?

1. US Department of State, "Berlin Wall;" Tůma, "Czechoslovakia's Velvet Revolution;" US Department of State, "Collapse of the Soviet Union," Wilson Center, "Yeltsin, Boris: 1931–2007."
2. Fukuyama, "The End of History?"
3. Fukuyama, "'Americans Are Not Very Good at Nation-Building.'"
4. Fukuyama, *End of History*, 152, Location 103.
5. Fukuyama, *End of History*, Location 150; quoted in Capaldi, *John Stuart Mill*, Locations 4388–4390; Fukuyama, *End of History*, 31.
6. Fukuyama, *End of History*, 362.
7. Fukuyama, *Identity*, Location 2284.
8. Fukuyama, *End of History*, 13–14.
9. Fukuyama, *End of History*, Locations 154, 2597.
10. Fukuyama, *End of History*, 14–15.
11. Definitions from Coppedge et al., "V-Dem Codebook v13, 287."
12. Fukuyama, *End of History*, 41–42.
13. Fukuyama, *Identity*, Location 66.
14. Fraser Institute, "Economic Freedom of the World."
15. Bateman et al., *Ghana's Cocoa Pricing Policy*, 2.18, Figures 6 and 2; Easterly, *Elusive Quest*, Location 2545.
16. Human Rights Watch, "Ghana," 17–18, 22; Amnesty International, "Ghana," 46, 47.
17. Summers, "The Great Liberator."
18. Sen, *Development as Freedom*, xiii; Pazzanese, "Amartya Sen's Nine-Decade Journey"; Sen, *Home in the World*, 289–290.
19. Sen, *Development as Freedom*, 286–288.
20. Sen, *Development as Freedom*, 5, 287–288.
21. Sen, *Development as Freedom*, 27.
22. Sen, *Development as Freedom*, 28, 112–116.
23. Sen, *Development as Freedom*, 112–116.
24. Sen, *Development as Freedom*, 223.
25. Connelly, *Fatal Misconception*, Locations 4614–4618.
26. Connelly, *Fatal Misconception*, Location 4421; original in McNamara, "Population and International Security," 49.
27. Connelly, *Fatal Misconception*, Location 4661.
28. Sen, *Development as Freedom*, 174.
29. Feng and Cai, "The End of China's One-Child Policy."
30. Sen, *Development as Freedom*, 223.

31. Sen, *Development as Freedom*, 288–289.

32. "Beijing Declaration"; data from World Bank Group, Women, Business & the Law, 2023: data for 1971–2023.

33. "Beijing Declaration," 49, 55, 92.

34. "Beijing Declaration," 56, 67, 92.

35. "Beijing Declaration," 24, 49.

36. "Beijing Declaration," 3, 36.

37. Rodrik, "Goodbye Washington Consensus," 969–983.

38. Easterly, "In Search of Reforms for Growth."

39. Joseph Stiglitz, quoted in Martin, "Stiglitz Tells Us Why 'Neoliberalism Is Dead'"; Levitz, "Biden Administration Declared the Death of Neoliberalism."

40. For Chubais in Russia, see Rutland, "Neoliberalism and the Russian Transition."

41. Cirium, "International Flying to and from Africa"; Dodd, "Supporting Economic & Social Development."

42. Fisher, "In Tunisia"; Fahim, "Slap to a Man's Pride"; de Soto, "The Real Mohamed Bouazizi"; Abouzeid, "Bouazizi:"; Watson and Karadsheh, "The Tunisian Fruit Seller"; Beaumont, "Mohammed Bouazizi."

43. Fukuyama, *Identity*, Locations 660, 683.

44. Davies, "Doubt over Tunisian 'Martyr.'"

Epilogue: Development in Search of Dignity

Banerjee and Duflo, *Good Economics for Hard Times*, xx.

1. Cole, "The White-Savior Industrial Complex," T. M. S. Ruge, "'Kony 2012' Is Not a Revolution."

2. Invisible Children, "KONY 2012"; C-Span, "Uganda's Joseph Kony."

3. Invisible Children, "KONY 2012."

4. Cole, "White-Savior Industrial Complex."

5. Cole, *Known and Strange Things*, 342–344; Kristof, "Viral Video, Vicious Warlord."

6. Cole, *Known and Strange Things*, 345.

7. Cole, *Known and Strange Things*, 342–344.

8. Sen, *Development as Freedom*, 136.

9. Marx, *The Eighteenth Brumaire.*

10. Holloway, with Grandi, "Dignity in Displacement"; Fehrenbach and Rodogno, "'Horrific Photo,'" 1121–1155.

11. Moyo, *Dead Aid*, 27, 31–32.

12. Wade, "Stop Raising Money."

13. Wade, "Stop Raising Money."

14. Fehrenbach and Rodogno, "'Horrific Photo,'" 1152; UN General Assembly, Code of Conduct; Manzo, "Imaging Humanitarianism," 632–657.

15. Van der Gaag and Nash, "Images of Africa," November 1987.

16. Holloway with Grandi, "Dignity in Displacement"; CONCORD, Code of Conduct on Images and Messages.

17. Dóchas, *Guide to Ethical Communications*, 4, 6, 11.

18. Ali and Murphy, "Black Lives Matter"; quoted in New York Times, "Foreign Aid."

19. Gerszon Mahler et al., "Stop Referring to the 'Developing World'"; Khan et al., "How We Classify Countries and People."

20. World Trade Organization, "Who Are the Developing Countries in the WTO?"; Yang, "China: We're Still a Developing Nation."

21. Opalo, "Who Is the African Child?"

22. Mamdani, "Kony."

23. Mamdani, "Responsibility to Protect," 58–59; Human Rights Watch, "Who Is Joseph Kony?"

24. US Department of State, "U.S. Relations with Uganda"; GlobalSecurity.org, "Uganda–US Relations"; data from World Development Indicators database.

25. Bush, "Presidential Address to the Nation."

26. Bush, "Radio Address."

27. Easterly, "Paradox of Aid"; Arezki et al., "Foreign Aid and Conflicts."

28. Nunn and Qian, "US Food Aid and Civil Conflict," 1630–1666; Zürcher, "What Do We (Not) Know?," 506–522.

29. Lincoln, *Speeches and Writings*, vol. 1, 1832–1858, 315–317.

30. Associated Press, "Putin Woos African Leaders"; Behnke, "Putin Searches for More Friends."

31. Kremlin, "Meeting with Heads of African Delegations."

32. Kremlin, "Meeting with President of Uganda."

33. Putin, "Speech at Annexation Ceremony."

34. Fukuyama, *Identity*, Location 694; Open Society, "Understanding Ukraine's Euromaidan Protests"; EU–Ukraine Association Agreement, "Quick Guide to the Association Agreement."

35. Banerjee and Duflo, *Good Economics*, 315–317.

36. Banerjee and Duflo, *Good Economics*, 321–322.

37. Banerjee and Duflo, "Mandated Empowerment," 333.

38. Duflo, "Human Values."

39. Duflo, "Human Values."

40. United Nations, *Summit on Sustainable Development*.

41. United Nations, "Transforming Our World," paragraph 38.

42. Moyo, *Dead Aid*, 145–146.

43. Wade, "African Aid."

44. Trade data by partner and by type of good in HS two-digit categories 2022, gathered from UN Comtrade Database, sorted in descending order by magnitude of trade flows, https://comtradeplus.un.org/TradeFlow?Frequency=A&Flows=M&CommodityCodes=AG4&Partners=800&Reporters=all&period=2022&AggregateBy=none&BreakdownMode=plus.

Index

Credit: Liz Dalton

William Easterly is professor emeritus of economics at New York University. He is the author of three previous books, including *The Tyranny of Experts* and *The White Man's Burden*. His writing has appeared in *The New York Times*, *The Wall Street Journal*, and the *Financial Times*. He lives in New York.

RAISING READERS

Books Build Bright Futures

Thank you for reading this book and for being a reader of books in general. We are so grateful to share being part of a community of readers with you, and we hope you will join us in passing our love of books on to the next generation of readers.

Did you know that reading for enjoyment is the single biggest predictor of a child's future happiness and success?

More than family circumstances, parents' educational background, or income, reading impacts a child's future academic performance, emotional well-being, communication skills, economic security, ambition, and happiness.

Studies show that kids reading for enjoyment in the US is in rapid decline:

- In 2012, 53% of 9-year-olds read almost every day. Just 10 years later, in 2022, the number had fallen to 39%.
- In 2012, 27% of 13-year-olds read for fun daily. By 2023, that number was just 14%.

TOGETHER, WE CAN COMMIT TO RAISING READERS AND CHANGE THIS TREND.

HOW?

- Read to children in your life daily.
- Model reading as a fun activity.
- Reduce screen time.
- Start a family, school, or community book club.
- Visit bookstores and libraries regularly.
- Listen to audiobooks.
- Read the book before you see the movie.
- Encourage your child to read aloud to a pet or stuffed animal.
- Give books as gifts.
- Donate books to families and communities in need.

Books build bright futures, and **Raising Readers** is our shared responsibility.

For more information, visit JoinRaisingReaders.com

Sources: National Endowment for the Arts, National Assessment of Educational Progress, WorldBookDay.org, Nielsen BookData's 2023 "Understanding the Children's Book Consumer"